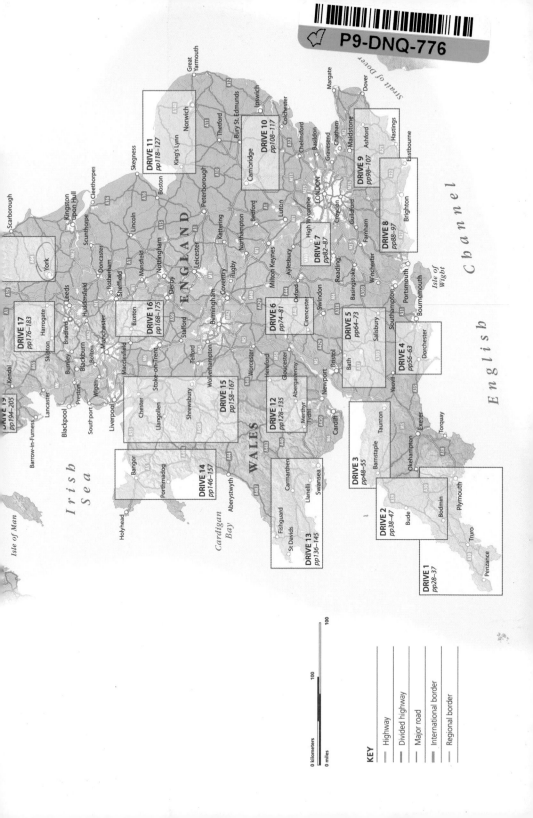

P9-DNQ-776

EYEWITNESS TRAVEL

BACK ROADS
GREAT
BRITAIN

EYEWITNESS TRAVEL

BACK ROADS
GREAT BRITAIN

CONTRIBUTORS

Pat Aithie, Robert Andrews, Donna Dailey,

Rebecca Ford, Gillian Harrison, John Harrison,

Nick Rider, Rose Shepherd, Roger Williams

LONDON, NEW YORK,
MELBOURNE, MUNICH AND DELHI
www.dk.com

PUBLISHER Douglas Amrine
LIST MANAGER Vivien Antwi
MANAGING ART EDITOR Jane Ewart
EDITORIAL Michelle Crane, Alastair
Laing, Georgina Palffy, Hugh
Thompson, Vicki Allen, Nichole
Morford
ART EDITORS Shahid Mahmood,
Kate Leonard
PRODUCTION CONTROLLER
Linda Dare
PICTURE RESEARCH Ellen Root,
Rhiannon Furbear
DTP Jason Little, Jamie McNeill
CARTOGRAPHY MANAGER
Uma Bhattacharya
SENIOR CARTOGRAPHIC EDITOR
Casper Morris
CARTOGRAPHY
Stuart James, Schchida Nand Pradhan,
Zafar-ul-Islam Khan, Hassan
Mohammad
JACKET DESIGN
Tessa Bindloss, Meredith Smith
ILLUSTRATIONS
Arun Pottirayil, Pallavi Thakur,
Dev Datta

Colour reproduction by
Media Development Printing Ltd, UK
Printed and bound in China by
South China Printing Co Ltd

First published in the United States in 2010 by
Dorling Kindersley Publishing, Inc., 375 Hudson
Street, New York 10014

First American Edition 2010

10 11 12 13 10 9 8 7 6 5 4 3 2 1

A CIP catalogue record is available from the
Library of Congress.

ISBN 978 0 7566 5913 4

CONTENTS

Above Sandy Porthmeor Beach with St Nicholas chapel
beyond it on the Island, St Ives, Cornwall

Above The Circus, an elegant 18th-century terrace designed by John Wood, Bath

Above Silbury Hill, Europe's largest man-made ancient monument, Avebury

Above King's College Chapel from The Backs, Cambridge

Below left Crescent Gardens in bloom, Harrogate, North Yorkshire **Below center** Road sign near Aysgarth, Wensleydale, in the rolling green Yorkshire Dales **Below right** Fishing port of Whitby with St Mary's Church on the hill behind, North Yorkshire Coast

Title page: Ardnamurchan Forest on the West Coast of Scotland **Half-title page:** Track across fields near St Abb's Head in the Scottish Borders

About This Book

Away from the fast-track motorways and uniform city centers, these drives along the back roads of Britain take you to some of the less-visited towns and villages of Britain. Taken at a gentle pace, they allow the driver time to appreciate what makes Great Britain unique – the landscapes, villages, grand country houses, castles, and gardens. This book goes beyond the must-see tourist sights to lesser-known places that will reveal a more intimate experience of Britain's people and architecture. This island nation encompasses three countries – England, Wales, and Scotland – each with a distinct history and different traditions. The landscape ranges from hillside pastures to mountain peaks, wild coastlines and open moorland. Glimpses of past cultures can be seen in the prehistoric standing stones and Roman ruins. And the castles and villages document the emergence, over many hundreds of years, of a single nation. Expect delightful surprises around every bend, and the reward will be the timeless culture of Great Britain.

Getting Started

The front section of the guide will give all the practical information needed to plan and enjoy a driving holiday in Great Britain. It includes an overview of when and how to get there, advice on renting vehicles or bringing one into the country. The traveling advice ranges from driving rules to road conditions, to buying gasoline and breakdown/accident procedures – the kind of background knowledge that will help make a driving trip stress free. Tips on money, opening hours, and other practical matters will save you time and confusion. There is also advice on accommodation and dining options, whether visitors are looking for a luxury hotel or a farmhouse bed-and-breakfast, a gourmet meal or pub food, which will help them to sample the range of British hospitality.

The Drives

The main section of the guide is divided into 25 drives, ranging from two to five days in duration, leading from the tip of Cornwall to the north of Scotland. All tours can be driven in a standard car or other vehicle. No special driving skills are required.

The drives cover every region of the country. Each one begins with an overview of the highlights and a clear map of the itinerary to help plan the trip. There is useful advice on the best time of year to make the drive, road conditions, local markets, and festivals.

The tours contain descriptions of each sight, including opening times and contact details, where applicable, linked by clear driving instructions. Side panels offer information on authentic places to stay and eat. Tinted boxes provide background information and anecdotes.

Each drive features at least one mapped walking tour, designed to take a maximum of three hours at a gentle pace with stops along the way. Some walks cover the highlights of towns or cities, while others explore glorious countryside walks on safe, clearly marked paths.

The tours are flexible and can be linked to create a longer vacation; alternatively, they can be used to plan day trips within a region.

Using the sheet map

A pull-out road map of the entire country is attached at the back. This map contains all the information necessary to drive around the country and to navigate between the tours. All highways, major roads, airports – both domestic and international – plus all the ferry ports are easily identified. This makes the pull-out map an excellent addition to the drive itinerary maps within the book. The pull-out map has a comprehensive index to help find the places, and is further supplemented by a clear distance chart so drivers can gauge the distances between the major cities.

Top left The Church of St. Peter and St. Paul, Northleach **Top right** Cove at St Abb's Head, Berwickshire, Scotland **Center left** Fishing boats at Whitby **Center right** Edinburgh – a famous festival venue **Below left** Traditional sweetshop, Rye **Below right** Field of sunflowers, Cornwall

Above Driving through Langstrothdale Chase near Oughtershaw, North Yorkshire

Introducing Great Britain

The back roads of Great Britain are a refreshing antidote to the bustle of its world-famous cities. Though it is possible to zoom along highways from London to Manchester, Cardiff, Glasgow, or Edinburgh in a few hours, it's the smaller roads away from these urban centers which lead into the true heart of the country. Here, through castles and ruined abbeys, and mining, farming, and fishing villages, the rich history of Britain's regions is waiting to be discovered. Take time to appreciate the landscapes, from the Scottish Highlands to the Yorkshire Dales and the watery Fens. Britain's rural hills and fields, lined with stone walls and hedgerows, are quietly beautiful. The rest is stunning, from the Kent coast to the Welsh mountains. Follow the back roads to find the farmers' markets, pubs, festivals, gardens, and wildlife that form the heart of the country.

When to Go

The itinerary for each of the drives offers suggestions on the best times to visit. Some regions are known for their gardens, others for their seasonal produce, still others for outdoor activities from surfing to climbing. Festivals and events can make for an unforgettable experience, so check with local tourist boards and consider these when planning your trip. The weather varies by region. July and August generally guarantee the hottest, sunniest weather. but for fewer crowds, April to June and September to October are a better bet. Summer's other advantage is the long hours of daylight, especially in Scotland, where darkness doesn't fall until 10 or 11pm. Scenery is another factor – spring can be magical with bluebells, daffodils, colorful blossoms and the brightest greens. Autumn brings red and gold to the trees and purple heather on the moors. Winter may be wetter and colder, but off-season rates are cheaper and most attractions are open year-round.

Times to Avoid

As mentioned already, July and August are the busiest times to visit – when British schools are on summer holiday and when the majority of foreign tourists arrive. Prices are also highest and traffic is heaviest, especially around popular coastal resorts. Throughout summer, biting insects known as midges are common in the western Highlands of Scotland. November–March has the rainiest,

coldest weather and days are shorter, especially the further north you go, with dusk falling as early as 4pm.

Climate

Thanks to the Gulf Stream, Britain's climate is moderate year-round and seldom drops below freezing. Snow is rare, except in mountainous areas. Average winter temperatures are 40–50°F (5–10°C), while summers average 65–77°F (18–25°C), although they can rise to over 90°F (32°C). In general, temperatures in the north are a few degrees lower than the south. Spring comes first to the southwest, with gardens in Devon and Cornwall budding out in February and March. The western coast is usually rainier and warmer than the east.

Festivals

Many festivals and events, in villages and market towns, center around regional produce from apples to oysters to cheeses to wines, craft fairs, music, and the arts. Some traditional celebrations date back centuries and involve clog dancing, inter-village football, and other bizarre sports. Famous events include the Hay Festival of Literature (May), Cambridge Folk Festival (Jul), and Highland Games, held in Scottish towns Jun–Aug. Across the country, bonfires blaze and noisy fireworks flare into the sky on Guy Fawkes' Night (5 Nov).

Public Holidays

New Year's Day (Jan 1)
Good Friday (Fri before Easter)
Easter Monday
May Day Holiday (1st Mon in May)
Spring Bank Holiday (last Mon in May)
Summer Bank Holiday (last Mon in Aug)
Christmas Day (Dec 25)
Boxing Day (Dec 26)

Left A quiet back road through the ancient and pristine forests of Argyll, Scotland

Above The pretty market town of Ashbourne in the Derbyshire Dales

Getting to Great Britain

Great Britain is an international travel hub. As the gateway to Europe and beyond for North American travelers, Britain's major airports enjoy direct transatlantic flights as well as a direct service from most of the rest of the world. London is the western terminus of Eurostar, the high-speed rail line from Paris, Lille, and Brussels, while other rail services connect with ferries across the English Channel and Irish Sea. Many ferry services link Britain to Europe and Ireland, and the Channel Tunnel provides road access from Europe via Calais, France. There is also low-cost coach service from Europe on Eurolines.

Above Colorful flower displays at Dovedale, in the Derbyshire Peak District

DIRECTORY

ARRIVING BY AIR

British Airways
0844 493 0 787 (UK);
www.britishairways.com

EasyJet
0905 821 0905 (calls cost 65p per minute; calls from mobiles and other networks may cost more); www.easyjet.com

Gatwick Airport
www.gatwickairport.com

Glasgow Airport
www.glasgowairport.com

Heathrow Airport
www.heathrowairport.com

London City Airport
www.londoncityairport.com

Luton Airport
www.london-luton.co.uk

Manchester Airport
www.manchesterairport.co.uk

Ryanair
0871 246 0000 (UK: calls cost 10p per minute); 0818 30 30 30 (Ireland: calls cost national rate); www.ryanair.com

Stansted Airport
www.stanstedairport.com

Virgin Atlantic
0870 5747 747; www.virgin-atlantic.com

Arriving by Air

Great Britain is served by most international airlines. From the United States and Canada, there are direct flights to London, Glasgow, and Manchester from major cities on international carriers, with internal connections to regional airports. Its own major carriers, **British Airways** and **Virgin Atlantic**, have direct flights from cities worldwide. In addition to the full service airlines, budget carriers such as **EasyJet** and **Ryanair** fly from Ireland and continental Europe to London, Glasgow and regional airports throughout the country, often with several flights a day in peak season. From Australia and New Zealand there are connecting flights via Bangkok and Singapore.

London is served by five airports. Most long-haul international flights arrive at **Heathrow**, 15 miles (24 km) west of the city center, or **Gatwick**, 27 miles (43 km) to the south. Heathrow is Britain's largest airport, serving around 90 airlines. It has five terminals. The newest, Terminal 5, is dedicated to British Airways. Most other long-haul and many European flights arrive at Terminals 3 and 4. Terminal 2 deals with mainly European flights, while all

domestic as well as some European and long-haul flights go through Terminal 1. London Underground trains and the Heathrow Express train connect the airport to the city center.

Gatwick has two terminals. The North Terminal serves British Airways and charter flights, while the South Terminal is home to around 50 airlines. The Gatwick Express to Victoria Station is the fastest way into the city center.

Luton Airport, 30 miles (48 km) north of London, and **Stansted Airport**, 35 miles (56 km) northeast, have many flights to/from Ireland, Europe, and beyond, on full service and budget airlines. Both have good connections to central London. **London City Airport** in East London serves domestic and European destinations.

Glasgow International Airport, is 8 miles (13 km) from the city center, and **Manchester International Airport**, 10 miles (16 km) south of its city, also handle international flights. Bristol, Cardiff, Birmingham, Liverpool, Newcastle, and Edinburgh are among Britain's many regional airports.

Flight times to London are: Paris 1 hour, Dublin 1¼ hours, New York 6½ hours, Montreal 7 hours, Los Angeles 10 hours, Sydney 21½ hours.

Arriving by Sea

The easiest way to compare the many services, routes, and prices is online at *www.directferries.com*.

From France: **Seafrance** and **P&O Ferries** have frequent crossings between Calais and Dover (travel time 1½ hours). **Transmanche Ferries/LD Lines** has ferry services between the French ports of Dieppe and Le Havre, and Newhaven and Portsmouth on England's south coast. LD Lines also runs between Dover and Boulogne. **Condor Ferries** has fast ferry services (4½–5½ hours) from St. Malo and Cherbourg to Weymouth, Poole, and Portsmouth, and **Brittany Ferries** plies similar routes to Britain's south coast with overnight and fast crossings. **Norfolkline** has frequent crossings from Dunkerque to Dover (2 hours).

From the rest of Europe: P&O Ferries serves Great Britain from Belgium, Netherlands, Spain, and Ireland, as does **DFDS Seaways** from Germany, Poland, Netherlands, Denmark, Norway, and Sweden. **Stena Line** has daily crossings from the Hook of Holland to Harwich (6¼ hours). P&O North Sea Ferries sails overnight from Zeebrugge in Belgium (13½ hours), and also from Rotterdam, Netherlands (11 hours) to Hull.

Brittany Ferries has overnight crossings from Santander in Spain to Plymouth (18 hours) or Portsmouth (24 hours), while P&O has a Bilbao to Portsmouth route (29 hours).

From Ireland: Norfolkline crosses between Belfast and Liverpool (8 hours). There are also services from Belfast to Stranraer in southwest Scotland (2 hours) and from Larne to Fleetwood in northwest England (8 hours) with Stena Line, and from Larne to Cairnryan (1 hour) or Troon (2 hours) in southwest Scotland with P&O Irish Sea. Dublin to Liverpool routes

(8 hours) are operated by P&O Irish Sea and Norfolkline. **Irish Ferries** runs 2-hour crossings from Dublin to Holyhead in North Wales, as does Stena Line from Dublin and Dun Laoghaire. Irish Ferries crosses from Rosslare to Pembroke in South Wales (4 hours), while Stena Line has daily 2-hour crossings from Rosslare to Fishguard.

Arriving by Train

Eurostar is the fastest and easiest way into Great Britain from Europe by train. This high-speed train travels through the 31-mile (52-km) Channel Tunnel. Passengers board at Brussels, Paris, Lille, or Calais to Ashford in Kent, Ebbsfleet International or London's St. Pancras Station. The journey from Paris to London can be as little as 2¼ hours. From London, there are train connections to all parts of the country through the British Rail network.

If traveling by train from Ireland, there are combined train and ferry tickets direct to most destinations in Britain. For information contact **Irish Rail**.

Arriving by Road

Cars can also be taken through the Channel Tunnel on the **Eurotunnel** rail shuttle, which runs between Sangatte near Calais and Folkestone in Kent. Travel time is 35 minutes. Passengers remain with their car. LPG-powered vehicles are not permitted. The terminals link to the A16 motorway in France and the M20 in England.

Eurolines provides long-distance coach (bus) service to Britain from cities across Ireland and Europe. Journey times can be long, but the fares are relatively inexpensive.

Below left Departure lounge at Gatwick airport
Below center Ferry terminal, Dover Harbour
Below right Boeing 747, Heathrow Airport

Practical Information

Traveling in Great Britain is easy, thanks to its generally up-to-date infrastructure. Public services usually operate smoothly and its health care system is among the best in the world. Police and security services may appear low-key, but they are highly trained to deal effectively with any emergency. Communication networks from broadband and Wi-Fi to mobile phone services are usually good, and most banks have ATM machines for out-of-hours use. In smaller towns and villages, shops are often closed Sundays.

Above Easily identifiable green pharmacy sign displayed outside a chemist's shop

Passports and Visas

Travelers from the United States, Canada, Australia, New Zealand, and South Africa do not need a visa if they are staying for less than six months. For longer stays, or for student or working visas, apply well in advance of departure. Nationals of European Union countries and Switzerland, Iceland, Norway, and Liechtenstein may enter Great Britain with a passport or national identity card. Irish citizens do not need a passport or visa if they are entering from Ireland.

However, it is generally advisable to always have a valid form of photo identification handy, as most airlines and ferry companies will require either a passport or driving license. If you don't have a passport, check with the carrier to see if an alternative form of ID is acceptable. All other visitors must have a passport, ideally with at least six months validity remaining to avoid problems at entry.

Other nationalities may require a visa, and visitors should contact the British Embassy, Consulate, or High Commission in their home country prior to traveling. Check the website of the Foreign and Commonwealth Office for details.

Travel Insurance

All travelers are strongly advised to take out comprehensive travel insurance. In addition to medical insurance (see below), a full policy will normally cover travelers for loss or theft of luggage and belongings, personal accident, damage to a third party, delayed or canceled flights, and in some cases the cancellation of your trip due to personal illness or that of a family member. Most policies also cover some legal costs. A standard travel policy will not cover hazardous sports, so anyone planning to go surfing, skiing, or rock-climbing must check their cover; it can usually be added for a small premium.

Read the terms to see what the excess is, and what cover is on valuable items such as cameras and jewelry.

Check to see what cover, if any, is offered under home insurance policy. Some credit card companies offer limited travel insurance if the card is used to book the trip or rental car, but these are often not as good as specialist travel policies.

Health Services

Currently no vaccinations or immunization documents are required to enter Great Britain unless traveling from a country where infectious diseases such as yellow fever are present.

There are no undue health hazards in Great Britain. Tap water is safe to drink and bottled water is available everywhere. In summer, the Highlands of Scotland are plagued with tiny biting flies called midges, so buy some strong insect repellent if planning to hike or camp.

Standard over-the-counter remedies can be bought in local pharmacies or chemists, but make sure to bring enough prescription medication from home to last throughout the trip, otherwise it will take a visit to a doctor to obtain a prescription. Pack them in carry-on luggage with their original labels to avoid problems at airport security.

In the unlikely event of an illness while traveling, the hotel staff should be able to locate a doctor or dentist. In the event of a genuine medical emergency, dial 999. **NHS Direct** provides round-the-clock medical advice by phone and has walk-in centers in many cities and larger towns. Most pharmacies – look for a green cross – are open Mon–Sat during regular business hours. If they are closed there is often a sign in the

Above left European Union passports **Above center** An ATM or Cashpoint machine **Above right** British policemen, on patrol at a train station

window advising of the nearest all-night chemist. Pharmacists are highly trained, too, and can usually advise on minor medical matters.

Visitors from countries outside the EU are strongly advised to have private medical insurance, as they will only be eligible for free emergency treatment. Without insurance, they will have to pay for follow-up care, doctor's visits, medication, etc. Check home health insurance plans for cover when abroad. Alternatively, travel insurance with medical coverage is a simple option and will give peace of mind.

Visitors from Ireland and other EU countries are covered for medical treatment in Great Britain under the EU's social security regulations, but they must see an NHS (National Health Service) doctor. To be eligible, they will need identification and a European Health Insurance Card (**EHIC**), which has replaced the old E111 form. Otherwise visitors will be liable for NHS charges. Obtain the card at home before traveling to the UK.

Personal Security

Great Britain is a relatively safe country. Alhough most serious crime takes place in inner-city areas where visitors are unlikely to go, they should take the normal precautions against petty crime as they would anywhere, especially in large towns.

Areas where there is a high volume of tourists are frequently targeted by petty thieves. Leave passports, jewelry and valuables in the hotel safe, if possible. Keep an eye on handbags and wallets, particularly in crowds and on public transport, and don't carry large amounts of cash around. Never leave bags, cameras, or luggage unattended or visible in cars, even if locked. If it's not possible to take them with you, it's best to put them in the car trunk before arriving at an attraction, as parking lots are sometimes watched by thieves.

British police are generally pleasant and helpful. Street officers wear dark blue uniforms (and often the famous domed hat), but do not usually carry firearms. If unfortunate enough to be a victim of crime, contact the police who can provide victim support. To telephone the **Emergency Services** – police, fire, or ambulance – dial 999.

Below far left Pedestrian road crossing, known as a zebra crossing **Below left** Emergency ambulance **Below center** Police on horseback, a common sight at football matches **Below right** Busy scene at Barnstaple's Pannier Market

DIRECTORY

PASSPORTS AND VISAS

American Embassy
24 Grosvenor Square, London W1; 020 7499 9000; www.usembassy.org.uk

Australian High Commission
Australia House, The Strand, London WC2; 020 7379 4334; www.australia.org.uk

British Foreign and Commonwealth Office
www.fco.gov.uk

Canadian High Commission
Macdonald House, 38 Grosvenor Square, London W1; 020 7258 6600 www.international.gc.ca/ Canada-europa/united_kingdom

Irish Embassy
17 Grosvenor Place, London SW1; 020 7235 2171; www.ireland.embassyhomepage.com

HEALTH SERVICES

NHS Direct
0845 4647; www.nhsdirect.nhs.uk

EHIC
www.nhs.uk/EHIC/Pages/About.aspx

PERSONAL SECURITY

Emergency Services
For Police, Fire or Ambulance dial 999

Telephone System

Telephone service is provided by British Telecom (BT). Phone numbers in Great Britain have an area code of four or five digits beginning with "0", followed by a local number. When dialing within the country, use the full area code. When dialing from abroad, drop the initial 0. When calling within the same area code, you only need to dial the local number.

To call Great Britain from abroad: first dial your country's international access code, followed by the country code for Britain (44), and the local area code (minus the initial 0), and number.

Public pay phones take either coins or phonecards. These are the cheapest way to make calls and you can buy cards at newsagents and post offices in various amounts. International phonecards can be an even cheaper way to call abroad. Making calls from your hotel room is generally expensive, as most hotels add a surcharge. Check the charges at reception before using the telephone.

Peak period is Mon–Fri 8am–6pm. Both local and international calls are cheaper after 6pm and on weekends. There is a charge for using Directory Enquiries, but you can look numbers up for free on the internet. Calls to cell phones are more expensive. Numbers beginning with 0845 are charged at a local rate and 0870 at national rate. 0800 and 0808 numbers are toll-free. Avoid numbers beginning with an 09 prefix – these premium rate lines cost up to £1.50 per minute.

Cell phones are convenient but find out what the roaming charges will be.

Great Britain is part of the GSM system – US phones need to be tri-band or quad-band and have international roaming activated to work here. Check with your supplier before leaving. If you plan to make a lot of calls, consider buying a cheap "pay-as-you-go" cell phone in the UK.

Internet and Mail Services

You'll find internet cafes in all the large towns and cities. Many hotels and guesthouses have internet access and there are Wi-fi hotspots at coffee shops around the country.

The national postal system is **Royal Mail**. In addition to main post offices, there are sub-post offices in shops and newsagents throughout the country, where you can send packages as well as letters and cards. You can also buy stamps at many newsagents. First-class mail within the country takes 1–2 days. Allow 3–10 days for International air mail, depending on the final destination. Post boxes are painted red.

Symbol for a Tourist Information Point

Banks and Money

Sterling is the currency in Great Britain. One pound is divided into 100 pence. There are £5, £10, £20, £50 and £100 notes, and 1p, 2p, 5p, 10p, 20p, 50p, £1 and £2 coins. Scotland issues its own bank notes, which are usable in England. However some shops south of the border won't accept them, so it's best to ask for change in English notes if you're nearing the end of your stay.

Traveler's cheques are a safe way to carry money abroad, but they have been largely replaced by Cash Passports – a prepaid currency card.

Above Foreign newspapers for sale on a newspaper stand

These can be loaded up with money before traveling and used in various shops and ATMs abroad. They are available from **Travelex** retail branches across the United States. Most airports have foreign exchange counters, but it is easier to use a debit or credit card to withdraw cash from one of the many ATMs or "cashpoints" around. Check with your bank or card provider what they will charge you for using your card abroad. Symbols on the ATM will tell you which cards it accepts. Cirrus and PLUS are widely used in Britain.

Major credit cards including Visa, Mastercard, and American Express are accepted at most hotels, restaurants, shops and gas stations, but you will need cash at pubs, small shops, guesthouses, and B&Bs. Credit card companies are increasingly vigilant against fraud, so it is wise to let them know you will be using the card abroad, so that they don't put a block on its use. It is also a good idea to carry a different card for back-up.

Great Britain has largely converted to the Chip-and-Pin system, which requires the purchaser to enter the card's pin number rather than a signature. If your card does not have a chip and uses the magnetic strip and signature system, then it may not be accepted.

Above left Logo of the Scottish Tourist Board **Above center** An ATM or Cashpoint showing the different cards accepted **Above right** Old clock face, Cambridge

Tourist Information

Visit Britain is the national tourism authority and its website has a wealth of information including destination guides, maps, and an accommodation booking service. The websites **Enjoy England**, **Visit Scotland,** and **Visit Wales** offer similar visitor information. There are also local tourist information centers (TIC) in most towns and tourist areas that serve drop-in visitors; hours vary and some are only open seasonally. You'll find links and contact details on the main websites. At the **Britain & London Visitor Centre** you can find information about most regions of the country. For castles, stately homes and gardens, contact **English Heritage**, **The National Trust,** and the **National Trust for Scotland**.

Opening Hours

Normal business hours are Mon–Fri 9 or 9.30am to 5.30 or 6pm. Shops open on Saturdays too and some have late-night shopping until 8 or 9pm on Thursdays. Supermarkets stay open later, and some are open 24 hours. Sunday trading hours, limited by law, are generally 11am or 12pm to 4 or 5pm; in smaller places shops do not open on Sundays.

Banks are open Mon–Fri 9.30am–4.30pm. Larger branches have longer hours and may open on Saturdays. Post offices are open weekdays from 9am to 5.30pm and Saturdays from 9am to 12.30pm or later. Small sub-post offices may close for lunch or on Wednesday afternoons.

Disabled Facilities

Many visitor attractions are accessible to wheelchair users, and a growing number of hotels and restaurants also provide facilities for guests with disabilities. The **Holiday Care Service** helps disabled and older travelers and can offer advice and information.

Time and Electricty

Great Britain is on Greenwich Mean Time (GMT). The clocks are put forward one hour during Summer (Daylight Saving) Time, from mid-March to the end of October.

Britain's electric current is 220-240 volts AC (50 cycles). Plugs have 3 pins. Many visitors will need a transformer and a plug adaptor to operate appliances from abroad. You can buy them at airports and electrical shops.

Below far left Old-fashioned telephone boxes **Below left** Shopping street reflected in a shop window selling tourist souvenirs **Below center** A traditional wall-mounted postbox **Below right** One of York's narrow shopping streets

DIRECTORY

TELEPHONE SYSTEM

International Access Codes
US and Canada: 011; Ireland: 00;
Australia: 0011; New Zealand 0170

Country Codes
US and Canada: 1; Ireland: 353;
Australia: 61; New Zealand 64

Directory Enquiries
118 500 (BT), www.bt.com; for business numbers, www.yell.com

International Directory Assistance
118 505 (BT)

INTERNET AND MAIL SERVICES

Royal Mail
www.royalmail.com

BANKS AND MONEY

Thomas Cook
www.thomascook.com

Travelex
www.travelex.co.uk

TOURIST INFORMATION

Visit Britain
www.visitbritain.com

Enjoy England
020 8846 9000;
www.enjoyengland.com

Visit Scotland
0845 22 55 121;
www.visitscotland.com

Visit Wales
08708 300 306; www.visitwales.com

Britain and London Visitor Centre
1 Regent Street, Piccadilly Circus,
London SW1; no phone

English Heritage
0870 333 1181;
www.english-heritage.org.uk

The National Trust
0844 800 1895;
www.nationaltrust.org.uk

The National Trust for Scotland
0844 493 2100; www.nts.org.uk

DISABLED FACILITIES

Holiday Care Service
0845 124 9971; www.holidaycare.org.uk

Driving in Great Britain

It's easy to travel the length and breadth of the country on Great Britain's major roads. Although many of these are scenic, running through beautiful countryside, the most memorable views are to be found off the beaten track. Driving along single-track roads in the Scottish Highlands, down the winding lanes of rural England and across the mountains of Wales, reveals many more facets of this diverse country. To make the most of your trip, it's best to learn the basics of driving in Great Britain before setting off.

Above Typical B-road sign, pointing to villages and indicating the distance

Insurance and Breakdown Coverage

Third-party motor insurance is compulsory in Great Britain, with a minimum cover level of £1,000,000. If you bring your own car to Britain, you must have an insurance certificate that is valid in this country. You do not need a green card if you are an EU national, but you should check with your insurer before traveling to make sure you are covered on the trip. Most companies give you automatic coverage in EU countries for up to 90 days. Citizens of other countries will need green card insurance. If your policy has breakdown cover, check if it applies abroad. If not, it is worth purchasing additional breakdown and accident cover. Motoring organizations such as the AA and RAC *(see p18)* may also provide assistance.

What to Take

In order to drive in Great Britain, you must have a valid driving license issued in your home country, or an International Driving Permit. Drivers whose documents are not in English should bring an official translation from their embassy or internationally recognized motoring association. If your license does not have a photograph, carry your passport or other form of official photo ID. If you are bringing your own vehicle, or trailer or motorcycle, bring the vehicle registration. If it is not registered in your name, bring a letter of authorization from the owner.

Great Britain does not yet require that you carry the visibility vests that are compulsory in many EU countries, though this may soon be extended throughout the EU. Although it's not compulsory to carry a first aid kit, it is a good idea. A warning triangle, flashlight (torch) and petrol container are also highly recommended.

Road Systems

Main roads in Great Britain are classified in three categories. Highways, or motorways have the prefix "M". In theory they are the fastest way of driving long distances, but traffic jams are common around large cities such as London and Birmingham, and you may experience long delays. Primary roads are indicated by the prefix "A" and may be either single or dual-carriageway. "B" roads, or secondary roads, are usually single-carriageway (one lane in each direction). These, along with the smaller, unclassified roads in rural areas, may offer some of the most rewarding and enjoyable driving.

There is currently only one toll road in Britain, the M6 Bypass at Birmingham. Tolls are charged at several river crossings, including the Dartford Tunnel, Humber Bridge, and the Severn Suspension Bridge. If you have to drive into central London, you will have to pay the **Congestion Charge** (currently £8 per day). Information on how to pay is posted on the Transport for London website. Similar schemes are being considered in other cities and on busy roadways to help reduce the volume of traffic.

Speed Limits and Fines

Speed limits are given in miles per hour throughout the country. Unless otherwise posted, the speed limits are 70 mph (112 kph) on highways and dual carriageways, 60 mph (96 kph) on single carriageways, and 30 mph (48 kph) in towns and built-up areas.

Police cannot make on-the-spot fines for speeding violations in Great Britain. Speed cameras, however, are widely used; fines are automatic and tickets are sent to the address of the vehicle's registration. You won't escape the penalty by driving a rental car. The car rental company will bill you for the

Above left Narrow Cornish street during the busy summer period **Above right** The only toll motorway in Great Britain, the M6 bypass at Birmingham

ticket, along with an administration fee. Speed camera detectors are illegal and will be confiscated.

Do not drink and drive. The laws are very strict and penalties are high. The legal limit is 80mg per 100ml of blood – about equal to a pint of strong beer. Police are authorized to administer a breathalyser test or a blood test at any time, and you can be prosecuted if don't agree to take one or the other.

Rules of the Road

Driving is on the left in Great Britain. Most visitors get used to it quickly, but pay extra attention at crossroads and roundabouts, where it is easy (and dangerous) to forget or get confused. Always turn left into a roundabout, and yield (give way) to traffic already in the roundabout and approaching from the right. Drive clockwise, staying in the right hand lane until you are approaching your left-hand exit.

Pass on the right. Do not pass if there is a continuous white line in the center of the road. At a junction where no road has priority, yield to traffic coming from your right.

Seat belts must be worn at all times, by the driver and all passengers, front seat and back. Using a hand-held cell phone while driving is illegal and

carries a fine and penalties.

Pedestrian crossings, often called zebra crossings, are marked by white striped lines on the road. Many have orange lights at either end to make them more visible at night. Drivers must yield to pedestrians if they step out into a zebra crossing and also at crossings when the "green man" is flashing, signaling it is safe to cross. Buy a copy of the *British Highway Code* from newsagents and gas stations for more information.

Please note that some signs in Wales may be in Welsh *(see right)*.

Buying Petrol

There are gas stations all over Great Britain, and unleaded gas as well as diesel is widely available – if renting a car, find out which type of fuel it uses. Most gas stations are self service and nearly all take major credit cards. Many stations on highways are open 24 hours. In remote areas, opening hours are shorter and some may be closed on Sunday.

Gas is sold by the litre and is expensive because it is highly taxed. Supermarket gas stations, on the outskirts of larger towns, are among the cheapest places to fill up your tank, highways the most expensive.

DIRECTORY

ROAD SYSTEM
London Congestion Charge
www.cclondon.com

SOME WELSH ROAD SIGNS
Araf *Slow*
Arafwch Nawr *Reduce Speed Now*
Bwsiau yn unig *Buses only*
Canol y dref *City center*
Cerddwyr ymlaen *Pedestrians ahead*
Dim Mynediad *No Entry*
Dim o gwbl *At any time*
Gyrrwch yn ofalus *Please drive carefully*
Ildiwch *Yield*
Un Ffordd *One Way*
Ramp o'ch blaen *Ramp ahead*
Rhybudd *Warning*

Below far left Multiple signage entering a popular Cotswolds town **Below left** Prices advertised outside a gas station at night **Below center** Self service at a gas station **Below center right** Road winding through the dramatic Cheddar Gorge **Below right** Single-lane road over a small bridge in the countryside

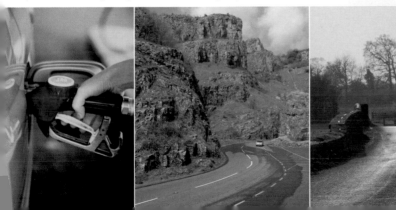

Above left A warning road sign **Above center** A pay-and-display parking ticket machine **Above right** Parking along the roadside in a Cotswolds village

Road Conditions

Most roads in Great Britain are well surfaced and maintained. Distances are given in miles, and roads are usually well marked. Many parts of the country suffer from traffic congestion, not only in and around the major cities but also in parts of the country popular for holidays and weekend breaks. Traffic to the West Country (Dorset, Devon and Cornwall) in summer can be maddeningly slow. Many people make an early getaway on holiday weekends, resulting in busy roads from Thursday evening through Monday night. Rainy weather can also slow things down. Get up-to-date reports on traffic conditions online or by phone from the **Met Office**, **Highways Agency**, or **AA Roadwatch**.

In the Highlands of Scotland and in some other rural areas, the roads are single-track. Slow down for sheep, cattle, and other animals who may run out in front of your car. These roads are often so narrow that one car will have to pull over to the side and let an oncoming car pass. Courtesy dictates that the car closest to a wide spot waits. There are designated passing places along these roads. When you meet oncoming vehicles, always pull in to the closest one on your left. You may need to reverse to

find a space. It is easier for a car to reverse than farm machinery or large vehicles. Always give drivers who yield to you a friendly wave.

Taking a Break

If you are feeling tired or lost, it's a good idea to pull over and take a break. Many roads have marked areas where you can pull off and stretch your legs, have a snack, and consult your map. The scenery can be a distraction, so if you find it hard to keep your eyes on the road, it's best to stop and admire the view. Parks and areas with nature trails also make good picnic stops. Highway service stations are generally well marked along the route. They have coffee bars, sit-down restaurants, fast food, snacks, toilets, shops, and other public facilities, as well as gas stations. On the A and B roads, services are smaller and public toilets are often found in petrol stations or restaurants.

Breakdown and Accident Procedures

If you have car trouble, try to park safely and turn on your hazard lights or put out a warning triangle to alert other drivers. There are SOS telephones at regular intervals along the hard shoulder (spare lane on the far left) of

a highway. It is dangerous to walk along any highway, so take care when getting out of your car.

Car rental companies will normally give you a number to call in case of breakdown or problems with the vehicle. They will advise or arrange for assistance, and can usually provide a replacement vehicle. You should not undertake any repairs to a rental car without the company's permission. If you belong to a motoring association in your country, the UK motoring services – **Automobile Association** (AA) and **Royal Automobile Club** (RAC) – may have a reciprocal arrangement of co-operation – check before leaving.

If you have an accident you must stop and exchange name, address, and car registration details with the other parties involved. Police must be notified within 24 hours if anyone is injured, and a report will be filed. Call the emergency services (see p13) if there are serious injuries. Be sure to get the insurance details of the other driver, and give them yours. You must also notify your car rental company as soon as possible.

Circumstances can be confusing at the time of an accident, so don't admit fault for the accident, accept liability, or give money to any party. If possible, take down any details from

Above left Traditional signpost and brown tourist sign in the Avon Valley **Above right** Old stone cottages in West Witton, Yorkshire Dales

independent witnesses. It's also a good idea to take photographs of the vehicles and the accident scene.

Parking

Finding a place to park is one of the most frustrating aspects of driving in Great Britain. Parking is prohibited at all times on a double yellow line. A single yellow line means no parking during business hours – these will be displayed on a sign nearby. Signs with a red "P" in a circle crossed by a diagonal line also indicate a no-parking zone. A red line is a clearway and you cannot stop at all. Don't be tempted to flout the rules and park illegally, even for a few minutes. Traffic wardens are eager to write expensive tickets. Wheel-clamping and towing companies are even more predatory and expensive.

Park in designated lots, which will be indicated by a blue sign with a white "P". These are often pay-and-display – obtain a ticket from a nearby machine and display it on your windscreen (windshield). Disc parking is another system used in many towns, whereby you must buy a scratch card from nearby shops and scratch off the date and time before displaying it in your car. In larger cities there are parking

garages such as NCP; these may be more expensive, but you don't have to worry about the time as you pay for your stay when you leave.

It is often possible to park on the street, but read the signs along the pavement carefully. Many streets have residents' parking only, with visitors restricted to particular hours and/or parking vouchers – if you are visiting someone who lives there, they may have a voucher for you. Others are pay-and-display, with the meter somewhere along the pavement.

In many rural towns and villages, there is little room for parking in the center, but there are parking lots, usually free, at the edge of town. In the countryside, be sure not to block farmers' gates or private roads if you are walking or exploring. On single-lane roads, never park in passing places as this is a traffic hazard.

Maps

Free tourist maps are widely available, but they are seldom useful for back-roads driving. It's well worth buying an up-to-date road atlas for more detailed coverage. There are several good ones published by Michelin, the AA, and A–Z. Buy them at gas stations, bookshops, newsagents, and tourist information centers.

DIRECTORY

ROAD CONDITIONS
Met Office
0870 900 0100; www.metoffice.gov.uk

Highways Agency
08700 660 115;
www.highways.gov.uk/traffic

AA Roadwatch
401100 (from mobile phones);
www.theaa.com/travelwatch/
travel_news.jsp

BREAKDOWN AND ACCIDENT PROCEDURES
Automobile Association (AA)
0870 600 0371 (UK) or +44 161 495
8945 (from abroad); www.theaa.com

Royal Automobile Club (RAC)
08705 722 722; www.rac.co.uk

Below far left Farmer's sign reminding drivers to close the gate through grazing land near Oban, Scotland **Below left** Prices outside a petrol station **Below center** Narrow country road between Cirencester and Chedworth in Gloucestershire **Below right** Horse riders on a quiet lane flanked by hedgerow near Lower Slaughter in the Cotswolds

Trailers and Motorhomes

Trailers (caravans) and motorhomes (RVs) are subject to the same rules of the road as other vehicles. However, camper vans or cars towing trailers are restricted to speeds of 50 mph (80 kph) on regular roads and 60 mph (96 kph) on motorways. Many of Britain's back-country roads, particularly in remote parts of Scotland, are narrow and winding and not suitable for trailers, motorhomes, or towed

Above A station wagon driving into a camp site just outside Brecon in Powys, Wales, towing a caravan

vehicles. Signs are often posted, but they are easy to miss. Ask locally about the conditions before setting out on these roads. Narrow bridges, sharp bends, and steep gradients can be dangerous for large vehicles, so pay attention to warning road signs.

If you are bringing your own trailer to Britain, you must be sure that your LP gas has been turned off correctly for the ferry crossing. With Eurotunnel, the valves must be sealed and your roof vents opened for safety.

You can also rent motorhomes and trailers. Some, such as those available from **Just Go**, come with XBox 360, DVD/CD players and other creature comforts. **Motorhomes Direct** has a huge selection of luxury models for rent nationwide, while **Cool Campervans** caters for travelers on a budget. There is a wide network of camping and RV parks. For online directories try **Camping and Caravanning UK** and **UK Caravan Parks and Campsites Directory**.

Motorbikes

All motorcyclists and passengers must wear protective helmets. Drivers must have a valid driving license to cover a motorcycle or moped and an insurance policy. You may not carry a passenger if

you hold a provisional license; you must have a full license and an insurance policy that allows you to do so. Motorcycles must have rear number plate lighting. Low-beam headlights during the day are not required, but they are recommended to make you more visible.

The rules of the road are the same for motorcyclists as for other drivers, though you should take additional safety precautions. Go slow when filtering or driving between traffic lanes. Give other vehicles a wide berth when overtaking them, and be aware they might not always see you.

Driving with Children

Drivers must ensure that all children under the age of 14 wear seat-belts or sit in an approved child restraint, if required. Older teenagers must wear adult seat-belts. If a child is around 4 ft 5 in (under 1.35 m) tall, a baby seat, child seat, booster seat or booster cushion suitable for the child's height and weight must be used. The correct child restraint must be used in both the front and back seats. Babies must never be placed in a rear-facing child seat in the passenger seat if there is an active airbag fitted, as it can cause serious injury or death to the child in a crash. Children must not sit behind the

rear seats in an estate car or other vehicle unless a special child seat has been fitted. Remember to request any necessary child seats in advance when making your car rental reservation.

Disabled Drivers

Drivers with disabilities should contact **Mobilise**, a charity that promotes mobility and represents the interests of disabled drivers, for advice on obtaining a UK blue badge for disabled parking spaces or using their Disabled Parking cards in the UK. If you are bringing your own car through Ireland first, you may be able to get a discount from the ferry company on some sailings. Contact your motoring association (or the **Disabled Drivers' Association** in Ireland) for a form.

Car Rental

Most of the big international car rental companies, such as **Budget**, **Avis,** and **Hertz**, have locations at airports and ferry ports, and in all the larger cities, and offer a wide range of vehicles. A good local firm with offices in Scotland and Northern England is **Arnold Clark Car and Van Rental**. To rent a car you will need a valid driver's license and a credit card. Normally, drivers must be between the ages of 21 or 23 and 75, but

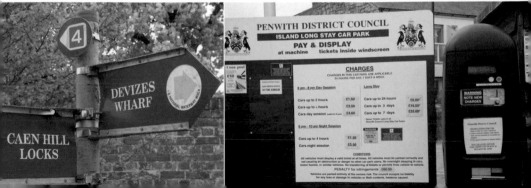

Above left Sign for a guest house in Bude, Cornwall **Above right** Camp site in a field in Dorset, tucked away behind the trees

check before you make your reservation regarding their age restrictions. It's highly recommended that you book in advance, especially during peak season – you will often get a better rate. Rental rates usually include unlimited mileage, but double check. Most rental cars in Great Britain are manual (standard) shift. Automatic cars are available, but they cost more and must be booked in advance. Consider renting a smaller car than you may be used to at home, as they are much easier to handle on narrow country roads than big SUVs. If you need a child seat, these should be booked in advance as well.

Third-party insurance is compulsory and is included in the rate. Some rental agreements also include Collision Damage Waiver (CDW) which limits your liability for damages to the rental car, theft loss cover, and personal injury insurance; others charge additional fees for these items. Be sure to read your agreement carefully so that you fully understand what your coverage and liabilities are. Some drivers may be able to use insurance from a personal credit card to claim CDW, but check carefully with your card company to make sure they cover your trip abroad and be prepared to show proof of cover.

Driving in Bad Weather

When conditions reduce light levels, low-beam headlights should be used. Turn on fog lights whenever visibility is less than 328 ft (100 m). If you bring a left-hand drive vehicle with you, adjust the headlights. Buy beam adjusters at ferry terminals, or check with your motoring organization.

Always reduce speed in adverse conditions, as you will need a greater braking distance, and poor visibility gives less time to react. In Scotland and other mountainous areas, you may encounter ice and snow in winter. Slow down, especially for curves and turns, and make your actions steady and deliberate to avoid sliding out of control. If you find the car skidding, take your foot off the accelerator – do not brake – and turn the wheel into the skid until the car corrects itself. Watch out for "black ice," especially on bridges and overpasses, which freeze up first. If you hit a patch, do not brake or turn the wheel, but keep as straight as possible and coast over it.

Below far left Signs on the Kennet and Avon Canal **Below left** Pay-and-display ticket machine, Penwith, Cornwall **Below center** Old-fashioned road sign at Lacock in the Cotswolds **Below right** Sheep by the roadside in Ashdown Forest, the home of Winnie the Pooh, Sussex

DIRECTORY

TRAILERS AND MOTORHOMES
Camping and Caravanning UK
http://camping.uk-directory.com

Cool Campervans
01332 661 342;
www.coolcampervans.com

Just Go
0870 240 1918 (UK); +44 1582 842 888
(from abroad); www.justgo.uk.com

Motorhomes Direct
0800 612 8719 (UK); +44 1954 718750
(from abroad);
www.motorhomesdirect.co.uk

UK Caravan Parks and Campsites Directory
www.uk-sites.com

DISABLED DRIVERS
Disabled Drivers' Association
+353 (0) 94 936 4054; www.ddai.ie

Mobilise
01508 489 449; www.mobilise.info

CAR RENTAL
Arnold Clark Car and Van Rental
0844 576 5425;
www.arnoldclarkrental.com

Avis
0844 581 0147; www.avis.co.uk

Budget
0844 544 3407; www.budget.co.uk

Hertz
08708 44 88 44; www.hertz.co.uk

Where to Stay

The picturesque views seen while driving the back roads of Great Britain will perhaps raise the question: what would it be like to live here? The accommodation in each of the driving tours has been selected to give a taste of life in this varied country, whether it be a cozy bed and breakfast in the Scottish Highlands, a boutique hotel on the Cornish coast or even an ancient castle. There is also a range of luxury golf and spa resorts, and camp sites with heavenly views from forest to mountains to seaside.

Above Doorway to cottage accommodation displaying its grading

Hotels and Inns

Great Britain is known for its traditional hotels, many of which have been operating for over a century. Historic inns offer some of the most charming accommodation, often in village pubs, converted mills, or old coaching inns which served travelers as far back as the 17th century. Because of the age of the buildings, some rooms may be small, compared to modern hotels. Many inns have excellent restaurants or pub menus.

Country-house hotels usually have beautiful grounds and bigger rooms. Food is often a highlight here, with more formal dining rooms, creative set menus, and top chefs in the kitchen. Be aware that some may not cater for young children.

Boutique hotels are not just for cities anymore. Chic, high-concept hotels dot the smaller towns and resort areas, with everything from the reception area to the bathroom sinks (faucets) featuring the best in modern design. These establishments usually have lively bars and restaurants, too.

National and international chain hotels offer accommodation in all price ranges, and these can be found in the larger towns and cities or along the highways throughout Britain. Depending on their quality rating,

hotels will normally have at least one restaurant and a bar. Most include breakfast in the room rate, but some do not. Most hotel rooms have ensuite bathroom facilities, and some also offer family rooms and suites.

Guest Houses

Guest houses are smaller and usually less expensive than hotels. Many were formerly large family homes, with all or several rooms converted for guests, often with simple but charming décor. Those with higher ratings will have ensuite bathrooms. Breakfast is usually included in the rate, but most guest houses do not have restaurants or bars, though they may have snacks and drinks available for guests. In the countryside, pubs and increasingly restaurants have guest rooms available and this can be a good way to enjoy the local nightlife without worrying about driving afterwards.

Bed-and-Breakfasts (B&Bs)

Bed-and-breakfast accommodation is offered in private homes around the country, from town centers to country farmhouses. They usually have several guest rooms – often ensuite, but sometimes with shared bathrooms. Facilities and décor vary, but they are usually clean and comfortable. Some

hosts will offer an evening meal for an additional charge, but this must be arranged in advance. B&Bs are often cheaper than hotels and guest houses, and are a great way to meet local people and pick up local tips.

Castles and Historic Homes

Stunning accommodation can be found in the castles and historic homes that have opened some of their rooms to overnight visitors. You will certainly pay for the privilege, but a night or two in one of these glorious landmark buildings can be the most memorable of your trip – book early.

Luxury Resorts

Golf resorts have long been popular, especially in Scotland, and now most luxury resorts feature spa facilities, too. These establishments offer a range of activities as well as fine dining and casual restaurants – an attractive option when you want a relaxing break from the road.

Making Reservations

It's essential to book ahead for July and August, and during festivals, events, and busy holiday periods, to ensure you get your choice of accommodation. Book by phone or (in most cases) online directly with

Above left Traditional inn, Chipping Campden, made out of the local stone **Above right** Smart interior of a Chipping Campden hotel

the establishment, using a credit card. Or take advantage of the service offered by tourist boards *(see p15)*. Some local tourist offices in Scotland will book accommodation ahead at your next night's destination for a deposit and small service charge. You can also find properties of character and luxury through organizations such as **Great Inns of Britain**, **Welsh Rarebits**, **Scotland's Hotels of Distinction**, and **Distinction Hotels**.

Be sure to check if the rate quoted is per person or per room – B&Bs and guest houses are almost always per person, as are many hotels. Rates in Britain generally include VAT (tax), but double-check in the pricier city hotels.

Facilities and Prices

British hotel rooms usually have a double or twin beds; if you need a cot or child's bed, request it when booking. Coffee- and tea-making facilities are a welcome standard. Most places serve a full "English" breakfast with eggs, bacon, sausage, and all the trimmings, although "Continental" breakfasts are usually also available.

All types of accommodation, from camping parks to luxury hotels, are rated from one to five stars in their respective categories. The rating system has finally been standardized across the various tourist boards and

other rating agencies, such as the AA. Properties are visited and assessed every year. Be aware that many establishments with lower star ratings still offer excellent quality, but simply have fewer facilities and services.

Generally, the higher the star rating, the more expensive the room, but prices also vary seasonally. Check for special offers, and remember that some of the lowest rates are offered online through the hotel website.

Camping

Camping is very popular in Great Britain, and there is a broad network of sites throughout the country. These are graded for their quality and facilities, similar to other types of accommodation. The **Camping and Caravanning Club** is a good source of information. Wild camping (outside of designated camp sites and RV parks) is not legal in England and Wales. It is permitted in Scotland, but you should always obtain permission from the landowner before parking your RV or pitching your tent.

Below far left Cozy room at the Abbotsbury Hotel, Dorset **Below left** Four-poster bed in the hotel at Amberley Castle, Sussex **Below center** Ees Wyke Country House hotel in the Lakes **Below right** Camp site by Glencoe, Scotland

DIRECTORY

PRICE BANDS IN THE BOOK
Hotels
For a double room for 1 night, breakfast and all taxes included.

Inexpensive – under £80

Moderate – £80–150

Expensive – over £150

BOOKING A HOTEL
Distinction Hotels
www.distinctionhotels.com

Great Inns of Britain
01423 770 152: www.greatinns.co.uk

Scotland's Hotels of Distinction
www.hotels-of-distinction.com

Welsh Rarebits
01686 668 030: www.rarebits.co.uk

CAMPING
Camping and Caravanning Club
0845 130 7632 or 024 7647 5448; www.campingandcaravanningclub. co.uk

Where to Eat

Britain's love affair with food has bloomed in recent years, inspired by TV chefs and innovative restaurateurs, and there is an enticing array of top-notch eating places at all prices. At the top end, British chefs are racking up Michelin stars in village restaurants, and there are countless fun, fashionable eateries with international themes as well as impressive gastro-pubs that won't break the bank. Menus increasingly feature local, seasonal produce, and there are shops and markets where you can stock up on gourmet goodies. But never fear – traditional favorites such as cream teas and fish and chips are as popular as ever, too.

Above Sign listing the food and facilities of the Castle Coffee House, Dunster

Practical Information

A full cooked breakfast at your guesthouse or hotel can set you up for the day – and don't be afraid to try local specialities such as black pudding (blood sausage), kippers (split, smoked herring) or Welsh laverbread (minced seaweed). Lunch is usually served from noon until 2 or 3pm; in smaller towns, restaurants and cafes may stop serving at 2.30pm. Dinner is the main meal of the day in Great Britain. Restaurant opening times vary widely. Most open at 6 or 7pm. In larger towns and tourist areas they may serve until 10 or 11pm, but in smaller towns and villages they often close at 9pm, with last orders half an hour earlier. Many pubs serve bar food from lunchtime until 9pm. High-end restaurants often close one or two days per week (usually Mondays), but many smaller establishments in busy areas stay open seven days. Off the beaten track, they may close out of season. It's always wise to phone ahead.

Credit cards are widely accepted, but pubs, tea shops, and take-out establishments may take cash only. Tax is always included in the bill, but the service charge varies. If it is added,

it will be listed separately on the bill; if it isn't, leave 10–15 percent for the wait staff. You can also leave an extra tip for excellent service.

Casual dress is acceptable in most restaurants, though you may want to dress smartly for more expensive establishments. Most places are wheelchair accessible, but check in advance for older buildings. Some upmarket restaurants may not welcome children under a certain age. Children are allowed in pubs with their parents until 9pm; look for those which are family friendly with gardens and play areas. Smoking is banned inside all restaurants and bars.

Menus are generally displayed outside beside the door or window and fine dining establishments usually offer a set-price (prix fixe) menu as well as à la carte. These can be great value, especially at lunchtime, and allow you to enjoy a top restaurant at an affordable price.

Restaurants

Restaurants in Great Britain run the gamut from cozy, casual eateries to impressive dining rooms with beautifully laid tables and crystal

chandeliers. Famous chefs run top restaurants specializing in seafood, game, or local produce all around the country, and you'll need to book well ahead to get a table. Look for quality symbols such as the **Taste of Scotland** restaurants, which feature creative menus based on regional produce.

Nearly all restaurants feature at least one vegetarian option, usually more. Fine dining establishments have full wine lists, and often feature a wide selection of whiskies and other spirits.

Ethnic restaurants and those specializing in European cuisine are popular around the country. Along with a multitude of Indian and Chinese restaurants, you'll find Italian, French, Greek, Turkish, Polish, Spanish, and many other offerings.

Pubs and Bars

Many pubs offer simple, inexpensive meals at lunchtime and usually in the evenings, too. Shepherd's pie, lasagne, fish and chips, and ploughman's lunch (cheese, bread and pickles) are standard offerings. Sunday lunch is popular at many pubs, often with a carvery serving roast meats, Yorkshire pudding (batter), and vegetables.

Above left The Pump Room Restaurant, Bath **Above center** Ice cream and candy floss kiosk, Weymouth beach **Above right** Café in Bradford-upon-Avon, near Bath

In a class of their own are gastro-pubs (short for gastronomic pubs). These are traditional pubs that have upgraded their menus with a range of exciting dishes featuring innovative and often local cuisine. You can enjoy restaurant-quality meals in a relaxed atmosphere – often at lower prices.

Bars and wine bars sometimes have sandwiches or light meals on offer at various times of the day.

Cafés and Take-aways

The weather is not conducive to a café culture in Britain similar to that in other parts of Europe. But whenever it's warm and sunny, you'll find restaurant, pub, and café tables spilling out onto every available pavement space.

Cafés are generally open for breakfast and lunch, but most close by 6pm. Most museums and visitor attractions have cafés where you can get light refreshments. The coffee craze has taken Britain by storm, and coffee-shop chains are ubiquitous in larger cities. Many sell sandwiches, muffins, and pastries as well. Not to be missed are traditional tea shops, where you can have a pot of tea or coffee along with homemade cakes, breads, and local specialities – often in delightful surroundings. Be sure to try a traditional cream tea with scones, clotted cream and jam, especially if

you're touring Devon and Cornwall. Fast-food chains are plentiful, but far more satisfying are the local versions. Look for small shops selling fish and chips, Cornish pasties, or even shish kebabs, which make quick, filling, and usually inexpensive take-away meals.

Picnics

Nearly every high street in every town will have at least one sandwich shop, where you can grab ready-made picnic supplies. Supermarkets also sell sandwiches and snacks. More fun are the independent food shops and delis, which sell a great range of meats, cheeses, and tasty local delicacies.

Best of all are the local markets. Always colorful, they are a showcase for regional producers. Look for picnic supplies of artisan breads, locally made cheeses, honey, and preserves, or apple varieties that you can't buy in a supermarket – they can also be a good place to find great presents or souvenirs. Each driving tour notes the location and days of the week for markets around the region.

Below far left Retro-style tea-shop window **Below left** Colorful fresh fruit and veg stall, selling good-value produce **Below center** The pretty Rising Sun Hotel, Lynmouth **Below center right** Café in the heart of Hay-on-Wye **Below right** Rick Stein's Seafood Restaurant, Padstow

DIRECTORY

PRICE BANDS IN THE BOOK

Restaurants
Three-course meal for one with half a bottle of wine and including VAT (tax).

Inexpensive – under £25

Moderate – £25–50

Expensive – over £50

RESTAURANTS

Taste of Scotland
www.taste-of-scotland.com

ROCHESTER
Upchurch
Iwade
Chap. and
Isle
Harr
and
Isle
the Welles

Woldham
Boxley
Cap ston
Milton Chu
Milton
Murston
Tong
Lyding
Chap.
Rainham
Bobbing
Tenham
Wood
Bredherst
Newington
Buckland
Borcham
Hartlip
Bor den
Siltingbourn
Banchild
Luddingham
Guilsted Str.
Hill Green
Stockbury
Bredgate
Tunstall
Rodmersham
Norton
Boxley
Stockb. Valley
Bickivor
Linsted
Aylesford
Delling
Hucking
Wormsell
Hogshare
Kingsdown
Ospringe
Sandling
Thornham
Frinsted
Newnham
Maidstone
Hollingborne
Wichling
Eastling
Sheld
the Bower
Otham
Leeds
Bromfield
Lenham
Throwley
Stallsfield
E. Farley
Hertewood Str.
Dane Str.
Langley
Kings Wood
Charing
W. Farley
Loose
Ulcomb
Broughton
Pete
Linton
Chart juxta Sutton
Challock
Boughton
Munchelsea
Sutton Valence
Egerton
Westwell
Eastwell
Muttenden
Frogin Fostle
Lit. Chart
Wilmerton
Hedcorne
Paweington
the
Twist
Crofs hand
Beula R.
Pluckley
Hothfield
Marden
Smarden
Goddenton
Willesborn
Downe
Romden
Bunsill
Great Chart
Staplehurst
Hamden
Surrenden
Shingleton
Fritenden
New Street
Goudhurst
Biddenden
WEALD
Mer
Camdens
Hill
Biddenden
Green
High Halden
Shadoxherst
Bilsing
Cranbrook
Bromley Green
Goford
Green
of KENT
Orlesto
High Street
Woodchurch
Warhorn
Ror
Benenden
Rolvenden
Tenderden
Sandhurst
Broad Tenterden
Kenarton
Newenden
Smallhythe
Horn Pla.
Snave

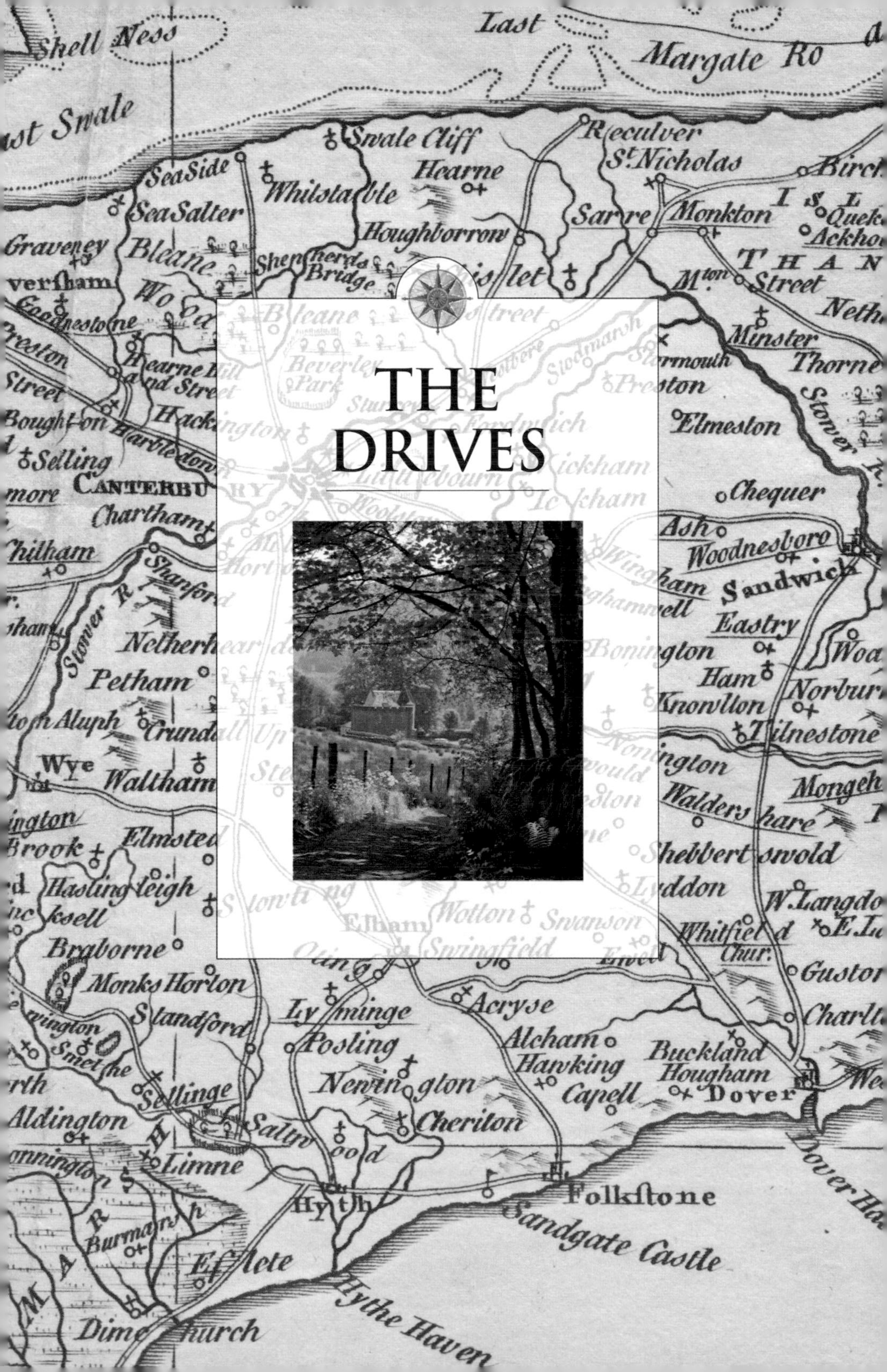
Shell Ness
Last
Margate Ro
East Swale
Swale Cliff
Reculver
St. Nicholas
Birch
Sea Side
Whitstable
Hearne
Sea Salter
Sarre
Monkton
ISL
Queks
Ackho
Graveney
Bleane
Houghborrow
Faversham
Shepherds Bridge
Wood
Chislet
THAN
Mton Street
Goodnestone
Neth
Preston
Hearne Hill and Street
Minster
Thorne
Boughton
Harble down
Hackington
Stourmouth
Preston
Elmeston
Stower R.
Selling
CANTERBURY
Chequer
Chartham
Ash
Woodnesboro
Chilham
Shanford
Wingham
Sandwich
Stower R.
Eastry
Netherhear
Bonington
Ham
Petham
Knowlton
Norburn
Chilham Aluph
Crundall Up
Tilnestone
Wye
Waltham
Nonington
Mongeh
Waldershare
Elmsted
Brook
Shebbertswold
Hastingleigh
Lyddon
Elham
Wotton
Swanson
W. Langdon
Braborne
Whitfield
Swingfield
Ewell
Chur.
Guston
Monks Horton
Standford
Acryse
Lyminge
Charlton
Posling
Alcham
Hawking
Buckland
Hougham
Smeethe
Newington
Capell
Dover
Sellinge
Aldington
Saltwood
Cheriton
Limne
Folkstone
MARSH
Hyth
Sandgate Castle
Burmarsh
Eastbridge
Dimchurch
Hythe Haven
Dover Ha

THE DRIVES

Lizard Point and the South Cornwall Coast

St Ives to Tavistock

Highlights

- **Artists' haven**
  Picturesque St Ives, home to national museums and brimming with galleries

- **Cape Cornwall and the Lizard**
  Wild, rugged and beautiful coastal scenery at England's extremities

- **Porthcurno**
  Perfect Cornish cove below the Minack Theatre, cut into the cliffside

- **Gardens galore**
  The South West has some of the UK's best gardens, thanks to its mild climate

- **Roseland Peninsula**
  Beautiful and unspoiled peninsula with the picturesque St. Justus Church

Classic Cornish cove at Porthcurno, a gem of a beach in an area of outstanding natural beauty

Lizard Point and South Cornwall Coast

The coastline around the most southerly part of the British mainland is outstandingly beautiful – dramatically rugged with tiny coves punctuating the shore below granite and serpentine cliffs. Seabirds such as fulmars, gannets, cormorants, and shags wheel and cry overhead while basking sharks, seals, and dolphins can often be seen in the water when the sea is calm. Ancient standing stones and redundant mine workings are evidence that the area has been well used by man for millennia, but never more so than today. Visitors pour in to enjoy vacations in and around the beaches and quaint old fishing villages which previously thrived on huge catches of pilchards. The area's mild climate has also contributed to its rich legacy of exotic gardens, some planted in previous centuries by keen local horticulturalists.

ACTIVITIES

Enjoy Cornish clotted cream on scones with jam or in ice cream

Take on the Atlantic surfing in St Ives or kite-surfing at Marazion

Admire great art in St Ives and invest in a piece of work from one of the small galleries there

Go underground at the Geevor tin mine in Pendeen

Enjoy a clifftop drama at the Minack Theatre, Porthcurno

Explore an exotic garden at Trebah, the Lost Gardens of Heligan or the Eden Project

Take a boat trip from Fowey for the scenery, wildlife and seabirds

Below The Lizard Lighthouse at England's most southerly point, *see p34*

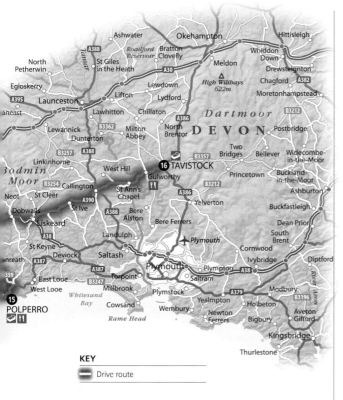

PLAN YOUR DRIVE

Start/finish: St Ives to Tavistock.

Number of days: 4–5, allowing half a day to visit the galleries in St Ives. Visits to a garden, especially Heligan or the Eden Project, will take up to half a day at least, as will a trip to Dartmoor.

Distance: 171 miles (275 km).

Road conditions: Although well-paved and marked, many of the country roads are narrow. Those leading down to old fishing harbors are often steep and tend to be congested in high season.

When to go: Cornwall is a popular tourist region so the whole area gets very crowded in July and August. In winter, when the weather is usually still comparatively mild, towns return to 'normal' but villages can be very quiet. Because of the number of tourists, most places have well-marked parking lots, usually pay-and-display. At peak times, look for park-and-ride schemes.

Opening times: Museums and attractions are generally open 10am– 5pm, but close earlier (or are closed altogether) Nov–Easter. Shops are often open longer. Churches are usually open until dusk.

Market days: St Ives: Thu; Tavistock: Pannier Market, Tue–Sat; **Moreton- hampstead:** last Sat of month, Apr–Nov.

Shopping: Local crafts, paintings, Cornish pasties, and clotted cream.

Major festivals: St Ives: September Festival; **Porthcurno:** Minack Theatre season May–Sep; **Helston:** Furry Dance Festival on May Day; **Widecombe:** Widecombe Fair, 2nd Tue in Sep.

DAY TRIP OPTIONS

Enjoy the **sandy beaches** and **art galleries** of St Ives, then head down the coast to explore old **tin mines**, **cliff tops** and the spectacular **Porthcurno theater**. On the Lizard, swim in the **Atlantic surf** or visit a **seal sanctuary**. From St Austell or Fowey, see the **Lost Gardens of Heligan**, learn about **shipwrecks** at Charlestown, or visit the amazing Eden Project with its **space-age biomes**. For full details, see p37.

Above View across the beautiful estuary from Polruan to Fowey, a popular yachting destination, see p36

VISITING ST IVES

Parking
The steep streets get very congested.
Park at the top of town and walk down
to the harbor. Upper Trenwith parking
lot provides a shuttle bus down.

Tourist Information
*The Guildhall, Street an Pol, TR26 2DS;
01736 796 297; www.visit-cornwall.
com; closed Sat pm, Sun*

WHERE TO STAY

ST IVES

Rivendell *inexpensive*
Award-winning family-run guesthouse
near sea and town center; offers dinner,
packed lunches, and a parking lot.
*7 Porthminster Terrace, TR26
2DQ; 01736 794 923;
www.rivendell-stives.co.uk*

Boskerris Hotel *moderate–expensive*
Smart but friendly hotel above Carbis
Bay with 15 stylish rooms (most with sea
views), a decked terrace and a garden.
*Boskerris Road, TR26 2NQ; 01736 795
295; www.boskerrishotel.co.uk*

AROUND ZENNOR

Gurnard's Head *moderate*
Small and cozy inn in an imposing
building near the sea amidst a wild
Cornish landscape. Excellent restaurant.
*Treen, TR26 3DE (2 miles/3 km/
west of Zennor); 01736 796 928;
www.gurnardshead.co.uk*

❶ St Ives
Cornwall; TR26 2DS

Once Cornwall's busiest pilchard-fishing port, St Ives suffered as fish
stocks declined at the start of the 20th century. Help had arrived with
the advent of the railway in 1877, as the trains brought holidaymakers
to the town. Artists, including Turner, were also drawn by the clear
light there, and many of the harborside net lofts were now converted
to artists' studios. The fishing never recovered, but the visitors kept
coming, attracted by the fine sandy beaches and many art galleries.

A two-hour walking tour

Walk downhill from the **Tourist
Information Center (TIC)** ❶. Turn left
along St. Andrew's Street to Market
Place, which is overlooked by the
15th-century **St. Ia's** ❷, built in the
local textured granite, with a
80-ft (24-m) tower. It has
carved sandstone pillars,
choir stalls, a gilded roof,
and a *Madonna* sculpture
by Barbara Hepworth.

Turn right to join **Wharf
Road** ❸ which leads around
the harbor to a tiny 16th-
century chapel on **Smeaton's
Pier** ❹ where, nowadays, just a few
fishermen still land their catch.

A warren of cobbled streets climbs
steeply up into Downalong, the oldest
part of town, once home to the fishing

community. Go along Sea View Place
to **St Ives Museum** ❺ *(open Easter–Oct,
closed Sun)* in Wheal Dream which tells
the town's history – one gallery has
paintings from the 1880s when the
celebrated St Ives School of Artists
was formed. Continue down
a narrow walkway to steps
above the sea and around
the parking lot above the
tiny Porthgwidden Beach
and its excellent café. With
the sea on your right, continue
onto the grassy headland of the
Island, which has the tiny
St. Nicholas Chapel ❻ at the
top. Drop down again to the parking
lot. Carry on along Porthmeor Road
and right into Back Road West and
right again onto the seafront for the
Tate St Ives Gallery ❼ *(Mar–Oct, open
daily; Nov–Feb, closed Mon)*, a striking
white building with a large convex
window. It features artists painting in
Cornwall in the mid-20th century.

Walk back along the seafront,
bearing right into The Digey and
right again into Fore Street, the main
street. Fork right uphill, following
signs to the **Barbara Hepworth
Museum and Sculpture Garden** ❽
*(Mar–Oct, open daily; Nov–Feb, closed
Mon)* on Barnoon Hill. The sculptor, a
key figure in the development of
abstract art in Europe, worked in the
house for 26 years, and her sculptures
are dotted around house and garden.

Head downhill from the museum,
turn right and go steeply uphill at the
next junction signed Trewyn Gardens.
Cross these to the far exit leading to a
T-junction. Turn left towards the High
Street. Return to the TIC via Tregenna
Place, past the Library which, like many
of the galleries in town, displays work
by local artists or created locally.

🚗 *Exit on the B3306 towards St Just
and Land's End. Zennor is just off the
road on the right after 8 km (5 miles).*

*St Ives
Museum sign*

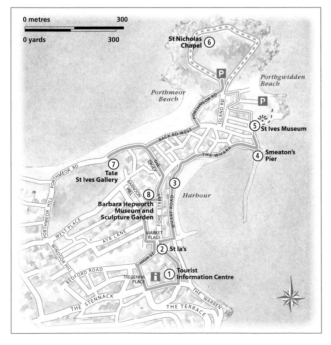

② Zennor

Cornwall; TR26 3DA

Did the mermaid depicted on a pew in the 12th-century church of **St. Senara** really lure a chorister to his death by her singing? Or did the story serve to discourage outsiders from venturing down to the cove, a local smugglers' haunt? Whatever the truth of the tale, the factual side of Zennor's history since the Bronze Age is shown in the **Wayside Museum** *(open daily, Apr–Oct)* housed in a 16th-century miller's cottage. The great Methodist evangelist John Wesley preached in Zennor in the mid-18th century and another notable visitor was the writer DH Lawrence during World War I. He stayed with his German wife, Frieda, at the Tinners Arms pub, while writing *Women in Love*. The **Zennor Quoit** burial chamber, just southeast of the village on Amalveor Downs, is one of the area's many prehistoric remains.

🚗 *Continue on B3306 to Pendeen. Geevor Tin Mine parking lot is on right.*

③ Pendeen

Cornwall; TR19 7NL

The ruined stacks and engine houses dotted along the coast, a UNESCO World Heritage site for Cornish mining, are reminders of the area's boom time in the 19th century. At Pendeen, **Geevor Tin Mine** *(closed Sat)* shows how tin was mined and processed. Continue on the B3306, past granite outcrops, where remains of prehistoric habitation, such as standing stones and burial mounds, can often be seen amongst the bracken. Turn right at St Just to **Cape Cornwall**, a windswept headland topped by a slender chimney stack that evokes a true end-of-the-world feeling. In fact, **Land's End** lies slightly further west,

but much of the majesty of the site has been lost due to the development of the area.

🚗 *Take the B3306 to St Just and take the A3071, then turn right onto B3306 (marked Land's End). Turn right onto A30. After Sennen, turn left onto B3315, then right to Porthcurno. Follow signs and park at the Minack Theatre.*

④ Porthcurno

Cornwall; TR19 6JX

The unique feature of this small sandy cove is the **Minack Theatre**, hewn out of the cliffs above it. With the sea as a backdrop, the Greek-style theater, created in the 1930s, has an incomparable setting. The visitor center tells its story *(open daily; performances May–Sep; www.minack. com)*. A small white pyramid on the cliff marks the spot where the first transatlantic telephone cable was laid in 1880. The history of telegraphy is told in the **Porthcurno Telegraph Museum** *(Mar–Oct, closed Wed; Nov–Apr, open Sun, Mon only)*.

🚗 *Return to B3315; after 8 km (5 miles), turn right for Mousehole parking lot.*

Above left Shop selling traditional beach toys, St Ives **Above center** The Tate St Ives building overlooking Porthmeor Beach **Above** The stage and beautiful setting of the Minack Theatre, Porthcurno

EAT AND DRINK

ST IVES

Sloop Inn *inexpensive*
Overlooking the harbor and noted for its seafood, this is one of Cornwall's oldest inns. It dates back to 1312 with wood beams, slate floors, and cobbles. *The Wharf, TR26 1LP; 01736 796 584; www.sloop-inn.co.uk*

Porthgwidden Café *moderate*
Small white stone building with terrace at Porthgwidden Beach. Noted for its steak, fresh fish, and waffles. *Porthgwidden Beach, TR26 1PL; 01736 796 791*

AROUND PORTHCURNO

Logan Rock Inn *inexpensive–moderate*
Pub known for its real ales and home-cooked food – pasties, steaks, and crab. Open fire in winter, beer garden, and pre-Minack theater dinners available. *Treen, TR19 6LG (1 mile/1.5 km east of Porthcurno); 01736 810 495*

Below Smeaton's Pier and the harbor at low tide, St Ives, Cornwall

Above The Castle, dominating St Michael's Mount, off Marazion **Top right** Picturesque harbor and granite houses at Mousehole **Right** Sign at Lizard Point, mainland England's most southerly point

WHERE TO STAY

AROUND THE LIZARD PENINSULA
Mullion Cove Hotel
moderate–expensive
Originally built for wealthy Victorians, this gleaming white clifftop hotel enjoys extensive sea views.
Mullion Cove, TR12 7EP; 01326 240 328; www.mullion-cove.co.uk

AROUND TREBAH
Budock Vean *expensive*
Large hotel in vast parklands beside the Helford River. Award-winning restaurant, sports activities, and natural health spa.
Helford Passage, Mawnan Smith, TR11 5LG (½ mile/1 km from Trebah); 01326 250 288; www.budockvean.co.uk

ST JUST-IN-ROSELAND
Round House Barns *moderate*
A Cornish cream tea greets guests at this award-winning B&B in a tastefully converted 17th-century barn.
St Just-in-Roseland, TR2 5JJ; 01872 580 038; www.roundhousebarnholidays.co.uk

ST MAWES
Tresanton *expensive*
Award-winning hotel stylishly created in a cluster of old houses. Rooms and restaurant have sea views.
27 Lower Castle Road, TR2 5DR; 01326 270 055; www.tresanton.com

---

⑤ Mousehole
Cornwall; TR19 6SD
This quintessential Cornish fishing village – pronounced "mouzel" – with a granite sea-walled harbor held over 400 pilchard fishing boats in the 19th century. A tangle of steep narrow lanes lead down past pretty cottages to waterside pubs, cafés, and shops. **Mousehole Bird Sanctuary** on Raginnis Hill cares for injured sea birds *(open daily)*.
🚗 *Return to the B3315 to Newlyn and join A30 (toward Truro). Turn right to Marazion at the junction with A394. Follow signs to St Michael's Mount.*

⑥ St Michael's Mount
near Penzance, Cornwall; TR17 0EF
This islet, looming out of the sea near Marazion, is dramatically topped by a 12th-century **castle** *(open daily Apr–Oct)* – in turn church, priory, fortress and now private home. At low tide it can be reached on foot across a causeway first used by pilgrims in the Middle Ages; a small ferry runs from Marazion at other times. A cobbled path leads up to the castle past terraced gardens. Home of the St Aubyn family since 1660, it has a mix of architectural styles.
🚗 *Return to the A394 to Helston, then turn right on the A3083 to the Lizard Peninsula. Turn right at signs for Kynance Cove after Mullion.*

---

⑦ The Lizard Peninsula
The tip of this windswept peninsula is England's most southerly point. Paths trace around the cliffs of this jagged coastline, dropping to secluded coves and harbors. Rare wildflowers grow on the heathland where ponies graze.

At much-photographed **Kynance Cove**, tilted pinnacles of rock stand like giants paddling in the sea off the sandy beach surrounded by cliffs.

At the end of the A3083, the **Lizard Point Lighthouse** is the most powerful in England, visible for 21 miles (34 km) in one of the world's busiest shipping lanes. In summer, basking sharks can often be seen just offshore.

Back up the A3083, to the right, tucked below the cliffs, lies **Cadgwith**. Here, pretty white-washed thatched cottages surround a tiny harbor whose fishermen entered the record books in the 19th century by landing 1.3 million pilchards in one day. Now they mainly catch lobster and crab which can be sampled with a glass of real ale at the Cadgwith Cove Inn.

Drive though Ruan Minor and Kuggar, turning left onto the B3293 to the **Goonhilly Satellite Earth Station** (with car park). On the open heathland stands a cluster of huge, futuristic satellite dishes – the largest is 151 ft (46 m) high – transmitting millions of messages every day. The **Future World** interactive exhibition *(open Tue–Sun)* suggests what life may be like in the next hundred years. Guided tours include a look inside a satellite dish.

Carrying on the B3293, turn off right to Gweek. Children of all ages will love the **Gweek Seal Sanctuary** *(open daily)*. Above Helford estuary, the sanctuary cares for sick or injured seals. There are also otters, ponies, goats, and a children's play area.

🚗 *From Gweek, continue toward Falmouth; at Constantine, turn right at sign to Mawnan Smith where Trebah Gardens and parking lot are marked.*

Above Winged cherub statue in the leafy, green Lost Gardens of Heligan

⑧ Trebah Gardens
Mawnan Smith, Cornwall; TR11 5JZ
In the 1830s, prosperous shipping agent and enthusiastic horticulturalist Charles Fox collected a wealth of sub-tropical plants and trees from around the world to create **Trebah Gardens** *(open daily)*. This lush paradise, set in a wooded ravine which descends 200 ft (61 m) to a private beach on Helford River has tumbling waterfalls, a pool of giant koi carp and great banks of blue and white hydrangeas. Paths lead under the shaded canopy of giant gunnera leaves and through a bamboo maze and flower borders.

🚗 *Return to Mawnan Smith, follow signs to Penryn. Turn left onto A39. Next take B3289 right to the King Harry Ferry (toll) across the Fal and back on B3289 to St Just-in-Roseland.*

⑨ St Just-in-Roseland
Cornwall; TR2 5HY
Designated an Area of Outstanding Natural Beauty for its leafy lanes and seascapes, the Roseland peninsula includes **St Just-in-Roseland** whose 13th-century St. Justus Church with its squat crenellated tower nestles beside a wooded tidal creek, framed by trees – a truly picture-postcard scene. The churchyard, entered either

through a 17th-century lych (roofed) gateway or via the beach, is notable for its subtropical plants and borders of granite stones inscribed with Biblical texts and hymns.

🚗 *Head south on A3078 to St Mawes. Fork right for castle; park in parking lot.*

⑩ St Mawes
Cornwall; TR2 5DE
Terraces of old cob cottages and smart modern houses command glorious seaviews from their position above the harbor. The views and two sandy beaches make St Mawes a popular spot for holidays and retirement, as well as for sailing and walking. The **castle**, the best preserved of Henry VIII's coastal fortresses, has gun ports on the three huge circular bastions overlooking the busy Carrick Roads waterway, a large natural harbor created during the Ice Age.

🚗 *Head north on A3078. After Ruan High Lanes, turn right (signed Portloe) and follow signs to Mevagissey through Tippetts Shop and Tubbs Mill. The gardens (with parking lot) are on right.*

⑪ Lost Gardens of Heligan
Pentewan, Cornwall; PL26 6EN
The "lost" gardens of Heligan *(open daily)* were restored in the 1990s after 75 years of neglect to their original designs, laid out between 1766 and World War I, including Italian and New Zealand gardens, summer houses, a rocky ravine, crystal grotto, and wishing well. Just as remarkable is the story of Tim Smit, the force behind this restoration (and the Eden Project, see p36), who took it on after a successful career in pop music.

🚗 *Turn right out of the gardens then left onto B3273 toward St Austell. Turn right to Charlestown.*

Above Futuristic satellite dish at Goonhilly Satellite Earth Station on the Lizard Peninsula

Above The beautiful and luxuriant gardens at Trebah, near Mawnan Smith

Above left Close up of one of the biome domes, the Eden Project **Above center** Inside the "Temperate" biome at the Eden Project **Above right** View of Fowey across the estuary, seen from Polruan

VISITING FOWEY

Tourist Information
5 South Street, PL23 1AR; 01726 833 616; www.fowey.co.uk

Ferry services
Take the Bodinnick car ferry, and then follow signs to Polruan Ferry (car park). The passenger ferry crosses to Fowey every 15 minutes (last ferry back 11pm). *www.looe.org/ferries.html*

WHERE TO STAY

AROUND THE EDEN PROJECT

Boscundle Manor *expensive*
Comfortable 18th-century country house with gardens and pools.
Boscundle, PL25 3RL (1 mile/1.5 km south of the Eden Project); 01726 813 557; www.boscundlemanor.co.uk

FOWEY

Old Quay House *expensive*
Elegant modern interiors and an award-winning restaurant overlookng the estuary grace this 150-year-old hotel.
28 Fore Street, PL23 1AQ; 01726 833 302; www.theoldquayhouse.com; no under-12s

POLPERRO

Claremont Hotel *inexpensive*
Traditional, small family-run hotel, partl dating back to the 17th century, in the heart of the village.
The Coombes, PL13 2RG; 01503 272 241; www.theclaremonthotel.co.uk

TAVISTOCK

Bedford Hotel *inexpensve*
This stately, castle-like building, on the site of a Benedictine abbey, was once the residence of the Dukes of Bedford.
1 Plymouth Road, PL19 8BB; 01822 613 221; www.bedford-hotel.co.uk

⑫ Charlestown
Charlestown, St Austell; PL25 3NJ

Soon after china clay was discovered 250 years ago in the downs north of St Austell, a major industry evolved. The "white gold" was exported around the world from Charlestown dock, formerly just a small fishing harbor. The **Shipwreck Museum** *(Mar–Oct, open daily)* on the quayside evokes local history through tableaux, models and photographs; visitors can also enter dark tunnels through which clay was conveyed in trucks to the dock-side. Today, the dock is quiet once more, home to three full-size replicas of historic sailing ships, used on film locations. Tours of ships available when in dock *(Easter–Oct, open daily)*.

🚗 *Turn right and take A390 through St Austell. Follow signs to Eden Project.*

⑬ The Eden Project
Bodelva, St Austell, Cornwall; PL24 2SG

Moving on from Heligan, Tim Smit's next visionary idea was the **Eden Project** *(open daily)* which has turned a huge disused china clay quarry into a "living theater of plants and people." The result is a series of incredible geodesic "biomes," the largest greenhouses in the world, in which different environments have been created – rainforest, temperate and arid, all surrounded by gardens. There is also a schedule of seasonal events and exhibitions.

🚗 *Rejoin A390, turning right onto A3082 to Fowey. Parking can be found opposite the Tourist Information Center on Albert Quay. For a car-free visit see left.*

⑭ Fowey
Cornwall; PL23 1AR

Two ruined blockhouses, one in Fowey (pronounced "foy"), the other across the estuary in Polruan, are a reminder of medieval times when a defensive chain stretched between them to demast any undesirable ships trying to enter the deep anchorage. Today the river is busy with pleasure craft, and neat Edwardian terraces linked by narrow streets climb up from the busy water's edge. The town's focal point is

Above Historic Square Sail Rigger at Charlestown harbor, near St Austell

Walking on Dartmoor

Much of Dartmoor National Park can only be explored on foot by fairly experienced walkers. However, the going is easier around the edges, where gentle woodland footpaths run beside small rivers, for example along Lydford Gorge and by the East Dart at Bellever. The **High Moorland Visitor Center** *(Tavistock Road, Princetown)* is a good starting point for circular walks, detailed in a free leaflet; other walks start from visitor centers at **Haytor**, **Postbridge** and **Newbridge**. In addition, there is a year-round schedule of guided walks graded by length and difficulty, see **www.dartmoor-npa.gov.uk**.

the 15th-century **St. Fimbarrus Church** with a Norman font. The nearby **Daphne du Maurier Literary Center** *(5 South St; open daily)* reveals local literary connections and houses the Tourist Information Center. Look for the original Elizabethan panelling and ceiling in the **Ship Inn**, *(Trafalgar Square)*. Take a boat trip from **Fowey Marine Adventures** *(35 Fore St, Fowey; 01726 832 300)* to see the many cliff-nesting sea birds and, perhaps dolphins, seals, or even basking sharks.

🚗 *Take the Bodinnick car ferry and follow signs to Polperro. The village is car-free, so park at the top, then either walk down to the harbor or ride in one of the "trams."*

Above The small ferry town of Polruan, looking across the estuary toward Fowey

⑮ Polperro

Cornwall; PL13 2QR

A single main street of whitewashed cottages, old mill houses, inns, and boathouses, with the little River Pol beside them, runs down a wooded valley to the fishing harbor and tiny stone Roman Bridge. With seagulls wheeling and crying overhead, this 13th-century former pilchard-fishing village is almost too pretty for its own good, as it gets very busy in summer.

🚗 *Leave Polperro on A387 (signed Looe), turning left onto B3359. At the junction with A390, turn right to Tavistock (25 miles/40 km). Park in Bedford Square.*

Plaque outside the Town Hall, Tavistock

⑯ Tavistock

Devon; PL19 0AE

Gateway to Dartmoor National Park, Tavistock became a prosperous market town during the 19th century, thanks to the discovery of copper in mines owned by the 7th Duke of Bedford. As a result, he paid for the remodeling of the town hall in grand Gothic style and built other buildings around Bedford Square in the local grey-green Hurdwick stone, including the Bedford Hotel and the Pannier Market. A small local history **museum** *(Easter–Oct, open daily)* is housed in the monastery gatehouse on the square.

To the east lies the wild moorland of **Dartmoor**, populated by ponies and sheep and dominated by granite tors. In the center, Princetown, famous for its prison built in Napoleonic times, is the highest town in England. Near the edges lie interesting old market towns such as **Moretonhampstead** and Chagford, as well as atmospheric villages like **Buckland-in-the-Moor** and **Drewsteignton**, both with pretty thatched stone cottages and small granite churches. The 120-ft (36-m) tower of St. Pancras Church at **Widecombe-in-the-Moor**, a village immortalized by the folk song about its fair, is a landmark for miles around.

Above left View over the Tamar Valley, seen from Kit Hill near Tavistock

VISITING TAVISTOCK

Tourist Information
Bedford Square, PL19 0AE; 01822 612 938; www.devon-information.co.uk

EAT AND DRINK

FOWEY

Sams *moderate*
Popular small restaurant specializing in seafood and American diner-style dishes.
20 Fore Street, PL23 1AQ; 01726 832 273; www.samsfowey.co.uk

POLPERRO

Three Pilchards *inexpensive*
Traditional old pub a small roof garden; renowned for its ales and food.
The Quay, PL13 2QZ; 01503 272 233

Couch's *moderate*
Smart restaurant that mixes old-world charm with modern influences.
Big Green, PL13 2QT; 01503 272 554; www.couchspolperro.com; open evenings only

AROUND TAVISTOCK

Chipshop Inn *inexpensive*
18th-century pub in a village with a mining heritage. Large garden, real ales and meals based on local produce.
Gulworthy, PL19 8NT (2.5 miles/4km west of Tavistock on the A390)

DAY TRIP OPTIONS

As well as the beauty of its coastline, Cornwall has a wealth of superb gardens thanks to its mild climate.

Culture and Coast
Explore St Ives ❶ and its galleries in the morning, then grab a pasty and head along the coast to pretty Zennor ❷, Pendeen ❸ and Cape Cornwall – for a clifftop picnic. Finish the day watching the sun sink into the sea at the Minack Theatre, Porthcurno ❹.

Follow the B3306 from St Ives on to St Just and then take the B3315.

The Lizard
The Lizard Peninsula ❼ offers plenty of attractions for both kids and adults. Take a dip at Kynance Cove, visit the Lizard Lighthouse and have lunch at Cadgwith. Drive past the futuristic Goonhilly Satellite Earth Station to see the seals at Gweek. Then, if there's still time, explore the gardens at Trebah ❽.

Use the A3083; then take the B3293 to Goonhilly and Gweek and drive on to Trebah.

Harbors and Gardens
Find the Lost Gardens of Heligan ⑪ and then learn about shipwrecks in Charlestown ⑫. Tour the Eden Project ⑬ before returning to Fowey to end the day by the water's edge ⑭.

The B3273, A390 and A3082 connect Fowey to Heligan, with Charlestown and the Eden Project well marked on the way.

Eat and Drink: inexpensive, under £25; moderate, £25–£50; expensive, over £50

Headlands and Coves

Bideford to Bodmin Moor

Highlights

- **Magnificent coastal scenery**
  Walk along grassy clifftops where Atlantic surf breaks onto rocks below and headlands frame distant beaches

- **Legendary King Arthur in Tintagel**
  On a windswept promontory, explore the ruins of the medieval castle that inspired tales of royal chivalry

- **Gourmet cuisine**
  Eat out in Padstow, home of chef Rick Stein, who has turned this small fishing port into a gastro heaven

- **Literary connections**
  Visit locations immortalized by writers Charles Kingsley, Daphne du Maurier, and Henry Williamson

Fishing trawlers and yachts moored side by side in Padstow's picturesque harbor

Coves and Headlands

The coast that runs south-west from north Devon into Cornwall is extremely dramatic. Grassy clifftops fringed by rocks are pounded by Atlantic waves. In places the cliffs drop down to stunning sandy beaches and coves, while jutting headlands stretch into the distance on either side. Find a place to leave the car and walk along a section of the South West Coast Path to enjoy the best views or, for a contrasting moorland panorama, head inland to Bodmin Moor and climb up one of its windswept tors. The area's rich scenery is complemented by fine historic houses and beautiful gardens as well as plenty of opportunities to sample some of England's freshest and best-cooked seafood.

ACTIVITIES

Cycle along the Tarka Trail between Bideford and Great Torrington, or by the Camel Estuary from Padstow to Bodmin

Laze on the beach at Bude or surf the waves as they roll onto the sand

Discover the ruined castle at Tintagel, the legendary gathering place of King Arthur's knights

Take a ferry ride to Rock from Padstow or enjoy a day trip by boat to Lundy Island from Bideford

Savor a plate of fresh fish and chips at a waterside fish restaurant in Appledore, Bude, or Padstow

Walk a stretch of the South West Coast Path or climb to the top of Brown Willy on Bodmin Moor

Left *Cliffs plunge to the bay below the medieval castle of Tintagel, see p45*

0 kilometres 8

0 miles 8

Hartlan Poir
HARTLAND
PENINSULA
Hartland Quay *Sto*
Docton Mi

Morwenstow

Bude
Bay

Stibb

Strattor

BUDE 6

Marhamchurch

Widemouth Bay

Widemouth

St Gennys

Week St Ma

Crackington Haven

Walnhouse Corner
A39

Boscastle   B3263

Canworthy Water

TINTAGEL 7   B3266

Tresmeer

B3263   Davidstow

A39

DELABOLE
SLATE 8   Camelford

Laneast

Port Isaac
Bay   B3314   West Downs

Port Isaac   *Rough Tor*
400m

Altarnun

St Endellion   St Teath   Michaelstow

Brown Willy
419m

Trevose
Head   St Minver   St Kew   A39

PADSTOW 9   Rock   B3314   B3266

CORNWALL   Bolventor

St Merryn   Blisland   A30   13

B3276   A389   St Issey   Wadebridge   BODMIN
MOOR

St Eval   St Breock   A389   10 PENCARROW   Cardinham   St Neot

B3274   A39   Washaway

Withiel   11 BODMIN   *Fowey*   A38

St Wenn   A391   12

Lanivet   LANHYDROCK

A30   B3268

Lostwithiel

Lundy Island

Barnstaple or Bideford Bay

Lundy Island

APPLEDORE
WESTWARD HO!

Barnstaple

B3233

Instow

A39

Dishop's Tawton

River Taw

Hartland Abbey

Abbotsham

BIDEFORD

Alverdiscott

Clovelly

A386

Hartland
Higher Clovelly

A39

Landcross

Weare Giffard

B3232

Atherington

B3248

Edistone
Tosberry

Woolfardisworthy

Monkleigh

B3227

B3217

Deptford

Frithelstock

GREAT TORRINGTON

A39

West Putford

Stibb Cross

B3227

Little Torrington

Kilkhampton

Bradworthy

Langtree

A386

Merton

A3124

Torridge

DEVON

Milton Damerel

Buckland Filleigh

A388

Chilsworthy

Bradford

A3072

Holsworthy

B3254

Clawton

Whitstone

North Tamerton

Tamar

Ashwater

A388

St Giles in the Heath

North Petherwin

Warrington

Egloskerry

B3254

Launceston

A30

South Petherwin

Lewannick

KEY

Drive route

Below The seaside town of Bude, framed by hills covered with a patchwork of fields, *see pp44–5*

PLAN YOUR DRIVE

Start/finish: Bideford to Bodmin Moor.

Number of days: 3–4, allowing half a day for a coastal walk in Bude.

Distance: 128 miles (205 km).

Road conditions: Well-paved and marked throughout, including some busier roads as well as winding country lanes that sometimes have steep gradients.

When to go: The area is busy from June to September, particularly along the coast, which is very popular for family holidays. Spring and autumn benefit from mild weather, but winter can be stormy. Many attractions and some places to stay and eat are closed from November to Easter.

Opening times: Museums and attractions are generally open 10am–5pm, but close earlier (or are closed altogether) Nov–Easter. Shops are often open longer. Churches are usually open until dusk.

Market days: Bideford: Tue and Sat; **Great Torrington:** Pannier Market, daily; **Bude:** Mon.

Shopping: Pasties and clotted cream; surf and beach equipment.

Major festivals: Bideford: Regatta, Sep; **Appledore:** Visual Arts Festival, late May; **Bude:** re-enactment at Stratton of Battle of Stamford Hill in 1643, May; Jazz Festival, last week in Aug; **Padstow:** 'Obby Oss' spring festival, with procession and dancing through streets, May 1.

DAY TRIP OPTIONS

Spend a day visiting the tranquil **Hartland Peninsula** or, a favorite with children, **exploring Tintagel** with its castle situated on a dramatic headland. Indulge in some **gourmet eating** in **Padstow**, then work it off **cycling** along the **Camel Estuary**, towards Bodmin, or **walking** the **South West Coast Path**. For full details, *see p47*.

Above left A sign advertises traditional pasties
Above right Bideford's Pannier Market hall

① Bideford
Devon; EX39 2QQ

Described 150 years ago by local writer Charles Kingsley as "the little white town which slopes upward from its broad river tide", Bideford is still much the same, busy with fishing vessels, pleasure craft and the MS *Oldenburg*, which ferries visitors to the National Trust's **Lundy Island** bird sanctuary, 11 miles (17 km) away. The promenade beside the Taw Estuary has been set off since the 13th century by the 24-arch **Long Bridge**, originally built from wood but encased in stone since 1535. Narrow old streets crowded with small shops and pubs lead up from the water to the **Victorian Pannier Market hall**, named for the baskets in which farmers' wives used to bring produce for sale. **Burton Art Gallery** *(open Tue– Sat & Sun pm)* in Victoria Park on the riverside has sections on the town's history. It's possible to hire a bike nearby and cycle along the **Tarka Trail** to Great Torrington.

🚗 *From the Victoria Park parking lot, turn right onto Kingsley Road (B3235) and cross A39 onto A386, marked to Appledore. Park in parking lot on quay.*

② Appledore
Devon; EX39 1QS

Along tiny streets and alleyways, color-washed Georgian cottages with bow windows line the Taw and Torridge estuaries; no wonder Appledore has become a favorite with local artists – several galleries show their work. Fishing and ship-building were the town's life blood for centuries, as shown in the small **North Devon Maritime Museum** in Odun Road *(open Easter–Oct, daily; May–Sept, Mon–Fri)* and fishing trips are available from the quay.

🚗 *Follow signs to Westward Ho!*

③ Westward Ho!
Devon; EX39 1QS

The neighboring seaside resort, named after Charles Kingsley's novel of Elizabethan seafarers, is notable mainly for having England's oldest golf links, a long sandy beach, and a pebble ridge.

🚗 *Take B3236 and A39 to Bideford, take A386 to Great Torrington, follow signs to Dartington Crystal. Park in parking lot.*

Far left Fishing boats moored at the quay at Appledore **Above left** Wall sculptures created by one of Appledore's artists **Below left** A statue of local author Charles Kingsley in Bideford

④ Great Torrington
Devon; EX38 8AA

It's a scenic drive beside the River Torridge to Great Torrington, home of **Dartington Crystal**, where visitors can see glass being hand blown and pick up bargains in the shop *(tours Mon–Fri; visitor center and shop daily)*. At the **RHS Rosemoor Gardens**, there are areas devoted to roses, fruit and vegetables, a lake, and an arboretum *(open daily)*. The Battle of Torrington – a Royalist rout in the English Civil War – is brought to life at the **Torrington 1646 visitor center** with displays of 17th-century weaponry *(open Feb–Nov, Tue–Fri; Jun–Sep, Mon–Sat)*.

🚗 *From Great Torrington, take B3227 to Stibb Cross; turn right on minor road*

Lundy Island

This car-free island 11 miles (17 km) off the coast is a sanctuary for puffins with a resident human population of 30 – joined in summer by hordes of day-trippers who come to go seal watching, visit its 13th-century castle, and have a drink at Marisco Tavern.

---

to go through *Woolfardisworthy to A39 (marked Bude). At Higher Clovelly, turn right onto B3248 to Hartland, then follow signs on minor road through Stoke to Hartland Quay; park in lot. Return to Stoke and turn right down tiny lane to Docton Mill at Milford.*

⑤ Hartland Peninsula
North Devon; EX39 6DU

This blissfully quiet rural pocket is crisscrossed by narrow country lanes leading to windswept **Hartland Quay**, where dramatic cliffs give way to a tiny 16th-century harbor with a small shipwreck museum *(open Easter–Oct, daily)*. In **Stoke**, St Nectan's 14th-century church is known as the cathedral for its 128-ft (350-m)-high tower. Nearby are 16th-century stately **Hartland Abbey** *(open Mar–Oct Sun, Wed & Thu)* and pretty **Docton Mill Gardens** *(open Mar–Oct daily)*, where tea is served by the mill pond.

🚗 *From Docton Mill, take minor road via Eddistone and Tosberry to rejoin A39 to Bude. Park in canalside Tourist Information Centre parking lot.*

Above left Windswept headlands of Hartland Peninsula **Above right** Docton Mill Gardens **Below** Mill pond at Docton Mill Gardens

---

EAT AND DRINK

AROUND BIDEFORD

Boathouse *moderate*
Lively waterside restaurant and bar looking across the Torridge Estuary to Appledore.
Marine Parade, Instow, EX39 4JJ (take B3233 out of Bideford along the estuary towards Barnstaple); 01271 861 292; www.instow.net/boathouse; no reservations

Decks *expensive*
Smart restaurant next to the Boathouse, specializing in English and French cuisine using local produce.
Marine Parade, Instow, EX39 4JJ; 01271 860 671; www.decksrestaurant.co.uk; open Tue–Sat

APPLEDORE

Beaver Inn *inexpensive*
Atmospheric old pub beside the Torridge Estuary, with panoramic views from its terrace. Noted for its fresh fish dishes.
Irsha Street, EX39 1RY; 01237 474 822; www.beaverinn.co.uk

The Royal George *inexpensive*
An old beamed pub with a dining area overlooking the estuary.
Irsha Street, EX39 1RY; 01237 474 335

HARTLAND PENINSULA

Docton Mill Gardens Tea Room *inexpensive*
Small café in the delightful gardens serving snacks and award-winning Devonshire clotted cream teas.
Lymebridge, EX39 6EA; 01237 441 369; www.doctonmill.co.uk; open Mar–Oct

Eat and Drink: inexpensive, under £25; moderate, £25–£50; expensive, over £50

Above Dinghies lined up against the wall on Bude's quayside

VISITING BUDE

Parking
Park in Crescent parking lot beside the canal, marked to the right from town.

Tourist Information
Crescent parking lot, EX23 8LE; 01288 354 240; www.visitbude.info

Raven Surf School
Lessons on Bude's beaches.
01288 353 693; www.ravensurf.co.uk; From £25 for a 2½ hour lesson.

WHERE TO STAY

BUDE

Falcon Hotel *moderate*
Originally a lodging house for sea captains, this hotel has sea and canal views and a walled garden.
Breakwater Road, EX23 8SD ; 01288 352 005; www.falconhotel.com

Stratton Gardens House *moderate*
Cozy six-bedroom guesthouse in a 16th-century house with a garden; excellent home-cooked meals.
Cot Hill, Stratton, EX23 9DN; 01288 352 500; www.stratton-gardens.co.uk

TINTAGEL

Lewis's Tea Rooms *inexpensive*
Comfortable B&B in a stone house built in 1586. Noted for its cream teas.
Bossiney Road, TL34 0AH; 01840 770 427

Below Stone milepost marking the path on clifftops above Bude

❻ Bude
Crescent car park, Bude; EX23 8LE

Bude is more than just a popular seaside resort. As well as two large sandy beaches, it has some of Britain's best coastal walks along its grassy clifftops. There are reminders, too, of its past, when it was a battlefield, a busy port, and home of Cornwall's "forgotten inventor."

A two-hour circular walk

The walk starts from the parking lot at the **Tourist Information Centre** ① in Bude, where a good selection of local guidebooks is on sale *(open daily, except Sun in winter)*. The restored stretch of canal beside it is the remains of a 56-km (35-mile)-long canal built in the early 19th century to transport lime-rich beach sand inland as fertilizer.

Heading toward the sea, cross the canal bridge – originally a swing bridge to let ships through – and continue past the impressive white **Falcon Hotel** ②. Opposite it, the canal-side castle now houses the excellent **Castle Heritage Centre** ③ *(open daily)*, where the town's varied story is imaginatively told, alongside working models of Sir Goldsworthy Gurney's pioneering Victorian inventions; these included a steam engine, sewer ventilation system and revolving lights for lighthouses.

Buckets and spades for sale at Bude

Heading on along the path toward the sea you come to a restored **sea lock** ④, which enabled boats to "lock in" to unload their cargoes at a quay rather than on the beach. Turning left, the path climbs sharply to the coast path, marked for Widemouth, 3 miles (5 km) away. From the clifftop there are views over Bude Haven beach, where the small River Neet flows into the sea. Before it silted up, this was a thriving harbor. Because of its trade, the village of Stratton, inland, was granted a royal charter by King John in 1207.

A long breakwater stretches out to Chapel Rock, lit in medieval times by a light to guide ships into port. The curious octagonal **tower** ⑤, known as the pepper pot, was a Victorian

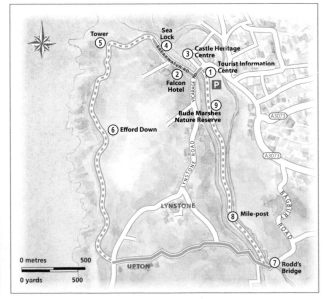

Tower ⑤
Sea Lock ④
Castle Heritage Centre ③
Tourist Information Centre ①
Falcon Hotel ②
⑨
Bude Marshes Nature Reserve
⑥ Efford Down
BREAKWATER RD
VICARAGE RD
A3073
A3073
LYNSTONE ROAD
BAGBER ROAD
LYNSTONE
⑧ Mile-post
UPTON
⑦ Rodd's Bridge

0 metres 500
0 yards 500

coastguard's hut, erected in Grecian style as a symbol of Bude's ambitions.

Look back past the Haven over twin sandy beaches Summerleaze and Crooklets; in Victorian times Crooklets was for women's use only.

The path along the clifftop crosses **Efford Down** ⑥. Here, in 1643, Cornishmen in the Royalist Army camped on the eve of the English Civil War battle of Stamford Hill, where they defeated the Parliamentarians.

At Upton, turn left inland and follow the lane down to the canal at **Rodd's Bridge** ⑦. Turn left along the towpath, noting the stone **milepost** ⑧ beside it, dating from 1820, and carry on along the towpath that flanks **Bude Marshes nature reserve** ⑨, where a variety of wild birds and flowers flourish, back to the start.

🚗 *Turn left out of parking lot and leave Bude on small clifftop road marked for Widemouth Bay, to rejoin A39 toward Camelford. Turn right onto B3263 to Boscastle and then Tintagel, where several parking lots are marked in village and near castle.*

⑦ Tintagel
Cornwall; PL34 0HE

Was this clifftop castle the birthplace of the legendary King Arthur? Did the medieval kings of Cornwall live there? Mystery surrounds the ruins perched on a rocky headland beyond the village's single main street. The **castle's** ruined battlements *(open daily)* date back to the 13th century and are well worth the steep climb for exhilarating views of the dramatic coastline. In the village

itself are the 14th-century **Old Post Office** *(open Mar–Oct daily)* and **King Arthur's Great Halls** *(open daily)*, telling the legend of the king. On the rugged clifftop you can see the 12th century church of St Materiana.

🚗 *Return to B3263 in direction of Camelford, turning right at sign to Delabole on B3314. Delabole Slate quarry is signed to the left in the village. Park in quarry parking lot.*

⑧ Delabole Slate
Cornwall; PL33 9AZ

The largest man-made hole in Britain, at Delabole Slate, has been quarried for more than 600 years. Over half a mile (1 km) across and nearly 500 ft (1,500 m) deep, the hole is Europe's oldest continuously worked quarry, producing 120 tons of slate a day. *(tours of surface works May–Aug, Mon–Fri).*

🚗 *Leaving Delabole Slate, turn left onto B3314 and left at Westdowns onto B3267 to join A39 toward Wadebridge. After Wadebridge, turn right at St Breock onto A389 to Padstow. Prideaux Place is on the edge of Padstow, off B3276 towards Newquay. Park on the quay or in Prideaux Place parking lot.*

Above left Bude's grassy clifftops **Above right** Life's a Beach café at Summerleaze

EAT AND DRINK

BUDE

Pengenna Pasties *inexpensive*
Beef, lamb, cheese & onion, vegetable, or vegan is the choice of traditional Cornish pasties at this small bakery. *Arundell House, Belle Vue, EX23 8JL; 01288 355 169; www.pengenna pasties.co.uk*

The Castle *moderate*
Smart restaurant with sea-facing terrace in the Castle Heritage Centre; strong emphasis on local produce. *The Wharf, EX23 8LG; 01288 350 543; www.thecastlerestaurantbude.co.uk; closed Sun eve*

AROUND BUDE

Life's A Beach *daytime: inexpensive; evening: expensive*
By day this is a popular beachside café; at 7pm it turns into a sophisticated restaurant, specializing in fish. *Follow signs from Bude to Summerleaze Beach (1 mile), EX23 8HN; 01288 355 222; www.lifesabeach.info*

TINTAGEL

Cornishman Inn *cheap*
Atmospheric, beamed pub with a restaurant noted for its steaks; 10 rooms. *Fore Street, PL34 0DB; 01840 770 238; www.cornishmaninn.com*

Below left The rocky headlands of Tintagel **Below right** Medieval battlements at Tintagel Castle

Eat and Drink: inexpensive, under £25; moderate, £25–£50; expensive, over £50

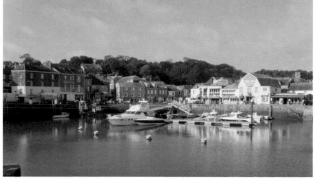

Above The still waters of Padstow's harbor reflect yachts and wharf buildings

VISITING PADSTOW

Parking
Park on the quay, or at Prideaux Place.

Tourist Information
Red Brick Building, North Quay, PL28 8AF; 01841 533 449; www.padstow-cornwall.co.uk

Padstow Cycle Hire
South Quay, PL28 8BL; 01841 533 533; www.padstowcyclehire.com

WHERE TO STAY

PADSTOW

Old Ship Hotel *moderate*
Centrally located hotel with estuary views whose bar has live music. Restaurant noted for its fresh fish.
Mill Square, PL28 8AE; 01841 532 357; www.oldshiphotel-padstow.co.uk

St Petroc's Hotel *expensive*
A short walk uphill from the harbor, this 10-room hotel in a white wisteria-clad Georgian building is one of Rick Stein's properties.
4 New Street, PL28 8BY; 01841 532 700; www.rickstein.com

Below The imposing façade of Bodmin Gaol, which now houses a pub and brasserie

⑨ Padstow
Cornwall; PL28 8AF
Fame has been bestowed on this small port on the Camel Estuary thanks to a fish restaurant opened in a Victorian drill hall in 1975 by a local chef, Rick Stein. Now famous for his TV appearances, he has four restaurants in the town, plus gourmet shops and a cooking school, making it a gastro heaven.

Alternatives to eating include clifftop walks, a ferry trip across to Rock, a stop at the intriguing fishery *(open daily)*, where lobsters are hatched, or a visit to **Prideaux Place** *(open May–Oct, Sun–Thu)*. This sumptuously furnished, family-owned Elizabethan manor has often been used as the location for period films, among them *Oscar and Lucinda*, Trevor Nunn's *Twelfth Night* and several Rosamund Pilcher novels. From Padstow bikes can be rented to cycle along the River Camel to Bodmin.

🚗 *From Padstow, return to the A389 past Wadebridge toward Bodmin. Pencarrow is marked off to the left 4 miles (6 km) after Wadebridge. Park in parking lot.*

⑩ Pencarrow
Washaway, Cornwall; PL30 3AG
Tall conifers from around the world soar above the long drive leading to this Georgian mansion, owned by the same family since it was built in the 1770s. In spring, rhododendrons, camellias and azaleas create patches of vivid color in the gardens. The house is notable for its Adam furniture, upholstered in rose silk damask that matches the curtains – "treasure" captured from a Spanish ship in 1762. Joshua Reynolds painted many of the portraits on show *(open Easter–mid-Oct: house Sun–Thu; gardens daily)*.

🚗 *From Pencarrow, continue to Bodmin on A389. There are several parking lots marked, one on left as you enter town, at end of Camel Trail.*

Literary Connections
Westward Ho! is the only town in England to be named after a book – and to have an exclamation mark! Charles Kingsley wrote his historical romance while living in Bideford; after its publication entrepreneurs developed the resort. Daphne du Maurier found inspiration for her novel *Jamaica Inn* while staying at the coaching inn on Bodmin Moor, a notorious smugglers' haunt, in 1930. Henry Williamson's 1927 story *Tarka the Otter* is set in North Devon. The places he describes in it are now linked by a 180-mile-long trail, including a section between Bideford and Great Torrington.

⑪ Bodmin
Cornwall; PL31 2DQ
Guilty or not guilty? Visitors to Courtroom One in **Shire Hall** *(tours Mon–Sat)*, the old county court, can decide the verdict in a realistic reenactment of a famous murder trial held here in 1844, and then visit the cells. The life of an 18th-century prisoner is depicted in the former **Bodmin Gaol**, a forbidding building that now houses various eateries. The 500-year-old **St Petroc's Church**, which has a 12th-century font and the saint's ivory casket, is the largest medieval church in Cornwall.

🚗 *Take B3268, signed Lostwithiel, out past the station. Lanhydrock is signed to the left after 3 miles (2 km). Park in parking lot.*

Where to Stay: inexpensive, under £80; moderate, £80–£150; expensive, over £150

⑫ Lanhydrock

near Bodmin, Cornwall; PL30 5AD
After this stately 17th-century house
was gutted by fire in 1881 it was
rebuilt, battlements and all, to match
the surviving north wing and
gatehouse. The interior was
replanned to include the latest
amenities – central heating,
bathrooms, and "modern" servants'
quarters, all in typical Victorian style.
The gardens, laid out at the time of
rebuilding, feature rhododendrons,
magnolias, and camellias, with
woods and parkland leading down
to the banks of the River Fowey *(open
Mar–Nov Tue–Sun)*.

🚗 *Return toward Bodmin and
follow signs to join A30 towards
Launceston. Blisland is marked to the
left, from where minor roads take you
to the tors. The A30 continues across
the moor, passing Jamaica Inn at
Bolventor. Turn right there toward
Liskeard and after 5 miles (8 km) turn
left to Minions.*

⑬ Bodmin Moor

**Blisland: PL30 4LT; Jamaica Inn: PL15
7TS; Minions: PL14 5LJ**
With its small 11th-century church,
St Protus and St Hyacinth, **Blisland**
is typical of the quiet villages that
nestle in leafy valleys on the western
slopes of the moor. In complete
contrast, the wild and often desolate
uplands are strewn with huge
boulders, dotted with ancient
standing stones and topped by
brooding tors like **Rough Tor**, an Iron
Age fort, and **Brown Willy**, which at
1,377 ft (420 m) is the moor's highest
point. Around **Minions**, on the south
side of the moor, darkly picturesque
relics of the mining industry can be
seen – chimneys, engine houses,
and spoil dumps. **Jamaica Inn** at
Bolventor, an 18th-century slate-
hung inn which inspired Daphne
du Maurier's novel of the same
name, is mainly notable for its bleak
evocative setting – and gets very
crowded in high season.

Above left Passenger ferry departs Padstow
for Rock **Above right** A signpost in Blisland
indicates its old-fashioned charms

EAT AND DRINK

PADSTOW

Custard *moderate/expensive*
Modern diner-style restaurant
specializing in simple but good quality
food, from cakes to full meals.
*1A The Strand, PL28 8AJ; 0870 1700
740; www.custarddiner.com;
closed Tues in winter*

Seafood Restaurant *expensive*
This is the Rick Stein place that started
Padstow's rise to culinary fame in the
1970s. Bright and airy, it's just across
the quay from where the lobster boats
and trawlers tie up. A less exalted
option (eat-in or take-away), but just
as special, is **Stein's Fish & Chips café**
on *South Quay, PL28 8BL*. Another
option is to hone your own talents by
signing up for a cooking course of
1, 2, 4, or 6 days.
*Riverside, PL28 8BY; 01841 532 700;
www.rickstein.com*

DAY TRIP OPTIONS

A great range of day trips is possible
along this route, taking in bike rides,
beautiful coastline and historic sites.

Tarka Country

Hire a bike at Bideford ❶ and
spend a leisurely day cycling along
the Tarka Trail up the Torridge Valley
to Great Torrington ❹, looking out
for otters on the river banks. Visit
Dartington Crystal and RHS
Rosemoor Gardens before cycling
back to Bideford. Drive to the head
of the Taw and Torridge estuaries at
Appledore ❷ and then relax over a
well-earned drink and a fish supper
at the atmospheric old Beaver Inn or
Royal George.

*Park in the Victoria Park parking lot
at Bideford and rent a bike at Bideford
Cycle, Surf and Kayak Hire. Follow
driving instructions from Bideford to
Appledore and park on the quay.*

Castles and Cliffs

Whatever the weather, the castle at
Tintagel ❼ on its dramatic headland
is an exciting place to explore, and
the clifftop coast path provides
magnificent sea views. Discover the
legend of King Arthur, then drive to
Bude ❻ to build sandcastles inspired
by the medieval ruins, surf, or simply
laze on one of its twin sandy beaches.
Pick up traditional pasties for a picnic
from Pengenna Pasties, or lunch at
Life's a Beach café.

*Park in parking lot closest to Tintagel
Castle, if you can, to visit the ruins. Take
B3263 to Boscastle, then join A39 to
Bude, exiting left at Widemouth.*

Gourmet Padstow

Take a boat trip across the Camel
Estuary to Rock, see how the lobsters
are hatched, and work up an
appetite for a fish lunch at Rick
Stein's Seafood Restaurant or fish
and chips on the quayside. Energetic
types can rent a bike and cycle
beside the River Camel to Bodmin
with its weighty judicial past;
alternatively visit the Elizabethan
manor at Prideaux Place.

Park on the quay at Padstow.

Eat and Drink: inexpensive, under £25; moderate, £25–£50; expensive, over £50

North Devon Coast and Exmoor

Taunton to Barnstaple

Highlights

- **Historic steam-train ride**
  Take a trip back in time through the lovely, rolling countryside on the preserved West Somerset Railway

- **Exmoor and its outlaws**
  Explore exhilarating moorland scenery and learn the legend of the Doone family, 17th-century outlaws

- **Coastal pleasures**
  Relax on swathes of golden sand or be awed by cliffs and crashing waves along the South West Coast Path

- **Market bound**
  Discover the rich heritage of historic market towns such as Taunton, Dunster, and Barnstaple

The South West Coast Path and spectacular coastline on the way to Morte Point, Devon

North Devon Coast and Exmoor

The countryside of Somerset and North Devon is as varied as any in Europe. Secluded coves, sand dunes, and wide sandy beaches, washed by powerful Atlantic waves, make the area a top choice for beach lovers – families and surfers alike. The windswept moorlands of Exmoor National Park are bordered by grassy clifftops which run along the dramatic coastline. Here and there a patchwork of fields covers gently rolling hillsides dotted with thick woods and crossed by clean and swift-flowing streams. The interior is dotted with small towns and pretty villages. All of this route lies is prime walking country, with spectacular coastal paths and a network of trails inland.

KEY

Drive route

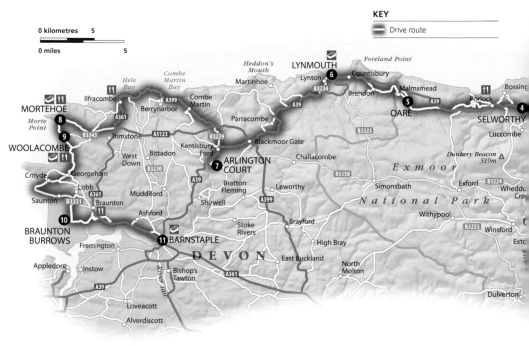

ACTIVITIES

Catch a vintage steam train through the Somerset countryside from Washford

Indulge in a Devon cream tea – soft scones topped with thick clotted cream and fruity strawberry jam

Explore Exmoor on foot and enjoy outstanding views from Dunkery Beacon, its highest point

Cycle along the scenic Tarka Trail, part of Cycle Route 27 which runs from Ilfracombe to Barnstaple

Ride the wild Atlantic rollers at Woolacombe Bay by renting a wet suit and body board

Go bargain-hunting for crafts and antiques in Barnstaple's airy and atmospheric Pannier Market

Below The Museum of Barnstaple and North Devon, Barnstaple, *see p55*

Above Beautiful Woolacombe Bay – a wide, sandy beach with great surf, *see p55*

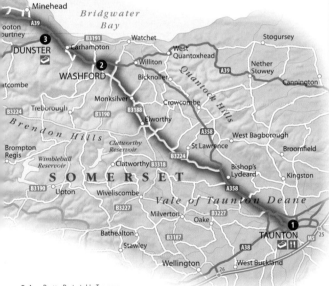

Below Pretty Periwinkle Tearoom, Selworthy, *see p53*

PLAN YOUR DRIVE

Start/finish: Taunton to Barnstaple.

Number of days: 2–3 days.

Distance: 84 miles (134 km).

Road conditions: Well-paved and marked, country roads are often narrow and winding. Be prepared to stop in a passing place if there is oncoming traffic. On Exmoor, watch out for ponies or sheep on the road. Most places have well-marked parking lots, usually pay-and-display.

When to go: In April–May, wild flowers border the roadsides; autumn sees the leaves turn rich brown and the moors are splashed with purple heather. During July and August, families crowd into the area for seaside holidays. It can get very busy. In winter, the weather is often relatively mild and towns return to "normal," but villages can be quiet.

Opening times: Museums and attractions are generally open 10am–5pm, but close earlier (or are closed altogether) Nov–Easter. Shops are often open longer. Churches are usually open until dusk.

Market days: Taunton: Farmer's Market, Thu; Barnstaple: Pannier Market: local produce, Tue, Fri, Sat; antiques and books, Wed; also crafts, Apr–Dec Mon & Thu.

Shopping: Look out for Devonshire clotted cream, local cider, surfing gear, and beachwear.

Major festivals: Taunton: Carnival, Oct; Exmoor: Walking Festival, May; Mortehoe: Scarecrow Festival, Aug; Barnstaple: North Devon Festival, June.

DAY TRIP OPTIONS

Beach lovers can enjoy the **golden sands** and **surging surf** at Woolacombe Bay before enjoying a **Devon cream tea**. Walkers can explore the **windswept expanses** and **hidden valleys** of Exmoor, home of the legendary outlaws, **the Doones**. From Taunton and Washford, step back in time by visiting **ancient churches**, an **abbey** and a **restored steam train**. For full details, *see p55*.

VISITING TAUNTON

Parking
Park in the parking lot near the bus station and castle.

Tourist Information
Paul Street, TA1 3XZ; 01823 336 344; www.heartofsomerset.com

VISITING EXMOOR

Exmoor National Park Centre
For more information about Exmoor National Park including walks, events and activities: open Mar–Oct.
Dunster Steep, Dunster, TA24 6SE; 01643 821 835; www.exmoor-nationalpark.gov.uk

WHERE TO STAY

TAUNTON
The Castle *expensive*
This wisteria-covered family-run hotel in the town center provides historic accommodation. It has an award-winning restaurant and a brasserie.
Castle Green, TA1 1NF; 01823 272 671; www.the-castle-hotel.com

DUNSTER
Luttrell Arms *expensive*
Small 15th-century hotel facing the Yarn Market. Used in medieval times as a guesthouse by the Abbots of Cleeve, it has several rooms with four-poster beds.
32–6 High Street, TA24 6SG; 01643 821 555; www.luttrellarms.co.uk

LYNMOUTH
Rock House Hotel *moderate*
Family-run small hotel in 18th-century building at the harbor entrance. It has a cozy restaurant with sea views.
Manor Green, EX35 6EN; 01598 753 508; www.rock-house.co.uk

Below left The 15th-century Luttrell Arms Hotel, Taunton **Below right** One of the pristine, tidily thatched cottages of Selworthy

① Taunton
Somerset; TA1 3XZ
This county town, in the heart of apple and cider country, centers around its triangular former market place, Fore Street. The cattle market moved to the outskirts in 1929, but the 200-year-old red brick **Market House** still dominates. Parts of 12th-century **Taunton Castle** survive, now home to the **Museum of Somerset** *(due to re-open after renovation in 2010)*. Nearby in Hammet Street, the richly sculptured tower of **St. Mary Magdelene Church**, founded 1308, soars up 163 ft (50 m) and is a landmark visible for miles.

🚗 *Turn left out of parking lot along Corporation Street, left at roundabout onto North Street (A3207), and left onto A358 out of town; take B3224 left just after Bishop's Lydeard, then B3188 right to Washford. Park at Cleeve Abbey parking lot, on left as you enter village.*

② Washford
Somerset; TA23 0PS
Cleeve Abbey *(open daily Apr–Oct)*, founded by Cistercian monks in 1188, is the most complete set of monastic cloister buildings in England, including a gatehouse, small chapel, dormitory, and large 15th-century refectory with an arched wooden ceiling known as a waggon roof. Washford is also on the **West Somerset Railway** *(daily mid Mar–Oct; www.west-somerset-railway. co.uk)*, a 20-mile (32-km) stretch of

Right One of the gatehouses of the impressive Dunster Castle, Dunster

track offering trips in veteran carriages often hauled by steam locomotives.

🚗 *Turn left from parking lot onto B3188, then left onto A39 toward Minehead, turning left into Dunster. Parking lots are just off A39 and in castle grounds.*

③ Dunster
Somerset; TA24 6SL
The quaint 400-year-old open-sided octagonal **Yarn Market** is a reminder of the village's once-thriving wool industry. The nearby **Doll Museum** *(open daily Apr–Sep; Sat–Sun pm only)*, displays ancient and modern dolls. Turreted Norman-style **Dunster Castle** *(open daily Mar–Dec)*, was home of the Luttrell family for 600 years until 1976. Perched on a hilltop and surrounded by terraced gardens, it was extensively remodeled in Victorian times. Dunster is a good base for visiting Exmoor.

🚗 *Continue on A39 past Minehead; look out for a sign for Selworthy off to the right. Park opposite church.*

④ Selworthy

Somerset; TA24 8TJ

This is a picture-postcard hamlet of thatched cottages with a splendid view over the Vale of Porlock and a white 14th-century Perpendicular church framed by woods. It is part of the Holnicote Estate which extends from Porlock Bay to Dunkery Hill on Exmoor, its spectacular moorland dotted with woods and medieval villages. Home to wild ponies and horned sheep, the moor is criss-crossed by footpaths. On the way to Oare, **Dunkery Beacon** is the highest point on Exmoor (1,260 ft/ 519 m), with extensive views in all directions.

🚗 *From Selworthy, take A39 toward Porlock, turning left at sign for West Luccombe, then right at sign for Dunkery Beacon. Return to A39, forking right at Porlock onto New Road (toll) to avoid very steep Porlock Hill. Rejoin A39. Turn left at sign for Doone Valley after half a mile (1 km). Follow road to Oare.*

⑤ Oare

Somerset; EX35 6NU

Oare's diminutive grey stone church, in a quiet valley overlooking Oare Water, was the setting in RD Blackmore's famous story, *Lorna Doone*, for the heroine's wedding to John Ridd; 18th-century box pews lead to the altar where the ceremony was interrupted by a shot fired through one of the windows. A plaque by the oak door commemorates the author who brought the area such fame.

🚗 *Go through Malmsmead and Brendon to rejoin A39 toward Lynmouth. Follow signs to town parking lots.*

⑥ Lynmouth

Devon; EX35 6EQ

Picturesquely set at the foot of the wooded valleys of the East and West Lyn rivers, this former herring fishing village is best known for the terrible flood in August 1952. After torrential rain, flash floods washed away the harbor and nearby houses, killing 34 people. The **Flood Memorial Hall** commemorates the disaster with a scale model of the village as it was. From the seafront, an ingenious water-powered cliff railway, opened in 1888, glides 862 ft (263 m) up a steep track to **Lynton** – an exciting two-minute

The Story of Lorna Doone

Stories of an outlaw family, the Doones, who terrorized Exmoor in the 17th century fired the fertile imagination of local author RD Blackmore. In his 1869 novel *Lorna Doone*, he tells the story of John Ridd, an Oare farmer who falls in love with the Doones' adopted daughter, Lorna. He vividly describes the countryside, disguising many of the real locations. Today, leafy footpaths run from Oare and Malmsmead to the so-called Doone Valley. Beyond Blackmore Memorial by Badgworthy Water, look out for Lank Combe Water – was this the secret waterfall that John Ridd climbed?

ride with fabulous coastal views *(open daily mid-Feb–Oct)*. Lynton is a small town looking out to sea with a pretty **church**, which has a Norman font and a 13th-century tower.

🚗 *Take B3234 to Lynton, then A39 (signed Barnstaple). Turn left for onto minor road (marked) for Arlington Court 1 mile 1.5 km) after Kentisbury Ford.*

⑦ Arlington Court

Arlington, Parracombe; Devon; EX31 4LP

This Regency house *(open Mar–Nov: Sun–Fri; 01271 850 296; www.national trust.org.uk)* is packed with treasures, from model ships to 18th-century tapestries. The stables in the Deer Park house over 50 horse-drawn carriages; rides available most days.

🚗 *Return to Kentisbury Ford on A39, turn left on B3229 and follow signs to Ilfracombe on A399. Take A361 out of town, turn right onto B3343, and follow signs to Mortehoe on minor road to right. Park in the village.*

Above Pretty harbour town of Lynmouth, rebuilt after the flood of 1952

EAT AND DRINK

TAUNTON

Willow Tree *moderate*
Set in a 300-year-old gabled building in an alley, this restaurant is noted for imaginative dishes and vibrant decor.
3 Tower Lane, TA1 4AR; 01823 352 835; open eves Tue–Sat; booking essential

SELWORTHY

Periwinkle Tearoom *moderate*
This amazingly picturesque 17th-century thatched cottage (National Trust) is perfect for a cream tea or snack.
Selworthy Green, TA24 8TP; 01643 862 769; open in daytime Easter–Sep; closed Mon Easter–Jun

AROUND SELWORTHY

Piggy in the Middle *moderate*
Small family-run restaurant specializing in local game, meat, and seafood.
2 High Street, TA24 8PS (4 km/2.5 miles on A39 from Selworthy); 01643 862 647; open lunch Easter–Sep; also lunch Easter–Sep; closed Feb

Below Visitors enjoying a carriage ride around the grounds of Arlington Court

Eat and Drink: inexpensive, under £25; moderate, £25–£50; expensive, over £50

Above The graveyard of St. Mary's Church, Mortehoe, with graves of shipwrecked sailors

VISITING BARNSTAPLE

Parking
Green Lanes Shopping Centre, Boutport Street, EX31 1UL.

Tourist Information
The Square, EX32 8LN; 01271 375 000; www.staynorthdevon.co.uk

WHERE TO STAY

MORTEHOE

Town Farmhouse *inexpensive*
Former farm B&B opposite the church.
EX34 7DT; 01271 870 204; www.townfarmhouse.co.uk; open Feb–Nov

WOOLACOMBE

Woolacombe Bay *expensive*
Large seafront hotel overlooking the beach with plenty of sporting facilities.
EX34 7BN; 01271 870 388; www.woolacombe-bay-hotel.co.uk

BARNSTAPLE

Royal & Fortescue Hotel *moderate*
Former coaching inn, centrally situated, with restaurant, bistro and cafe-bar.
Boutport Street, EX31 1HG; 01271 342 289; www.brend-hotels.co.uk

❽ Mortehoe
Devon; EX34 7DT

This is one of the most spectacular stretches of the South West Coast Path, England's longest National Trail. A footpath leads along the clifftops from Mortehoe over grassy slopes to Morte Point. In the ancient village of Mortehoe, mentioned in the Domesday Book, a handful of pubs and tea rooms cluster around the picturesque 13th-century St. Mary's Church, and just around a headland is the golden sandy beach of Woolacombe.

A two-hour clifftop walk

Start at the pay-and-display parking lot at the end of Station Road and visit the **Heritage Centre** ① *(open Easter–Oct: Sun–Thu; Jul–Aug: daily)* to learn about the history of the area.

Exit the parking lot, turn left toward the church passing the Post Office and Village Store – good for provisions. Go through the Victorian lych gate for a look inside **St. Mary's Church** ②. Though the entrance porch dates from around 1500, the barrel-roofed nave and chancel were built during the 13th century. The square belfry, which houses six bells, dates from 1275. Much of the decoration is Victorian; the pretty stained-glass windows were re-glazed at this time.

To the right of the church a sign points to the coastal path. Walk to the left of the village cemetery along the path fringed with bracken and gorse. Over a sheep-dotted hillside, the path drops sharply down to a stream where it meets the 630-mile (1,000-km) South West Coast Path running along the clifftop.

There are views past Woolacombe south across Morte Bay to the next

headland, Baggy Point, and beyond. Lundy Island is visible out to sea 17 miles (27 km) away and the South Wales coast is just discernible. Walk along the clifftop toward Morte Point, watching the waves crash onto jagged slate rocks. Just past the aptly named **Windy Cove** ③, sticking out of the sea, is Morte Stone (Death Stone), a reminder of the dangers of the rocky reef. In the winter of 1852, five ships were lost off this treacherous coast. Continue to **Morte Point** ④ itself, and rest on one of the white boulders to admire the seascape – look out for seals on the rocks below. Follow the path around the point to go eastward.

Turn inland at the sign to Mortehoe and return via a wide grassy path. For a short detour, walk up to the 450-ft (137-m) viewpoint (marked on left) and the megalithic tomb, known as the Cromlech, nearby. Finally, retrace your steps back to the village for a cream tea or a glass of heady local scrumpy cider.

🚗 *Follow signs along a narrow seaside road to Woolacombe and park in the beach parking lot.*

Below The road down to lovely Woolacombe Bay, North Devon

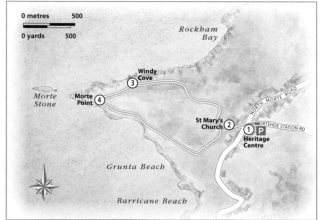

| 0 metres | 500 |
| 0 yards | 500 |

Rockham Bay

Windy Cove ③

Morte Stone *Morte Point* ④

NORTH MORTE ROAD

St Mary's Church ②   ① P **Heritage Centre** *MORTEHOE STATION RD*

Grunta Beach

Barricane Beach

Where to Stay: inexpensive, under £80; moderate, £80–150; expensive, over £150

⑨ Woolacombe
Devon; EX34 7DL

Woolacombe's beach, which stretches for nearly 3 miles (5 km), is regularly voted one of the world's best. Backed by dunes and washed by Atlantic waves, the beach attracts surfers year round. **Nick Thorn Surf School** (www. nickthorn.co.uk) offers lessons. Clamber over rocks at the north end to Barricane Beach to hunt for shells washed here from the Caribbean. Above the beach is a memorial to American forces who trained there for the D-Day landings in 1944.

🚗 *Follow signs along minor roads to Croyde. Then take B3231 toward Braunton, turning right (opposite sign to Lobb) onto a narrow road to Braunton Burrows parking lot.*

⑩ Braunton Burrows
Braunton; EX33 2NU

Behind Saunton Sands, Braunton Burrows is the largest area of sand dunes in England, stretching 4 miles (7 km). With 500 species of wild flowers and 33 of butterflies, the area is a SSSI (Site of Special Scientific Interest) and part of North Devon's UNESCO Biosphere Reserve. Kestrels,

skylarks, and curlews can often be seen flying overhead. The site of practice beach landings during World War II, the dunes are still used by the army for 10 days a year.

🚗 *Return on the same road, but take first right (unmarked narrow road) to join A361 to Barnstaple. Park in Green Lanes Shopping Centre.*

⑪ Barnstaple
Devon; EX32 8LN

The town's fortunes as a sea port have declined but Barnstaple's market still bustles with life in the 150-year-old timber-framed **Pannier Market** (Apr–Dec: open Mon–Sat; Jan–Mar: closed Sun, Mon, Thu). On the Strand riverside promenade, the town's 18th-century maritime heyday is depicted in the **Heritage Centre** (closed Sun, Mon). At the end of the Strand is the **Museum of Barnstaple and North Devon** (closed Mon) with an eccentric collection of local archaeology, natural history, and crafts. The best views of the scenic Taw Estuary can be enjoyed by cycling the **Tarka Trail**, along a riverside stretch of old railway track. Rent bikes from **Tarka Trail Cycle Hire** (The Railway Station; 01271 324 202; www.tarkatrail.

Above The wooden-framed Pannier Market (1855), Barnstaple **Above right** South West Coast Path on the way to Mortehoe, Devon

EAT AND DRINK

MORTEHOE

Chichester Arms *inexpensive*
Next to the church, this 16th-century pub was once the vicarage. It serves good ales and food with a beer garden. *EX34 7DU; 01271 870 411*

AROUND MORTEHOE

The Quay *expensive*
Artist Damien Hirst's fish restaurant has dining rooms facing harbor and sea. *Take B3343 and turn left on A361 to Ilfracombe; 11 The Quay, Ilfracombe, EX34 9EQ; 01271 868 090; www.11thequay.com*

WOOLACOMBE

Red Barn *inexpensive*
Lively bar-restaurant near the beach, popular with surfers and families. *The Esplanade, EX34 7DF; 01271 870 264*

AROUND BRAUNTON BURROWS

Squire's Fish Restaurant *moderate*
Renowned as the best place in the area for traditional fish and chips – large portions and top quality. *Exeter Road, Braunton, EX33 1JR; 01271 815 533; closed Sun*

DAY TRIP OPTIONS

There is a variety of great days out based anywhere around Exmoor.

West Somerset Railway
Start at Taunton ❶ to see St. Mary's Church; then it's on to Washford ❷ to visit Cleeve Abbey, before taking a trip on this preserved railway line through the Somerset countryside.

Take the A358 north from Taunton and then left on the A39 to Washford.

Beaches and Coastal Trails
Work up an appetite building sandcastles at Woolacombe ❾, hike the South West Coast Path at Mortehoe ❽ and then indulge in a cream tea.

Follow the B3343 to Woolacombe's

parking lots, off A361, then follow signs to Mortehoe and park in the village.

Lorna Doone Country
Visit the castle at Dunster ❸, then climb Dunkery Beacon for views of Exmoor and follow the Lorna Doone Trail from Oare ❻.

Dunster and Oare are both off the A39.

Hardy Country and the Jurassic Coast

Swanage to Sherborne

Highlights

- **Rolling Dorset hills**
  Meander through Dorset's inland hills and valleys, adorned with giant chalk figures and medieval castles

- **Dinosaur coast**
  Admire the striking formations of Durdle Door, Chesil Beach, and fossil-rich Purbeck and Portland

- **Thomas Hardy's home town**
  Explore Thomas Hardy's Dorchester and the remnants of its Roman and prehistoric past

- **Ancient abbeys and churches**
  Marvel at the medieval craftsmanship of tiny churches and the inspiring fan-vaulting of Sherborne Abbey

Spectacular Durdle Door and Bay with the chalk cliffs of the Jurassic Coast

Hardy Country and the Jurassic Coast

Dorset is one of England's comeliest counties, renowned for its soft, undulating hills, and cliff-backed coastline. There are few conurbations to blot the landscape, instead gentle sheep-speckled slopes and mellow green prospects soothe the traveler's eye. The past looms large here, from the fossil-rich Jurassic Coast to ancient British sites, and from Roman remains to medieval monuments. Literary types know the region for its associations with Thomas Hardy and his works, in which it appears as "Wessex," while Hardy's own town of Dorchester ("Casterbridge") offers plenty of entertainment for children and adults alike.

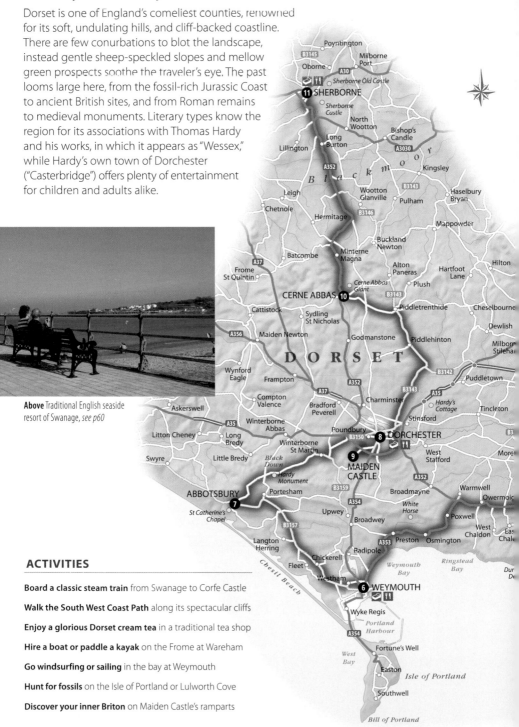

Above Traditional English seaside resort of Swanage, see p60

ACTIVITIES

Board a classic steam train from Swanage to Corfe Castle

Walk the South West Coast Path along its spectacular cliffs

Enjoy a glorious Dorset cream tea in a traditional tea shop

Hire a boat or paddle a kayak on the Frome at Wareham

Go windsurfing or sailing in the bay at Weymouth

Hunt for fossils on the Isle of Portland or Lulworth Cove

Discover your inner Briton on Maiden Castle's ramparts

Above The peaceful country village of Abbotsbury, *see p61*

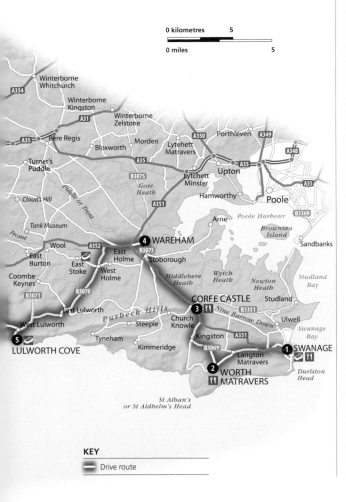

KEY

— Drive route

PLAN YOUR DRIVE

Start/finish: Swanage to Sherborne.

Number of days: 3 days allowing a half-day's tour of Dorchester.

Distance: Around 80 miles (129 km).

Road conditions: Good roads, but sometimes narrow and steep.

When to go: It is possible to tour the area any time of year, but best to try and avoid public holidays and summer weekends, when traffic is heaviest around the coast.

Opening times: Museums and attractions are generally open 10am–5pm, but close earlier (or are closed altogether) Nov–Easter. Shop opening hours are longer. Churches are usually open until dusk.

Main market days: Swanage: Tue (Apr–Oct); **Wareham**: Thu & Sat; **Weymouth**: Thu; **Dorchester**: Wed; **Sherborne**: Thu & Sat, also Farmer's Market on 3rd Fri of month.

Shopping: Dorset is famed for its creamy Blue Vinny cheese; sweet cinnamon-rich Dorset apple cake, and delicious locally produced chutneys and jams.

Major festivals: Swanage: Jazz Festival, Jul; **Wareham**: Music Festival, Sep; **Weymouth**: Seafood Festival, Jul; Weymouth Regatta, Jul–Aug; **Dorchester**: Dorchester Festival (various arts events) Jun.

DAY TRIP OPTIONS

Dorchester's many **museums** and **ancient sights** have something for everyone – but especially **dinosaur hunters**; follow the learning with some practical **fossil hunting** on Chesil Beach and Portland. From Swanage, enjoy a ride on a **steam train**, visit a **crumbling Norman castle**, and then head to the coast to explore the **beach** and awesome **rock formations** near Lulworth. For full details, *see p63*.

Above The pretty stone-quarrying town of Worth Matravers

VISITING SWANAGE

Parking
There's a short-term parking lot behind the tourist office, on Horsecliffe Lane, off Victoria Avenue. There's also a longer term parking lot on Victoria Ave (A351).

Tourist Information
The White House, Shore Rd, BH19 1LB; 0870 442 0680; www.swanage.gov.uk

WHERE TO STAY

SWANAGE

Grand Hotel Swanage *moderate*
This old-fashioned Victorian palace has terrific views over the Bay, a splendid lawn, and an award-winning restaurant. *Burlington Rd, BH19 1LU; 01929 423 353; www.grandhotelswanage.co.uk*

AROUND WAREHAM

Kemps Country House *expensive*
This former Victorian rectory offers clean, modern, and well-equipped rooms. *East Stoke, BH20 6AL (5 km/3 miles on A352 and B3070 west from Wareham); 0845 862 0315; www.kempscountryhouse.co.uk*

LULWORTH COVE

The Beach House *moderate*
This whitewashed Edwardian hotel has contemporary rooms overlooking the sea or an adjacent duck pond. *West Lulworth, BH20 5RQ; 01929 400 404; www.lulworthbeachhotel.com*

WEYMOUTH

Chandlers Hotel *moderate*
Small pristine hotel within walking distance of the center. *4 Westerhall Rd, DT4 7SZ; 01305 771 341; www.chandlershotel.com*

① Swanage
Dorset; BH19 1LB
This is a quintessential Victorian resort with a seafront promenade, Punch and Judy shows, and a fine sandy beach that curves around Swanage Bay. For something wilder, head 4 miles (7 km) north to **Studland Bay** – the tourist office by the beach has maps for walkers, or take bus no. 50 from Shore Rd. The town is not without interest either. The stone façade of the **Town Hall**, built in 1833, was taken from the Mercers' Hall in London (designed by Christopher Wren) when it was being remodeled – notice the cherubs holding cloths for the Virgin Mary. Board a **Swanage Railway** *(Apr–Oct)* steam train for a visit to Corfe Castle.

🚗 *Leave on A351, left on B3069, and left to Worth Matravers. Park behind pub.*

② Worth Matravers
Dorset; BH19 3LF
This tiny village's attractions include **The Square and Compass** pub *(see right)*, inspiring views (can be enjoyed from the pub's outdoor tables), and a graceful Norman church, **St. Nicholas**. Dating from the late 12th century, the church has a wood-beamed roof and a jagged chancel arch. This is a great place to enjoy a walk along the **South West Coast Path**, starting on one of the footpaths that radiate from the village to the coast on either side.

🚗 *Turn left out of parking lot, then left onto B3069 to A351, then left to Corfe village, castle, and parking lot.*

Lawrence of Arabia in Dorset
T E Lawrence – dubbed "Lawrence of Arabia" for his World War I exploits – spent his post-war life in quiet Dorset. See his effigy in Wareham and cottage at **Clouds Hill** *(late Mar–late Oct: open Thu–Sun)*. From here, it's possible to walk to the site of his fatal motorbike crash, to his grave in **Moreton** and to **Bovington Camp** where he briefly served – now a **tank museum** *(open daily)*.

③ Corfe Castle
Dorset; BH20 5EZ
The silhouette of the crumbling castle ruins *(open daily)* that dominate this village presents a truly romantic

Lawrence of Arabia, Wareham

vista. This once mighty Norman bastion owes its present decrepit state to the English Civil War (1641–51), when Lady Bankes defended it against Parliamentarian troops, who finally blew the castle up after a six-week siege.

🚗 *Continue on A351, then take B3075 toward Stoborough, for Wareham. Parking lot is on right over river.*

④ Wareham
Dorset; BH20 4LU
Located on the River Frome close to the sea, Wareham was an important port in Saxon times. Now a pretty backwater, it preserves the layout of its old town walls. **St. Martin's Church** also has much of its Saxon structure, medieval frescoes, and a romantic effigy of T E Lawrence *(see box above)*. Rent a rowing boat or kayak at the bridge and enjoy a river trip from

Below The historic restored railway line at Swanage, with steam trains for Corfe Castle

Far left Corfe Castle's dramatic Norman hilltop ruins **Left** The peaceful town of Wareham, located on the River Frome

Wareham Boat Hire *(01929 550 688; www.warehamboathire.co.uk; Mar–Oct).*

🚗 *Leave town on A352, turn left on B3070, signed Lulworth Cove, through West Lulworth to cove and parking lot.*

⑤ Lulworth Cove
Dorset; BH20 5RQ
Below the Purbeck Hills with dramatic chalk cliffs lie a series of enticing shingle and shale beaches, reached by the coastal path. One of these, the nearly circular **Lulworth Cove** fills with small vessels in summer and offers sheltered swimming. A 15-minute walk west stands spectacular **Durdle Door**, a natural limestone archway in the sea at the popular beach, Durdle Bay. Purbeck's seaboard forms part of the **Jurassic Coast**, a World Heritage Site whose geological makeup has yielded a rich trove of fossil finds.

🚗 *From West Lulworth, follow signs for Dorchester, passing the turn for Durdle Door. Turn left on A352 and left again on the A353 to Weymouth and the town centre – park at ferry terminal.*

⑥ Weymouth
Dorset; DT3
With its sandy beach and promenade, Weymouth is a typical traditional English resort. Sailing, kitesurfing, and windsurfing are popular activities here – try **SailLaser** *(0845 337 3214; www.sail-laser.com)* for sailing courses – and the

town is set to host sailing events in the 2012 Olympics. To the south, the **Isle of Portland**, connected to the mainland by a causeway, has a wild coastline worth exploring – dinosaur footprints have been found here. Northwest stretches the 18-mile (29-km) pebble strand of **Chesil Beach**, a bleak, unearthly expanse backed by the Fleet Lagoon, a nature reserve.

🚗 *Take the B3157 northwest, following signs to Abbotsbury.*

⑦ Abbotsbury
Dorset; DT3 4JT
A 15th-century tithe barn – the only remaining building of a Benedictine Abbey – now houses a **Children's Farm** *(mid-Mar–early Sep & half-term: open daily; mid-Sep–Oct: open weekends)*, where kids can get close to a range of animals. There is also a garden filled with exotic plants, and the **Swannery** *(mid-Mar–mid-Sep: open daily)*, home to a colony of mute swans, best visited in June, when the swans nest and the young hatch. Climb up to the hilltop **St. Catherine's Chapel** for stupendous views (and the path to the Swannery).

🚗 *Turn right at Strangeways Hall and leave via Back St on a steep, narrow ascent with great coastal views. Cross over the junction, following signs to the Hardy Monument. Turn right onto B3159 and left to Dorchester. Park in town center off Acland Road.*

EAT AND DRINK

SWANAGE
Ocean Bay *moderate*
Enjoy fabulous beach views from this modern eatery with a strong seafood menu. Try the ale-battered haddock, sea-bass fillets, or ribeye steak. Also serves salads, snacks, and breakfasts.
2 Ulwell Rd, BH19 1LH; 01929 422 222; www.oceanbayrestaurant.com

WORTH MATRAVERS
The Square and Compass *inexpensive*
Great pasties and real ales are served at this excellent flagstoned pub with great views and a small museum of fossils and other local finds.
Worth Matravers, BH19 3LF; 01929 439 229

CORFE CASTLE
Morton's House *inexpensive–moderate*
This 16th-century manor house has been tastefully converted into a smart hotel-restaurant. Lunch on soups, salads, and snacks in the bar, or guinea fowl or halibut in the more formal restaurant.
East St, BH20 5EE; 01929 480 988; www.mortonshouse.co.uk

WEYMOUTH
Old Rooms Inn *inexpensive*
Right by the fishing harbor, with tables outside, this pub offers a range of snacks from salads to burgers and grills, as well as real ales.
Cove Row, DT4 8TT; 01305 771 130

Crab House Café *moderate*
On Fleet Lagoon, this is not much more than a shack, with a few wooden tables and a view of the sea, but serves superb fresh seafood such as Portland crab and huge prawns in tarragon butter.
The Oyster Farm, Ferryman's Way, DT4 9YU; 01305 788 867; www.crabhousecafe.co.uk

Below left Traditional seaside facilities at Weymouth's sandy beach **Below right** The naturally sheltered harbor of Lulworth Cove

ICE CREAM CHIPS

Above The impressive Maumbury Rings, Dorchester **Above center** The view down High Fast Street in the center of Dorchester **Above right** The remains of the Roman Town House, discovered 1937

VISITING DORCHESTER

Tourist Information
11 Antelope Walk, DT1 1BE; 01305 267 992; www.westdorset.com

Parking
Park in the town centre, off Acland Road. There is an additional car park nearby on Durngate Street.

WHERE TO STAY

DORCHESTER

Westwood House *inexpensive*
This centrally located B&B in a smart Georgian town house offers six well-equipped rooms. Good breakfasts are served in an airy conservatory.
29 High West St, DT1 1UP; 01305 268 018; www.westwoodhouse.co.uk

The Casterbridge *moderate*
A range of cozy rooms are available at this family-run hotel on the main street, including one with a four-poster, one with its own patio, and a family room.
49 High East St, DT1 1HU; 01305 264 043; www.casterbridgehotel.co.uk

SHERBORNE

The Bakehouse *inexpensive*
Dating from the 18th century, this friendly B&B with flagstone floors has plenty of period character. The rooms are comfortable and a good size.
1 Acreman St, DT9 3NU; 01935 817 969; www.bakehouse.me.uk

The Eastbury Hotel *moderate*
Close to the Abbey, this Georgian hotel offers luxury and old-fashioned charm. Public rooms are welcoming, bedrooms are spacious, and the staff are friendly. The smart restaurant is worth trying, too.
Long St, DT9 3BY; 01935 813 131; www.theeastburyhotel.co.uk

⑨ Dorchester

Dorset; DT1 1BE

With Georgian architecture, tree-lined avenues, and quirky museums, Dorchester is associated with Thomas Hardy as the Casterbridge of his novels. Look, too, for reminders of the infamous Judge Jeffreys (1645–89), the Tolpuddle Martyrs, and the town's early Roman inhabitants.

A two-hour walking tour

From the parking lot, head south, then left onto tree-lined South Walks Rd and on to the **Dorset Martyrs** ① – three bronze figures carved in 1986 by modernist sculptor Elisabeth Frink. Cross Icen Way, then go left on a path across Salisbury Fields to Salisbury St. The **Teddy Bear Museum** ② is at the end of this street, in the same building as the **Terracotta Warriors Museum** *(both open daily)*, dedicated to the red clay army of China's first emperor. Exit left into I ligh East St, and left again into Icen Way to find the entertaining **Dinosaur Museum** ③ *(open daily)*. From here, turn right and follow Durngate St, then left on South St to **Barclays Bank** ④, said to have been the Mayor of Casterbridge's house in Thomas Hardy's novel. Retrace your steps up South St, which becomes Corn Hill. On the left, the entrance to the **Antelope Walk Shopping Arcade** ⑤ was once the Antelope Hotel, mentioned in *The Mayor of Casterbridge* and where Judge Jeffreys held his "Bloody Assizes" condemning 74 of those rebelling against James II to death in 1685.

At the top of Corn Hill, turn left into High West Sreet. **St. Peter's Church** ⑥, on the right, is mainly 15th century (Thomas Hardy helped to restore it as an apprentice in the 1850s). To the left of the church is the **Dorset County Museum** ⑦ *(closed Sun, except Jul)*, detailing the cultural and geological history of the region. Past the museum is the **Old Crown Court** ⑧ *(open Mon–Fri)*, where the Tolpuddle Martyrs were sent to Australia for trying to form an agricultural union in 1834. Over the road the **Tutankhamun Exhibition** ⑨ *(open daily)* gives an insight into the life and burial of the Egyptian boy-king.

Cross back over High West St and turn into Glyde Path Rd,

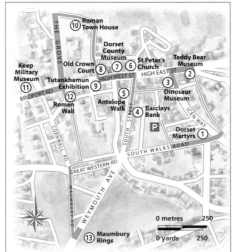

following it to the **Roman Town House** ⑩ *(open daily)*. The ruins reveal the elaborate heating system and mosaic floors. At the end of Northernhay, turn left into The Grove, and on to a statue of Thomas Hardy. Cross The Grove and walk up Bridport Rd to the fascinating **Keep Military Museum** ⑪ *(Apr–Sep: open Mon–Sat; Oct–Mar: open Tue–Sat)*, revealing the history of local army regiments. From here, return to High West St to see a fragment of **Roman Wall** ⑫ by Princes St. Cross here and follow West Walks, turning right at the end then left into Cornwall Rd; cross Gt Western Rd into Maumbury Rd, and head to the **Maumbury Rings** ⑬, a Neolithic henge, then a Roman amphitheater and later a place of public execution. Return on Weymouth Ave to South Walks Rd, back to parking lot.
🚗 *Head south on Weymouth Ave, turning right on Maiden Castle Rd.*

⑨ Maiden Castle
Dorset; DT1 2AB, DT2 8QJ
Prehistoric **Maiden Castle** *(open daily)* is the largest Iron-Age hillfort in Europe. The vast and complex structure of 20-ft (6-m) ramparts and trenches is

Above The chalk carving of the Cerne Giant, possibly a fertility symbol

now all grassed over but the undulating banks vividly evoke the ancient fortification (450–300 BC), overcome by the Romans in AD 43.
🚗 *Return to A35, heading east around Dorchester, turn left on B3150 and right on B3143. At Piddletrenthide, turn left, following signs for Cerne Abbas, up a narrow, steep lane.*

⑩ Cerne Abbas
Dorset; DT2 7JF
Amid the timbered, golden houses of Cerne Abbas stands **St. Mary's Church**, dating from the 13th century and boasting a rare stone chancel screen. However, the village is most famous for the **Cerne Giant**, a chalk carving on a hillside north of the village. Little is known about the origins of the 180-ft (55-m) figure, wielding a club and proudly displaying his manhood. It was first recorded in 1694, though some historians believe it dates from around 190 AD, possibly depicting Hercules – it has long been the site of fertility rituals. To view it, turn up Duck St from Long St, following signs for the Giant and a parking area.
🚗 *Turn right out of the viewing area, on the A352, marked Sherborne. Follow signs to Abbey and park opposite.*

⑪ Sherborne
Dorset; DT9 3NL
The chief glory of this charming stone town is **Sherborne Abbey**, a fine example of Perpendicular architecture whose fan-vaulted ceiling is studded with colorful bosses depicting such images as a mermaid, an owl, and a dog with a bone. To the east of town stand the ruined **Old Castle** *(late Mar–Oct: open daily)*, dating from the 12th century, and the **New Castle** *(late Mar–Oct: open Tue–Thu & Sun; Sat pm)*, built for Sir Walter Raleigh in 1594, with grand state rooms, a Tudor kitchen and now with parkland by "Capability" Brown.

Above Sherborne Abbey, featuring Saxon, Norman, and Perpendicular architecture

EAT AND DRINK

DORCHESTER
Potters *inexpensive*
This casual but smart café offers a healthy selection of home-cooked food, from snack lunches to cakes.
19 Durngate St, DT1 1JP; 01305 260 312

Judge Jeffreys *inexpensive*
Great Italian cuisine is served in this former residence of the infamous Judge Jeffreys, with paneled dining areas.
6 High West St, DT1 1UJ; 01305 259 678; www.prezzoplc.co.uk

The Fridge *inexpensive*
Blue Vinny cheese, Dorset Apple Cake, and other local specialities are stocked in this award-winning delicatessen.
17 Tudor Arcade, DT1 1BN; 01305 269 088; www.thefridge.biz

SHERBORNE
Aspire 2 Eat *inexpensive*
Close to the Abbey, this bistro/wine bar serves dishes such as mushroom risotto, grilled goat's cheese, and crab tagliatelle.
Digby Rd, DT9 3NL; 01935 389 666; www.aspire2eat.co.uk

The Green *moderate*
Sophisticated modern European cuisine is featured in this semi-formal restaurant where all the ingredients are fresh and locally sourced.
3 The Green, DT9 3HY; 01935 813 821

DAY TRIP OPTIONS
Dorchester and Swanage are both good bases for exploring the coastline, beaches and museums.

Jurassic Adventure
Spend a morning at **Dorchester's** ⑧ Dinosaur Museum and Dorset County Museum, pack a picnic, and head to

Weymouth ⑥ for some fossil-hunting on Chesil Beach or Portland – keep away from the cliffs. If time, make a trip to Abbotsbury ⑦ with its children's farm and swannery.

Weymouth is on the A354 from Dorchester, then use the B3157 for Chesil Beach; return as per drive.

Coast and Castles
From Swanage ❶, ride a steam train before lunching at Worth Matravers ❷. Then head on to Corfe Castle ❸ and Wareham ❹, and finish the day off at Lulworth Cove ❺ or Durdle Door.

Take the A351, B3069, A351, and B3070; skip Wareham, if short of time.

Eat and Drink: inexpensive, under £25; moderate, £25 £50; expensive, over £50

A Spiritual Journey

Salisbury to Glastonbury

Highlights

- **Medieval Salisbury**
  Unearth the medieval wonders of Salisbury, crowned by its venerable cathedral and the tallest spire in the UK

- **Neolithic stone circles**
  Experience the different character of England's prehistoric stone circles, from the majesty of Stonehenge to the solemnity of Avebury

- **Inland waterways**
  Soak up the tranquility of the Kennet and Avon Canal on foot, by bike, or on a gentle boat cruise

- **Georgian Bath**
  Follow in the footsteps of Jane Austen in this panoply of Georgian architecture, and tour the ancient, naturally-heated baths

The elegant and stately architecture of Bath, by the River Avon

A Spiritual Journey

From the lovely city of Salisbury, dominated by its iconic cathedral spire, to the graceful Georgian terraces of Bath, and west to medieval Wells, this drive takes in some of England's most compelling historic centers. En route, there are appealing stretches of countryside: the grand swathes of Salisbury Plain and the rolling pastures of Somerset, studded by the Mendip Hills, an Area of Outstanding Natural Beauty. And along the way are many reminders of the distant past, in which ancient religions have left their mark: Stonehenge is the most famous of Britain's prehistoric stone circles, but lesser-visited circles exist at Avebury and Stanton Drew. The final stop is Glastonbury, where religion, history and myth are all magically mixed together.

Below Elaborate pinnacles of Bath Abbey, seen across the River Avon, Bath *see pp71–2*

ACTIVITIES

Stroll through Salisbury's water meadows to find the spot from which Constable painted his Salisbury Cathedral picture

Take a tour of the Wadworth Brewery, Devizes

Hire a skiff or canal boat from Devizes or Bradford-on-Avon to tour the Kennet and Avon Canal

Rejuvenate at Thermae Bath Spa, the modern bathing complex at the heart of Bath

Hike in the Mendip Hills around the beautiful Ebbor Gorge

Rent a bike in Glastonbury and experience the tranquility of the Somerset Levels, west of town

0 kilometres 5

0 miles 5

KEY

Drive route

PLAN YOUR DRIVE

Start/finish: Salisbury to Glastonbury.

Number of days: 4, allowing for a half-day each in Salisbury and Bath.

Distance: 112 miles (180 km).

Road conditions: Good, but allow for congestion in and around Bath.

When to go: Weekdays are best for Salisbury, Stonehenge, and Bath, to miss the crowds. Glastonbury is very busy either side of the last weekend of June, when the festival takes place.

Opening times: Attractions are generally open 10am–5pm, but close earlier (or close completely) Nov–Easter. Shops stay open longer. Churches are usually open until dusk.

Market days: Salisbury: Charter Market, Tue & Sat; Farmers' Market, 1st & 3rd Wed of month; **Devizes**: Thu & Sat; **Bath**: Farmers' Market, Sat (Green Park Station); Indoor Market, Mon–Sat (Guildhall).

Shopping: Look out for authentic Cheddar cheese in the Mendip Hills – especially in the Cheddar Gorge, and discounted Clark's shoes in Street, south of Glastonbury. Anyone interested in New Age trinkets will enjoy Glastonbury.

Major festivals: Salisbury: International Arts Festival (2 wks May–Jun); Food and Drink Festival (mid-Sep); **Bath**: International Music Festival (18 days May–Jun); Jane Austen Festival (10 days late Sep); **Glastonbury**: Music Festival (around last weekend Jun).

DAY TRIP OPTIONS

From Salisbury, take in the **prehistoric stone rings, ancient monuments,** and **ditches** of Old Sarum, Stonehenge, and Avebury. Fans of **architecture** and **shopping** can happily spend several hours exploring Bath followed by a trip to Bradford-on-Avon for **Anglo-Saxon buildings** and then to **medieval** Lacock Abbey. A morning spent touring Wells and Glastonbury will appeal to lovers of **medieval churches**, while cavers and nature-lovers will appreciate the **walks, gorges, and wildlife** found among the Mendip Hills. For full details, *see p73*.

Below Narrow boats on the Kennet And Avon Canal, near Bradford-on-Avon, *see p70*

Above Salisbury Cathedral, with the highest spire in the UK **Top right** Canal boat on the Kennet and Avon Canal, Devizes **Bottom right** Ruins of the Bishop's Palace, Old Sarum

VISITING SALISBURY

Parking
The best parking lot in Salisbury is Central Car Park (signed) by the Playhouse.

Tourist Information
Fish Row, SP1 1EJ; 01722 334 956; www.visitsalisbury.com

WHERE TO STAY

SALISBURY

Cathedral View *moderate*
Intimate B&B behind the Cathedral and with views of it from the front rooms; (all four rooms are ensuite).
83 Exeter St, SP1 2SE; 01722 502 254; www.cathedral-viewbandb.co.uk

Red Lion Hotel *moderate–expensive*
This charming coaching inn is nearly 800 years old and filled with curios and period pieces. There is limited parking.
Milford St, SP1 2AN; 01722 323 334; www.the-redlion.co.uk

DEVIZES

The Bear Hotel *moderate*
This hotel has numbered royalty among its guests. Rooms are comfortable, and there's live jazz in the cellar on weekends.
Market Place, SN10 1HS; 01380 722 444; www.thebearhotel.net

AVEBURY

The Lodge *expensive*
Wake within sight of the stones in this lovely Georgian upmarket vegetarian B&B. Only two rooms so book ahead.
High Street, SN8 1RF; 01672 539 023; www.aveburylodge.co.uk

① Salisbury
Wiltshire; SP1 1EJ
One of Britain's great cathedral cities, Salisbury has a compact center that is ideal for a leisurely stroll. **Salisbury Cathedral** *(open daily)*, built over a period of just 38 years in the 13th century, is an unusually fine example of Early English Gothic. The soaring 404-ft (123-m) tower can be explored on a guided tour and the library holds an original copy of Magna Carta. Learn more about the city's history, as well as that of Old Sarum and Stonehenge in the **Salisbury and South Wiltshire Museum** *(open Mon–Sat; daily Jul–Aug)*, behind the cathedral. Finally, take a short stroll west of the cathedral to the water meadows, to enjoy the classic city views painted by John Constable.
🚗 *From the center, head north on Castle St onto the A345; park on site.*

Below The huge, impressive Neolithic stone complex at Stonehenge

② Old Sarum
Wiltshire; SP1 3SD
On a windswept hilltop, formidable earthworks and scanty Norman remains mark the site of Old Sarum *(open daily)*, an important settlement that flourished from around 500 BC. Occupied later by the Romans and Saxons, it was then fortified by the Normans who also built a cathedral here in the 12th century. The site was abandoned in the next century, when Salisbury became the regional center.
🚗 *Turn left out of Old Sarum onto A345, then left to Upper Woodford. Follow the road until it joins A303, turn right for Stonehenge. Bear right on the A344 past the stones to the parking lot.*

The riddle of the stones
Composed of a ring of upright stones topped with lintels, a horseshoe of trilithons (two uprights and a lintel), and a ring of bluestones, Stonehenge remains a mystery. Why was it built? How were the stones moved here, some from as far away as the Preseli Hills in Wales? The most extraordinary fact is that the whole complex was built without any more sophisticated tools than picks made from antlers and shovels made of bone.

③ Stonehenge
Wiltshire; SP4 7DE
England's grandest and best preserved stone circle appears dwarfed by the expanse of Salisbury Plain. Built in stages between 3,000 BC and 1,600 BC, the huge stones and earthworks originally formed part of a much larger complex. The exact function of Stonehenge *(open daily)* is obscure but, given the alignment of the stones relative to the rising and setting sun, it is likely to have been astronomically connected to religious rituals. Its

Where to Stay: inexpensive, under £80; moderate, £80–£150; expensive, over £150

location at the heart of a dense area of Neolithic and Bronze Age monuments and burial mounds adds to its aura of spirituality. There is no direct access to the stones (visitors must follow a path around them) but free audioguides provide an informative commentary.

🚗 *Turn right out of the parking lot and continue northwest along the A344 and A360 to Devizes.*

Above Elegant façade of Bowood House, one of the finest stately homes in England

④ Devizes

Wiltshire; SN10 1JG

This historic market town has one of the finest main streets in the region, graced by elegant buildings from all eras. On Long St, the **Wiltshire Heritage Museum** *(open daily)* traces the history of the county from earliest times and has an excellent prehistoric collection. Take an enlightening tour of the Victorian **Wadworth Brewery** *(open Mon–Sat; 01380 732 277; www. wadworth.co.uk)*, on New Park St, with samplings on most days. A brief walk west of town along the **Kennet and Avon Canal** leads to Caen Hill Locks, an extraordinary succession of 29 locks. The canal, which stretches for nearly 60 miles (96 km) between Newbury and Bath, dates from 1810. Explore the outstanding beauty of this great waterway on a canal boat rented from **Devizes Marina**, north off the A361 *(01380 725 300; www.devizesmarina.co.uk)*.

🚗 *Head northeast along A361, turn right at a roundabout, through Horton and past a white horse on the chalk hills. Turn left toward Marlborough, then left for East Kennett. Turn left on the A4, then right onto the A4361 for Avebury. Pass West Kennet Avenue, a procession of stones leading to Avebury. Park onsite.*

⑤ Avebury

Wiltshire; SN8 1RE

Sprouting out of the earth like broken teeth, the three concentric stone circles of Avebury *(open daily)* are less famous than Stonehenge but far more accessible. Erected between 2,850 BC and 2,200 BC, the rough-hewn stones extend through the village and beyond and are ringed by a huge ditch and earth mound. The site has suffered much over the years, and the stones largely owe their present appearance to Alexander Keiller, an amateur archaeologist who excavated and re-erected many of them in the 1930s. Other sites within walking distance include **Silbury Hill**, Europe's largest man-made ancient monument, and **West Kennet Long Barrow,** a 330-ft (100-m) chambered tomb mound.

🚗 *Take the A4361 west, then take the A4 through Calne, follow signs on to Bowood House on the left.*

⑥ Bowood House

Calne, Wiltshire; SN11 0LZ

"Capability" Brown and Robert and James Adam were among the garden designers and architects who worked on Bowood House *(open mid-Mar–early Nov)*, a superb stately home dating mainly from the 18th century. Inside are displays of costumes, porcelain and Indian artistry, and the laboratory where Joseph Priestley discovered oxygen in 1774. There are spectacular rhododendron walks in the grounds – at their best April to June – as well as grottoes and an adventure playground.

🚗 *Exit to the A4 west, then south on the A342, then right at Sandy Lane for Lacock. The parking lot is on the left.*

Above Silbury Hill, one of several major Neolithic sites close to Avebury

Above Caen Hill Locks on the Kennet and Avon Canal, Devizes

EAT AND DRINK

SALISBURY

Polly Tea Rooms *inexpensive*
There are both indoor and outdoor tables at this buzzing tearoom and restaurant opposite St. Thomas' Church. Grilled goat's cheese, baked potatoes and lasagne feature on the menu as well as lip-smacking pastries and artisan chocolates.
8 St. Thomas's Square, SP1 1BA; 01722 336 037; www.thepolly.com; open daytime only

AROUND DEVIZES

The George & Dragon *moderate*
Inventive modern dishes are served in this welcoming gastro pub on the A342 3.4 km (2 miles) north of Devizes. Spicy crab risotto and game dishes are among the specialities. It also has some stylish rooms.
High St, Rowde, SN10 2PN; 01380 723 053; www.thegeorgeanddragonrowde.co.uk

AROUND AVEBURY

The Waggon and Horses *inexpensive*
This large thatched inn lies 2 km (1 mile) from Avebury's monuments on the A4. Tuck into steaks, pies, and traditional English dishes, as well as curries and lasagne. There's also a pleasant garden.
Beckhampton, SN8 1QJ; 01672 539 418

Above Half-timbered houses lend charm to the picturesque village of Lacock

VISITING BATH

Parking
There are parking lots off Charlotte Street and Avon Street. Or use the park-and-ride and leave your car on the outskirts and catch a bus into the center.

Tourist information
Abbey Churchyard, BA1 1LY; 0906 711 2000; www.visitbath.co.uk

Thermae Bath Spa
Hot Bath St, BA1 1SJ; 01225 331 234; www.thermaebathspa.com; 9am–10pm (last entry 7.30pm) daily

WHERE TO STAY

BRADFORD-ON-AVON

The Swan Hotel *moderate*
Stylishly refurbished rooms offset the traditional exterior of this cozy hotel, which has broadband and flatscreen TVs. There's a good restaurant, too.
1 Church St, BA15 1LN; 01225 868 686; www.theswan-hotel.co.uk

BATH

Apsley House Hotel *moderate*
Antiques adorn this stately house built in 1830. Some rooms have four-poster beds, and there is a garden suite. The hotel is located just over 1 mile (2 km) west of the city center.
Newbridge Hill, BA1 3PT; 01225 336 966; www.apsley-house.co.uk

Tolley Cottage *moderate*
This Victorian B&B with just two small but bright rooms lies a 10-minute walk from Bath's center. Breakfast can be enjoyed on the patio in fine weather.
23 Sydney Buildings, BA2 6BZ; 01225 463 365; www.tolleycottage.co.uk

Royal Crescent Hotel *expensive*
Stay in the best address in Bath – the Royal Crescent. Rates are high, but a luxurious stay is assured, and the facilities and restaurant are rightly acclaimed.
16 Royal Crescent, BA1 2LS; 01225 823 333; www.royalcrescent.co.uk

⑦ Lacock
Wiltshire; SN15 2LG
Meticulously preserved by its owners, the National Trust, this village has half-timbered houses and a predominantly sleepy flavor. Its unspoiled air has led to many appearances in TV and film productions, including *The Other Boleyn Girl* and the Harry Potter films. At one end of the main street is the cloistered **Lacock Abbey** *(open Mar–Oct: Wed–Mon pm)*, founded in 1232 and gracefully converted into a home after the 16th-century Dissolution of the Monasteries. A separate **museum** *(Feb–Oct: open daily; Nov–Jan: open Sat & Sun)* features the work of photography pioneer William Fox Talbot (1800–77).

🚗 *From Lacock, turn left onto A350 to Melksham. Take B3107 to Bradford-on-Avon. Cross the bridge, bear right, and park by the tithe barn on the right.*

⑨ Bath
Somerset; BA1 1SU

Museum og Costume
Roman Baths

With its golden-hued terraces around a vast natural amphitheater, Bath is one of England's most congenial cities. At its heart, the Roman Baths and the Abbey are the most compelling of the many attractions to be appreciated on a stroll. Its maze of lanes lined with smart boutiques will tempt shoppers; gastronomes will savor the range of great restaurants, and culture addicts will enjoy the year-round program of festivals.

A two-hour walking tour
From Avon Street Car Park, walk along Broad Quay and Dorchester St, past the railway station and up Manvers St to reach Orange Grove. Turn left here down York St for Abbey Churchyard. The small piazza is grandly overlooked

⑧ Bradford-on-Avon
Wiltshire; BA15 1LF
Rising up from the river, this engaging town deserves a lingering visit. The wealth earned from the cloth trade is evident in the historic buildings, such as the Anglo-Saxon **Church of St. Laurence**, possibly founded in AD 705 and the early 14th-century **Tithe Barn**, used to store food owed to the church, and one of the oldest in England. See the Norman bridge – with two original pointed arches – but rebuilt in the 17th century, and enjoy a stroll along the River Avon and the Kennet and Avon Canal or rent a boat from **MV Barbara McLellan** *(Mar–Oct; Wharf Cottage, BA15 1LE; 01225 868 683; www.katrust.org)*.

🚗 *Exit west on B3108, turn right on A36 and left to Claverton Down. Turn left, then right down Widcombe Hill into town. Cross the river and go left to park.*

by the tall façade of **Bath Abbey** ① *(open Mon–Sat & Sun pm)*, mainly 16th-century with a magnificent fan-vaulted ceiling. To one side are the **Roman Baths** ② *(open daily)*, built on natural hot springs between the first and fifth centuries AD and displaying

Below Pulteney Bridge, designed by Robert Adam, spanning the River Avon

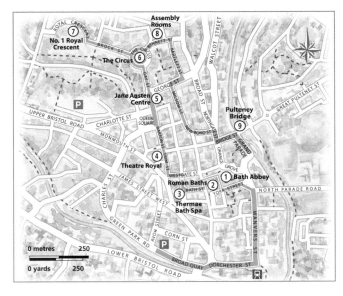

EAT AND DRINK

LACOCK

At the Sign of the Angel *moderate*
Antiques and open fires set the tone of
this ancient hostelry (with rooms, too).
Menu features traditional British cuisine.
*6 Church St, SN15 2LB; 01249 730 230;
www.lacock.co.uk*

BRADFORD-ON-AVON

Mr Salvats Coffee Room *inexpensive*
A unique, fun coffee house (c.1700) that
offers hot and cold snacks and more
substantial dishes in "olde worlde" style.
*Town House, 44 St. Margarets St, BA15
1DE; 01225 867 474; open Thu–Sun*

The Tollgate Inn *moderate*
First-class gastro-pub in a village east of
Bradford, with a cozy ambience. The
menu features British dishes with a
Mediterranean slant. It also has rooms.
*Ham Green, Holt, BA14 6PX; 01225 782
326; www.tollgateholt.co.uk*

BATH

Sally Lunn's *inexpensive*
The city's oldest house and home of the
Bath bun, this popular eatery serves
salmon, duck breast, and coq au vin.
*2 North Parade Passage, BA1 1NX;
01225 461 634; www.sallylunns.co.uk*

Demuths *moderate*
Classy vegetarian restaurant close to
the Abbey. The menu is inspired by
global tastes such as beetroot blinis,
falafel with tzatziki, and Sri Lankan curry.
*2 North Passage Parade, BA1 1NX;
01225 446 059; www.demuths.co.uk*

finds from the Temple of Minerva.
The adjacent 18th-century Pump
Room was the venue of an elegant
salon during Bath's fashionable
heyday, and now offers a range of
refreshments, as well as samples of
the famous spa waters.

Turn left and then right out of
Abbey Churchyard into Bath Street. At
the end of this on the left is **Thermae
Bath Spa** ③, a stunning bath complex
opened in 2006, sporting a rooftop
pool. Turn right, past the Little Theatre,
into St. Michael's Place, then left and
right to pass the 19th-century **Theatre
Royal** ④. Continue up Barton St into
Queen Square. Just past the square, on
the right, explore the world of Jane
Austen at the **Jane Austen Centre** ⑤
(open daily). Austen lived at various
addresses in Bath and set some of her
fiction here.

At the top of Gay Street stands **The
Circus** ⑥, an elegant terrace designed
by John Wood and his son (also John
Wood) in the 18th century. Note the
528 individual carvings on the frieze
running along the buildings, including
serpents, theatrical masks, and possibly
druidic and masonic symbols. From
here, Brock Street leads to the grandest
of Bath's terraces, Royal Crescent, the
work of John Wood the Younger, and
fronted by a graceful sweep of lawn.
Have a look inside one of the houses at
No. 1 Royal Crescent ⑦ *(closed Mon)*.
Retrace the route to The Circus and

walk up Bennett Street for the Georgian
Assembly Rooms ⑧ *(open daily)*, built
in 1769 with a plain exterior but
sumptuous within. In the same
building, the Fashion Museum *(open
daily)* gives an entertaining overview of
costumes and clothing through the
ages. From here, head down Bartlett
Street, turning right and then left at
George Street for Milsom Street, one of
Bath's main shopping areas. Bear left
into New Bond Street, turn right at
Northgate Street and then left at
Bridge Street to **Pulteney Bridge** ⑨,
the elegant shop-lined crossing over
the pretty River Avon, designed by
Robert Adam in the 1770s. To get the
best view, walk down Grand Parade,
past ornamental gardens and back to
Orange Grove, then return to the
parking lot..

🚗 *Follow signs for A4 toward Bristol,
turn off onto A39. Fork right to Compton
Dando, turn left then right. Turn right
towards Woollard. Right onto A37, left
onto B3130 and left at a thatched toll
house. Follow signs to the stone circles.*

Below top right Nave and fan vaulting at
Bath Abbey **Below** Grand, impressive sweep
of the Royal Crescent, Bath

Above Stanton Drew Stone Circle in its delightful rural setting

VISITING THE MENDIPS

The B3135 runs through the **Cheddar Gorge** which offers rock climbing, caving, and nature walks *(01934 742 343; www.cheddarcaves.co.uk)*. Look out also for authentic Cheddar cheese – the production process can be viewed at **Cheddar Gorge Cheese Company** *(01934 742 810; www.cheddargorge cheeseco.co.uk)*. **Ebbor Gorge** (with parking lot) has several nature-filled walks –the area is famous for bats, butterflies, and mosses and lichens; carry on east to **Wookey Hole** *(01749 672 243; www.wookey.co.uk)*. This has many indoor attractions that will appeal to kids.

WHERE TO STAY

THE MENDIP HILLS

Wookey Hole Inn *moderate*
This Inn provides funky accommodation with a young Bohemian ambience. It also offers a great selection of zesty Belgian beers.
Wookey Hole, BA5 1BP; 01749 676 677; www.wookeyholeinn.com

WELLS

Canon Grange *inexpensive*
Enjoying a prize location opposite Wells Cathedral, this period-furnished B&B has five rooms, friendly, helpful hosts, and good breakfasts. Reserve ahead for a room facing the cathedral.
Cathedral Green, BA5 2UB; 01749 671 800; www.canongrange.co.uk

GLASTONBURY

The George and Pilgrim *moderate*
Reputedly haunted and full of character and history, this inn has been in business for 500 years. Some rooms have four-posters and there is a choice of bars for relaxing and eating.
1 High St, BA6 9DP; 01458 831 146; www.relaxinnz.co.uk

Right The winding B3135 through the Cheddar Gorge **Far right** The sublime symmetry of Wells Cathedral nave

⑩ Stanton Drew Stone Circle
Stanton Drew, Somerset
After Avebury, this is the second largest of England's Neolithic stone circle complexes and, like Avebury – and unlike Stonehenge – it's an unfenced site, the irregular-shaped rocks sprouting out of meadows where cattle quietly graze. There are three circles here, the largest at 367 ft (112 m) contains 27 stones and is aligned with a burial chamber known as the Cove 1,640 ft (500 m) away, in what is now a pub garden. Originally, avenues of standing stones lead up to the circles. Many of the stones have been damaged over the years, so the structure of the complex is not easy to see. However, it remains a calming and mesmerizing site. A local myth tells that the stones are a wedding party whose musicians were tricked by the devil into playing on into the Sabbath, at which point they were turned to stone.

🚗 *Return to B3130 west and fork left on B3114. Turn right on A368 and turn left at Compton Martin to B3371 and then right onto B3135, to the Cheddar Gorge. Carry on to A371 east and fork*

left at Draycott, back to B3135 and on to Priddy. Fork right here for Ebbor Gorge and Wookey Hole. Park on site.

⑪ The Mendip Hills
Somerset
Running for some 25 miles (40 km) and not rising above 1,067 ft (325 m), the Mendip Hills are a comparatively low-key range, but they present a stark contrast to Somerset's gentle, rolling landscape. They are characterized by bare heathland over the higher areas, and deep limestone gorges riddled with cave systems that invite further exploration *(see left)*. The **Cheddar Gorge** and **Wookey Hole** *(both open daily)* can get busy and are both somewhat overdeveloped, but there's lots to do here, especially for children, and the caves are spectacular. Unspoiled **Ebbor Gorge**, west of Wookey Hole, is an important National Nature Reserve and has some inviting marked walking trails. The grassland areas are criss-crossed by dry-stone

Mystic Glastonbury
Nowhere else in England has quite the same mix of history and New Age romance, religion and superstition, magic and myth, as Glastonbury. Jesus' uncle, Joseph of Arimathea, is said to have visited here; the Chalice Well on Chilkwell St (and Glastonbury Tor) is supposed to have been the hiding place of the Holy Grail. In the grounds of the Abbey, it is claimed that King Arthur is buried alongside Guinevere. Above the town, ley lines are said to cross on Glastonbury Tor. Believe it or not, there's something special about Glastonbury.

walls and are an important habitat for wildflowers, insects and wildlife such as dormice and the peregrine falcon.

🚗 *From Wookey Hole continue down the High St onto Wells Rd, following signs into the center of Wells.*

⑫ Wells
Somerset; BA5 2RP

England's smallest city, Wells has a **cathedral** that is one of the crowning glories of early English Gothic architecture. Fronted by a swathe of lawn, its stately west façade is a marvel of medieval statuary, and the interior houses an incredible 600-year-old astronomical clock. Close to the cathedral, admire the medieval **Vicars' Close,** said to be the oldest planned street in Europe, and the beautiful walled and moated 13th-century **Bishop's Palace,** from whose springs the city took its name.

Carving on the Market Cross, Glastonbury

🚗 *Follow the A39 southwest, turning right at roundabout. Carry on past Glastonbury Abbey to parking lot on left.*

⑬ Glastonbury
Somerset; BA6 9EL

A magnet for "New Agers" and those seeking "alternative" lifestyles, medieval Glastonbury is awash with legend and religious symbolism. Close to its heart near the Market Cross, lie the majestic ruins of **Glastonbury Abbey** *(open daily)*, once one of the most powerful abbeys in the land, but razed during the Dissolution of the Monasteries. The abbey dates mostly to the 12th and 13th centuries, but a stone church was built here as early as AD 705. To the east, topped by the ruins of St. Michael's church, stands the cone of **Glastonbury Tor** – variously said to be a portal to the fairy kingdom, King Arthur's stronghold, or where the Holy Grail was kept. Climb up here for fabulous views over the Somerset Levels – reclaimed marshes whose atmosphere is best appreciated by bike. To do so, visit **Monkey Motion** *(3a Silver St, BA6 8LX; 07530 104 215)* who have a wide range of bikes for rent .

Above left West façade of Wells Cathedral, built between 1209–50 **Above center** The ruins of St. Michael's Church on top of Glastonbury Tor **Above right** The romantic ruins of Glastonbury Abbey, set in picturesque parkland

SHOPPING IN GLASTONBURY

For genuine Clark's shoes often at a discount, visit *Clark's Factory Shop (Clarks Village, Farm Rd, Street, BA16 0BB; 0844 499 3805; www.clarks.co.uk)* in Street, south of Glastonbury.

EAT AND DRINK

WELLS

The Good Earth *inexpensive*
This is the ideal place for a coffee or snack, serving wholesome, simple fare such as soups, quiches, pizzas, and baked potatoes and takeaway items.
4 Priory Rd, BA5 1SY; 01749 678 600; www.thegoodearthwells.com; open daytime only except Sat eve

GLASTONBURY

Hundred Monkeys *moderate*
In a town renowned for its hippy cafés, this has a refreshing, down-to-earth feel and serves various main meals as well as great cakes.
52 High St, BA6 9DY; 01458 833 386; open daytime only; closed Sun

---

DAY TRIP OPTIONS
Salisbury and Bath are both good bases for day trips; staying at Glastonbury enables visits to Wells and a trip into the Mendips, with the opportunity for some walking or outdoor activity.

Salisbury and the stones
Learn about the prehistory of the area in Salisbury museum ❶, then see it for real at Old Sarum ❷, Stonehenge ❸ and Avebury ❺. Active families will have most fun in the outdoor sites and might want to consider stopping off in Devizes ❹ for a jaunt on the Kennet and Avon Canal.

From Salisbury, follow the directions to visit Old Sarum, Stonehenge, Devizes and Avebury – return via A361 and A342 for speed and convenience.

Beautiful buildings
Explore the amazing architecture of Bath ❾, with its inspiring mix of elegant houses and buildings, its museums, and impressive range of shops and restaurants. The Roman Baths are an essential sight. See too, Bradford-on-Avon ❽ for some Anglo-Saxon and medieval treats and Lacock Abbey ❼ for its intriguing blend of medieval and 16th-century design.

From Bath, take the A36/B3108 to Bradford and the B3107/A350 to Lacock.

Glastonbury and the gorges
Staying at Glastonbury ⑬, enjoy the romantic abbey ruins and a scramble up Glastonbury Tor for the views. On to wonderful Wells ⑫ for a tour of the cathedral and adjacent sights, and then a drive through the Mendip Hills ⑪ via Cheddar, Ebbor, and Wookey Gorges, stopping off at will.

The A39 connects Wells to Glastonbury; follow the drive's instructions in reverse for the gorges. Return via A371 and A39.

Eat and Drink: inexpensive, under £25; moderate, £25–£50; expensive, over £50

The Villages of the Cotswolds

Cirencester to Broadway

Highlights

- **Picture-perfect scenery**
  Enter a world of thatched cottages, flower gardens, and streams, framed by the gentle Cotswold landscape

- **A miscellany of museums**
  Explore a range of nostalgic museums displaying everything from old musical instruments to cars and bikes

- **Cotswold "wool churches"**
  Admire the late-Gothic architecture of the area's magnificent churches, built from the wealth of the wool trade

- **Art and antiques**
  Discover the designs of the Arts and Crafts movement that flourished here a century ago, and browse the many antique shops that grace the villages

Sezincote House and Garden, built in the Moghul Indian style

The Villages of the Cotswolds

From the heart of Gloucestershire to the edge of Worcestershire, this drive takes in some of the most enchanting villages and hamlets of the Cotswold Hills – mellow, dreamy vistas dotted with sheep grazing amid drystone walls. A journey through the Cotwolds will reveal honey-hued cottages, thickly thatched pubs, and great mansions built by farmers and merchants trading in what was once the finest wool in Europe. Many local wool merchants showed off their wealth by erecting or improving rural churches and filling them with grand memorials – those at Cirencester, Northleach, and Chipping Campden are among the most exquisite. There's an abundance of quality food and accommodation available, and also an array of independent outlets, galleries, and workshops selling antiques and handicrafts.

Above Thatched cottage in the village of Chipping Campden, *see p80*

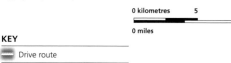

0 kilometres 5

0 miles 5

KEY

Drive route

ACTIVITIES

Browse among the alluring antiques shops for which the Cotswolds are famous

Take an aromatic tour around the perfume factory in Bourton-on-the-Water

Saddle up for a bike ride in the beautiful country around Chipping Campden

Take a hike on the 100-mile (160-km) Cotswold Way between Chipping Campden and Bath

Fill your plate and support the Great British Pud at Mickleton near Hidcote Manor Garden

Climb up the hilltop folly of lofty Broadway Tower

Drive off the first tee of Broadway Golf club

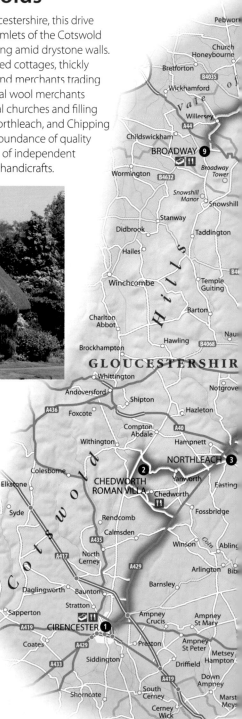

Above Hidcote Manor Garden, an Arts and Crafts masterpiece, *see p81*

Below Early morning view of St. James' Church, Chipping Campden, *see p80*

PLAN YOUR DRIVE

Start/finish: Cirencester to Broadway.

Number of days: 2–3 days.

Distance: Around 55 miles (90 km).

Road conditions: Mainly straight A- and minor roads, but often narrow – watch out for tractors and people on horseback around unsighted bends.

When to go: In summer, some Cotswold villages can be overrun at the weekends by tourists, day trippers and coach parties – it is best to try and visit during the week.

Opening times: Museums and attractions are generally open 10am–5pm, but close earlier (or are closed altogether) Nov–Easter. Shops are often open longer. Churches are usually open until dusk.

Market days: Cirencester: Charter Market, Market Place, Mon & Fri; Craft Market, Corn Hall, 2nd & 4th Sat of month; Stow-on-the-Wold: Farmers' Market, 2nd Thu of month; **Moreton-in-Marsh**: Tue.

Shopping: Look out for antiques and handicrafts throughout the area – including hand-blown glass and hand-thrown pottery, jewelry, and ceramics. Foodwise, expect fine local beers, meats – especially lamb – and cheeses such as the famous Stinking Bishop.

Major festivals: Cirencester: Beer Festival, late Apr; **Chipping Campden**: Music Festival, mid-May; Olympick Games, late May.

DAY TRIP OPTIONS

A few day trips can take in the very best of the Cotswolds region. Families with children will appreciate the combination of the **Roman museum** at Cirencester, Chedworth **Roman villa,** and the **instruments**, **toy collections**, and **model railway displays** of Northleach and Bourton-on-the-Water. Arts and Crafts devotees can take in the **antiques shops**, **galleries**, **museums,** and **workshops** at Stow-on-the-Wold, Chipping Campden, and Broadway. For full details, *see p81*.

Parking
There are plenty of parking lots close to the center of town and Market Square.

Tourist information
Corinium Museum, Park St, GL7 2BX; 01285 654 180; www.cotswold.gov.uk

WHERE TO STAY

CIRENCESTER

The Fleece Hotel *moderate*
This rambling old inn at the heart of town is an atmospheric place to stay. The rooms are on the small side, but functional and pleasant. There are two restaurants, and a patio for drinks.
Market Place, GL7 2NZ; 01285 658 507; www.fleecehotel.co.uk

BOURTON-ON-THE-WATER

Chester House Hotel *moderate*
This small, traditional-looking hotel has a relaxed atmosphere with modern décor and genial staff. Rooms are all fresh and airy, some with four-poster beds. Family rooms are also available.
Victoria St, GL54 2BU; 01451 820 286; www.chesterhousehotel.com

STOW-ON-THE-WOLD

The Limes *inexpensive*
Simple Victorian B&B run by a friendly young couple on the northern outskirts of Stow, on the A424 (a 5-minute walk from the center). There are five guest rooms and a lovely garden with a fish pond and aviary.
Evesham Rd, GL54 1EJ; 01451 830 034

Stow Lodge Hotel *moderate*
Country-style accommodation in the heart of Stow, with a perfectly groomed garden overlooking the main square, good food, and a comfortable living room with a log fire.
The Square, GL54 1AB; 01451 830 485; www.stowlodgehotel.co.uk

MORETON-IN-MARSH

Redesdale Arms *inexpensive*
This old coaching inn has cozy log fires and well-equipped rooms with clean, modern bathrooms. Breakfasts are excellent and tasty meals are served in the bar or restaurant.
High St, GL56 OAW; 01608 650 308; www.redesdalearms.com

Manor House Hotel *expensive*
Old but charming and well-maintained, this hotel on the main street has period furniture and modern fixtures. Staff are courteous and attentive, and Mulberry's Restaurant rustles up first-class meals.
High St, GL56 OLJ; 01608 650 501; www.cotswold-inns-hotels.co.uk

Near right St. John the Baptist Church in the heart of Cirencester **Far right** Chedworth Roman Villa: dining room mosaics

Above The village of Northleach, built of traditional Cotswold stone

① Cirencester
Gloucestershire; GL7 2BX

This compact, relaxed market town's importance in Roman Britain – it was the second largest town – is revealed in the superb **Corinium Museum** *(open daily; Sun closed am)*. The town kept its wealth in the medieval era, as can be seen in the huge church of **St. John the Baptist** – the south porch with fan vaulting dates to 1490. The church dominates **Market Square**, home to one of the biggest markets in the Cotswolds. Visit **New Brewery Arts** *(open daily)* for galleries, shops, events, and workshops.

🚗 *Follow the A429 (Stow Road) north toward Stow-in-the-Wold for about 8 km (5 miles). Turn left at the signpost for Chedworth Roman Villa, then continue to follow the signs to the villa and the on-site parking lot .*

② Chedworth Roman Villa
Yanworth, Gloucestershire; GL54 3LJ

Nestled amid woods, this absorbing site, discovered in 1864, displays part of the bath houses and dining areas of a substantial Romano-British villa *(closed Mon)* inhabited from the 2nd to 4th centuries AD. Vivid mosaics, underfloor heating systems, plunge pools, and the latrine can be seen while audioguides fill in the history. The grounds make a nice picnic area.

🚗 *Follow signs for Yanworth, then for Northleach. Park in the center of town.*

Stone relief, Corinium Museum

③ Northleach
Gloucestershire; GL54 3ET

This unassuming village has one of the finest Cotswold "wool churches". The oldest parts of **St. Peter and St. Paul** date from around 1300, and on the floor, brasses show merchants, with sheep, woolpacks and many children. Look out for the carved corbels (stone brackets) in the porch, depicting such images as angels and a cat playing a fiddle. On the High St, **Keith Harding's World of Mechanical Music** *(open daily)* is well worth a visit, displaying an array of period pieces, ably explained and demonstrated on a guided tour.

🚗 *Take the A429 following signs for Stow-on-the-Wold and Bourton-on-the-Water. Park off Rissington Road.*

④ Bourton-on-the-Water

Gloucestershire; GL54 2AN

This classic, relaxing Cotswold village nestles around an extended village green and the gentle River Windrush, and has something for everyone to enjoy. The **Cotswold Motoring Museum and Toy Collection** *(open daily)* is a nostalgic wallow in the style and technology of yesteryear; the **Model Railway Exhibition**, has an elaborate layout with more than 40 trains *(Jun–Aug: open daily; Sep–Dec & Feb–May: open Sat & Sun; Jan: limited opening)*; the **Model Village** *(open daily)*, is a detailed 1: 9 replica of Bourton; and the **Cotswold Perfumery** *(open daily; 01451 820 698; www.cotswold-perfumery.co.uk)* is a fascinating factory-museum-shop that makes its scents by hand; tours are available.

🚗 *Rejoin A429, following signs for Stow-on-the-Wold. Park in the town square or on A429 north of the center.*

Cotswold Antiques

The Cotswolds are one of the most rewarding areas for shopping for antiques, though don't expect to find many bargains. The main centers are Stow-on-the-Wold, Moreton-in-Marsh, Chipping Campden, and Broadway, but it's always worth looking in smaller places, and look out for antiques fairs – local tourist offices should have a list.

⑤ Stow-on-the-Wold

Gloucestershire; GL54 1BN

Eight roads – one of them the Roman Fosse Way – meet at this Cotswold market town, crammed with antiques shops, delicatessens, and smart hotels. Stop here for some window-shopping and a bite to eat, with pubs and cafés surrounding the huge main square – once a busy market at the heart of the Cotswold wool trade. Look out for the stocks here, and the **King's Arms**, where Charles I spent a night in 1645 during the Civil War; the following year, nearby **St. Edward's Church** was used as a prison for defeated Royalist troops after the Battle of Stow.

🚗 *Continue north along the A429 for Moreton-in-Marsh; park on the High St.*

⑥ Moreton-in-Marsh

Gloucestershire; GL56 0AF

This lively Cotswold center is known for its Tuesday Market – the county's largest outdoor market. A short way on the A44 towards Evesham there's a collection of interesting places to visit. **Sezincote** is an onion-domed stately home built in the Mughal Indian style in 1810 *(House: May–Sep: open Thu & Fri pm, no children; Garden: Jan–Nov: open Thu & Fri pm)*. Opposite is the **Batsford Arboretum**, a fabulous collection of exotic trees and shrubs *(Feb–Nov: open daily; Dec–Jan: closed Wed)*. And just next door, families will enjoy watching the gripping live demonstrations at the excellent **Cotswold Falconry Centre** *(mid-Feb–mid-Nov: open daily)*.

🚗 *Take A429 north out of town, left toward Batsford. Follow the signs to Draycott, passing through the village, then pass through Broad Campden. In Chipping Campden, park on High St.*

Above left Picturesque bridge at the center of Bourton-on-the-Water **Above right** Typical Cotswold tea room in Moreton-in-Marsh

SHOPPING FOR LOCAL CHEESE

Cotswold cheeses are rightly renowned. In **Stow-on-the-Wold** pack a picnic from the cheeses, breads, pâtés, and pies at **Maby's** *(Digbeth St, GL54 1BN; 01451 870 071; www.mabys.co.uk)*. For more than 50 cheeses (including Stinking Bishop) and other local specialities in **Moreton-in-Marsh**, try the **Cotswold Cheese Company** *(High St, GL56 0AH; 01608 652 862; www.cotswoldcheesecompany.co.uk)*.

EAT AND DRINK

CIRENCESTER

Harry Hare's *moderate*
Friendly, charming brasserie serving snacks or full meals such as belly of pork, Barbary duck, and Gorgonzola risotto. *3 Gosditch St, GL7 2AG; 01285 652 375; www.harryhares.co.uk*

CHEDWORTH ROMAN VILLA

Seven Tuns *moderate*
This traditional family pub serves snacks and upmarket meals next to a warming fire or in the patio-garden. *Queen St, Chedworth, GL54 4AE; 01285 720 242*

STOW-ON-THE-WOLD

Digbeths *inexpensive*
Inviting café with stone floors and a delectable array of cakes and snacks. *Digbeth St, GL54 1BN; 01451 831 609*

The Old Butcher's *moderate*
This highly rated brasserie serves quality modern British fare such as local grouse, shin of veal, and lemon posset. *7 Park St, GL54 1AQ; 01451 831 700; www.theoldbutchers.com*

MORETON-IN-MARSH

Tilly's *inexpensive*
Breakfasts and sweet and savoury snacks are served in this friendly tea room with a courtyard for fair weather. *18–19 High St, GL56 0AF; 01386 701 043; open in daytime only*

Left View of the countryside around Stow-on-the-Wold

Above Campden House with St. James' Church, Chipping Campden **Below** Flower baskets outside the Eight Bells, Chipping

VISITING CHIPPING CAMPDEN

Tourist Information
The Old Police Station, High St, GL55 6HB; 01386 841 206; www. visitchippingcampden.com

Cotswold Country Cycles
Longlands Farm Cottage, GL55 6LJ; 01386 438 706; www. cotswoldcountrycycles.com

WHERE TO STAY

CHIPPING CAMPDEN

Eight Bells *moderate*
Originally built in the 14th century for the stonemasons at work on St. James Church, this inn has chic and modern rooms and an excellent restaurant.
Church St, GL55 6JG; 01386 840 371; www.eightbellsinn.co.uk

BROADWAY

The Broadway Hotel *expensive*
Timber beams and creaking floors add character to this traditional hotel. Enjoy the friendly staff and big breakfasts.
The Green, WR12 7AA; 01386 852 401; www.cotswold-inns-hotels.co.uk

The Lygon Arms *expensive*
Stay here to enjoy luxury and old-world charm. Try the first-class leisure facilities and then dine in the Great Hall.
High St, WR12 7DU; 01386 852 255; www.barcelo-hotels.co.uk

❼ Chipping Campden
Gloucestershire; GL55 6JE

This uncommercialized Cotswold village was one of the centers for the Arts and Crafts movement that flourished in the Cotswolds at the turn of the 20th century. It still has a vibrant craft movement as well as the Court Barn Museum, devoted to art and design. The village is also the start of the Cotswold Way, a 100-mile (160-km) walking trail to Bath, and ideal for cyclists, who can explore the country on rented bikes.

A three-hour walking tour

Start your walk from the High Street at the parking lot next to the old **Market Hall** ①, dating from 1627. Walk through the archway to the left of the Noel Arms Hotel, and on to George Lane, turning left into Badgers Field. Pass through a kissing gate (designed to contain livestock) into a field. The path cuts across the field and over a stream with views of 17th-century **Campden House** ②, burnt down in the Civil War.

The path ends at Station Rd, turn left for a good look at **St. James' Church** ③. Dating from the 16th century, it is one of the finest Cotswold "wool churches." Note the sumptuous memorials and Jacobean pulpit and lectern. Nearby is the **Court Barn Museum** ④ *(closed Mon)*, dedicated to local art, design, and crafts. Walk down Church St, past a pretty row of **Almshouses** ⑤ on the right, built in 1612. Turn left into the High St, and back to the Market Hall.

Continue along the High St, taking a detour down Sheep St on the left, to visit the **Old Silk Mill** ⑥, once home to CR Ashbee's Guild of Handicrafts and still dedicated to craft products. Browse the displays and maybe even buy a little souvenir.

Return to the High St and turn right at the Catholic **St. Catherine's Church** ⑦, a Gothic revival building with early

20th century stained glass windows, designed in the Arts and Crafts style by local artist Paul Woodroffe. Follow signs for the Cotswold Way down West End Terrace and Hoo Lane, which soon becomes a footpath to Kingcombe Lane. Turn left here, then after about 100 paces, right onto another path, also marked Cotswold Way. This leads to The Common, an area of parkland with a path to **Dover's Hill** ⑧, where there are benches for just soaking up the views. The hill is the venue of the "Olympick Games" – originating in the 17th century, and involving sports such as wrestling and shin-kicking. Brass bands, Morris dancers, and a torchlight procession add to the fun, on the Friday after Spring Bank Holiday.

From Dover's Hill, turn left onto the road, cross Kingcombe Lane and head down Dyers Lane. Follow Dyers Lane, then bear left onto Park Road, which leads back to Chipping Campden's High Street.

Dover's Hill lies on the way marked Cotswold Way and is a great place for a walk, so pick up route maps from the tourist office. Cyclists can rent bikes from **Cotswold Country Cycles** *(see left)*.
🚗 *Take the B4035 toward Shipston-on-Stour and turn left to Ebrington. After the level crossing, turn left and follow signs for Hidcote Manor Gardens.*

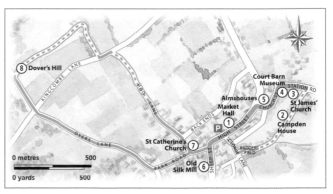

Above High Street shops in the well-preserved village of Broadway

Arts and Crafts

Britain's Arts and Crafts movement flourished in the years around 1900, especially in the Cotswolds. Inspired by the writing of John Ruskin and reacting against industrialization, its followers relied on traditional skills. Its most famous exponents included artist and designer William Morris, furniture maker Gordon Russell and CR Ashbee, who designed jewellery and printed books. Examples of their works can be viewed in museums in Broadway and Chipping Campden.

⑧ Hidcote Manor Garden

Gloucestershire; GL55 6LR
There is no shortage of gardens in the Cotswolds, but Hidcote (*mid-Mar–Jun, Sep & Oct: open Sat–Wed; Jul–Aug: open Fri–Wed*) is one of the finest in the country. It was created in 1907 by an American, Major Lawrence Johnston, who designed a series of "outdoor rooms," each one following a specific style, separated by tall hedges and walls, and often with exquisite topiary. Highlights include the White Garden, the Bathing Pool and the informal Old Garden. Think about having lunch –

and a traditional pudding –at **Three Ways House** in Mickleton.

🚗 *Turn left out of Hidcote, then next right to Mickleton. Turn right, then left at the mini-roundabout onto B4632. Park off Broadway High St and Church St.*

⑨ Broadway

Worcestershire; WR12 7DT
The elegant main street of this well-preserved Cotswold village is lined with immaculate stone houses, smart shops, and a handful of cozy pubs and hotels. The **Gordon Russell Museum** (*closed Mon*) displays examples of the graceful furniture designed by the famous local artisan, along with metalwork and glassware.

Take the High St east to the A44, turn right and first right to **Broadway Tower** (*Apr–Oct: open daily; Nov–Mar: open Sat & Sun*). This castle-like folly was built in 1799 and offers stunning panoramas, displays of local history, and a deer park – it's a good area for walking, too.

Go south on Church St to **Snowshill Manor** (*mid-Mar–Oct: Wed–Sun pm*), built of Cotswold honey-yellow stone with an Arts and Crafts garden. The house is full of curiosities from around the world, from clocks to cow bells, and from toys and bicycles to musical instruments and Samurai armour. Close by is the very scenic **Broadway Golf Club** (*Willersey Hill, WR12 7LG; 01386 853 683; www.broadwaygolfclub.co.uk*).

Above Looking north towards Birmingham from Broadway Tower

EAT AND DRINK

AROUND CHIPPING CAMPDEN

Ebrington Arms *moderate*
This Cotswold stone inn serves great homemade and locally sourced food. *Ebrington, GL55 6NH (2 miles/3 km from Chipping Camden on the B4035); 01386 593 223; www.theebringtonarms.co.uk*

AROUND HIDCOTE MANOR

Three Ways House *moderate*
Award-winning restaurant (with rooms) serving fabulous traditional and modern British food. It also houses the Pudding Club, dedicated to saving and raising the profile of the Great British Pudding. *Mickleton, GL55 6SB (turn left out of Hidcote and right to Mickleton); 01386 438 429; www.puddingclub.com*

BROADWAY

Tisanes *inexpensive*
This tea room provides cream teas as well as breakfasts, and light lunches. *21 The Green, WR12 7AA; 01386 853 296; www.tisanes-tearooms.co.uk*

Russell's *moderate–expensive*
Modern restaurant (with rooms) with excellent food – try fried sweetbreads, dover sole, and sticky toffee pudding. *20 High St, WR12 7DT; 01386 853 555; www.russellsofbroadway.co.uk*

Left The seemingly haphazard planting in the Old Garden at Hidcote Manor Garden

---

DAY TRIP OPTIONS

Cirencester and Stow-on-the-Wold are good bases for exploring the area.

Romans and Toys
Families with children will love the Roman Museum at Cirencester ❶, Chedworth Roman Villa ❷, the exhibition of mechanical music at

Northleach ❸, and the engaging toy displays at Bourton-on-the-Water ❹.

Cirencester, Northleach, and Bourton-on-the-Water are all linked by the A429.

Antiques and design
In the morning, browse the antique shops at Stow-on-the-Wold ❺. Next,

tour a mansion with a difference – Sezincote in Moreton-in-Marsh ❻. In the afternoon, visit Chipping Campden ❼ and Broadway ❾ to explore local arts, crafts, and design.

Stow-on-the-Wold is extremely well-connected – the A424 goes to Broadway and the B4081 to Chipping Campden.

Through the Chilterns

Chalfont St Giles to Henley-on-Thames

Highlights

- **Paradise found**
  Peek inside the sweet 15th-century cottage where John Milton wrote his masterwork, *Paradise Lost*

- **History at large**
  Roam among sheep-dotted open parkland and woods among the many historic buildings at the Chilterns Open Air Museum

- **Phizz-whizzing inspiration**
  Fire up the imagination of adults and children alike at the fascinating Roald Dahl Museum and Story Center

- **Perfect English villages**
  Enjoy the sturdy flint churches, half-timbered houses and welcoming pubs of these picturesque gems, nestling among gentle hills and ancient woods

Springtime in the gently rolling countryside of the Chiltern Hills

Through the Chilterns

This drive begins just 25 miles (40 km) away – but a whole world – from the turmoil of central London, in the pretty village of Chalfont St Giles, and takes a route through the Chiltern Hills, a designated Area of Outstanding Natural Beauty. Through necessity, some stretches run along main roads, but there are also lovely country lanes with no significant traffic. The proposed stops along the way are varied – grand, quaint, beautiful – while the destination town of Henley offers plenty to absorb the visitor for a day.

Above Cobstone windmill, Turville, see p86

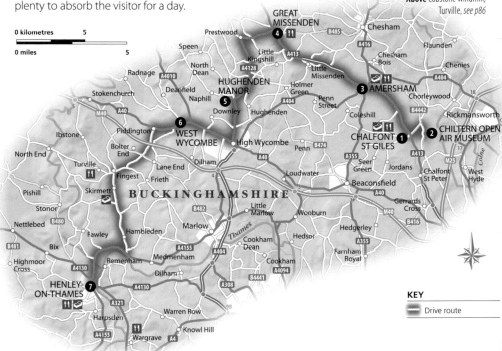

KEY

Drive route

PLAN YOUR DRIVE

Start/finish: Chalfont St Giles to Henley-on-Thames.

Number of days: 2 days.

Distances: 56 km (35 miles).

Road conditions: Very good; some lanes can be narrow; good signage with brown tourist signs.

When to go: From late May through to autumn.

Main market days: Amersham: Amersham Country Market, Fri am; Henley-on-Thames: Market Day, Thu; Farmers' Market, last Thu of month, am.

Major Festivals: Amersham: Charter Fair (and market), Sep 19–20; Henley-on-Thames: Henley Royal Regatta, beginning of Jul; Henley Festival of Music and Arts, Jul.

Above The Red Lion Hotel, Henley-on-Thames, dating back to the 14th century, see p87

1 Chalfont St Giles
Bucks; HP8 4JH

With village green, duck pond, old inns, and beamed cottages, this has been hailed as "Britain's most perfect village". Follow a sign just outside the village to **Milton's Cottage** *(open Mar–Oct, closed Mon; www.miltonscottage.org),* the 16th-century home of poet John Milton. After fleeing London in 1665 to escape the plague, he wrote his masterwork, *Paradise Lost,* here. The cottage contains, among other treasures, first editions of *Areopagitica,* Milton's essay on free speech, and *Eikonoklastes,* his riposte to Charles II's defence of the Divine Right of Kings.

Drive on towards Seer Green and turn left at the sign for Quaker Meeting House. Enter the village of Jordan's but bypass the right turn to the center marked "Jordan's village". On the left is a sign for **Jordan's Quaker Meeting House**, one of England's first and dating back to 1688. William Penn, the founder of Pennysylvania, who died in 1718, is buried in the graveyard.

Back in Chalfont St Giles, gourmets can buy top-quality oils, vinegars, spirits, and liqueurs from **Vom Fass** *(closed Sun),* on the High Street.

🚗 *Head up High St and Pheasant Hill; go over double roundabout onto Vache Lane, then right down narrow Gorelands Lane. Follow signs to museum.*

2 Chiltern Open Air Museum
Newland Park, Gorelands Lane, Chalfont St Giles, Bucks; HP8 4AB

In an ambitious initiative, 30 vernacular buildings of past generations, typical of this region, have been rescued and rebuilt here in a natural setting *(open Apr–Oct; 01494 871 117; www.coam.org.uk).* Explore a 19th-century farm with animals; wander through a village with a green, cottages, forge and chapel; find out what a 16th-century wood-framed hall house is really like inside, and peer into the tiny Henton Mission Room, a "tin tabernacle" made after the invention of corrugated, galvanized iron in 1882. And, of course, pet the resident shire horse. Other buildings include a 1940s prefabricated bungalow and cast-iron public convenience from1906.

🚗 *Return to A413, turn right at roundabout and drive on to Amersham. Follow signs for old town. Park on street.*

3 Amersham
Bucks; HP6 5AH

There's no stand-out attraction in Old Amersham *(www.amersham.org.uk),* the heart of the town, it's just very pretty. See its almshouses, coaching inns, half-timbered cottages, and **Market Hall**, topped off with a clocktower and holding the original town jail, and maybe enjoy a nice lunch. Dominating Broadway (the main street) is the flint **Church of St. Mary**, built in the12th century with 14th- and 15th-century additions. The Memorial Gardens and tiny River Misbourne are just nearby.

🚗 *Continue up High St to A413. Go right, then left at roundabouts, following signs to Great Missenden. Use main parking lot on right in Link Rd.*

4 Great Missenden
Bucks; HP16 0AL

Another appealing small town, at the head of the Misbourne Valley, its main street is lined with lovely half-timbered and Georgian buildings. For 36 years, the children's author Roald Dahl (1916–90) lived and worked in Gt Missenden and the "flushbunkingly gloriumptious" **Roald Dahl Museum and Story Centre** is a major attraction *(closed Mon; www.roalddahlmuseum.org).* Here, visitors learn about Dahl, man and boy, see where he wrote, and admire artwork, photographs, correspondence, and manuscripts in progress. With plenty to fire everyone's imagination, a truly whizzpopping time is guaranteed.

🚗 *Follow A4128 toward Prestwood. Continue on this road toward High Wycombe, then take a right, following signs to Hughenden Manor (last one is after a blind bend and easy to miss).*

Above Fountain in the Memorial Gardens, beside the Church of St. Mary, Amersham

Above Milton's Cottage, the poet's 16th-century home, Chalfont St Giles

VISITING CHALFONT ST GILES

Parking
From A413, head down Pheasant Hill into Deanway. Free parking at Milton's Cottage and at Quaker Meeting House.

WHERE TO STAY

CHALFONT ST GILES

The White Hart Inn *moderate*
This inn has 11 comfortable rooms with ensuite bathrooms in a purpose-built block. It has a good restaurant, too.
Three Households, HP8 4LP; 01494 872 441; www.whitehartstgiles.co.uk

AMERSHAM
The Crown *moderate*
This Elizabethan coaching inn has a cool yet traditional style and featured in the film *Four Weddings and a Funeral.*
16 High Street, HP7 0DH; 01494 721 541; www.dhillonhotels.co.uk

EAT AND DRINK

CHALFONT ST GILES

The Crown *moderate*
Smart popular pub (booking advised) with pub food in the bar and full menu in the dining room – it serves honest, modern British cooking with flair.
High Street, HP8 4QQ; 01494 875 156; www.the-crown-csg.co.uk

AMERSHAM

Gilbey's *moderate*
Well-regarded bar and restaurant with garden, serving modern European food such as rack of English lamb, and lemon tart with gin-and-tonic ice cream.
1 Market Square, HP7 0DF; 01494 727 242; www.gilbeygroup.com

GREAT MISSENDEN

Nags Head *moderate–expensive*
A 15th-century pub (with rooms) aiming high and sourcing tip-top organic produce. Try the steak and kidney in ale; not much for vegetarians.
London Rd, HP16 0DG; 01494 862 200; www.nagsheadbucks.com

Eat and Drink: inexpensive, under £25; moderate, £25–£50; expensive, over £50

Above The gardens and rear of Hughenden Manor, once Disraeli's country home

VISITING HENLEY-ON-THAMES

Parking
On the way in, follow signs to short term parking (maximum three hours) on Market Street or Gray's Road.

Tourist Information
King's Arms Barn, Kings Road, RG9 2DG; 01491 578 034

Thames Cruise
To rent self-drive (or even chauffeured) motor launches for relaxing trips along the river; or take a scheduled cruise, try **Hobbs of Henley** on Station Rd *(01491 572 035; www.hobbs-of-henley.com)*.

WHERE TO STAY

AROUND WEST WYCOMBE

Frog Inn *inexpensive–moderate*
Pretty family-run inn with attractive ensuite rooms and rural views. The inn is situated directly south of Fingest, close to Turville. Also serves good food.
Skirmett, RG9 6TG (8 km/5 miles west of West Wycombe); 01491 638 996; www.thefrogatskirmett.co.uk

HENLEY-ON-THAMES

Milsoms Hotel *moderate*
In a listed, red brick former bakery above the Loch Fyne Bar and Grill *(see right)*. Five smallish, tasteful en suite rooms. Kippers for breakfast!
20 Market Place, RG9 2AH; 01491 845 789; www.milsomshotel.co.uk

Hotel du Vin *moderate-expensive*
This boutique hotel, part of a small chain, has 43 luxurious rooms offering style, attention to detail and bistro cooking.
New Street, RG92BP; 01491 848 400; www.hotelduvin.com

Red Lion Hotel *expensive*
This red brick 16th-century inn by the bridge has 35 substantial, well-furnished rooms, some with river views.
Hart Street, RG9 2AR; 01491 572 161; www.redlionhenley.co.uk

⑤ Hughenden Manor
High Wycombe, Bucks; HP14 4LA
Time has not stood still at Hughenden Manor, despite access up a steep, unpaved, and rutted track *(house and garden open Mar–Sep: Wed–Sun pm; park open daily all year; 01494 755 565; www.nationaltrust.org.uk)*. The country home of Queen Victoria's trusted Prime Minister Benjamin Disraeli (1804–81) has seen some alterations, but a few rooms are as they would have been in "Dizzy's" day. The gardens recreate an original design by his wife, Mary Anne. Mementoes, books, and paintings bring the interior alive, but low lighting, while kind to furnishings, can be less kind to eyes. There are some beautiful walks in the surrounding parkland with glorious views of the countryside.

🚗 *Rejoin the A4128 toward High Wycombe. In town, follow signs to A40 west. Turn left at Pedestal roundabout to West Wycombe. After village, turn right, past caves entrance, for free parking.*

Below left The "Royal River" running through the heart of Henley-on-Thames **Below right** The half-timbered Old Granary, originally a warehouse

⑥ West Wycombe
Bucks; HP14 3AH
West Wycombe's main attractions are found at **West Wycombe Park** *(Apr–Aug: open Sun–Thu; house open Jun–Aug)*. The Italianate house is set in landscaped gardens dotted with follies, statues, and ornamental lakes. The estate is also home to the **Hellfire Caves** *(open daily; www.hellfirecaves.co.uk)*, excavated in the 1740s on the orders of Sir Francis Dashwood and running nearly over half a mile (1 km) underground under West Wycombe Hill. See the Gothic "church" entrance and descend dank passages through the Banqueting Hall, past chambers with portrayals of members of Dashwood's infamous Hellfire Club (1749–60). The final destination is the "Inner Temple," across the "River Styx." Here were held the bacchanals of the club, whose members included such luminaries as the then Prince of Wales, the Marquis of Granby, and artist William Hogarth. Despite tales of devil worship, the main activities were probably drinking and pornography. Not suitable for anyone with claustrophobia, the caves are reputed to be haunted by the spectre of a steward of the Hell Fire Club who kept a tally of drinks consumed. On the hilltop above the caves stand the imposing **Dashwood Mausoleum** and the distinctive **Church of St. Lawrence**, its tower topped by a large golden sphere that is said to served in the past as a venue for covert meetings.

🚗 *Take A40 through Piddington and turn left, toward Bolter End. Cross B482 to Fingest. It is possible to fork right here for the pretty village and pub at Turville. Otherwise turn right, then right again onto A4155 to Henley-on-Thames.*

⑦ Henley-on-Thames

Oxfordshire RG9 2EB

In its leafy setting on the Thames, this Georgian market town, famous for its July Royal Regatta, offers a mix of the historical and fashionable. A graceful 18th-century, five-arched bridge spans the river – a dynamic and defining presence; beautiful, recreational and a haven for wildlife.

A one-hour walking tour

From the parking lot, walk down Market Street and cross Bell Street to Hart Street, dominated by the red brick **Victorian Town Hall** ①, built in 1901. Walk down Hart Street to the **Church of St. Mary** ② with its 16th-century stone and flint tower. The stucco almshouses to the west date from 1830 and the red brick ones on the east were originally built in the 1660s and rebuilt in 1884. Beside them is the Grade I listed 16th-century Chantry House, overlooking the churchyard (with Dusty Springfield's grave) and the river. At the bottom of Hart Street look across the bridge (built in 1786) to the headquarters of the Henley Royal Regatta to the left and the Leander Club – the world's oldest rowing club – to the right. Turn right for a saunter down Thames Side, passing the half-timbered **Old Granary** ③, located on the corner of Friday Street. Next, go past the **Hobbs of Henley Boatyard** ④, a good place to start a motor launch trip or a cruise along the river. Head down Meadow Rd to the **River and Rowing Museum** ⑤ (open daily; www.rrm.co.uk) with its fun Wind in the Willows Gallery. Children will be enchanted by the models of Mr Toad, Ratty, and Mole, faithful to the illustrations of Ernest Shepard. Retrace the route to turn left onto Friday Street and right onto Duke Street, noticing **Tudor House** ⑥, a venerable-looking antiques' shop – actually a pastiche built in 1934.

Cross Hart Street and go down Bell Street, where, on the left, is the **Bull Inn** ⑦, one of the oldest inns in Henley, with walls 3 ft (up to a metre) thick. It is rumored to be haunted by the ghost of a young woman. Turn right onto New Street to pass the **Kenton Theatre** ⑧ (www.kenton theatre.co.uk), opened in 1805, and the former Brakspear's Brewery, opened in 1779 and now the Hotel du Vin. Turn right again onto Riverside and once more, onto Hart Street to return to the parking lot.

To extend the walk, follow the Thames Path from Thames Side south for 2 miles (3 km), crossing the river at Marsh Lock to Shipton. Or cross the bridge and walk 2 miles (3 km) north to Hambleden Lock. For more walks and information, visit www.thames-path.org.uk.

Henley On Thames sign of bridge

Above The 16th-century Church Loft with original clock, West Wycombe

EAT AND DRINK

AROUND WEST WYCOMBE

Bull and Butcher *moderate*
This 16th-century real-ale pub, in Turville near Fingest on the route to Henley-on-Thames, serves dishes such as rib-eye steak, and hearty puddings.
Turville, RG9 6QU (9 km/5 miles from West Wycombe); 01491 638 283; www.thebullandbutcher.co.uk

HENLEY-ON-THAMES

Loch Fyne Bar and Grill *moderate*
This popular restaurant and oyster bar, part of a small chain, serves fresh and smoked fish, shellfish, and meat options.
20 Market Place, RG9 2AP; 01491 845 780; www.lochfyne.com

Green Olive Meze Bar & Restaurant *inexpensive–moderate*
There is something for everyone – including veggies – here, on the pick-and-mix menu of light bites and mains.
28 Market Place, RG9 2AH; 01491 412 220; www.green-olive.co.uk

AROUND HENLEY-ON-THAMES

St George & Dragon *moderate*
Cross the river and go south on A321 for 5 km (3 miles) to this riverside pub offering plain or more ambitious fare.
High St, Wargrave, RG10 8HY; 01189 404 474; www.stgeorgeanddragon.co.uk

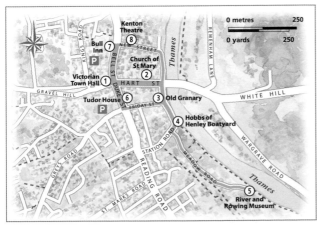

Eat and Drink: inexpensive, under £25; moderate, £25–£50; expensive, over £50

Exploring the South Downs

Beachy Head to Chichester

Highlights

- **Historic country life**
  Experience traditional farm life at a wide range of open-air museums

- **Enjoying the ups of the Downs**
  Walk along the South Downs Way – a superb walking path with great views

- **Antiques paradise**
  Hunt for antiques in the shops and galleries of Petworth, Arundel town, and Brighton's Lanes

- **A treasury of modern art**
  Country retreats, gardens, cathedrals, sculpture parks, and galleries – see a wealth of novel modern art venues

- **Wildlife wonderland**
  Spot flowers, birds, and butterflies in Cuckmere Valley, and waterbirds in the Arundel Wildfowl and Wetlands Centre

Market hall and other historic buildings, Weald and Downland Museum

Exploring the South Downs

The great grassy humped back of the chalk Downs, kept trim by sheep and topped with the remnants of Iron-Age forts, holds plenty of rare treats for the visitor and is a beautiful area to explore at leisure. Along its ridge runs the glorious 100-mile (160-km) South Downs Way, and around its base lie scattered flint-stone farms, pretty thatched cottages, and friendly pubs. Although the main roads through the area can get busy, there is a surprisingly remote country feel to the back roads, and the life of bygone days conjured in its open-air museums doesn't seem far away.

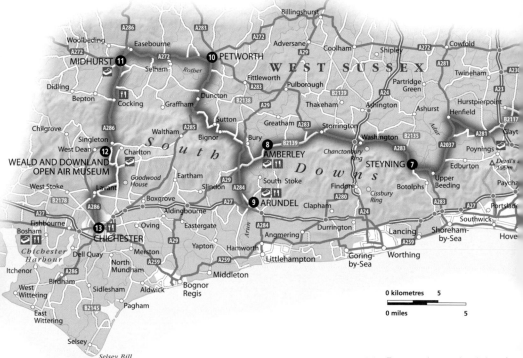

Below The open road running along the base of the South Downs near Beachy Head, *see p92*

ACTIVITIES

Go on a nature ramble in the Cuckmere Valley near Alfriston

Cool off in the sea at Brighton or the Witterings

Breach the defences of Iron-Age hill forts at Steyning

Take a boat on the River Arun or Chichester Harbour

Go birdwatching in the wetlands of Arundel

Watch a dashing game of polo in Midhurst

Enjoy a day at the races at Glorious Goodwood

Above Sheep grazing on the upper slopes of the South Downs, near Steyning, *see p94*

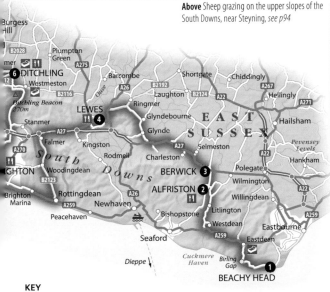

KEY

🚌 Drive route

Below Beachy Head Lighthouse at the foot of the spectacular white cliffs, *see p92*

PLAN YOUR DRIVE

Start/finish: Beachy Head to Chichester.

Number of days: 3–4, allowing for half a day in Brighton.

Distance: Around 100 miles (160 km).

Road conditions: The roads are mostly in good repair. Prepare for the steep hills of the Downs, and be ready to squeeze by other cars on the narrow roads.

When to go: The drive can be enjoyed at any time: spring brings perky lambs; in summer the larks are rising, the sea tempting, and the roads at their busiest; autumn delivers golden harvest days and winter bracing temperatures, when pub fires burn bright.

Opening times: Museums and attractions are generally open 10am–5pm, but close earlier (or are closed altogether) Nov–Easter. Shops are often open longer. Churches are usually open until dusk.

Market days: Brighton: Big Sunday Market, Railway Station car park, Sun; Arundel: Farmers' Market, 3rd Sat of the month; Chichester: 1st and 3rd Fri of the month.

Shopping: Arts and crafts (Lewes), antiques (Brighton, Arundel, and Petworth), pottery (Amberley) and silver and leatherware (Ditchling).

Major festivals: Charleston: Literary Festival, May; **Lewes**: Bonfire Night, 5 Nov; **Brighton**: Brighton Festival, a major cultural event, May; **Arundel**: Music Festival, Aug.

DAY TRIP OPTIONS

Brighton has plenty to enjoy: from **shopping, restaurants** and **museums** to its **beach** and famous **pier**. Then head to the countryside – visiting Ditchling for the **Beacon's views** and a **local museum**. For those interested in art history, visit Lewes, Charleston, and Berwick for **arts and crafts**, the work of the **Bloomsbury set**, and **tea in the garden**. Explore Arundel with its **antiques shops** and **castle, river,** and **wetlands centre**. Head to Chichester for the **cathedral** and **a Roman palace, harbor fun,** or a **trip to the beach**. For full details, *see p97*.

Above The chalk cliffs at Birling Gap, near Beachy Head

VISITING BRIGHTON

Parking
Park in one of the North Laine parking lots, on Church Street or North Road, or in Trafalgar Street, near the train station.

Tourist Information
Royal Pavilion, BN1 1EE; 0906 711 2255; www.visitbrighton.com

WHERE TO STAY

BEACHY HEAD

Birling Gap Hotel *inexpensive*
The splendid clifftop location is a key feature of this Victorian colonial villa.
Seven Sisters Cliffs, East Dean, BN2 0AB; 01323 423 197; www.birlinggaphotel.co.uk

BRIGHTON

Brighton Wave *moderate*
In the heart of trendy Brighton, this small and friendly boutique hotel by the sea epitomizes the style of the town.
10 Madeira Place, BN2 1TN; 01273 676 794; www.brightonwave.com; minimum two-night stay at weekends

AROUND BRIGHTON

Manor Farm *inexpensive*
On the South Downs Way this flint farmhouse has three simple rooms.
Poynings Rd, BN45 7AG (13 km/ 8 miles left off the A281 from the A23); 01273 857 371; www.poyningsmanorfarm.co.uk; open May–Oct

Below The ancient George Inn, Alfriston, first licensed in 1397 **Below right** Straw bales on a farm near Lewes, East Sussex

❶ Beachy Head
Eastbourne, East Sussex; BN20
The white chalk cliffs of Beachy Head, set against the deep blue sea are an awesome sight, as though the South Downs have just been snapped off to let the English Channel through. At the cliff's giddy edge, look down to the lighthouse 530 ft (162 m) below. The **Beachy Head Countryside Centre** *(www.beachyheadcountrysidecentre.co.uk)* and parking lot has displays about the history and nature of the area. A little way along the loop road, past Birling Gap (more excellent views) and close to the A259, is the **Seven Sisters Sheep Centre** *(open Mar–Sep: Sat & Sun all day; Mon–Fri pm only)* where young children can feed and pet the sheep.

🚗 *Head to the A259 and turn left. At the Seven Sisters Country Park, turn right (on a sharp left bend) past the small chalk white horse on the left and through Litlington. Turn left down Lullington Road, toward Alfriston, then left and left again. Park in parking lot on left on way into village.*

❷ Alfriston
East Sussex; BN26 5TA
The most attractive village in Sussex has a High Street of handsome old inns, shops and teahouses, and a large green with the medieval thatched **Clergy House** *(closed Tue, Fri)* by the river. Shopping in town, buy old-time music from Music Memorabilia, and pack a picnic from the excellent deli in the old Post Office and Village Store to take on a hike in Cuckmere Valley. Follow the footpaths along the tidal Cuckmere River as it meanders to the sea, supporting a wide variety of wild birds, butterflies, and plants.

🚗 *Backtrack north out of village, but carry straight on to A27. Turn left, then first left for Berwick and fourth left for Charleston, after Selmeston.*

❸ Berwick
East Sussex; BN26 6SZ
The ancient **St. Michael and All Angels Church** was decorated in 1943 with paintings by Bloomsbury Group artists, Duncan Grant and Vanessa Bell, and their son Quentin Bell. The Bloomsbury Group were avant-garde intellectuals, writers, and artists who first met in Bloomsbury, London in 1905 to share and promote their philosophical and artistic ideas. Other notable members included writers, Virginia Woolf and Lytton Strachey, critic Roger Fry and economist John Maynard Keynes.
In 1916, Vanessa and Duncan moved to nearby **Charleston** *(open Mar–Oct; closed Mon)*, a lovely 18th-century farmhouse which became the set's country meeting place. Tours give an inspiring insight to the Group's life.

🚗 *Head west on the A27, turn right through Glynde. At the llama farm, the road winds left past Glyndebourne, the opera venue. At the B2192 go left for the A26 to Lewes. Park on left over bridge.*

❹ Lewes
East Sussex; BN7 2QS
Tom Paine (1737–1809), "Father of the American Revolution," lived in this feisty county town, which today is such a good place to shop that it has its own currency. Spend "Lewes pounds" in craft shops and galleries such as the **Sussex Guild Shop** *(Southover Grange; 01273 479 565)*. Take a break at **Pelham House** *(see right)* for tea in a sculpture garden. Get a taste of history in the 14th-century **castle** *(closed Mon in Jan)* and walk down the High Street and across the bridge to visit **Harvey's Brewery**.

🚗 *Follow signs for A27 (Brighton). Turn left onto B2123 to coast at Rottingdean, and right onto A259, then Marine Drive. At pier turn right, and follow "P" signs to North Laine parking lots.*

Where to Stay: inexpensive, under £80; moderate, £80–£150; expensive, over £150

⑤ Brighton

East Sussex; BN1

There is a lot to see and do in this city of old smugglers' lanes, Bohemian hang-outs, shops, museums, cafés, and elegant squares. Time on the beach could easily make a visit last a full day.

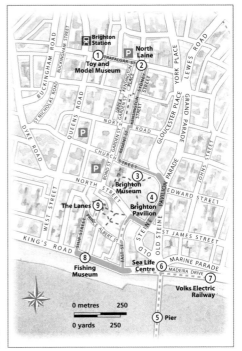

Two-hour city walk

Walk down Trafalgar Street under the forecourt of the train station to the **Toy and Model Museum** ① *(closed Sun, Mon)* for a nostalgic return to childhood, then continue to **North Laine** ②. Here is a myriad of alternative shops selling herbal remedies, fashions, crafts, and world food. Go down the fifth right, Sydney St, and almost directly across into Kensington St and then Regent St opposite. Turn left at the end into Church St, past the Dome to **Brighton Museum** ③ *(closed Sun pm and Mon except Bank Hols)*, on the corner, with a great art deco and fashion collection. Continue right into Pavilion Parade for the **Brighton Pavilion** ④ *(open daily)*, an Indian-styled folly built in the early 1800s by the Prince Regent (later George IV), with its wonderfully lavish interiors. Cross North St and follow East St down to the seafront and turn left for the **Pier** ⑤ *(open daily)*. Enjoy the arcades and rides, see the fish tanks at the **Sea Life Centre** ⑥, *(open daily)* and ride the **Volks Electric Railway** ⑦ *(Apr–Sep: open daily)*, which

goes to the naturist beach and Marina. Walk onto the shore and head westwards, past the arches. This is the liveliest stretch of seafront, cafés, funfair rides, and the small **Fishing Museum** ⑧ *(open daily)*.

Return to the road, crossing at the traffic lights to go down Ship St by the Ship Hotel. Take the first right, doubling back along Prince Albert St toward the Town Hall. Head left into the maze of alleys known as **The Lanes** ⑨. Once the old fishing town, these are now full of shops selling clothes, antiques, and jewelery. To return to the start, cross North St into Bond St and carry on along Gardner St, Upper Gardner St, and Kensington Place.

🚗 *Follow one-way system down through North Laine to bottom of hill and turn left toward A23. Pass to right of St. Peter's Church on a huge traffic island, turn left then right up Ditchling Rd. At T-junction, go left and right to Ditchling Beacon and village. Parking lot right at main crossroads.*

Left Jewellers in The Lanes, Brighton **Below right** Indian-style entrance to the Brighton Pavilion **Below left** Paddling on Brighton beach

---

EAT AND DRINK

ALFRISTON

Wingrove House Hotel *moderate*
This smart restaurant in the stables of Wingrove House, built in 1870, has a sunny terrace and modern European cooking.
High St, BN26 5TD; 01323 870 276; www.wingrovehousehotel.com

LEWES

Pelham House *moderate*
Dine in handsome rooms overlooking the hotel's garden and the Downs.
St. Andrew's Lane, BN7 1UW; 01273 488 600; www.pelhamhouse.com

BRIGHTON

The Regency Restaurant *inexpensive*
For excellent fish and chips, this is a good-value spot by West Pier.
131 King's Rd, BN1 2HH; 01273 325 014; www.theregencyrestaurant.co.uk

Hotel du Vin *moderate*
Whacky mock-Gothic-Tudor building houses this Parisian-style bistro, close to the seafront. Has a strong winelist.
2–6 Ship St, BN1 1AD; 01273 718 588; www.hotelduvin.com

Terre à Terre *moderate*
Top vegetarian restaurant in The Lanes with an eclectic approach to cooking.
71 East St, BN1 1HQ; 01273 729 051; www.terreaterre.co.uk; closed Mon

WHERE TO STAY

DITCHLING

The Bull *moderate*
With four smart, themed rooms (with ensuite walk-in showers), this cozy village pub is a friendly place to stay. It serves good local food, too.
2 High St, BN6 8TA; 01273 843 147; www.thebullditchling.com

AROUND DITCHLING

Blackberry Wood *inexpensive*
This is a real rural campsite, complete with cheery birdsong, in the woods 3 miles (5 km) east of Ditchling. All the usual facilities, plus caravans to rent.
Streat Lane, Streat, BN6 8RS (take Lewes Rd from Ditchling through Westmeston then fourth on the left); 01273 890 035; www.blackberrywood.com

AMBERLEY

Amberley Castle *expensive*
Spend a noble night in this fantastic castle with walled gardens. Four posters, of course, jacket-and-tie fine dining, and a portcullis which closes at midnight – so no returning late from the pub.
BN18 9LT; 01798 831 992; www.amberleycastle.co.uk

ARUNDEL

The Thatched Barn *moderate*
This converted 17th-century barn and cattlesheds in Wepham were on the Duke of Norfolk's estate, and have views across the Arun valley to Arundel castle.
105 Wepham, BN18 9RA; 01903 885 404; www.thethatchedbarnwepham.co.uk; minimum two-night stay at weekends

Below Pretty thatched cottage at Amberley, West Sussex

⑥ Ditchling
East Sussex; BN6 8TB

Before reaching this classic Downland village, the road winds up **Ditchling Beacon**, at 886 ft (270 m) the highest point on the Downs with glorious views. The excellent village **museum** *(open mid-Mar–mid–Dec: Tue–Sat, pm only on Sun)* reveals what traditional rural life was like. It also features the work of two local artists: Eric Gill (1892–1940), sculptor and designer of the Gill Sans typeface, and Edward Johnston (1872–1944), creator of the London Underground typeface. More art is on show at the **Turner Dumbrell Workshops**, on the High Street, where work can be bought directly from artists' studios. Take tea in the garden of Chestertons *(see right)* at the crossroads, or visit the Bull pub *(see left)*.

🚗 *Go west along West Street/B2116 to Hurstpierpoint, then south on the B2117, over the A23, and right on the A281 into a left-hand bend. At Henfield, turn left on the A2037 all the way to the A283 (skirting Upper Beeding) and turn left to Steyning. Park on the street.*

⑦ Steyning
West Sussex; BN44 3YE

Half-timbered and quaint, Steyning is a typical Downs market town and worth a stop for a stroll and some tea in the **Steyning Tea Rooms** in the High Street. Take a look at the latest mini-furnishings in **The Dolls House Shop** and don't miss the handsome Norman **church**. The town is a great base for walks to the Iron-Age hill forts of **Cissbury Ring**, the second

Above View of the rolling green countryside of Sussex, from Ditchling Beacon

largest in England, dating from c. 300 BC, and **Chanctonbury Ring**, marked by a beech copse. A round route from Steyning will take about 4 hours, although Cissbury can be reached in under an hour and Chanctonbury can be more easily conquered up an easy track, a short drive west, off the A283.

🚗 *Continue west along the A283 (passing Chanctonbury Lane on the left). At the roundabout, just after Storrington, take the second exit onto the B2139 to Amberley. Park on street.*

⑧ Amberley
West Sussex; BN18 9LT

This small village of honey-colored cottages is one of the prettiest and most thatched in Sussex. **Amberley Village Pottery** *(open daily)*, in an old chapel in Church Street, is where Caroline Seaton makes pots in Amberley Blue, a deep-colored glaze which she developed in 1964. **Amberley Castle** is actually a manor house and has been turned into an

Below The Steyning Tea Rooms in the old market town of Steyning, West Sussex

impressive hotel *(see left)*. There is a useful village shop by the Black Horse pub. Several hours can be enjoyably spent at **Amberley Working Museum** *(open mid-Mar–mid-Oct: Wed–Sun; daily during school holidays)* in a nearby former chalk pit where craftsmen include broom, clay-pipe, and walking-stick makers, plus lime kilns and displays of historic transport.

🚗 *Continue along the B1239 to join the A284 to Arundel. Park by the river on Mill Road, opposite castle entrance.*

Above Dominating the skyline, the turrets and towers of Arundel Castle

Above An example of a half-timbered house, Petworth, West Sussex

9 Arundel

West Sussex; BN18 9AB

Dating from the Norman conquest but largely Victorian, **Arundel Castle** *(open Apr–Oct; closed Mon except in Aug and bank holidays)* dominates this pleasant market town of antiques shops and tearooms – the oldest of which is 16th-century Belinda's in Tarrant Street. Try a 1-hour cruise on the River Arun from **Arundel Boatyard** *(open Mar–Oct)* by the Riverside Tea Gardens, or hire a motor boat. Carry on along Mill Road past the parking lot to **Swanbourne Lake** and rent a rowing boat before visiting Swanbourne Lodge Tea Rooms for a cream tea. Glide through reed beds and waterways on a boat safari at the wonderful **Arundel Wildfowl and Wetlands Centre** *(open daily)*.

🚗 *Return up A284, then A29 towards Pulborough. At Bury Hill turn left to Bignor (signed) and carry on past roman villa and Sutton to A285. Turn right to Petworth and central parking lot.*

10 Petworth

West Sussex; GU28 0AE

Petworth town is dominated by the vast **Petworth House and Park** *(open Mar–Nov: Sat–Wed)* whose extensive

grounds were designed by Capability Brown. The house holds the National Trust's biggest art collection, with works by JMW Turner. The town itself has a reputation as an antiques center, and the dealers' wares are like museum pieces. On the High Street is the delightful **Petworth Cottage** *(open pm only, Tue–Sat)*, kept in a time warp at 1910, when it was occupied by Mary Cummings, a local seamstress.

🚗 *Take the A272 to Midhurst. There is a parking lot on the left at the road enters town, or park on Main Street.*

The South Downs Way

This walking route runs for more than 100 miles (160 km) along the ridge of the Downs from Eastbourne to Winchester in Hampshire. It takes 6–9 days to complete, but can be done in handy stages on weekends. The route is a bridleway, so horse riders and cyclists can enjoy it, too. **Footprints of Steyning** does baggage transfers *(01903 813 318; www.footprintsofsussex. co.uk)*. For shorter loop walks, see *www.nationaltrail.co.uk/Southdowns*.

EAT AND DRINK

DITCHLING

Chestertons *inexpensive*
More than just a tea shop, this is a fabulous deli selling local produce.
1 High Street, BN6 8SY; 01273 846 638

AMBERLEY

The Sportsman *inexpensive*
This country pub near the back of the village is popular with South Downs walkers for its views. Serves good food and has five ensuite rooms.
Rackham Rd, BN18 9NR; 01798 831 787

ARUNDEL

The Black Rabbit *moderate*
The setting beside the River Arun with views across to the castle made this pub famous. Its good food, service and long bar have maintained its popularity.
Mill Road, BN18 9PB; 01903 882 828; www.hall-woodhouse.co.uk

Swanbourne Lodge Tea Rooms *inexpensive*
Beautiful building by the lake serving snacks and refreshments.
Mill Road, BN18 9PA; 01903 884 293

Right An antiques shop on the steep High Street, Arundel

Eat and Drink: inexpensive, under £25; moderate, £25–£50; expensive, over £50

Above left In the heart of the market town of Midhurst, West Sussex **Above right** Modern art in the woods, Goodwood Sculpture Park

VISITING CHICHESTER

Parking
There are five city-center 2-hour parking lots, and several longer-term parking lots just a few minutes' walk from the center.

Tourist Information
Town: *29a South Street, PO19 1AH; 01243 775 888; www.visitchichester. org;* **Harbour:** *01243 513 275; www.conservancy.co.uk*

BOAT TRIPS

Chichester Harbour Water Tours
01243 670 504; www.chichesterharbour watertours.co.uk

Chichester Ship Canal
01243 771 363; www.chichestercanal.org.uk

WHERE TO STAY

MIDHURST

The Spread Eagle Hotel and Health Spa *expensive*
For top-class pampering, try this spa. It is comfortable and modern, yet still maintains its Tudor roots.
South Street, GU29 9NH; 01730 816 911; www.hshotels.co.uk

AROUND CHICHESTER

Woodstock House Hotel *inexpensive*
There are 13 ensuite rooms in this converted farmhouse. Good choice for Goodwood and the Downs.
Charlton Road, Charlton, PO18 0HU (12 km/7.5 miles on A286); 01243 811 666; www.woodstockhousehotel.co.uk

Millstream Hotel *moderate*
In a lovely spot, with a garden and a excellent restaurant serving innovative modern dishes, this small hotel offers apartments as well as B&B rooms.
Bosham, PO18 8HL; 01243 573 234; www.millstream-hotel.co.uk

Where to Stay: inexpensive, under £80; moderate, £80–£150; expensive, over £150

⑪ Midhurst
West Sussex; GU29 9DS
This attractive half-timbered market town, with more than 100 listed buildings, has a broad main street, plenty of pubs and top-class hotels. The distinctive yellow paintwork on some houses shows that they belong to the Cowdray Estate. This includes the romantic **Cowdray Ruins** *(open mid-Mar–Nov: Wed–Sun)*, once a Tudor mansion built in 1520 and partially destroyed by fire in 1793. **The Cowdray Estate** *(www.cowdray.co.uk)* organizes fly fishing and clay pigeon shooting and has holiday cottages. Check for fixtures of Cowdray Park Polo Club *(May–Sep)*.

🚗 *Head out of town on the A286 towards Chichester. After the village of Singleton turn left to the Weald and Downland Museum (signed).*

Below The boat house at Bosham, one of the inlets of Chichester Harbour

Glorious Goodwood
This huge estate encompasses a motor racing circuit, aerodrome and "Glorious Goodwood," a flat-racing course. The grounds also include a golf course, the Richmond Arms, the elegant Goodwood Park Hotel, and an organic Farm Shop. Art lovers are not forgotten either, with a great collection of paintings at the 18th-century Goodwood House and the Sculpture Park, a superb woodland space with top-rank pieces. (www.goodwood.co.uk).

⑫ Weald and Downland Open Air Museum
Singleton, West Sussex; PO18 0EU
Allow at least 3 hours to explore the ancient buildings of this excellent museum *(www.wealddown.co.uk; mid-Feb–Dec: open daily; Jan–mid-Feb: open Wed, Sat, Sun)*. Displays of traditional agricultural methods and crafts – with steam tractors and shire horses – bring the rural past to life. Next door, the award-wining **West Dean Estate Gardens** *(www.westdean.org.uk; open daily)* include a fine kitchen garden and extensive Victorian glasshouses. The vast grounds of **Goodwood** offer much of interest *(see above)*.

🚗 *Continue past the museum toward Goodwood. At a tight left-hand bend, a cul-de-sac on the right leads to The Trundle, with great views. Go past Goodwood race course and House, turning left on the A286 to Chichester. Park in the town center.*

⑬ Chichester
West Sussex; PO19 1NB

This peaceful county town is centred on a market cross from which North, South, West, and East Streets radiate. The **Festival** and **Minerva Theatres** (*www.cft.org.uk; 01243 784 437*) are renowned, and **Pallant House** (*closed Sun am, Mon*), is a superb modern art gallery. Don't miss **Chichester Cathedral**, consecrated in 1108, with Graham Sutherland's small painting *Noli Me Tangere* (1962), John Piper's dramatic 1966 altar tapestry, and Marc Chagall's striking stained-glass window

Above The tapestry designed by John Piper, Chichester Cathedral

(1978). The recumbent figure of Richard Fitzalan, 10th Earl of Arundel, with his wife, Eleanour of Lancaster, inspired Philip Larkin's 1956 poem *An Arundel Tomb*, which can be read alongside it.

There's also much to see just outside Chichester. Head west on the A27 and turn left on the A259 for the impressive mosaics of **Fishbourne Roman Palace** (*Feb–mid-Dec: open daily; mid-Dec–Jan: open Sat & Sun*). Further along the A259 lies **Bosham**, one of the many inlets of **Chichester Harbour**. Bosham has a pretty Saxon church; the supposed burial place of King Cnut's daughter, the church is depicted in the Bayeux Tapestry and is the oldest Christian site in Sussex. At low tide, drive (or walk) from the village to **Bosham Hoe**, and return to the famous Anchor Bleu pub. The harbor inlets are in an Area of Outstanding Natural Beauty, one of the best boating areas on the south coast, so consider taking a boat trip for the scenery, birdlife or to go fishing (*see left*). Other inlets can be reached by heading south from Chichester on the A286 to charming **Dell Quay** and **Itchenor**. Finish a tour of these wet flatlands with a walk on the sandy beach at **West Wittering** or the more pebbly one at **East Wittering**, a short drive to the south.

Above left Traditional beach huts at sandy West Wittering **Above right** Surfer negotiating the pebbles at East Wittering

EAT AND DRINK

AROUND MIDHURST

Moonlight Cottage *inexpensive*
This is a very English tea room in a 200-year-old cottage with a pretty garden, 3 miles (5 km) south of Midhurst. Also does B&B and roasts on Sundays.. *Chichester Rd, Cocking, GU29 OHN; 01730 813 336; www.moonlightcottage. co.uk; open daytime only, Wed–Sun*

CHICHESTER

St Martin's Organic Tea Rooms *inexpensive*
Home-made snacks, soups, bread, cakes, and ice cream are served in this friendly café. The handsome period building has a garden and a nice log fire in winter. *3 St. Martins St, PO19 1NP; 01243 786 715; www.organictearooms.co.uk; open in daytime only; closed Sun*

The Dining Room at Purchases *moderate*
This is an excellent restaurant in a Georgian mansion. Try rabbit with pearl barley, local game, or Selsea crab. *31 North St, PO19 1LY; 01243 537 352; www.thediningroom.biz; closed Sun*

AROUND CHICHESTER

Anchor Bleu *inexpensive*
Good food in a friendly pub with terrace. *The High Street, Bosham, PO18 8LS; 01243 573 956*

DAY TRIP OPTIONS

Explore the area from buzzy Brighton, arty Lewes, or pretty Arundel.

Town and Country
Spend the morning in Brighton ❺ with its museums, arty shops, pavilion, and restaurants. There's plenty for children, with a pier, aquarium, and mini-railway. When the seaside glitz

palls, drive up Ditchling Beacon ❻ for views and down to the village for tea.

Follow the drive route to Ditchling.

Arts and crafts
In Lewes ❹, browse the crafts shops before heading over to Charleston and Berwick ❸ to see the Bloomsbury circle's art.

Follow the drive route in reverse.

Historic Waterland
Explore Arundel ❾ with its castle, antiques shops, and wetlands center. Then, off to Chichester ⑬ for the cathedral, ancient Roman art, and a boat trip or a walk on the beach.

Follow the A27.

Eat and Drink: inexpensive, under £25; moderate, £25–£50; expensive, over £50

The Garden of England

Ashdown Forest to Battle

Highlights

- **Wildlife and wilderness**
  Spot the natural flora and fauna of
  Ashdown Forest, Romney Marshes,
  Rye Nature Reserve and Bewl Water

- **Produce from the garden**
  Sample fruit-rich jams, saltmarsh lamb,
  hoppy ales, wine, cider and smoked fish

- **Medieval Winchelsea**
  Walk around the gridded streets of
  this ancient town with vaulted cellars

- **Gardens in bloom**
  Relax at Great Dixter and Sissinghurst,
  two of Britain's most celebrated gardens

- **Film-set castles**
  Storm the bastions of the South Coast,
  the mighty Scotney and Bodiam castles

Shady picnic spot with a view in the high
heathland of Ashdown Forest

The Garden of England

Between the North Downs and the coast, this itinerary starts in Ashdown Forest and loops through winding river valleys to the flat wetlands of Romney Marsh and back up to the forests of the High Weald and Bewl Water. The roads twist and turn, diving through woodland and opening into farmlands – so often there are wonderful and unexpected views. Weatherboard villages, elegant windmills, distinctive oast houses and handsome hall houses make it one of Britain's most architecturally diverse regions. Called the Garden of England for its orchards of fruit trees and farmland bursting with produce, the area also contains some of the finest and most original gardens in the country.

ACTIVITIES

Enjoy a cream tea on a glorious country estate at Penshurst

Windsurf on the sea or row on the canal at Hythe

Go birdwatching at RSPB Dungeness or on a walk in Rye

Take a dip in the sea at Camber Sands

Board a vintage train from Tenterden to Bodiam or Hythe to Dungeness

Sample wine from excellent English vintages at Tenterden

Visit the glorious gardens at Sissinghurst and Great Dixter

Rent a bicycle to ride around the forest at Goudhurst

Try a day's tranquil fishing on Bewl Water

KEY

Drive route

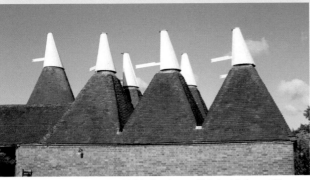

Above **Traditional oast houses at Sissinghurst Castle, see p106**

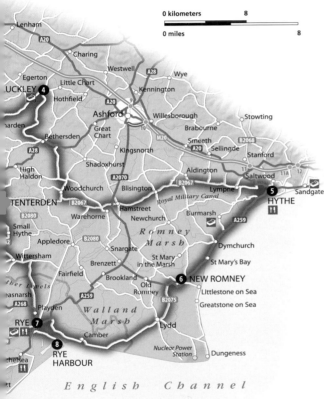

0 kilometers　　　　8

0 miles　　　　8

Above **Fisherman's hut at Rye Harbour, see pp104–5**

PLAN YOUR DRIVE

Start/finish: Ashdown Forest to Battle

Number of days: 3–4, allowing for a half day's walk at Rye.

Distance: Around 175 miles (280 km).

Road conditions: The roads are generally well maintained. Some lanes are narrow and hedgerows can get wild, so be careful not to scratch your paintwork.

When to go: May to June is a good time to visit, when apple and cherry blossom paints the area pink and white. July and August are often the warmest months but are also the busiest. September is harvest time, when the sea is still warm.

Opening times: Museums and attractions are generally open 10am–5pm, but may close earlier (or be closed altogether) Nov–Easter. Shops are often open longer. Churches are usually open until dusk.

Main market days: Tonbridge: 3rd Sat in month; Yalding: Farmers' Market: every 3rd Sat; **Hythe**: Tue 8am–4pm; Rye: every Wed 10am–1pm; **Battle**: Fri 10am–11.15am; Farmers' Market: every 3rd Sat.

Shopping: Look out for Winnie the Pooh memorabilia in Ashdown Forest; teapots on Tea Pot Island, Yalding; pottery and antiques in Rye, and smoked fish in Dungeness.

Major festivals: Hythe: Venetian Fête, Aug 2011 (every two years); Rye: RX Wildlife Festival, May; Arts Festival, Sep; A Taste of Rye, Oct; Tenterden: Folk Festival, Oct.

DAY TRIP OPTIONS

For a good family trip, visit the **church** at Hythe and picnic on the **beach** before riding the **steam train** along the coast for some **birdwatching**. Historians will enjoy visiting the **abbey** and **battlefield** at Battle, lunching at the Great Dixter **gardens** and exploring the fairytale **castle** at Bodiam. Another day out might take in the **ghosts** of Pluckley and the **gardens** at Sissinghurst followed by a **castle** and a **lakeside stroll**. For full details, see p107.

VISITING ASHDOWN FOREST

Getting There
From East Grinstead take the A22 south. After three roundabouts (6 miles/10 km) turn left at traffic lights down Colemans Hatch Rd. The Forest Centre is on the left.

Ashdown Forest Centre
Wych Cross, Forest Row, RH18 5JP, 01342 823 583; www.ashdownforest.org

WHERE TO STAY

AROUND PENSHURST

Whitepost Oast *inexpensive*
This oast house between Chiddingstone and Penshurst has wonderful views over the Weald and three ensuite rooms. *Chiddingstone Causeway, TN8 8JH (3 km/ 2 miles south on B2176); 01892 870 058; www.a1tourism.com/uk/whitepost*

AROUND YALDING

Leavers Oast *inexpensive*
The rooms are in the roundels of this handsome oast house in large grounds. *Stanford Lane, Hadlow, TN11 0JN (off A26 east of Yalding); 01732 850 924; www.leaversoast.co.uk*

PLUCKLEY

Elvey Farm *moderate*
This medieval house and stable block is a rural treat. The restaurant (open to non-residents) serves Kentish cuisine. *Elvey Lane, TN27 0SU; 01233 840 442; www.elveyfarm.co.uk*

AROUND HYTHE

Sandgate Hotel *inexpensive*
Book a room with a sea view – only £10 extra – at this excellent seaside hotel. *8–9 Wellington Terrace, The Esplanade, Sandgate, CT20 3DY; 01303 220 444; www.sandgatehotel.com*

Below left Attractive local stores and gas station, Penshurst **Below right** The fertile Kent countryside near Yalding

① Ashdown Forest
East Sussex; RH18 5JP
Probably most famous as the home for the children's character Winnie the Pooh, Ashdown Forest is filled with deer and sheep and provides walks, views, and picnic spots. The **Ashdown Forest Centre** *(open Sat & Sun; also Mon–Fri pm in summer)* helps visitors get the most out of the heathland. Pick up a map to the shop Winnie's creator AA Milne (1982–56) used to visit – **Pooh Corner** *(open daily)* at Hartfield (along Coleman's Hatch Rd to B2110, right, and then left on B2026). Buy the rule book for Poohsticks to play at **Poohsticks Bridge**, a 40-minute walk away, next to Cotchford Farm. This is where AA Milne brought up his son, Christopher Robin (and also where Rolling Stone Brian Jones drowned in 1966).

Pooh Corner shop sign, Hartfield

🚗 *From Hartfield, at the end of the High St turn right on B2110 all the way to an A264. Turn left, then first right down B2188 to Penshurst.*

② Penshurst
Kent; TN11 8DG
The stone bridge over the fledgling Medway is a delightful approach to this attractive village. Don't miss **Penshurst Place** *(open Easter–end Oct)* – one of the grandest estates in the county. Dating from 1346, the pretty crenellated manor house contains the largest original medieval hall outside Westminster as well as some great state rooms and galleries. It also has beautiful walled gardens, a small toy museum, and a children's playground. Stop off for a cream tea at the Fir Tree Tea Rooms, once part

of the estate. Visit St. Mary's church in **Speldhurst,** just off the B2176, to see windows by the 19th-century Pre-Raphaelites William Morris and Edward Burne-Jones. Try the impressive George and Dragon for a top-end pub lunch.

🚗 *Take the B2176 east, turn left on the A26. Keep right, turn right at the second roundabout and left at the third before turning off right onto B2017. Continue to the A228 and turn left. Turn right onto B2015, then take B2162 to Yalding.*

③ Yalding
Kent; ME18 6JB
The village lies on the River Beult, which joins the Medway at The Lees, where the medieval **Twyford Bridge** spans the river. Nearby is the 500-year-old, much flooded Anchor pub, opposite Tea Pot Island *(see right)* and Twyford yacht basin. Once a center of hop-growing, Yalding is an attractive village, with a farmers' market on the third Saturday of each month. Visit **Yalding Organic Garden**, south of the village, for home-grown inspiration *(www.yaldingorganics.com)*.

🚗 *Turn left on B2010, turn right and follow signs for B2163, right on A274. After Headorn, take third left to Smarden and on to Pluckley. Park on street.*

④ Pluckley
Kent; TN27 0QS
This is apple country, and the hedges along the lanes protect the orchards from winds. Pluckley has two claims to fame: as the most haunted village in England, and as the setting for the TV comedy *The Darling Buds of May*,

Above left Apple orchards are dense around Pluckley **Above right** The medieval Twyford Bridge at Yalding

based on the stories of HE Bates (1905–74) who lived in nearby Little Chart. A booklet on sale in the Post Office and the Black Horse pub outlines a tour of the village's dozen supposedly haunted sites, one of them being the pub itself.

🚗 *Turn right to Bethersden, past Pluckley station, right on Kiln Lane, then left onto the A28, and first right to Woodchurch. Turn left here onto the B2067 towards Lympne to Hythe. Use town parking lots.*

⑤ Hythe
Kent; TN27 OQS

One of the Cinque Ports, a group of towns formed in 1155 to provide ships for the Crown in return for a beneficial tax status, Hythe is now a breezy, open resort. The old town is set back from the sea and topped by **St. Leonard's Church**, dating as far back as 1090. Don't miss the fascinating ossuary, with the bones of around 2,000 people. The town fills up on Tuesdays when there is a big market in **St. John's Street Car Park** *(open 8am–4pm).*

Kentish Hops

The flowering part of the hop plant used as a flavouring for beer, hops have given Kent its distinctive red-brick oast houses – kilns used to dry fresh hops. Half a century ago, East Londoners would flock to Kent to spend their summers picking hops. Now only a handful of hop gardens remain. The **Hop Farm Country Park** *(www.thehopfarm.co.uk),* Beltring – between Yalding and Paddock Wood, explains all things hoppy, holds a hop festival in autumn and has attractions for kids, too.

Between the town and the sea, the 28-mile (45-km) **Royal Military Canal** has rowing boats for rent, and every two years holds a lavish Venetian Fête in August. Hythe is also the terminus for the 14-mile (22-km) **Romney–Hythe–Dungeness miniature railway** *(open Easter–Sep: daily; www.rhdr.org.uk).* Popular with windsurfers, the long sandy beach is safe and family friendly.

🚗 *Take the A259 toward Hastings, to New Romney. Park behind the High Street in pay-and-display parking lot.*

EAT AND DRINK

ASHDOWN FOREST

Piglit's Tea Room *inexpensive*
Have a little something in the tearoom that adjoins the Pooh Corner shop. *High Street, Hartfield, TN7 4AE; 01892 770 456; www.poohcountry.co.uk; open in daytime only*

PENSHURST

Fir Tree Tea Rooms *inexpensive*
Enjoy cream teas and great home-made cakes in an atmospheric building dating from the 16th century. *Penshurst, TN11 8DB; 01892 870 382; open Wed–Sun pm*

AROUND PENSHURST

George and Dragon *moderate*
Medieval oak-beamed inn that exudes character – local produce includes lobster, smoked eel, and Larkin Bitter. *Speldhurst Hill, Speldhurst, TN3 0NN (off the B2176, 4.3 km/2.7 miles south of Penshurst); 01892 863 125; www.speldhurst.com*

YALDING

Tea Pot Island *inexpensive*
Have a cream tea, a coffee, or a snack at this riverside setting, filled with teapots. Children can paint their own mugs. *Hampstead Lane, ME18 6HG; 01622 814 541; www.teapotisland.com; open in daytime only; Oct–Mar: call for opening times*

HYTHE

Hythe Bay Seafood *medium*
On the seafront, this large family-run restaurant is good for seafood. The menu runs from simple fish soup to a Hythe Bay shellfish platter and lobster. *Marine Parade, CT21 6AW; 01303 233 844; www.thehythebay.co.uk*

Below Windsurfers in Hythe, taking advantage of the open breezy beach

Eat and Drink: inexpensive, under £25; moderate, £25–£50; expensive, over £50

Above Rye Windmill Hotel, on the pretty Tillingham river, Rye

WHERE TO STAY

AROUND NEW ROMNEY

Haguelands Farm *inexpensive*
This is a comfy farmhouse B&B, off the A259 near Dymchurch, with farm shop, maize maze, restaurant, and alpaca farm.
Burmarsh Rd, TN29 OJR; 01303 872 273; www.haguelandsfarm.co.uk

RYE

Rye Windmill *inexpensive*
Near the quay, this hotel offers rooms with character and excellent breakfasts.
Mill Lane, TN31 7DW; 01797 224 027; www.ryewindmill.co.uk; usually minimum two-night stay at weekends

AROUND TENTERDEN

Barclay Farmhouse *inexpensive*
This 18th-century farmhouse, off the A262, offers comfort and hospitality.
Woolpack Cnr, Biddenden, TN27 8BQ; 01580 292 288; www.barclayfarm house.co.uk; usually minimum two-night stay at weekends

Below left The Old Lighthouse (1904), Dungeness **Below right** Film director Derek Jarman's Prospect Cottage, Dungeness

⑥ New Romney
Kent; TN28 8AH

New Romney is the capital of Romney Marsh, a low-lying area of expansive skies, narrow lanes, water channels, and fields dotted with sheep – look out for sweet Romney saltmarsh lamb in restaurants. Take the coastal road from Littlestone to the **nuclear power station** *(closed to visitors)* at **Dungeness**, on one of the largest shingle banks in Europe. Stop by **Prospect Cottage**, where film-maker Derek Jarman created an unusual garden from what he found on the beach. At the 131-ft (40-m) **Old Lighthouse** (1924–94), climb to the top to see the view and examine the great glass prisms. The area's special habitat has made it an important **RSPB site** *(open daily)* with trails for kids and regular sightings of bitterns, plovers and wheatears.

🚗 *Take the A259, turn left on B2075 for Lydd. Go through the High Street and follow signs to Camber and on to Rye. Park at the entrance to the town.*

⑦ Rye
East Sussex; TN31 7LA

It is a pleasure just to stroll around this pretty, ancient, and cobblestoned former port. Climb **St. Mary's Tower** for excellent views; on the High Street, pop into **Rye Art Gallery**, buy sweets from jars in Britcher & Rivers' 1920s shop, or pick up delicious picnic snacks from Rye Delicatessen. Head to the waterfront where the tar-black former warehouses are troves of bric-a-brac and antiques. Watch the fishing boats behind the bowling green landing the day's catch.

On the road in to Rye lie **Camber Sands**, a vast sweep of golden beach revealed when the tide races out across the flat shore. Popular with horse riders and sand yachters, the Sands get busy on summer weekends.

🚗 *Leave Rye on the Winchelsea Road and take the turning marked for Rye Harbour. Drive to the end and park in the parking lot, by the Nature Reserve Information Centre.*

⑧ Rye Harbour
East Sussex; TN31 7TU

Home to **Rye Harbour Nature Reserve** *(www.wildrye.info)*, these wetlands and reed beds are great for birdwatching. A network of paths cross the area, so it is easy to tailor a walk to the time available. Lime Kiln Cottage by the River Rother is the information centre.

A three-hour country walk

From the parking lot follow the river past **Lime Kiln Cottage** ① and continue past the bird hide to the sea. Turn right and follow the coast west, past the Ternery Pool on the right – a great place to see wildlife. Walk past the **Mary Stanford Lifeboat House** ② from where, in 1928, a lifeboat with 17 volunteers rowed out to help a storm-stricken ship; all were lost at sea. Turn inland by the marked footpath that runs right by the edge of the larger body of water – Nook Beach – and turn right, veering round to the left past Castle Farm barns. Continue on to a small cluster of houses, to Sea Road and walk up to

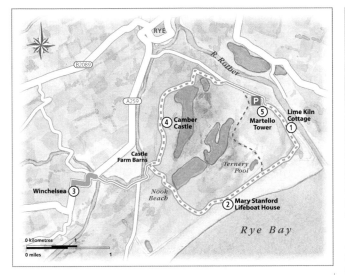

Above Camber Sands has seven miles of award-winning dune-backed beach

the roundabout, and take the first exit past the Bridge Inn. Then, turn first left up the steep Strand Hill under Strand Gate into **Winchelsea** ③.

Overlooking the wetlands and sea below, Winchelsea is laid out in the manner of a medieval Bastide town (from Southwest France) – on a grid pattern divided into quarters with wide streets. With little modern development, it feels as if nothing has changed since it was first designed by Edward I in 1288, following a series of storms in which Old Winchelsea all but disappeared. At the town's center is the large Church of St. Thomas the Martyr. Half ruined, its great chancel now serves as the nave, with brilliant stained-glass windows, including one to the victims of the 1928 Rye lifeboat disaster. A feature of Winchelsea's houses is their enormous cellars: look out for the stone steps leading to these vaulted undercrofts where wine was stored; tours are arranged on weekends in summer *(www. winchelsea.net)*. The town, which is not big enough to get lost in, merits a look, and offers several places to stop for refreshments or a cream tea.

Return down to the roundabout and back down Sea Road. Past the Castle Farm barns, just after the footpath begins, follow the signs left, along the track to **Camber Castle** ④, a ruined 16th-century fort. Take the path forking right that skirts the Castle Water. This is another great spot for

seeing more birdlife. Follow the path sharp left toward the road, then right, between the ponds and back onto the road. Turn right here back to the parking lot by the **Martello Tower** ⑤, one of a series of 74 bastions built along the south coast between 1805–08 during the Napoleonic Wars.

🚗 *Return to Rye, take A268 through the town center, forking right onto B2082 to Tenterden. Park free for 2 hours at the supermarket just before town.*

⑨ Tenterden
Kent; TN30 6AN
On the road to town, after a series of sharp bends, stop at **Smallhythe Place** *(open Sat–Wed; weekends only, in winter)*, home of the actress Ellen Terry (1847–1928). Dating from the 16th century, when Smallhythe was a center for shipbuilding, this pretty half-timbered house and cottage garden was the actress's home for nearly 30 years.

Also on the way, look out for **Chapel Down Vineyard** (with free tastings), and **Morgew Park Farm** selling organic potatoes from their honesty stall.

Antiques shops in Tenterden are open on weekends and the High Street is ideal for browsing. Visit the small local museum and step back in time at the **Kent & Sussex Light Railway Station** *(www.kesr.org.uk)*, which runs steam and classic trains to Bodiam.

🚗 *Drive through Tenterden turning left on the A28, signed to Ashford, then forking left on the A262 to Sissinghurst.*

EAT AND DRINK

RYE

Webbes at the Fish Cafe *moderate*
The best seafood restaurant in town – try the steamed selection of fish with shellfish – also serves meat dishes, too.
Tower Street, TN31 7AT; 01797 222 226; www.thefishcafe.co.uk

AROUND RYE HARBOUR

The Tea Tree *inexpensive*
This café-restaurant serves a wide range of wholesome snacks and daily specials
12 High St, Winchelsea, TN36 4EA (6 km/4 miles on A259); 01797 226 102

AROUND TENTERDEN

West House *moderate*
Eat Romney lamb and crème brulée with rhubarb at this excellent Michelin-starred restaurant, on the road to Sissinghurst, in the center of the village.
28 High St, Biddenden, TN27 8AH; 01580 291 341; www.thewesthouse restaurant.co.uk; closed Mon

Below The restored Kent & Sussex Light Railway Station, Tenterden

Eat and Drink: inexpensive, under £25; moderate, £25–£50; expensive, over £50

Above Rural scenery of wheat fields and hay bales near Sissinghurst, Kent

ACTIVITIES AT BEWL WATER

Bewl Water Outdoor Centre
Bewl Water, Lamberhurst, TN3 8JH; 01892 890 716; www.bewlwater.org

WHERE TO STAY

AROUND BEWL WATER

The Bull Inn *inexpensive*
West of Ticehurst, a short walk from Bewl Water, this excellent pub has four ensuite rooms and a smart restaurant. *Three Legs Cross, Ticehust, TN5 7HH; 01580 200 586; www.thebullinn.co.uk*

BATTLE

The Powder Mills *moderate*
Gorgeous Georgian country house hotel with fishing lake and grounds. Good restaurant open to non-residents. *Powder Mill Lane, TN33 0SP; 01424 775 511; www.powdermillshotel.com*

Below left The gatehouse of Sissinghurst Castle
Below right The splendid gardens and hall house of Great Dixter

⑩ Sissinghurst
Kent; TN17 2AB

One of the great National Trust estates in southeast England, **Sissinghurst Castle Garden** *(open Mar–Nov: Fri–Tue)* is not in fact a castle but the remains of a Tudor manor built around 1560. It became a "Castle" in 1756 when it was used to house French prisoners of war who called it "Le Château." The estate was bought by the parliamentarian Harold Nicolson and gardening writer Vita Sackville-West in 1930, who laid out the grounds as a series of "rooms," each with a distinctive theme and colour. The white garden, best in early July, is spectacular, but at any time of year there is something to see. An added attraction is the farm that is being revived by Harold and Vita's grandson Adam Nicolson and his wife, the culinary writer Sarah Raven, bringing home-grown food to the restaurant – "from plot to plate"

🚗 **Continue along the A262 to Goudhurst. Turn left at the village pond for free parking, just down on the right.**

⑪ Goudhurst
Kent; TN17 1AL

This is an idyllic village with a fine pond and lovely, uplifting views. The church tower is sometimes open, for even better views across the Weald. South from Goudhurst on the B2079 lie the green forests of **Bedgebury Pinetum**, with plenty for kids and

adults to do – adventure playgrounds, cycle trails, and educational activities. Rent some bikes, enjoy a picnic, or just stroll among the tall trees.

Also near Goudhurst, off the A262 is **Finchcocks** *(open Sun & Bank Hols; Wed–Thu in Aug; 01580 211 712; www. finchcocks.co.uk)*, a Georgian manor set in beautiful grounds with a museum of early pianos and other instruments. Return to the A262 and follow signs for the impressive **Scotney Castle** *(open Mar–Nov: daily)*. This magical, ruined 14th-century castle has towers, a moat, brightly-colored flower gardens, shady woodland, and a hop farm.

🚗 **Take the road out of Scotney Castle to the roundabout, turning left on the A21. Turn right to Bewl Water following the signs – park on-site.**

Butcher's sign, Goudhurst

⑫ Bewl Water
Kent; TN3 8JH

Built in the 1970s, the largest inland water in southeast England, **Bewl Water Outdoor Centre** *(open daily)* is encircled by a 14-mile (22-km) walk and riding path. There is a wide range of activities available, such as canoeing, windsurfing, sailing, fly fishing, and cycling. Alternatively take a lake cruise, explore an adventure playground or simply learn about the surrounding environment at the Visitor Center. After all that, enjoy a snack at the restaurant.

🚗 **Return to the A21, turn right and then left onto the A268 to Hawkhurst,**

Above left Bewl Water, the largest reservoir in southeast England **Above right** The almost complete exterior of Bodiam Castle

then turn right on the A229 and left on the B2244. Turn left to Bodiam Castle, marked and with on-site parking.

⑬ Bodiam Castle
Kent; TN32 5UA

When it comes to castles, few live up to the ideal as well as **Bodiam Castle** *(Feb–Nov: open daily; Dec–Jan: open Sat & Sun)*. Built in 1385 by the River Rother to defend the coast – now some miles away – it saw little action. A square bastion with corner towers and a carp-filled moat, the castle has been the backdrop to films such as *Monty Python and the Holy Grail*. Re-enact swashbuckling movie moments on the battlements, spiral staircases, and gatehouse with original portcullis.

🚗 *From the parking lot, turn left over the river and take first left. At a staggered junction turn left for Great Dixter House and Gardens. Park in the free on-site parking lot.*

⑭ Great Dixter
Kent; TN31 6PH

A beautiful medieval hall house, **Great Dixter** *(open Apr–Oct: Tue–Sun; garden 11–5pm; house 2–5pm)* is in fact the amalgam of two buildings. The original half-timbered house, built between 1440 and 1454, was bought by Nathaniel Lloyd in 1909. He transported another, similar Tudor house from Benenden nearby and commissioned the Arts and Crafts architect Edwin Lutyens, to meld them together and plan the gardens. Nathaniel's son, the garden writer Christopher Lloyd, was born here in 1906 and made the gardens some of the most inspiring in Britain, using innovative planting techniques. Since his death in 2006, Great Dixter has been managed by a charitable trust.

🚗 *Head back to town and take the A28 south. Turn right and follow the signs to Battle. Park by the Abbey.*

⑮ Battle
Kent; TN33 0AD

At **Battle Abbey** *(open daily)* stretch your legs with a stroll around the 100-acre battlefield where the Normans defeated the English in 1066: the audio tour is excellent. The Abbey itself was largely destroyed during the 16th-century Dissolution of the Monasteries. The market town of Battle sprang up around the Abbey and merits a short visit. Go down memory lane at **Yesterday's World** *(open daily)*, a museum of social history. A country market is held every Friday morning in the memorial hall.

EAT AND DRINK

GOUDHURST
Taywell Farm Shop *inexpensive*
Fabulous farm shop with homemade produce and some delicious ice cream. Stock up for the perfect picnic.
Cranbrook Road, TN17 1DY; 01580 211 881; www.taywell.co.uk

AROUND BEWL WATER
The Bistro *inexpensive*
This well-established restaurant in a vineyard is open for breakfast, lunch and cream teas. Try spit-roast chicken and lamb shanks and take home local wine and cheese from the shop.
The Down, Lamberhurst, TN3 8ER (from Bewl Water turn left on the A21, over the roundabout keeping straight on for 3 miles/2 km); 01892 890 412; www.lamberhurstvineyard.net

BATTLE
Nobles *moderate*
Good center of town restaurant with menus featuring local produce – try the Romney Marsh lamb. It has a terrace for sunny days and the set menus are great value. Probably best to book ahead.
17 High Street, TN33 0AE; 01424 774 422; www.noblesrestaurant.co.uk

DAY TRIP OPTIONS
Discover Kent's history and country-side from Hythe, Battle or Pluckley.

Coastal Marshes
In Hythe, ⑤ see its fine church, then buy provisions and head to the beach with a picnic. Next take the steam railway to New Romney ⑥ and on to Dungeness for a walk on the shingles and some birdspotting.

This trip doesn't require any driving.

War and Peace
At Battle ⑮, see the Abbey and walk the field where the decisive battle in the last successful invasion of England took place. Next, head for a peaceful lunch in the wonderful house and gardens of Great Dixter ⑭, before climbing the battlements of 14th-century Bodiam Castle ⑬.

Retrace the driving directions to Great Dixter and Bodiam Castle. To return, head northeast to A21, then south.

Ghosts, Gardens and Castles
Stay in the haunted village of Pluckley ④, then go to see the wonderful gardens and ancient buildings of Sissinghurst Castle ⑩. Drive through pretty Goudhurst ⑪ to Scotney Castle and if there is time, go to Bewl Water ⑫ for a lakeside stroll or a cycle ride.

Head south out of Pluckley, turn right on A28 and right on the A262. Retrace the journey to return to Pluckley.

Eat and Drink: inexpensive, under £25; moderate, £25–£50; expensive, over £50

The River Cam and Constable Country

Cambridge to East Bergholt

Highlights

- **A world-class university**
  Walk through the historical charms of Cambridge on the picturesque River Cam with its outstanding medieval architecture of college courtyards and churches – and then go punting

- **Galleries and museums**
  Undertake some further education at Cambridge and Saffron Walden's museums, see great art at Audley End, Gainsborough's House and gallery at Sudbury and Sir Alfred Munnings Art Museum at Dedham.

- **Constable Country**
  Tour the ancient wool towns, pretty villages, historic churches and rural landscapes captured by John Constable in his paintings

View across the River Cam towards King's College Chapel, Cambridge

The River Cam and Constable Country

This glorious drive begins only 64 miles (103 km) from central London but the places it visits are surprisingly rural, with a flavour and colour that is distinctly local. It traces a route from the venerable university architecture of Cambridgeshire through the unspoiled village greens of Essex to the fertile countryside of the Stour Valley and Dedham Vale, just straying across the border into Suffolk. Here are opportunities to explore a landscape of timeless beauty, immortalized by some of Britain's greatest artists. In this part of East Anglia, history is everywhere present in the ancient market towns, the villages whose cottages – many half-timbered, thatched and washed prettily in pink – seem almost to have sprung from the earth.

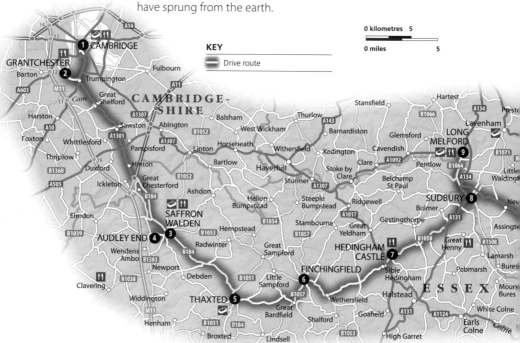

KEY

—— Drive route

0 kilometres 5

0 miles 5

ACTIVITIES

Go punting on the River Cam under the Bridge of Sighs and along the glorious Cambridge Backs

Take tea at "ten to three" at the pretty village of Grantchester, made famous by poet Rupert Brooke

Take your own snap of the village green in Finchingfield, supposedly the most photographed in England

Cross the moat bridge to look around historic Hedingham Castle and maybe watch a joust or two

Take a river cruise beside the lush meadows at Sudbury

Step into a gorgeous Constable painting by the House on Water Lane, Stratford St Mary

Walk along the banks of the Stour at East Bergholt

Below View across the mill pond on the River Cam, Grantchester, *see p113*

Above View across the graveyard to the windmill at Thaxted, built by local farmer John Webb at the turn of the 19th century, see p114

Below The Bridge of Sighs built in 1831, St. John's College, Cambridge, see p112

PLAN YOUR DRIVE

Start/finish: Cambridge to East Bergholt.

Number of days: 3–4 days, allowing at least a half day in Cambridge.

Distance: About 110 miles (177 km).

Road conditions: Good, well-paved, and well-marked. Off the main roads, lanes are narrow and can be busy.

When to go: Best from April to October as the weather is generally more pleasant and the countryside green and blooming.

Opening times: Museums and attractions are generally open 10am–5pm, but close earlier (or are closed altogether) Nov–Easter. Shop times are longer. Churches are usually open until dusk.

Main market days: Cambridge: Farmers' Market, Sun; **Saffron Walden**: Market (crafts, farm produce, etc), Tue & Sat; **Thaxted**: Market, Fri am; **Sudbury**: Market Thu & Sat; **Long Melford**: Farmers' Market, 3rd Sat of month.

Shopping: Long Melford is famous for its antiques, arts and crafts shops.

Major festivals: Cambridge: Summer Music Festival, mid-Jul to early Aug; Folk Festival, end Jul/Aug; **Thaxted**: Music Festival, end June/early July; Sudbury: Festival of Music, Speech and Dance, last week Feb & Mar.

DAY TRIP OPTIONS

Cambridge merits the best part of a day to tour its **colleges, galleries, churches**, and **picnic** on a **punt**, then head to pretty Grantchester for tea. For quintessential England, see Saffron Walden with its quirky **museum**, then tour the grand **mansion** Audley End, the **church** of Thaxted, Finchingfield **village green**, and the **ruins** of Hedingham Castle. **Sources of artistic inspiration** abound here, from **Long Melford**, with its two great halls linked to children's books, to the charming **villages of Constable Country**, which, with their cottages, churches, galleries and beautiful scenery, have all been immortalized in Constable's paintings. For full details, see p117.

Above Gothic cloisters at St. John's College, Cambridge University

VISITING CAMBRIDGE

Parking
Cambridge is not car-friendly and much of the center is pedestrianized. Park in one of the five park-and-ride lots ringing the city or, for the most central parking lot, follow signs to Grand Arcade.

Tourist Information
The Old Library, Wheeler Street, CB2 3QB; 08712 268 006; www.visitcambridge.org

College Opening
Visiting times vary from college to college, and some charge for entrance at certain times. Colleges may be closed to visitors in the exam period (Easter–Jul).

Punting
A plethora of firms offer chauffeur tours and self-punting. Well-established outfits include **Scudamore's** *(01223 359 750; www.scudamores.com)* and **Cambridge Chauffeur Punts** *(01223 354 164; www.punting-in-cambridge.co.uk)*.

WHERE TO STAY

CAMBRIDGE

Hotel du Vin & Bistro *expensive*
Choose from 41 rooms in a marvelous old building at the heart of the city. Emphasis on creature comforts, and on bistro classics in the restaurant.
15–19 Trumpington Street, CB2 1QA; 01223 227 330; www.hotelduvin.com

Hotel Felix *expensive*
This highly regarded hotel offers Victorian elegance overlaid with modern chic. Lovely bedrooms and bathrooms, large grounds, and local produce on the menu in the Graffiti Restaurant.
Whitehouse Lane, CB3 0LX; 01223 277 977; www.hotelfelix.co.uk

Where to Stay: inexpensive, under £80; moderate, £80–£150; expensive, over £150

❶ Cambridge
Cambridgeshire

This vibrant city – famed the world over for its medieval university – offers enrapturing architecture, a rich historic fabric, green spaces, and many activities for the visitor. Cambridge stands on the River Cam, amid beautiful green countryside. Dominated by its 31 colleges, the city enjoys the buzz generated by a large student population.

A three-hour walking tour

From the Grand Arcade parking lot turn right into Corn Exchange St and left into Wheeler St to pick up a map at the **Tourist Information Centre** ①. Turn right, then left onto King's Parade. After St. Catharine's College turn right onto Silver St. As you cross the bridge look right for the **Mathematical Bridge** ②, designed by William Etheridge and first built by James Essex the Younger in 1749. Constructed without nails, this wooden bridge was the first in the world to be designed according to mathematical analysis. To the left, next to the Anchor pub, there is punt rental on the River Cam. On the far side of the bridge, the walk leads via a footpath to the right along **The Backs** ③, with unmissable rear views of the colleges of Queens', King's, Clare, and Trinity Hall. At Trinity, where the path ends, continue along Queens Rd, then bear right on Northampton St. On the left, at the junction with Honey Hill, is **Kettle's Yard** ④ *(open Tue–Sun pm; www.kettlesyard.co.uk)*, for 16 years home to Harold Stanley Ede, the Tate Gallery's first modern art curator. Ring

Wrought-iron gate, Cambridge

the bell to explore the little museum, filled with paintings, sculptures, and found objects from Ede's collection. Behind is Cambridge St. Peter, the city's second-oldest church, and next door is the **Cambridge and County Folk Museum** ⑤ *(closed Sun am, Mon)*, where 20,000 objects and documents recall rural life in Cambridgeshire. Cross Northampton St, turn right onto Magdalene St and cross the bridge (punts can be rented here). In the Second Court of Magdalene College on the left is **Pepys Library** ⑥ *(closed Sun am, Mon)*, housing the diaries of Samuel Pepys, bequeathed to the college in 1703. Back on Magdalene St by Bridge St, on the right, are some fine half-timbered Tudor houses – erotic carvings hint that one may have been a brothel. At the corner of St. Johns St stands the **Church of the Holy Sepulchre** ⑦, one of four Norman round churches in England, dating from the 12th century. Head down St. Johns St for **St. John's College** ⑧, founded in 1511 by Lady Margaret Beaufort, mother of Henry VII, and enter First Court, the oldest part of the college. Signs lead to St. John's Chapel, designed by Sir George

Below Grantchester church, mentioned in one of Rupert Brooke's most famous poems

Left St. John's College and the romantic Bridge of Sighs, Cambridge

EAT AND DRINK

CAMBRIDGE

Fitzbillies *inexpensive*
A Cambridge institution established in 1922, this bakery is famed for its Chelsea buns, "probably the stickiest in the world". *52 Trumpington St, CB2 1RG; 01223 352 500; www.fitzbillies.co.uk; dinner served Fri & Sat only*

The Bun Shop *inexpensive*
Enjoy tapas-style global cuisine in a pub as idiosyncratic as its name. You might try garlic chicken, Merlot-braised chorizo, Cajun mussels or gorgonzola gnocchi. *1 King Street, CB1 1LH; 01223 366 866; www.thebunshop.com*

Cotto *moderate*
This café, deli, restaurant and gallery makes much of local organic produce. Dishes might include smoky celeriac and hazelnut soup or wood-roasted mackerel. *183 East Road, CB1 1BG; 01223 302 010; www.cottocambridge.co.uk; dinner served Thu–Sat; closed Sun*

Midsummer House *expensive*
Garlanded with rosettes and stars, this riverside restaurant is recommended for its professionalism and highly imaginative cuisine from a fixed-price menu. *Midsummer Common, CB4 1HA; 01223 369 299; www.midsummerhouse.co.uk*

GRANTCHESTER

The Orchard Tea Garden *inexpensive*
Tread in the footsteps of Rupert Brooke and relax over traditional tea or lunch in this idyllic spot, with its historic wooden pavilion and glorious orchard setting. *45–7 Mill Way, CB3 1RS; 01223 551 125; www.orchard-grantchester.com; closed over Christmas*

Gilbert Scott in 1863–9. Here a statue of William Wilberforce broods on the evils of slavery. Spanning the Cam is the Bridge of Sighs, designed by Henry Hutchinson in 1827. Turn right out of St. John's and enter **Trinity College** ⑨, founded in 1546 by Henry VIII, through its Great Gate. The Wren library was completed in 1695 to designs by the famous architect. Turn right out of Trinity to head back to **King's College** ⑩. Visit the chapel, probably the city's most spectacular building, to marvel at the magical architecture of its ceiling.

🚗 *Follow ring road to Trumpington St, signed M11 south. At Trumpington turn right to Grantchester. Use pay parking lot and continue on foot.*

② Grantchester

"Stands the church clock at ten to three, and is there honey still for tea?" wrote Rupert Brooke (1887–1915) in his gentle satire of English life, *The Old Vicarage, Grantchester*. It's a pretty village with thatched cottages and historic inns, not yet subsumed by its larger and more lively academic neighbor. See the memorial to the poet Brooke, and the Old Vicarage that was for a time his home; take a snap of the clock at ten to three – and enjoy traditional afternoon tea at the old Orchard Tea Garden.

🚗 *Return to the A1309 at Trumpington, turn right, then left to Great Shelford on A1301. After four roundabouts, take B184 to Saffron Walden. Follow signs for pay parking or look for free short-stay parking in the town center.*

Below Punters seen from The Backs as they glide past King's College, Cambridge

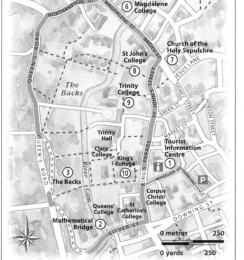

Above left Thaxted's picturesque 19th-century windmill **Above top right** The Tudor-style town hall in the heart of Saffron Walden, built in 1761 **Above right** Thatched cottage in traditional Suffolk pink, Thaxted

④ Audley End
Essex; CB11 4JF

Henry VIII gave Walden Abbey to Sir Thomas Audley, who transformed it into a splendid mansion *(closed Mon, Tue; www.english-heritage.org.uk)*. The third Baron Baybrooke, who came into the property in 1825, brought in works by Holbein, Canaletto and many more. There are 30 rooms to be seen, some designed by Robert Adam, as well as parkland designed by landscape gardener "Capability" Brown, and a Victorian kitchen garden.

🚗 **Return to Saffron Walden and take B184 south (clearly marked) to Thaxted. Park on the street.**

③ Saffron Walden
Essex; CB10

A gem of a medieval market town, Saffron Walden sits on the River Cam, in unspoiled Essex countryside. Dating in parts from the 12th century, the town has many half-timbered buildings, although the Tudor-style **town hall** was built as late as 1761. Opened in 1835, **Saffron Walden Museum** *(open daily; www.visitsaffronwalden.gov.uk)* is one of Britain's oldest public museums. It stands in a meadow, beside the ruins of 12th-century Walden castle and offers eclectic collections – from Egyptian sarcophagi and mammoth tusks to displays about the people and natural history of the region.

🚗 **From the center, follow signs on B1383 to Audley End and parking lot.**

Below Audley End, one of the finest Jacobean houses in England

⑤ Thaxted
Essex; CM6

A pleasing, small town which does not go out of its way to pull in tourists, but nevertheless boasts ancient, timber-framed houses and a 14th-century **Guildhall** complete with jail *(open to visitors for occasional exhibitions)*. There's also a windmill built in 1804, almshouses and, on the hilltop, the magnificent **Church of St. John the Baptist**. Dating to the 14th century, the "Cathedral of Essex" is held by some to be the finest parish church in the country. The town's famous residents have included composer Gustav Holst, who lived here 1914–25, when writing

VISITING SUDBURY

Tourist Information
Town Hall, Market Hill, CO10 1TL; 01787 881 320

River Stour Trust
The Granary, Quay Lane, CO10 2AN; 01787 313 199; www.riverstourtrust.org

WHERE TO STAY

SAFFRON WALDEN

Saffron Hotel *moderate*
This classic market-town hotel, dating back to the 16th century, offers 16 comfortable ensuite rooms in a handy central location.
8–12 High Street, CB10 1AZ; 01799 522 676; www.saffronhotel.co.uk

THAXTED

Swan Hotel *moderate*
A traditional coaching inn, this hotel has recently had a major refurbishment and provides spruce, comfortable accommodation at very reasonable prices. Check for special offers.
Bull Ring, CM6 2PL; 01371 830 321; www.swanhotel-thaxted.com

Where to Stay: inexpensive, under £80; moderate, £80–£150; expensive, over £150

his *Planets Suite,* and highwayman Dick Turpin (1705–39), whose cottage can be seen on the alley up to the church.

🚗 *Take Bardfield Rd right, marked The Bardfields, to Great Bardfield and B1057 left to Finchingfield. Park on street.*

⑥ Finchingfield

Essex; CM7

A picture-postcard village, reputedly the most photographed in England, with thatched cottages, village green, duck pond, windmill and Norman Church of St. John the Baptist. Dodie Smith, author of *The One Hundred and One Dalmatians,* once lived here.

🚗 *Cross the bridge and turn right past church to Wethersfield, head east along the High St to Sible Hedingham. Go left on A1017 and almost immediately right on B1058. Follow signs to parking lot.*

Above Ancient mulberry tree in the grounds of Gainsborough's House, Sudbury

⑦ Hedingham Castle

Essex; CO9 3DJ

Cross a dry moat by way of a Tudor bridge to reach the four-storey remains of this 12th-century castle *(mid-Apr–Oct: open Sun–Thu; www.hedinghamcastle.co. uk)*, with its tall keep, banqueting hall, and minstrels' gallery. The grounds and surrounding woodlands are especially lovely in spring when carpeted with bluebells. In summer, there may be jousting and other spectacles.

🚗 *Take B1058, then A131 to Sudbury. Join one-way system and follow signs to lot by Tourist Information Center.*

⑧ Sudbury

Suffolk; CO10

This ancient Suffolk wool town, amid sublime countryside in the Stour Valley, boasts no fewer than three medieval churches, a Victorian corn exchange,

and a **bronze statue** of the painter Thomas Gainsborough (1727–88), which presides over the market square. Modern commercial development has been at some cost to historic charm, but **Gainsborough's House** *(closed Sun and Christmas; www.gainsborough.org),* a typical Suffolk building, has a unique collection of the work of this master of portraiture and landscape. Loaned works and local artists are frequently on display, too. In the walled garden stands a 400-year-old mulberry tree. South of town, there are pleasant meadows to picnic in and river cruise boats operate from the quayside, run by the **River Stour Trust**.

🚗 *Follow signs round one-way system to Bury St Edmunds, A134. Branch onto B1064 to Long Melford.*

Above The imposing keep of 12th-century Hedingham Castle

Above War Memorial by the village green and pond at Finchingfield

EAT AND DRINK

SAFFRON WALDEN

Kim's Coffee House *inexpensive*
Home-baked cakes and scones, a wide choice of sandwiches and filled baguettes prepared to order and a vast choice of leaf teas in this friendly establishment in Georgian premises.
5 Hill Street, CB10 1EH; closed Sun

AROUND SAFFRON WALDEN

Cricketers *moderate*
Locally sourced, seasonal, organic food takes pride of place at this 16th-century inn, run by the parents of TV chef Jamie Oliver, 12 minutes' drive from Saffron Walden on the B1383/B10.8. The menu features chicken, "lots of fish," and homemade sausages.
Wicken Road, Clavering; CB11 4QT; 01799 550 442; www.thecricketers. co.uk; closed 25 & 26 Dec

CASTLE HEDINGHAM

Bell Inn *inexpensive–moderate*
Beamed and timbered 15th-century real-ale pub in extensive garden, serving freshly-prepared, honest food, much of it locally sourced. Home-made soup, sausages with mustard mash. Monday night is barbecued fish night – phone ahead to book your fish.
CO9 3EJ; 01787 460350; www.hedinghambell.co.uk

AROUND SUDBURY

The Henny Swan *moderate*
This inn with garden on the banks of the Stour, south of Sudbury, has numerous awards for its stylish gastropub cooking. For a novelty, book to come here for lunch from Sudbury aboard the eight-seater electric boat, the *Rosette.*
Henny St, Great Henny, CO10 7LS; 01787 269 238; www.hennyswan.com

Eat and Drink: inexpensive, under £25; moderate, £25–£50; expensive, over £50

Above Tudor mansion of Kentwell Hall, built in 1554, Long Melford

WHERE TO STAY

LONG MELFORD

Bull Hotel *moderate*
There are 25 comfortable ensuite rooms at this old but friendly and comfortable half-timbered inn set in a central location.
Hall Street, CO10 9JG; 01787 378 494; www.thebull-hotel.com

AROUND LONG MELFORD

Angel *moderate*
Nothing grand here, but there's decent pub accommodation and obliging service in this warm and friendly inn (first licensed in 1420) on the village square. Head north out of Long Melford on the A134 and turn right on Bridge St Rd at Bridge Street to get to Lavenham.
Market Place, Lavenham, CO10 9QZ; 01787 247 388; www.maypolehotels. com/angelhotel

DEDHAM

Dedham Hall and Fountain House *moderate*
This historic manor house hotel and restaurant set in expansive grounds also has an artists' studio and art school housed in a converted Dutch barn. The hotel offers 18 pleasant rooms (13 in an annexe for painting holidays). The place is run with a generous ethos.
Brook Street, CO7 6AD; 01206 323 027; www.dedhamhall.co.uk

Sun Inn *moderate–expensive*
There are five bedrooms furnished to a high standard in this 15th-century inn. The food on offer is good, too. Expect imaginative breakfasts and a restaurant featuring modern British cooking. Also prepares delicious picnics to order.
High Street, CO7 6DF; 01206 323 351; www.thesuninndedham.com

Right St. Mary's Church, Stoke-by-Nayland, a typical Suffolk "wool" church

9 Long Melford
Essex; CO10 9AA

This village is aptly named, with its long high street lined with specialist and independent shops, galleries and antiques emporia, bars, restaurants, and old inns. **Holy Trinity Church**, dating from the late 15th century, is grand and glorious and the **Old Bull Inn** (c. 1450) once played host to Beatle John Lennon. Delightful Georgian and Queen Anne cottages overlook the green, as does turreted **Melford Hall** (1554) *(open late Mar–late Oct: Wed–Mon pm; www.nationaltrust. org.uk)*, where Queen Elizabeth I once slept and where children's author Beatrix Potter sketched for her books by the fishponds. Then, it's into the car again and – "Parp, parp!" – head north, following tourist signs to the setting for the film *Toad of Toad Hall*. **Kentwell Hall** *(check online calendar for opening times: www.kentwell.co.uk)* is a moated, red-brick Tudor mansion, with gardens and a rare-breeds farm – home to Tamworth pigs, near-extinct Norfolk Horn sheep, and huge Suffolk Punch

horses. The humor and hospitality of Patrick Phillips – owner since 1970 – is everywhere in evidence.

🚗 *Head back towards Sudbury on B1064, then follow one-way system to A134 (signed Colchester). Turn off left onto B1068 to Stoke-by-Nayland. Park in the center.*

10 Stoke-by-Nayland
Suffolk; CO6 4QU

Another wonderful Suffolk village, on a hilltop in Constable Country, Stoke-by-Nayland has plenty of attractive half-timbered and traditional pink-washed cottages. **St. Mary's Church**, which features in a number of John Constable's paintings, was built from the profits of the local wool trade and dates mainly from the 14th and 16th centuries. It has a fine octagonal font and a well-preserved oak door, adorned with a Tree of Jesse.

🚗 *Rejoin B1068 to Higham. Here, turn right and right to Stratford St Mary. At the village sign turn left to parking lot.*

Constable Country

"The sound of water escaping from mill dams, willows, old rotten planks, slimy posts and brickwork, I love such things. These scenes made me a painter." So wrote John Constable (1776–1837), who would go on to be recognized, with JMW Turner, as one of the foremost landscape artists of the 19th century. The dramatic vistas, farmlands, water meadows and marshes of the Stour Valley and Dedham Vale, the big skies and distant church spires, all evoke Constable's true spirit.

Where to Stay: inexpensive, under £80; moderate, £80–£150; expensive, over £150

⑪ Stratford St Mary
Suffolk; CO7 6YG

The southernmost village in Suffolk, Stratford St Mary is another "Constable Country" location. On the road in, look out for the fine pair of striped half-timbered houses, the **Ancient House** and **Priest's House** *(not open to the public)*, opposite the Post Office. Continue under the A12 to find flint-faced **St. Mary's Church**. The building is mainly 15th century, but parts of it may date back to the 1200s. Further along the road (once known as Water Lane) stands **Ravenys**, a private house immortalized in Constable's painting *A House on Water Lane*.

🚗 *Continue on B1029 over A12 to Dedham and park by church.*

⑫ Dedham
Essex; CO7 6AZ

This village retains some fine timber-framed and early-Georgian buildings, and the **Church of St. Mary the Virgin**, built in 1492, whose graceful 131-ft (40-m) tower appears in Constable's paintings – his work *The Ascension* is on display inside. The painter attended the **Old Grammar School**, founded by Elizabeth I. Head east on Brook St and follow the road to the **Sir Alfred Munnings Art Museum** *(open Apr–Sep: Sun, Wed pm; Jul, Sep: open Wed, Thu, Sat,*

Sun pm; www.siralfredmunnings.co.uk), a showcase for this artist, famous for his studies of racehorses, who was also an excellent painter of landscapes.

🚗 *From the center, take Manningtree Rd, left at T-junction, left onto A137, and left at roundabout (still A137). Go left on B1070 to East Bergholt. Park by church.*

⑬ East Bergholt
Suffolk; CO7 6UP

The birthplace of John Constable, this village boasts more pubs than any other in Suffolk. The "ruined" flint towers of the **Church of St. Mary the Virgin** were never completed. The bells, however, had already been cast and now hang in a timber bell cage dating from 1531 – they are rung on Sunday mornings. Head down Flatford Rd (clearly signed) to visit **Willy Lott's Cottage** and **Flatford Mill** – settings for two of Constable's famous paintings, *The Hay Wain* and *The Mill Stream*. Nearby, there are lovely walks on both sides of the River Stour and rowing boats can be rented for waterborne adventures. The lovely **East Bergholt Place** *(Mar–Sep: open daily; www.placeforplants.co.uk)*, just off the B1070, described as "a Cornish garden in Suffolk," and laid out 1900–14, features an arboretum and specialist plant center in a Victorian walled garden.

Above left 16th-century half-timbered house, Stratford St Mary **Above center** Sign for a 15th-century coaching inn in pretty Dedham **Above right** View of the River Stour from the bridge, East Bergholt

EAT AND DRINK

LONG MELFORD

Bizzi Beans Café *inexpensive*
Handy for Kentwell Hall, this place offers homemade scones and cakes – including boiled fruitcake. Enjoy, too, baguettes and rolls, filled with free-range chicken and eggs, and speciality coffee. *Cherry Lane Garden Centre, High Street, CO10 9DH; 01787 464 800; www.bizzibeans.net*

Scutchers *moderate*
Tip-top cooking from a fairly short *à la carte* menu offers dishes such as fillet of wild halibut on a prawn, saffron and bacon chowder and pan-fried calves' liver with onion gravy. There's also a choice of two fixed-price menus. *Westgate St, CO10 9DP; 01787 310 200; www.scutchers.com*

STOKE-BY-NAYLAND

Crown Inn *moderate*
A changing menu based on local ingredients includes "catch of the day," Bradfield potatoes and Colchester asparagus, washed down with local ales. Upmarket but friendly. Eleven bedrooms and great breakfasts. *Park St, CO6 4SE; 01206 262 001; www.crowninn.net*

DAY TRIP OPTIONS
Take in the area's wealth of beautiful and historic buildings alongside idyllic English scenery.

A University Education
In Cambridge ❶, enjoy the walk around stunning architecture, some of it over 800 years old. Picnic and punt along the Cam, then drive the short distance to Grantchester ❷ for tea, before returning to Cambridge.

Follow Trumpington St, there and back.

Quintessential England
Staying at Saffron Walden ❸, see its town hall and museum, before touring the mansion at Audley End ❹. Then off to Thaxted ❺, for more half-timbered buildings and church. Drive on to pretty Finchingfield ❻, and finish the day with a visit to Hedingham Castle ❼.

Follow the drive instructions.

Creative Inspiration
From Long Melford ❾, see the two great halls with links to popular children's books. Visit Sudbury ❽, to learn about Gainsborough, then take the Constable tour through Stoke-by-Nayland ❿, Stratford St Mary ⑪, and Dedham ⑫, and East Bergholt ⑬, to see the places and countryside that inspired the great artist.

Follow the drive instructions.

The Broads and the North Norfolk Coast

From Norwich to Heacham

Highlights

- **Historic county town**
  Begin your tour with an exploration of endearing Norwich – the old county town of Norfolk that "has everything"

- **Wonderful waterworld**
  Discover the world-famous Norfolk Broads, filled with history and wildlife under the big skies of East Anglia

- **Seaside secrets**
  Escape the crowds on open sandy beaches, pretty fishing villages and quintessentially English seaside resorts

- **Coastal cuisine**
  Eat Cromer crab fresh off the boats, Stewkey Blue cockles on the beach, and fish and chips on the pier

Glorious sunrise scenery under the wide open skies of the Norfolk Broads

The Broads and the North Norfolk Coast

This drive begins in the bustling and historic county town of Norwich before cutting through the beautiful Norfolk Broads National Park, where the flat still waters magnify the sunlight streaming from wide skies. Then it heads to the sea, simply following the spectacular coastline west. It's one of the few places in the country where you can see the sun both rise and set in the ocean in a spectacular display of pinks, oranges and mauves. And if the drive ever feels a long way from the sea, simply turn off the main road to find safe, sandy beaches, fishing villages and old-fashioned English resorts. The trip is clearly best enjoyed in fine weather, with glorious opportunities for swimming and sunbathing, but lowering skies and storm-tossed seas also make for dramatic scenery. Walkers, birdwatchers, naturalists and photographers will be in their element among unspoilt salt marshes and wild shores.

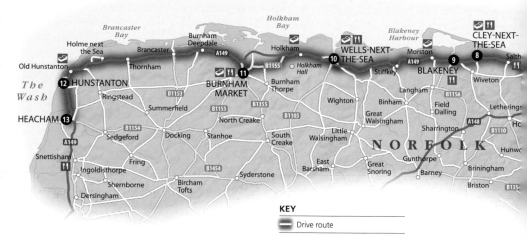

KEY

Drive route

ACTIVITIES

Canoe along the tiny creeks and shallow lakes of the Norfolk Broads from Horning

Hunt for crabs and shrimps in tidal pools at Mundesley

Catch a traditional end-of-the-pier show at Cromer

Walk along the Norfolk Coast Path at Sheringham

See a bittern or marsh harrier in the salt marshes at Cley-next-the-Sea

Take a boat to Blakeney Point to see the migrant terns, dunlin and wigeon and the resident seal colony

Picnic in the glorious sand dunes at Wells-next-the-Sea

Eat a cup of delicious Stewkey Blue cockles doused in plenty of vinegar, while sitting on the beach

Go shopping in Burnham Market, known as "Chelsea on Sea"

Watch the sun sink into the sea at stripy Hunstanton

Below Norwich's Art Nouveau Royal Parade, first opened in 1899, *see p122*

Above View from the pier of Cromer beach, washed by the North Sea, *see p124*

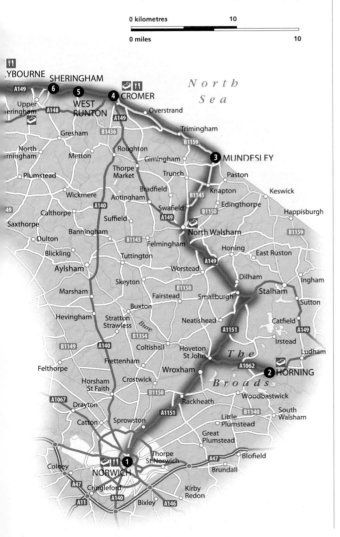

PLAN YOUR DRIVE

Start/finish: Norwich to Heacham.

Number of days: 3 days.

Distances: Around 100 miles (160 km).

Road conditions: Generally well-maintained and unchallenging.

When to go: From late May to September is best for sun, sand, sea.

Opening times: Galleries, museums, and attractions are generally open 10am–5pm, but often close earlier Nov–Easter. Shops are often open longer. Churches are usually open until dusk.

Main market days: Norwich: provisions market, Mon–Sat; **North Walsham**: Farmers' Market, 2nd Sat of month: **Cromer**: Fri; **Sheringham**: Sat and Mar–Oct also Wed; **Burnham Market**: Farmer's Market, 1st Sat and 3rd Fri of month; **Hunstanton**: Wed.

Shopping: Norwich has some good shops, especially the Royal Arcade, as does Burnham Market. Find great seafood – Cromer crab, Stewkey Blue cockles, and samphire – on the coast.

Major festivals: Norwich: Norfolk & Norwich Festival, May; Royal Norfolk Show, late Jun; Food Festival & Fringe Festival, Oct; **Cley**: Little Festival of Poetry, Oct; **Wells-next-the-Sea**: Holkham Country Fair, Jul; **Burnham Market**: Flower Show & Carnival, Jul, Concerts & Craft Fair, Aug; **Hunstanton**: Arts Festival, Jun, Jul; **General**: Festival of the Broads, Sep, venues within the National Park.

DAY TRIP OPTIONS

Something for everyone. From Norwich, spend half a day walking in the **historic center**, then go to Horning for a **canoe trail** through the Broads. Nature lovers can get close to some **marine animals,** then try a **boat trip** to see the **birds** and **seals** at Blakeney, and go **birdwatching** on the Cley marshes. Families can visit the **animal sanctuary** at West Runton, enjoy a **train ride** from Sheringham, and inspect the **tanks** at Weybourne. Alternatively, spend the morning at grand **Holkham Hall** before browsing in the shops of Burnham Market and enjoying the **aromas** of a lavender farm. For full details, *see p127*.

Above View to Norwich Cathedral, built in the 11th–12th centuries

VISITING NORWICH

Parking
The city center can be confusing for drivers. The largest central parking lots are Chapelfield and Castle Mall, or use park-and-ride facilities around the city.

Tourist Information
The Forum, Millennium Plane, NR2 1TF;
01603 727 927; www.norwich.gov.uk

WHERE TO STAY

NORWICH

By Appointment *moderate*
Restaurant with five rooms, lavishly furnished with swags and antiques, in three 15th-century merchants' houses. Breakfast menu includes local sausages, field mushrooms and fresh croissants.
25–29 George St, NR3 1AB; 01603 630 730; www.byappointmentnorwich.co.uk

Maids Head *moderate*
With ensuite four-star accommodation and guest parking, this is a handy city-center hotel. It also has a great old bar.
Tombland, NR3 1LB; 0844 855 9120;
www.foliohotels/maidshead

HORNING

Moorhen B&B *inexpensive*
A delightful old guesthouse with two garden rooms and two rooms looking right onto the River Bure.
45 Lower Street, N12 8AA; 01692 631 444; www.themoorhenhorning.co.uk

AROUND MUNDESLEY

Beechwood Hotel *moderate*
This charming, creeper-covered hotel has 17 ensuite rooms just off the A149 in North Walsham, south of Mundesley. The proprietors are friendly and welcoming. It's worth considering the hotel as a dining option, too.
Cromer Road, NR28 0HD; 01692 403 231; www.beechwood-hotel.co.uk

❶ Norwich

Norfolk; NR2 1TF
"Norwich has everything" wrote architectural historian Nikolaus Pevsner in 1962 – a cathedral and castle, grand halls, cobbled streets lined with ancient buildings, museums, theaters, bars, and restaurants, a 900-year-old market, many shops, and two rivers – the Wensum and Yare. The old county town of Norfolk, Norwich makes an ideal base for exploring the East Anglian countryside, the Fens, and Norfolk Broads.

Two-hour walking tour

Start at the magnificent **Cathedral** ①, with the second-tallest spire in the UK. It was built by the Normans 1096–1145, although the spire was not completed until 1480. Flanking the West Door, in niches, are two recent figures by David Holgate who used local people for his models. Turn right into Tombland from **Erpingham Gate** ②, where there is a bust of Edith Cavell, a Norfolk nurse executed by the Germans in World War I for helping British and French soldiers to escape. Turn right into Palace St and left and left again to walk down Quayside, along a short stretch of the Wesum. Take a left on Bridge St and right onto cobbled Elm Hill, lined with cottages and antique shops, noting the tiny **Church of St. Simon and St. Jude** ③, the second most ancient in Norwich. Fork right and right again onto St. Andrew's St and take a left on Bridewell Alley to find the **Bridewell Museum** ④ *(closed for restoration until 2011)*, which tells the story of Norwich. To continue, turn right and walk down

Stained-glass, Norwich Cathedral

Bedford St and Lobster Lane, then left onto Lower Goat Lane; continue to find **City Hall** ⑤ lording it over Market Square. Built in the 1930s, this has the longest balcony in England and its sonorous clock bell – Great George – is the largest in Europe. Descend into the square and head to the right to see the 15th-century **Church of St. Peter Mancroft** ⑥, dedicated to St. Peter and St. Paul, whose symbols appear on either side of the north porch. Wander through the market to emerge on to Gentleman's Walk and pass through the Art Nouveau **Royal Arcade** ⑦, designed by George Skipper and opened in 1899. The arcade is lined with traditional old shops. Exit to see **Norwich Castle** ⑧ *(open daily, pm only on Sun, www.museums.norfolk.gov.uk)*, looming above on a mound, with its Norman keep and garden. From 1345, this served as a prison and place of public execution. Since Victorian times it has been a museum with displays of art, archaeology, and history. Beyond the castle, go left on Market Avenue

Below Cobbled street and traditional shops in Elm Hill, Norwich

Where to Stay: inexpensive, under £80; moderate, £80–£150; expensive, over £150

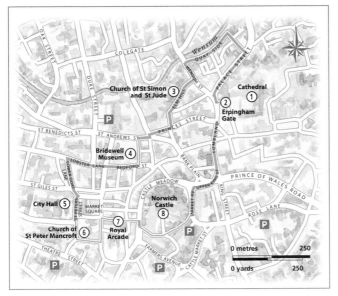

and right on Upper King St, back to Tombland and the cathedral.

🚗 *From the cathedral cross the river to A1151 to Hoveton St John, take a right on A1062; pay parking on the right.*

❷ Horning
Norfolk; NR12 8AA

This pretty village, downriver from charming but busy Wroxham, is blessed with thatched cottages, good shops, waterside inns, and restaurants. The **Galley** deli on Lower Street sells good picnic fare, perfect for an outing on the river. Summer guided canoe tours and trails provide the ideal way to explore the Broads, venturing into peaceful backwaters inaccessible to motor vehicles and walkers – try *01603 499 177; www.thecanoeman.com.*

🚗 *Return to Hoveton St John and turn right on to A1151, turn left onto A149; continue onto B1145 to Mundesley.*

❸ Mundesley
Norfolk; NR11 8JH

The golden, sandy beaches at this old-fashioned resort, with its gaily painted beach huts, are among the finest in Norfolk. At low tide, children splash around in the sun-warmed tidal pools. Above the beach there's a 10-ft (3-m) bomb-shaped **war memorial** to the 36 men killed clearing mines from the Norfolk coast after World War II and tiny **Mundesley Maritime Museum**

The Norfolk Broads

Britain's largest nationally protected wetland has a network of rivers, lakes (broads), and marshes that abound with rare flora and fauna. It's a haven for birds such as wigeon, teal, marsh harriers, or bitterns, plants such as the fen orchid or ragged robin, and large butterflies such as the swallowtail. Visitors can fish, take a boat trip, cycle, or walk through watery landscapes, admiring the villages, churches, and windmills. Contact *Broads Authority, 18 Colegate, Norwich, NR3 1BQ; 01603 610 734; www.broads-authority.gov.uk.*

(open May–Sep: daily) in a former coastguards' look-out, possibly the smallest museum in the country.

🚗 *Head northwest on the B1159, the coast road to Cromer.*

Below Thatched cottage in the attractive riverside village of Horning

BOAT TRIPS

For trips to Blakeney Point to see the seal and seabird colonies, try **Beans Boats** *(01263 740 038; www. beansboattrips.co.uk)* or **Temples Seal Trips** *(01263 740 791; www. sealtrips.co.uk)* at Morston Quay or **Bishops Boats** *(01263 740 753; www. bishopsboats.com)* at Blakeney Quay.

WHERE TO STAY

CROMER

Cliftonville Hotel *moderate*
Enjoy sea views in this Edwardian hotel – there's a good restaurant, open to non-residents – with a fine minstrels' gallery.
Seafront, NR27 9AS; 01263 512 543; www.cliftonvillehotel.co.uk

AROUND SHERINGHAM

Dales Country House Hotel *expensive*
Twenty good ensuite rooms are available here, in a former rectory in grounds by Sheringham Pk, south of town on B1157.
Lodge Hill, Upper Sheringham, NR26 8TJ; 01263 824 555; www.dalescountryhouse.co.uk

WEYBOURNE

Weybourne Forest Lodges *moderate*
Well-equipped, comfortable lodges in in a delightful sylvan setting.
Sandy Hill Lane, NR25 7HW; 01263 588 440; www.weybourneforestlodges.co.uk

CLEY-NEXT-THE-SEA

Cley Windmill
This lovely mill offers B&B or self-catering facilities and enjoy home-cooked dinner by candlelight in the dining room.
Cley Windmill, NR25 7RP; 01263 740 209; www.cleymill.co.uk

AROUND BLAKENEY

Morston Hall *expensive*
A luxurious Jacobean manor house with great sea views and tip-top food.
Morston, Holt, NR25 7AA (7 miles/ 12km on the A149); 01263 741 041; www.morstonhall.com

Below Traditional seaside pier with theater at Cromer beach

Above left Historic station on the North Norfolk Railway Poppy Line, Sheringham **Above top right** Horse grazing at the Hillside Animal and Shire Horse Sanctuary **Above right** Rhododendrons at Sheringham Park

④ Cromer
Norfolk; NR27 0AH

A resort of note since the 18th century, Cromer is best known for its delicious crabs. From April to September, boats ply to and from crab banks out to sea, landing the local delicacy. Along the front, tall Victorian houses look out to the ocean, over the sand-and-shingle beach. Overlooking the beach stands the **RNLI Henry Blogg Museum** *(closed Mon; Dec & Jan)* offering an interesting history of the RNLI and a cake in the café upstairs. The pier's **Pavilion Theatre** still hosts traditional end-of-the-pier shows. In town, the tower of **St. Peter and St. Paul Church** soars to a stunning (49 m) 160 ft and may be climbed at certain times for breathtaking views over the area.

🚗 *Head west on A149 to West Runton.*

⑤ West Runton
Norfolk; NR27 9QH

This attractive village is home to the **Hillside Animal and Shire Horse Sanctuary** *(Jun–Aug: open Sun–Fri; Apr–May, Sep–Oct: open Sun–Thu: closed winter; www.hillside.org.uk)*. The rescued animals include some magnificent heavy work horses, ponies, pigs, cattle, goats, alpacas, rabbits, ducks, and hens – many of them up for "adoption" (sponsorship). There's much to delight young children, and the wonderful collection of old carts, farm machinery, and wooden caravans, will occupy older minds.

🚗 *Keep west on A149 to Sheringham.*

⑥ Sheringham
Norfolk; NR26 8RA

A former fishing village, Sheringham is now a thriving, very English holiday resort, with clifftop gardens, arcades and golden sands. Its situation on the Norfolk Coast Path makes the resort an ideal base for walkers. From the A149 follow signs to **Sheringham Park** *(mid-Mar–Sep: open daily; Oct: open Wed–Sun; Nov–mid-Mar: open Sat & Sun)*, with paths through parks and National Trust gardens landscaped by Humphry Repton (1752–1818). Take a trip by steam or vintage diesel train on the **North Norfolk Railway Poppy Line** *(Jun–Sep: open daily; check at other*

times; 01263 820 808; www.nnrailway.co.
uk). With a "Rover" ticket for a day's
travel, board and alight at will. There
is a charming station building,
complete with period furnishings, at
the western terminus, just 5 miles
(8 km) from Sheringham and not far
from the flower-filled Georgian town
of **Holt**, a repeated finalist in the
Anglia in Bloom contest.

🚗 *Continue on A149 to Weybourne.*

Above Little station on the North Norfolk Railway
Poppy Line, Weybourne

⑦ Weybourne
Norfolk; NR25 7SZ
This attractive village (pronounced
"Webbon'") sits amid farm and heath
land and has a famously steep, pebbly
beach. It also boasts a delightful inn, a
historic station on the Poppy Line and
the **Muckleburgh Collection** *(Apr–Nov:
open daily; www.muckleburgh.co.uk)*,
Britain's largest private collection of
military vehicles and equipment.

🚗 *Take A149 west, via Salthouse,
stopping off at Cookies Crab Shop.*

⑧ Cley-next-the-Sea
Norfolk; NR25 7SZ
A thriving port in medieval times, Cley
is now some distance inland. In its
heyday, it exported wool to the
Netherlands – and imported curved
gables, Flemish bricks, and pantiles,
which mix happily with Georgian
architecture. **Cley Windmill** is an 18th-
century mill that has been converted
into a B&B with views of the salt marsh
and bird sanctuary. The owners usually
let visitors have a look inside. Visit the
Norfolk Wildlife Trust visitor centre on
the marshes, east of town. Facilities
include a remote camera, a café, hides
for bird watching, and an audio trail.

🚗 *Continue on A149 to Blakeney.*

⑨ Blakeney
Norfolk; NR25 7SZ
Like Cley, this was a busy port in
ancient times but, since the harbour
has silted up, only small craft can
navigate the creeks. The village is
delightful, with attractive flint cottages,
a 14th-century guildhall and places to
shop, eat, drink and stay. However, the
greatest draw for visitors are the boat
trips to **Blakeney Point**, which put out
from here and neighbouring Morston,
to the west. These trips, lasting one to
two hours, provide an excellent way to
view seabirds and basking seals in
their natural environment, without
unduly disturbing them. The seal
colony – a mix of Common and Grey
seals – numbers some 500. Common
seals have their young or pups Jun–
Aug; the Greys Nov–Jan.

🚗 *Take the A149 west to Stiffkey
(pronounced "Stewkey"), famous for its
cockles, with pretty flint cottages, salt
marshes, and reed beds.*

Above Sign for the village of Blakeney
painted according to Norfolk tradition

EAT AND DRINK

CROMER

**Rocket House Café and
Restaurant** *inexpensive*
Visit this stylish place above the RNLI
Henry Blogg Museum (with lift access),
for coffee and a cake, or a meal of local
seafood with unsurpassed sea views.
*The Gangway, Promenade, NR27 9ET;
01263 514 334*

WEYBOURNE

The Ship Inn *inexpensive–moderate*
Simplicity is key in this attractive old pub.
The short menu features delicious local
dishes such as seafood chowder.
*The Street, NR25 7SZ; 01263 588 721;
www.shipinnweybourne.co.uk*

AROUND WEYBOURNE

Cookies Crab Shop *inexpensive*
On the A149 to Cley, this is a café-shop;
buy some samphire and try the soups
and local fish. Bring your own alcohol.
*The Green, Salthouse, NR25 7AJ; 01263
740 352*

CLEY-NEXT-THE-SEA

The George *inexpensive–moderate*
Good, honest fare with a few flourishes
can be enjoyed in this birdwatchers'
paradise. Consider the rooms, too.
*High Street, NR25 7RN; 01263 740 652;
www.thegeorgehotelatcley.co.uk*

BLAKENEY

The Blakeney White Horse
inexpensive–moderate
This well-situated pub offers seasonal
seafood fresh off the boat, good local
produce and homemade bread and
desserts – and it also has a few rooms.
*4 High Street, NR 25 7AL; 01263 740
574; www.blakeneywhitehorse.co.uk*

Left Cley Windmill, set on the salt marshes and
popular with artists

Eat and Drink: inexpensive, under £25; moderate, £25–£50; expensive, over £50

Above Lobster and crab boats at the quayside Wells-next-the-Sea

WHERE TO STAY

WELLS-NEXT-THE-SEA

Globe Inn
Seven bright and airy ensuite rooms are available in this refurbished inn. The breakfast menu includes Cley smoked haddock with poached egg. Good-value bar snacks all day.
The Buttlands, N23 1EU; 01328 710 206; www.holkham.co.uk/globe

Victoria Hotel *moderate–expensive*
A historic hotel on the edge of the Holkham Estate, this has real-ale bars on the ground floor and an upmarket restaurant. The 10 ensuite rooms are beautifully done and some have views over the marshes. There are also three glorious self-catering lodges available.
Park Road, NR23 1RG; 01328 711 008; www.holkham.co.uk

BURNHAM MARKET

The Jockey *inexpensive–moderate*
This pub offers four decent bedrooms with ensuite shower rooms in the heart of this lovely village. There are hearty breakfasts and bar meals that make use of local ingredients.
Creake Road, PE31 8EN; 01328 738 321; www.thejockeyburnhammarket.co.uk

HUNSTANTON

Neptune Inn *moderate*
There are seven pleasant ensuite rooms at this handsome 18th-century coaching inn. The Michelin-starred restaurant uses mainly Norfolk ingredients in the restaurant and bar.
85 Old Hunstanton Road, PE36 6HZ; 01485 532 122; www.theneptune.co.uk

Right Winding creek through salt marshes into the harbor at Wells-next-the-Sea

⑩ Wells-next-the-Sea
Norfolk; NR23 1AN
A popular resort town, Wells got its name from the many clear springs in the area. Today, as a result of silting, it is more "near" than "next" the sea – vessels must sail some way up inlets to berth here, but the harbor is still a great attraction. Stroll up to the grassy Georgian square known as The Buttlands, for a drink in either of the village inns, the **Crown** or the **Globe**, or buy a picnic from the **Wells Deli** and head for the beach. Travel in style on the tiny, narrow-gauge, steam or diesel **Wells Harbour Railway** *(seasonal service)*. The beautiful sands are backed by expansive dunes and cooling pines.

Wells-next-the-Sea village sign

Just west, neighboring **Holkham Hall Estate** *(open spring–summer; park*

open daily; www.holkham.co.uk) is a fabulous Palladian-style country seat amid a deer park, home to Viscount and Viscountess Coke (pronounced "Cook"). It houses a treasury of statues, Old Masters' paintings, antiques and tapestries. The Statue Gallery contains one of the finest private collections of classical sculpture, including a statue of Diana and a bust of Thucydides from the 4th century BC. A notice on the piano on the way in, invites able musicians to sit down and play. The hall was a setting in the film *The Duchess*, starring Keira Knightley as Georgiana Spencer and Ralph Fiennes as the Duke of Devonshire.

🚗 *Carry on A149, then left on B1155. Park on-street.*

⑪ Burnham Market
Norfolk; NR23 1AB
Away from the coast, enjoy the fine Georgian cottages book-ended by two small churches in this riverside town, known as "Chelsea on Sea." Browse the hat and dress shops, art gallery, jewelers, fish shop, and delicatessen, then have a deserved drink at the handsome Hoste Arms.

🚗 *Head north on the B1355, then turn left on A149.*

Peddars Way

The Norfolk Coast Path forms part of the ancient Peddars Way, a scenic trail which starts at Knetishall Heath, near Thetford, and runs across 46 miles (74 km) of mainly flat fenland to the sea near Hunstanton, following an old Roman road. It hugs the coast eastward to Cromer before turning inland and joining the Weavers Way and Angles Way to Great Yarmouth.

12 Hunstanton

Norfolk; PE36 6BQ

An old-fashioned, bucket-and-spade sort of resort, "Sunny Hunny" has two distinct geographical features. Its award-winning sandy beaches are overlooked by cliffs striped red, white, and brown and, although an east coast town, it looks west, into glorious sunsets over the Wash. History buffs might like **Old Hunstanton** for its deeper roots and charm, but hidden away among traditional amusements on Hunstanton's Southern Promenade, (with pay parking), is the fascinating **Sea Life Sanctuary** (open daily; 01485 533 576; www.sealsanctuary.co.uk). This is dedicated to the rescue, rehabilitation and release back into the wild of sick and injured seals and other marine animals. Walk through an underwater glass tunnel and be mesmerized by sharks, seahorses, rays, and other sea creatures in this safe habitat.

🚗 *Head south on the A149.*

13 Heacham

Norfolk; PE31

This seaside village is a popular holiday destination with accommodation of all kinds, and the wide open sands attract kite-fliers and windsurfers. Like Hunstanton, Heacham looks west across the vast bay and enjoys the evening spectacle of a "highway to heaven" – golden sunsets reflected in the water. In 1614, the Algonquin Indian princess Pocahontas married the Heacham local John Rolfe – commemorated by a carving in the 13th-century Norman **St. Mary's Church**. Just outside the village, located in an old watermill, is **Norfolk Lavender** (open daily; 01485 570 384; www.norfolk-lavender.co.uk), with fragrant meadow garden, plant center, herb garden, and shop. Try lavender and lemon scones in the tea room or take a minibus tour of the blooming lavender fields in July.

Above left Local produce at Burnham Market
Above center Resident of the popular Sea Life Sanctuary, Huntstanton **Right** Bronze lioness, Holkham Hall, near Wells-next-the-Sea

EAT AND DRINK

WELLS-NEXT-THE-SEA

Crown Hotel *moderate*
The emphasis here is on local produce, seasonality and sustainability. The result is good, inventive but unfussy cooking. *The Buttlands, NR23 1EX; 01328 710 209; www.thecrownhotelwells.co.uk*

BURNHAM MARKET

Hoste Arms *moderate*
Eat in the bar or in comfortable dining-rooms from an imaginative menu of local produce – Brancaster oysters, Cromer crab and Norfolk pork. There are also plenty of good rooms – Horatio Nelson is said to have stayed here. *The Green, PE3 8HD; 01328 738 777; www.hostearms.co.uk*

AROUND HEACHAM

Rose and Crown *moderate*
Family-friendly, 14th-century beamed inn with walled garden– try the beef or lamb grazed on the salt marshes at Holkham, and fish and shellfish landed off the Norfolk and Suffolk coast. *Old Church Rd, Snettisham, PE31 7LX; 01485 541 382; www.roseandcrownsnettisham.co.uk*

DAY TRIP OPTIONS

There's lots of choice here for history buffs, nature lovers, families, and even those who like life a little slower.

Norwich and the Broads

Staying at Nowich ❶, explore the town in the morning – see the castle, cathedral, historic center and shops, then head for Horning ❷, to buy a picnic and spend the afternoon on the Broads in a canoe. Finally, enjoy a fish supper at Mundesley ❸ by the sea.

Follow the instructions in this drive.

Wildlife Adventure

From Hunstanton ⓬, visit the Sea Life Sanctuary to learn about the animals up close. Then drive over to Blakeney ❾ for a boat trip to see the sea birds and seals in their natural environment. Finish up at Cley-next-the-Sea ❽ birdwatching in the salt marshes.

Take the A149 there and back.

Family Fun

Starting at Cromer ❹, enjoy the traditional resort atmosphere then set off for West Runton ❺, to see the farm

animals at the sanctuary. Stop off at Sheringham ❻ for a railway ride and then head to Weybourne ❼ for the amazing collection of military vehicles.

Take the A149 there and back.

A Genteel Day

Take a tour the grand hall and estate at Holkham. Then drive to Burnham Market ⓫, for some quaint village life and a spot of shopping, before heading for Heacham ⓭ and a visit to the lavender farm.

Take the A149 there and back.

Eat and Drink: inexpensive, under £25; moderate, £25–£50; expensive, over £50

Borderlands to Beacons

From Hereford to Blaenavon

Highlights

- **Ancient and modern treasures**
  Wonder at Saxon and Norman architecture, medieval artifacts, and modern ecclesiastic art in Hereford, Kilpeck and Brecon

- **Idyllic valley landscapes**
  Travel through the Vale of Ewyas with its ancient priory, leaning church tower, and its pass over the Black Mountains

- **The book capital of the world**
  Rummage through the books in Hay-on-Wye, the world center for antiquarian and second-hand books

- **Industrial heritage**
  Step back in time and tour the extraordinary collection of Industrial Revolution sites at Blaenavon

Crickhowell countryside, on the eastern edge of the Brecon Beacons

Borderlands to Beacons

Beginning in the compact English borders city of Hereford, with its beautiful cathedral, this drive follows a route through the ecclesiastical highlights of the "Golden Valley" (Abbey Dore) and Vale of Ewyas (Llanthony Priory). It then crosses into Wales to Hay-on-Wye, the book capital of the world, and through the glorious landscape of the Brecon Beacons National Park before finishing in Blaenavon, a sprawling industrial World Heritage Site.

Above From farmland to wilderness – the varied landscape of the Brecon Beacons, *see p134*

ACTIVITIES

Map the 13th-century route to Jerusalem on the Mappa Mundi at Hereford Cathedral

Taste some fine cider at Hereford's Museum of Cider

Drive over stunning Gospel Pass for views of the Wye Valley

Go fishing, birdwatching, or take a boat out on the waters of Wales' second largest lake at Llangorse

Walk glorious trails in the Brecon Beacons

Trace the lineage of Jesus on the medieval Jesse sculpture inside St. Mary's Priory Church in Abergavenny

Go down a mine and reflect on South Wales' industrial past – a history that changed the modern world

Below Pointed, arched doorway at Hereford Cathedral, *see p132*

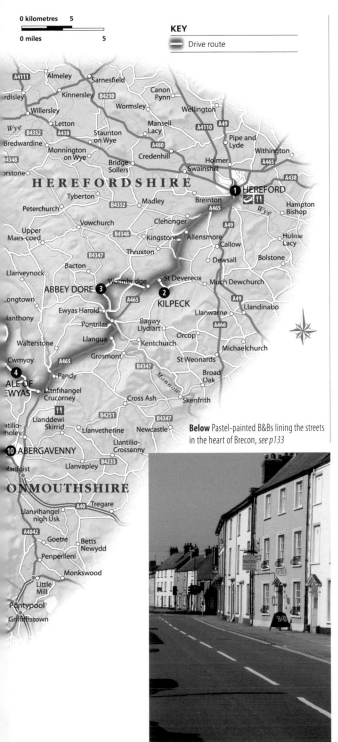

0 kilometres 5

0 miles 5

A4111 Almeley Sarnesfield
rdisley Kinnersley B4230 Canon Pynn
Willersley Wormsley Wellington
Wye Letton Mansell Lacy A4110 A49
B4352 A438 Staunton on Wye Pipe and Lyde
Bredwardine Monnington on Wye A480 Credenhill Holmer Withington
4348 Bridge Sollers Swainshill A465
orstone **HEREFORDSHIRE** ① **HEREFORD** A438
Tyberton Madley Breinton Hampton Bishop
Peterchurch B4352 A465 Wye
Vowchurch Clehonger A49
Upper Maes-coed B4348 Kingstone Allensmore Holme Lacy
Thruxton Callow
Bacton Dewsall Bolstone
Llanveynock Wormbridge St Devereux Much Dewchurch
ABBEY DORE ③ A465 ② **KILPECK** A49 Llandinabo
ongtown Ewyas Harold Llanwarne
lanthony Pontrilas Bagwy Llydiart A466
Walterstone Llangua Orcop Michaelchurch
Cwmyoy A465 Grosmont Kentchurch St Weonards
④ Pandy B4347 Broad Oak
ALE OF EWYAS Llanfihangel Crucorney Cross Ash Skenfrith
Llanddewi Skirrid B4251 B4347
Llanvetherine Newcastle
ABERGAVENNY Llantilio-Crossenny
⑩ Llanvapley B4233
ONMOUTHSHIRE Tregare
Llanvihangel nigh Usk A40
A4042 Goetre Betts Newydd
Penperlleni
Monkswood
Little Mill
Pontypool
Griffithstown

Below Pastel-painted B&Bs lining the streets in the heart of Brecon, *see p133*

PLAN YOUR DRIVE

Start/finish: Hereford to Blaenavon.

Number of days: 3, allowing half a day to explore Hay-On-Wye.

Distances: 110 miles (175 km).

Road conditions: Good roads in most places and well marked. Some roads are narrow and quite rural.

When to go: Spring is pleasant but summer is best for outdoor activities.

Opening times: Museums and attractions are generally open 10am–5pm, but close earlier (or are closed altogether) Nov–Easter. Shops are often open longer. Churches are usually open until dusk.

Main market days: Hereford: Indoor Retail Market, Wed & Thu; Butter Market (foods and miscellaneous), daily; Hay-on-Wye: Butter Market (food, antiques and bric à brac), Thu am; Brecon: Farmers' Market, second Sat of the month.

Shopping: Look out for apple juice around Crickhowell, as well as produce from the Black Mountain Smokery, Welsh venison, lamb, and Penderyn Whisky in the Brecon Beacons.

Major festivals: Hereford: Art Week (open studios, exhibitions – *www.h-art.org.uk*), Sep; Hay-on-Wye: Hay Festival (everything about books – *www.hayfestival.com*), a week at the start of Jun; Brecon: Jazz Festival (*www.breconjazz.co.uk*), Aug; Green Man Festival (music festival – *www.thegreenmanfestival.co.uk*), end Aug; Blaenavon: Spring Festival, May.

DAY TRIP OPTIONS

Church buffs can start at Hereford **cathedral** before heading to the fine **church** at Kilpeck. Visit the **abbey** at Dore and drive through the Vale of Eywas, past the **priory** and a **church** with a **leaning tower**. Last stop is the **book capital** at Hay-on-Wye. Families might prefer a visit to the **iron works** and a trip down the **mine** at Blaenavon, then the **castle** and **manor house** at Tretower, and **waterside activities** at Llangorse. For full details, *see p135*.

Above Dore Abbey, founded by French Cistercian monks in 1147

VISITING HEREFORD

Parking
One-hour parking in the center at Broad Street and King Street.

Tourist Information
1 King Street, HR4 9BW; 01432 268 430

WHERE TO STAY

HEREFORD

Somerville House *moderate*
This friendly boutique B&B is located in a Victorian villa a short walk from the station. Serves healthy breakfasts.
12 Bodenham Rd, HR1 2TS; 01432 273 991; www.somervillehouse.net

HAY-ON-WYE

The Swan at Hay *moderate*
This former coaching inn dates back to Georgian times and has 18 comfortable rooms and pretty gardens.
Church Street, HR3 5DQ; 01497 821 188; www.swanathay.co.uk

AROUND HAY-ON-WYE

The Old Post Office *inexpensive*
Set in a 17th-century building, southeast of Hay off the B4350, this good B&B offers three ensuite country-style rooms, with delicious vegetarian breakfasts.
Llanigon, HR3 5QA; 01497 820 008; www.oldpost-office.co.uk

AROUND BRECON

Felin Glais *inexpensive–moderate*
Restored 17th-century barn in fields to the northwest of Brecon off Cradoc Rd. It offers rustic chic and evening meals.
Aberyscir, LD3 9NP; 01874 623 107; www.felinglais.co.uk

Felin Fach Griffin *moderate*
This is a lovely rose-painted pub off the A470 northeast of Brecon. Its boutique rooms are stylish and comfortable.
Felin Fach, LD3 0UB; 01874 620 111; www.eatdrinksleep.ltd.uk

① Hereford
Herefordshire; HR1 0LW
With its gentle hills and gardens, it is easy to forget that in the Middle Ages Hereford saw fierce border skirmishes between the Welsh and English, even after the Saxon King Offa of Mercia (AD 757–96) invaded Wales and built his dyke. For earlier civilizations, visit **Hereford Museum and Art Gallery** *(closed Mon; Oct–Mar also closed Sun)* on Broad St and see a Roman mosaic and coins, keys, and bronzes found locally.

High above the River Wye, **Hereford Cathedral** has Saxon origins and fine Norman pillars, dog-tooth arches, and an ancient library. See, too, one of Britain's finest treasures, the Mappa Mundi, a map of the known world, drawn on deer vellum in 1290. Among the modern artworks are Simon Beer's silver corona, above the altar, and John Piper's tapestries.

Known for its apples, Hereford is a big cider producer, so follow signs to the **Museum of Cider** *(closed Sun)* to learn the secrets of cider production.
🚗 *Cross the river and take A465 until a sign to the left for Kilpeck; follow signs and park outside the church.*

② Kilpeck
Herefordshire; HR2 9DN
The crowning glory of this pretty village is the **Church of St. Mary and St. David**, perhaps the best 12th-century Norman Romanesque church in Britain. Look for exquisite Celtic and Norse-style carving dating from 1140 and the whimsical carved corbels of animals, wrestlers, and dancers below the roofline. To see the remains of the **motte and bailey castle** and for good views, walk up behind the churchyard and left over a stile up the hill.
🚗 *Return to A465 and turn left. Drop in to the Galanthus Gallery and café at Wormbridge (open Thu–Sun), then take next right and follow signs to Abbey Dore. Park on road by Antiques Center.*

③ Abbey Dore
Herefordshire; HR2 0AJ
Nestling in the fertile "Golden Valley," this village is home to the remains of the Cistercian **Dore Abbey**, founded in 1147 from wool trade profits. Only the eastern end still stands, but it is an impressive height. The abbey was dissolved in 1537 and reconsecrated

in 1634 as an Anglican church. There are fine examples of 13th-century roof bosses, a number of interesting wall paintings, and a wooden musicians' gallery, which dates from the 1700s.

Visit the **Antiques Center** next door, and the **Trappe Gallery** in Ewyas Harold (on the way back to the A465), for the exquisite paintings of Rob Ritchie.
🚗 *Take B4347 to A465 and turn right. Turn right to Llanfihangel Crucorney. Just before the Skirrid Inn, Wales's oldest pub, turn right to the priory and follow signs to Cymyoy. Turn left at T-junction by Coach House and right at end of road.*

④ Vale of Ewyas
Llanthony, Powys; NP7 7NN
This is a beautiful glaciated valley, with woodlands and fertile farmland, offering good horse riding. **Cwmyoy Church** sits on a geologically recent landslip which some say coincided with Christ's crucifixion. The ground is still settling, and the church's tower is said to lean even more than the one at Pisa. There is also a stone cross here similar to an Irish high cross. Return to the valley road and turn right to **Llanthony Priory** by the River Honddu. Legend has it that St. Peter and St. Paul visited here and that St. David, the patron saint of Wales, lived here as a hermit. In the 12th century, the knight William de Lacy was so impressed with its spirituality that he founded a church on the spot – later the site of Wales's first Augustinian priory. Carry on north over the Black Mountains to **Gospel**

Below Finely sculpted doorway at the Church of St. Mary and St. David, Kilpeck

Pass at 1,778 ft (542 m) with dramatic views over the Wye valley.

🚗 *Keep going north from Gospel Pass to Hay-on-Wye and park in the parking lot at the back of the castle on B4348.*

⑤ Hay-on-Wye
Powys; HR3 5DB
Hay is a charming Welsh market town with winding streets, built on a hillside beneath the ruins of a Norman castle. Home to cafés and many, many bookshops, Hay is considered by some the second-hand book capital of the world. The largest bookshop is that of **Richard Booth**, who has been promoting Hay as a book center since 1961. The Hay Festival of Literature (*www.hayfestival.com*) is held at the end of May and attracts high profile poets, writers, and politicians.

Take the B4351 from Broad St to **Clyro**, a pretty village on the outskirts of town that was once home to the Reverend Francis Kilvert, a great Victorian diarist, who depicted the rural life of his parish during the 1870s.

🚗 *Leave Hay on B4350 (toward Brecon) and join A438, then A479 through Talgarth. Turn right onto B4560, then right in Llangorse to lake parking lot.*

⑥ Llangorse Lake
Brecon, Powys; LD3 7TR
The largest natural lake in South Wales, **Llangorse Lake** was created during the last Ice Age. In the summer, it is a popular water sports center with boats for hire from the **Lakeside Caravan & Camping Park** (*www.llangorselake.co.uk*). The lake is also good for fishing and its reedy shallows attract waterfowl which can be viewed from lakeside hides. At the north edge of the lake is the tiny man-made islet, or crannog, **Ynys Bwlc**. This was built around AD 900 by piling stones and earth onto

brushwood and reeds, and held a royal hall and church and was linked to the shore by a causeway. At the **Llangorse Crannog Center** visitors can learn more about the lake. Enjoy lakeside walks to Llangorse village – a center for pony trekking, and a starting point for trails in the Brecon Beacons National Park.

🚗 *From the lake road, turn left back into Llangorse and follow the signs to Brecon on the A40 and B4601.*

⑦ Brecon
Brecon, Powys; LD3 9DP
An old market town at the confluence of the Honddu and Usk Rivers in the Brecon Beacons National Park, Brecon contains a mix of medieval, Tudor, Jacobean, and Georgian architecture around its central square, **The Bulwark**, and 16th-century Church of St. Mary's.

The central **Brecknock Museum and Art Gallery** (*closed 1st Mon of month*) has an interesting collection of artifacts such as a canoe from Llangorse Lake, dating from AD 760–1020, and one of Wales's best-loved spoon collections.

Visit also the **South Wales Borderers Museum** (*www.rrw.org.uk; open weekdays*) on the Watton (B4601), covering Welsh regimental history including the defence of Rorke's Drift (1879), where 139 soldiers faced 5,000 Zulu warriors.

Founded as a Benedictine priory in 1093, **Brecon Cathedral** has some of the best monastic buildings in Wales – mostly built in the 13th and 14th centuries. The decorated Norman font with its birds, grotesques, and beasts is the oldest object. The Havard Chapel has many millitary memorials and the regimental colors from Rorke's Drift. There's also a Heritage Center and café.

🚗 *Leave on the B4061, then take the A470 toward Cardiff. At Libanus turn right to the Brecon Beacons National Park Visitor Center.*

Above left Pastoral landscape in the fertile Vale of Ewyas **Above right** Hereford Cathedral, home to much ancient and modern art

EAT AND DRINK

HEREFORD
The Stewing Pot *moderate*
This contemporary restaurant serves local produce such as rib of Hereford beef or goat cheese tart.
17 Church Street, HR1 2LR; 01432 265 233; www.stewingpot.co.uk

HAY-ON-WYE
Old Black Lion *inexpensive–moderate*
A historic inn with a reputation for fine food, it serves traditional Welsh produce – guinea fowl in the restaurant, or hearty steak and kidney pie in the bar.
Lion Street, HR3 5AD; 01497 820 841; www.oldblacklion.co.uk

Kilverts *inexpensive-moderate*
This very popular pub serves good bar food, with a mix of traditional and Mediterranean flavors.
The Bullring, HR3 5AG; 01497 821 042; www.kilverts.co.uk

Other options
For delicious low-fat sheep milk ice cream, try **Shepherds** *inexpensive* (*9 High Town, HR3 5AE; 01497 821 898; www.shepherdsicecream.co.uk*). For wholesome food, with good vegetarian options, try the **Granary** *inexpensive* (*Broad St, HR3 5DB; 01497 820 790*).

Below The popular Granary Café, by the clocktower in Hay-on-Wye

Eat and Drink: inexpensive, under £25; moderate, £25–£50; expensive, over £50

Above View looking into the hills of the Brecon Beacons National Park **Below** Sheep grazing on the verdant upper slopes of the Brecon Beacons

VISITING BRECON BEACONS NATIONAL PARK

National Park Visitor Center
Libanus, Brecon, LD3 8ER; 01874 623 366; www.breconbeacons.org

WHERE TO STAY AROUND TRETOWER COURT AND CASTLE

Ty Gwyn *inexpensive*
Beautifully restored Georgian building, with three attractive ensuite rooms and lots of character, in Crickhowell on the A40 from Tretower to Abergavenny. There's a pretty garden and local produce for breakfast.
Brecon Rd (A40), Crickhowell, NP8 1DG; 01873 811 625; www.tygwyn.com

⑧ Brecon Beacons National Park
Powys; LD3 8ER

This walk is a figure of eight across a plateau in the shadow of the Brecon Beacons. While enjoying the scenery and waymarked trails, listen for birdsong – especially the sky larks in summer.

A two-hour walking tour

From the far end of the parking lot next to the **Visitor Center** ① walk straight on to the grassy track. A sign shows the way (do not veer left up the slope). Look out for gorse clumps with yellow flowers – these are popular with songbirds such as stonechats, meadow pipits, and chaffinches. The path then leads up a gentle incline with the Brecon Beacons landscape on the right. Follow the broad grassy path straight ahead, past the pond on the right and across a road, past a sign pointing back to the Visitor Center. After a while the path dips down to a farm road and then up again to the peak ahead. Cross the road and the boggy watercourse and head up the path to the trig point on top of **Twyn y Gaer** ②, the site of an Iron Age hillfort, at a height of 1,204 ft (367 m). From here there are great views around, and all the way down to Brecon. To return, take the worn pathway to the right of the pillar and follow it back around the

Sign from Blaenavon World Heritage Site

hill and down to the farm road again. Look for "pillow mounds" – banks of earth created in the 18th century for rabbits to breed and feed the growing populations of the industrial towns to the south. Cross over the road and head uphill, veering right toward the boundary fence where there is a clear pathway following a Roman road – **Sarn Helen** ③. This was the old route linking the Roman forts between Y Gaer and Coelbren, and is still traceable further along the common. Follow the path beside the fence until the fence turns abruptly right. Leave the fence and walk straight ahead, across gently sloping common land on the path downhill to a road. Cross the road keeping an area of flat land with a **pond** ④ on the left and follow the path back down to the Visitor Center, enjoying the dramatic vistas on the way.

🚗 *Return to Brecon and take the A40 east. Go left after the Kestrel pub and left at the end of the road, and park outside the gates of Tretower.*

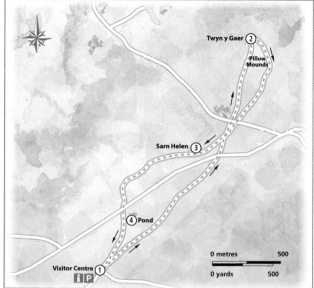

⑨ Tretower Court and Castle
Crickhowell, Powys; NP8 1RF
These two sets of buildings clearly illustrate the transition from castles to houses in the borders, indicating the advent of a more peaceful time. The **tower**, built by Picard c.1100, is one of a number of motte and bailey castles built during the Norman advance into Wales. In the 14th century, the **house** became the main dwelling place. It is a rare intact example of a medieval manor house with a walled front and courtyard, like an early Oxford college. Partly rebuilt in the 15th century by Sir Roger Vaughan, it has wonderful timber work and a garden.

🚗 *Continue along the road to return to the A40 and continue eastward to Abergavenny. Park in the town center.*

⑩ Abergavenny
Monmouthshire; NP7 5ND
Set in the Usk Valley with easy access to the Brecon Beacons, Abergavenny is superbly located. At its heart is **Abergavenny Castle**, a classic motte and bailey structure from the 11th century. It saw three centuries of fierce border fighting and was the scene of the infamous massacre of Welsh

Above St. Mary's Priory Church, Abergavenny, founded in the 11th century

chieftains by the Normans in 1175. A 19th-century hunting lodge, on the site of the keep, houses **Abergavenny Museum** *(open Mon–Sat; Mar–Oct also Sun pm)*, with displays of local social history. However, the star attraction is **St. Mary's Priory Church**. Founded in 1087 as a Benedictine priory, it is one of the finest churches in Wales. It has a huge 15th-century carved oak "Jesse" sculpture – tracing Jesus' lineage back to Jesse – which is unique in size and craftsmanship. Also admire the fine English School Renaissance alabaster tombs in the Herbert Chapel.

🚗 *Return to A40 east, taking A4143, then B4246 to Blaenavon. Park on site.*

⑪ Blaenavon
Gwent; NP4 9RN
Set on a mountainside in a bleak and awe-inspiring landscape, Blaenavon rose to prominence at the start of the Industrial Revolution and was given UNESCO World Heritage status in 2000. One of several heritage attractions on the site, **Blaenavon Ironworks** *(Apr–Oct: open daily; Nov–Mar: open Fri–Sun)* was the most advanced ironworks in the world when it was built in 1787. The vast infastructure includes mines, water towers, steam-powered blast furnaces, casting houses, and workers' cottages. The works fell into decline with the advent of large-scale steel making.

Part of the same heritage site, the **Big Pit: National Coal Museum** *(open daily)*, is where the coal that fired the furnaces came from. In this fascinating industrial museum, ex-miners escort groups around the mines, 300 ft (90 m) underground and reveal the harsh lives of the miners (men, women, and children) who worked in dark and damp conditions.

Above The ruined Norman tower of Tretower Castle, near Crickhowell

VISITING BLAENAVON

Blaenavon World Heritage Center
Church Rd, NP4 9AS; 01495 742 333; www.world-heritage-blaenavon.org.uk

EAT AND DRINK

AROUND TRETOWER COURT AND CASTLE

The Bear Hotel *inexpensive–moderate*
This atmospheric pub in Crickhowell, on the A40 outside Tretower, serves traditional food such as Gloucester Old Spot sausages, fishcakes and faggots. *High St, Crickhowell, NP8 1BW; 01873 810 408; www.bearhotel.co.uk*

Nantyffin Cider Mill *moderate*
This lovely old drovers' inn, on the A479 from Tretower to Crickhowell, offers a high standard of cuisine using produce from local farms and estates. *Brecon Rd, NP8 1SG; 01873 810 775; www.cidermill.co.uk*

AROUND ABERGAVENNY

The Walnut Tree *moderate–expensive*
This well-known restaurant, just off the B4521 northeast of Abergavenny, is part-operated by top chef Shaun Hill. The food is well-flavored modern British and the set lunch is excellent value. *Llanddewi Skirrid, NP7 8AW; 01873 852 797; www.thewalnuttreeinn.com*

DAY TRIP OPTIONS
Hereford and Abergavenny make excellent bases for these trips.

Churches, History and Books
Start in Hereford ❶, with its cathedral, and head to Kilpeck ❷ for its church, then on to Abbey Dore ❸ and the spectacular Vale of Ewyas

❹, stopping off at the church and priory. Drive over Gospel Pass for a stroll around Hay-on-Wye ❺.

Follow the driving instructions, but return to Hereford on the B4352.

Family Activity Day
Spend the morning touring the industrial sites at Blaenavon ⑪,

before heading to Tretower Court and Castle ⑨, and on to Llangorse Lake ❻ for a walk and some fishing or bird-watching. If there's still time, take a look around pretty Brecon ❼.

Follow the driving instructions from Abergavenny to Blaenavon and then follow the A40.

Eat and Drink: inexpensive, under £25; moderate, £25–£50; expensive, over £50

Wonders of West Wales

Llandovery to Newport

Highlights

- **Glorious Welsh gardens**
  Visit two striking, individual gardens: colorful and sculptural planting at Aberglasney and the exotic and futuristic National Botanic Garden

- **Majestic Welsh castles**
  Admire the crumbling bastions of Norman might from Carreg Cennen to Kidwelly and Carew, reminders of a turbulent Welsh history

- **Stunning Pembrokeshire coast**
  Walk along the rugged, splintered cliffs to rocky coves and wide sandy bays washed by the powerful Atlantic

- **One of Britain's oldest cathedrals**
  For over 1,400 years there has been Christian worship at St Davids Cathedral, an astonishing work of religious art

Tenby Harbour overlooked by Prince Albert's monument on Tower Hill

Wonders of West Wales

The drive heads west from Llandovery through some glorious Welsh gardens – The National Botanic Garden and Aberglasney – to the home of Dylan Thomas, one of the great poets of the 20th century, in the sleepy coastal town of Laugharne. The route is studded with solid Norman castles, built to control the land the French invaders had just conquered. Take some time out in the bustling resort of Tenby before visiting Britain's smallest city, St Davids, with its ancient cathedral. Walk the stunning wild clifftops, rich in religious myths in Britain's only National Coastal Park, and visit the seabirds on Ramsey Island. See the Neolithic burial monument of Pentre Ifan and walk the Preseli Hills, source of the mysterious blue stones at Stonehenge *(see p68)*.

ACTIVITIES

Cycle (or walk) around the Brecon Beacons from Llandovery

Climb up to the fabulous beauty spot of Carreg Cennan Castle

Take a boat to Ramsey or Caldey Islands to see the seabirds

Picnic in the grounds of Carew Castle and walk to the mill

Count the steps down and up to St. Govan's Chapel – it is said they are never the same

Listen to the sublime evensong at St Davids Cathedral

Surf the Atlantic rollers at Whitesands Bay, St Davids

Hike in the splendid Preseli Hills from Newport

Below Picturesque Laugharne, where poet Dylan Thomas lived, *see p141*

Above The mazy clifftop path of the Pembrokeshire Coast National Trail, close to St Davids, *see pp144–5*

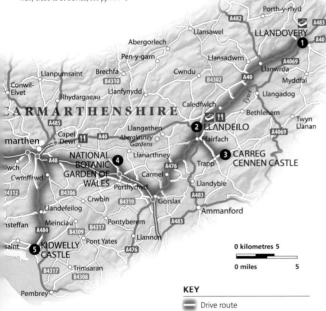

KEY

       Drive route

0 kilometres 5

0 miles   5

Below Pendine Sands with the tide out, once a favorite location for land-speed record attempts, *see p142*

PLAN YOUR DRIVE

Start/Finish: Llandovery to Newport.

Number of days: 4, allowing half a day at St Davids.

Distances: Around 168 miles (270 km).

Road conditions: Well-paved and marked. In remote areas the country roads can be very narrow.

When to go: Spring is very pretty, with wild flowers, and summer is best for outdoor activities. Many attractions and venues close during the winter.

Opening times: Museums and attractions are generally open 10am–5pm, but close earlier (or are closed altogether) Nov–Easter. Shops are often open longer. Churches are usually open until dusk.

Main market days: Llandeilo: Country Market, Civic Hall, Fri am; **Tenby**: Country Market, St. John's Hall, Fri am; **St Davids**: Country Market, Memorial Hall, Thu am; **Fishguard**: Country Market, Market Hall, Tue am; Farmers' Market, alternate Sat (every week in summer).

Shopping: Buy natural soaps from the Soap Shed at St Davids produce market, and jam and chutney from Miranda's Preserves at village stores in Llandovery and many local delis.

Major festivals: St Davids: Cathedral Festival, classical music, 1st week in Jun; **Fishguard**: Folk Festival, 4 days at end of May; International Classical Music Festival, one week late Jul–early Aug; Pembrokeshire's Jazz 'n' Blues Festival, 5 days at end of Aug.

DAY TRIP OPTIONS

Castle and garden lovers can stay at Llandovery to visit the **castle** and the **gardens** at Aberglasney, and climb up to Carreg Cennen **castle** before admiring the **Great Glasshouse** at the National Botanic Garden. **Families** will enjoy the beach at Tenby, Carmarthen Bay, a visit to the **museum** at Pendine, and the **castle** and **Dylan Thomas' house** at Laugharne; finish off with the **castles** at Kidwelly and Carew. For more **coastal fun**, stay at Newport, see Fishguard **harbor**, then on to St Davids for the **cathedral**, **walk**, and time at the **beach**. Enjoy a **fish supper** in Solva. For full details, *see p145*.

Right Aberglasney House set in the famous gardens, near Llandeilo

VISITING LLANDOVERY

Parking
Free parking by the castle and TIC.

Tourist Information
Kings Rd, SA20 0AW; 01550 720 693

WHERE TO STAY

LLANDOVERY

Kings Head Inn *moderate*
Lashings of history are available at this 16th-century inn with 14 ensuite rooms. There's a cozy bar and restaurant with traditional home-cooked Welsh food.
1 Market Square, SA20 0AB; 01550 720 393; www.wales-llandovery-hotel.co.uk

LLANDEILO

Fronlas *moderate*
This boutique, eco-friendly B&B in an Edwardian townhouse has three stylish rooms and serves organic breakfasts.
7 Thomas Street, SA19 6LB; 01558 824 733; www.fronlas.com

LAUGHARNE

The Boat House B&B *moderate*
This B&B in the heart of town has four light, airy, and contemporary rooms. It's just a short walk from here to Dylan Thomas' famous Boathouse.
1 Gosport Street, SA33 4SY; 01994 427 263; www.bed-breakfast-holiday.co.uk

Below left Pastel-colored inn on Market Square, Llandovery **Below right** Yellow daisy-like flowers at Aberglasney Gardens

① Llandovery
Carmarthenshire; SA20 0AP
This is a lovely Welsh market town with neat cottages and Georgian buildings. The ruined **Norman castle** by the river was built in 1110 and sacked by Owain Glyndŵr in 1403. Drive south on Bridge Street out of town over the river and then fork right to the village of **Myddfai**. A family of doctors, the "Physicians of Myddfai," lived here from the 14th to the 19th centuries, and were renowned for their herbal remedies. Walkers can use Llandovery as a base for hikes around the northern edge of the Brecon Beacons National park *(www.breconbeacons.org)*. Or rent bikes from **Myddfai Cycles** *(Myddfai Rd, Llandovery, SA20 0LQ; 0155 720 372)*. Pick up maps and leaflets from the tourist information center.

🚗 *From Llandovery re-cross the bridge and take the A40 west to Llandeilo.*

② Llandeilo
Carmarthenshire; SA19 8QH
This elegant town is perched on a bluff overlooking the Tywi, the longest river to flow entirely within Wales. At its center is 13th-century **St. Teilo's Church**, rebuilt in the 19th century by renowned Victorian revivalist architect George Gilbert Scott. The church has an exhibition on the St. Teilo Gospels, a local 8th-century illuminated book,

and the earliest known example of Welsh script. Head west on the A40 turning off left to Llangathen and **Aberglasney Gardens** *(open daily; www.aberglasney.org)*, a rare restored cloister garden dating back to the 15th century. It is a planter's paradise, with vast swathes of delphiniums and a yew tunnel. The mansion house has a splendid early Victorian Ionic portico, a shop, and a café. Enjoy the colorful profusion of butterflies attracted by the flowers in summer.

🚗 *From Llandeilo, take A483 south to Ffairfach, turn left at roundabout, right after a railway bridge, following signs to Trapp, then to castle and parking lot.*

③ Carreg Cennen Castle
Carmarthenshire; SA19 6UA
Just east of Trapp, on the western edge of the Brecon Beacons National Park, **Carreg Cennen Castle** *(open daily)* is a dramatic ruined fortification, set high on a stunning 325-ft (99-m) limestone bluff. There is evidence of prehistoric and Roman activity, but it was the 11th-century Welsh princes who first built on the site. Today's remains are those of the magnificent 13th-century Norman edifice. Walk up hill to the castle from the parking lot.

🚗 *Go back to Ffairfach and straight on to A476. Turn right on A48, then right on B4310 to the Botanic Garden (signed).*

④ National Botanic Garden of Wales
Carmarthenshire; SA32 8HG
Once the estate of 18th-century banker Sir William Paxton, Master of Calcutta Mint, the National Botanic Garden of Wales *(open daily; www.gardenofwales. org.uk)* is the most visited garden in Wales. Its central focus is the Great Greenhouse, designed by Norman

Foster. It is the largest single-span glasshouse in the world and houses a collection of rare plant species in a controlled climate. On the edge of the park is a double-walled garden with a Tropical House designed by John Belle, a New York-based Welsh architect. This is home to exotics such as pineapples, coconuts, palms, and cardamom. There is also a Japanese garden which won gold at the Chelsea Flower Show. Other features include a bee garden, an ice house, rare Welsh plants, and a mirror pool. The garden is wheelchair-friendly, and there are several available *(pre-booking advised; 01558 667 148)*.

🚗 *Head back to the A48 west towards Carmarthen and take the A484 south to Kidwelly (Cydweli). Follow signs to castle.*

⑤ Kidwelly Castle
Carmarthenshire; SA17 5BQ

An imposing fortification, built during the 13th–15th centuries on a bluff over the River Gwendraeth, **Kidwelly Castle** *(open daily)* was part of the Norman strategy to secure south Wales by controlling the river passes here and at Laugharne, Llansteffan, and Loughor. The earliest parts of the castle consist of the square inner ward with the four round corner towers and portcullis gates to the north and south. Further concentric defenses were added in the mid-13th century by its new owners, the de Chaworth family. The gatehouse is extremely well fortified and was designed so that it could be held independently if the rest of the castle was captured. The castle also contains two bakehouses and the remains of a chapel.

🚗 *Return to Carmarthen, head west on the A40, and turn left onto the A4066 south to Laugharne.*

Dylan Thomas
Dylan Thomas was one of the world's great 20th-century English-language poets. Born in Swansea, he wrote over half of his poems there including "And Death Shall Have No Dominion". He moved west to New Quay and Laugharne to write his masterpiece "Under Milk Wood," a play about night and day, set in the imaginary Welsh fishing village of Llareggub, which means something entirely different read backwards. He was a big success in America but died in New York aged only 39.

⑥ Laugharne
Carmarthenshire; SA33 4SD

This is a very picturesque coastal town with lovely cottages and Georgian houses set on the expansive Taf Estuary. The town and coastline is dominated by the ruins of **Laugharne Castle**. It was built by the Norman de Brian family in the 13th and 14th centuries and later turned into a grand Tudor Mansion in the 16th century by Sir John Perrot. During the Elizabethan period, the town was bigger than Cardiff and remained an English-speaking village within Wales.

The narrow fishing lane behind the castle leads up to Dylan Thomas's home, the **Boathouse** *(01994 427 420; www.dylanthomasboathouse.com)* with his modest writing-study in the garage. There is a nice café here, so enjoy a cup of tea while gazing out over pretty **Carmarthen Bay**. The poet is buried in a simple grave in the churchyard in the north of the town.

There are several interesting shops behind the clocktower and a jeweler, **Quicksilver**, who can craft designs in silver in just a couple of hours.

🚗 *From Laugharne continue on the A4066 to Pendine.*

EAT AND DRINK

LLANDEILO
The Angel Hotel *moderate*
This established inn has a relaxed bar – choose from the blackboard menu, or dine in the more formal bistro. There's always a vegetarian choice available. *60 Rhosmaen, SA19 6EN; 01558 822 765; www.angelbistro.co.uk*

AROUND THE NATIONAL BOTANIC GARDEN OF WALES
Y Polyn *moderate*
On the B4310 south of the A40, Y Polyn offers excellent Welsh produce, such as organic beef, in traditional dishes with a modern twist. Everything is homemade – even the bread. *Capel Dewi, Nantgaredig, SA32 7LH; 01267 290 000; www.ypolynrestaurant.co.uk*

LAUGHARNE
The Cors Restaurant *moderate*
Set in beautiful gardens and with a charming interior, this restaurant features local produce such as salt marsh lamb. It also has two "shabby chic" bedrooms. *Newbridge Rd, SA33 4SH; 01994 427 219; www.the-cors.co.uk; open Thu–Sat*

Below The imposing Carreg Cennen, in a superb setting **Below left** The Great Greenhouse, National Botanic Garden of Wales **Below right** Kidwelly Castle, one of a series of 13th-century Norman fortifications

Above left The smaller of Tenby's two lovely sandy beaches **Above top right** Tenby kiosk offering fishing and sightseeing trips **Above right** Fishing and pleasure boats buoyed just outside Tenby harbor

VISITING TENBY

Parking
Park in Rectory Fields Car Park, *South Cliff St, SA70 7EA* or the Somerfield multi-story parking lot, *Upper Park Rd, SA70 7LT*

Tourist Information
The Croft, SA70 8AP; 01834 842 402

WHERE TO STAY

AROUND PENDINE

Jabajak *moderate*
This small hotel in a renovated farmstead has rooms and suites, some with four-poster beds, and extensive grounds. To get here, head north at the Whitland roundabout on the A40.
Banc y Llain, Llanboidy Rd, Whitland SA34 0ED; 01994 448 786;
www.jabajak.co.uk

AROUND CAREW CASTLE

Poyerston Farm *inexpensive–moderate*
Enjoy the comfortable ensuite rooms on this friendly farm, just off the A477 near Carew, along with Aga-cooked breakfasts and a lovely conservatory.
Cosheston, Pembroke, SA72 4SJ; 01646 651 347; www.poyerstonfarm.co.uk

AROUND TENBY

Wychwood House *inexpensive*
Large ensuite rooms, a pretty garden, and lovely views can be found at this friendly B&B, just outside Tenby, south off the A4139. Also does evening meals.
Penally, SA70 7PE; 01834 844 387;
www.wychwoodhousebb.co.uk

⑦ Pendine
Carmarthenshire; SA33 4NY
This coastal town is best known for the flat sandy beach that made it ideal for land-speed record attempts. Malcolm Campbell in *Blue Bird* in 1924 reached 146 mph (235 km/h) and then raised it to 174 mph (280 km/h) in 1927. The **Museum of Speed** *(Easter–Sep: open daily; Oct: open Fri–Mon)* traces the history of these records. See *Babs*, the car buried in the dunes after crashing and killing its driver, Parry-Thomas, in a record attempt in 1927, now dug out and restored. In a repeat of history, Campbell's grandson set a UK electric car land-speed record here in 2002.

🚗 *Head west on B4314 to Red Roses, turn left onto A477 and left onto A478 to Tenby. Use the parking lot at the end of South Cliff St or in Upper Park Rd.*

Below The still impressive 14th-century ruins of Carew Castle

⑧ Tenby
Pembrokeshire; SA70 8EU
This 9th-century walled town marks the start of the Pembrokeshire Coast National Park. Sandwiched by two golden beaches, Tenby is a gem of a holiday resort with a busy nightlife. **St. Mary's Church** has a superb roof, and alabaster tombs of Tenby mayors John and Thomas White. The 15th-century **Tudor Merchants House** *(Apr–Oct: open Sun–Fri)* has *secco* wall paintings, and original fireplaces and furniture. No visit is complete without a walk up Castle Hill – with its statue of Prince Albert – for the views and **Tenby Museum and Art Gallery** *(open daily; closed Sat–Sun in winter)*, which has local history exhibitions. The **Wilfred Harrison Gallery** displays original paintings by siblings Gwen John (1876–1939) and Augustus John (1878-1961), both distinguished artists who grew up in Tenby. Consider taking a boat trip to **Caldey Island,** run by Cistercian Monks *(closed Sun; 01834 843 545; www.caldeyisland.co.uk)*. There are medieval churches, an abbey and quiet sandy bays.

🚗 *Leave on B4318, turn left onto A477 and then turn right on A4075. Park in free parking lot on left next to the cross.*

⑨ Carew Castle
Pembrokeshire; SA70 8SL
This is another magnificent example of the transition from Norman castle to Elizabethan manor house in Wales *(see also p135)*, although the castle is sadly ruined. Nevertheless, there are spectacular views of **Carew Castle** *(open daily; www.carewcastle.com)* from over the millpond, and the grounds

Where to Stay: inexpensive, under £80; moderate, £80–£150; expensive, over £150

are a good place for a picnic. Take a pleasant stroll to the only restored tidal mill in Wales, and inspect the 11th-century **Carew Cross** nearby, one of the best examples of its type in Wales, with fine Celtic knot work.

🚗 *Head back to A477 and turn right, fork left on A4075 to Pembroke, straight over roundabout and left on B4139 to Bosherston. Drive on to coast (road passes military firing range, closed Mon–Fri except Aug). Park at St. Govan's Head.*

🔟 St. Govan's Chapel

Bosherston, Pembrokeshire; SA71 5DP
An ancient Christian cell, **St. Govan's Chapel** is set into a steep cliff on the southernmost tip of Pembrokeshire. It was probably founded in the 6th century by the followers of St. Govan – the chapel is at least 11th century. St. Govan's identity is unknown, but most experts favor St. Gobham, Abbot of Dairinis in County Wexford, who visited and stayed until his death in AD 586. He is said to have lived as a hermit, keeping a look out for marauding pirates, the scourge of the local population, from Lundy Island. It is said that the number of steps to the chapel (approximately 74) is never the same on the way up as on the way down. Be sure to stop off at the little village of Bosherston to visit the craft shop, tea house, or pub and admire the gorgeous lily ponds.

Design from Solva Woollen Mill

🚗 *Return to Pembroke and on to A477 across the toll bridge, then A4076 to Haverfordwest. Drive through town on A487 to Solva. Park in the Harbour Inn parking lot at the near edge of town.*

1️⃣1️⃣ Solva

Solva, Pembrokeshire; SA62 6UU
The jewel of the Pembrokeshire Coast National Park, Solva is the ideal location for walking, sailing, or simply relaxing among the galleries, restaurants, and shops. Used as a smuggling center and later a busy port, Solva has a lovely harbor set in a cleft in the coastline. A walk on the cliffs above the inlet is recommended.

Solva Boat Trips *(01437 721 725; www.solva.net/boattrips)* leave from the quayside for sea fishing and sealife safaris. A little way north lies **Solva Woollen Mill** *(open most weekdays; www.solvawoollenmill.co.uk)*, with a working waterwheel, making flat-weave carpets and coverings.

🚗 *From the Woollen Mill, turn right past the quarry and on to A487. Turn left for St Davids. Park on outskirts by the visitor center and walk in, or continue on and over the roundabout to the cathedral parking lot on Quickwell Hill.*

Above The spectacular cliff coastline, home to St. Govan's Chapel

EAT AND DRINK

TENBY

The Bay Tree *moderate*
Set in charming Tudor Square, the Bay Tree has an excellent menu of hearty bistro-style food and a cordial ambience. *Tudor Square, SA70 7AJ; 01834 843 516; www.baytreetenby.co.uk*

Mews Bistro *moderate*
Freshly cooked food here includes fish caught in the local harbor. *Upper Frog Street, Tenby SA70 7JD; www.mewsbistrotenby.co.uk*

Ocean Restaurant *expensive*
Overlooking the harbor, the Ocean has a modern international menu ranging from sea bass to Welsh lamb. *St. Julien's Street, Tenby SA70 7AY; 01834 844 536; www.tenby-oceanrestaurant.co.uk*

AROUND TENBY

St. Brides Hotel Restaurant *moderate*
North of Tenby, on the A478, then B4316, this hotel restaurant has glorious sea views. The menu uses local produce such as crumbly goat cheese. *St. Brides Hill, Saundersfoot, SA69 9NH; 01834 812 304; www.stbridesspahotel.com*

SOLVA

The Old Pharmacy *inexpensive*
Enjoy Pembrokeshire spiced lamb kebabs or a bowl of bouillabaisse in this former chemist's shop. *5 Main Street, SA62 6UU; 01437 720 005; www.theoldpharmacy.co.uk*

AROUND SOLVA

The Rising Sun Inn *inexpensive*
A family-run inn serving food prepared with local produce and real ales, 10 miles (16 km) east on A487. *Pelcomb Bridge, Haverfordwest, Dyfed, SA62 6EA; 01437 765 171*

Above The pretty inlet harbor of Solva, once used for smuggling

Eat and Drink: inexpensive, under £25; moderate, £25–£50; expensive, over £50

Below St. Non's Chapel, on the St Davids coastline, built in 1934

Below Pretty pastel-painted houses of the village-like city of St Davids

⑫ St Davids
Pembrokeshire; SA62 6RH

More of a village than a city, St Davids' key attractions are its coastline and its cathedral. Set in the Pembrokeshire National Park, it is blessed with glorious beaches. This easy circular walk heads south to the Pembrokeshire Coast National Trail and back to the cathedral.

A two-hour walking tour

Start at the cathedral parking lot on Quickwell Hill, turning right and right again into Nun Street. Cross Cross Square and turn right into Goat Street and left down St. Stephen's Lane. Go left at the end and then first right into Pen-y-Garn. At the end of this road, turn right along a field to a sign for St. Non's Chapel. Take a left and keep on this path all the way to the coast. After three right-then-left turns and several gates and stiles, the modern **St. Non's Retreat** ①, its chapel built in 1934, is visible. Dedicated to St. David's mother, Non, it has lovely windows. Follow the path around the retreat to the remains of the original **Capel Non** ②, actually Non's house. A 7th–9th century creed stone with an incised Latin cross marks David's birthplace. See, too, the vaulted well said to have spouted during a storm when St. David was born around AD 500 – reputed to have healing powers. There is a small shrine to Mary on the right. Follow the path up steps to the **Pembrokeshire Coastal Path** ③ and

around the rocky headlands. The path goes up the side of the **Porth Clais** ④ inlet, once St Davids' port, with its tiny harbor and boats. At the end of the inlet, follow the path right, up the hill, and head for the campsite, keeping the buildings on the right. Go straight on and then take the track inland along the edge of the field. Continue straight up to the road next to the Warpool Court Hotel entrance. Cross the road, then turn left. Walk down the path into Bryn Rd to a sign for Dinas Tyddewi (St Davids City). Turn left into Mitre Lane, and carry on to the **Farmer's Arms** ⑤ on Goat St and back to the cathedral.

Built with local purple-red stone on the site of the 6th-century monastery of St. David, **St Davids Cathedral** ⑥ has long been a major pilgrimage site – two trips to St Davids equalled one to Rome. The present, 12th-century, cathedral has a magnificent interior. Admire the early 16th-century oak ceiling with wooden pendant ceiling bosses and beautiful 14th-century

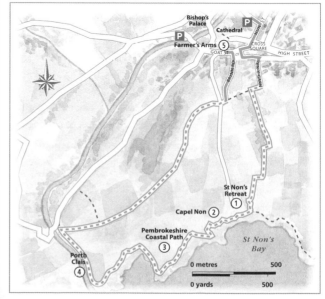

rood screen. Evensong is a delight *(Thu–Tue: 6pm)*. Across a little bridge, explore the stone ruins of the **Bishop's Palace** ⑦, built between 1280 and 1350, before returning to the parking lot, where the Tower Gate House has a display of religious stones.

West of town, on the B4853, lies **Whitesands Bay**, where legend tells that St. Patrick left Wales to take Christianity to Ireland. It is a stunning sandy surf beach. Visible just offshore lies **Ramsey Island**, an RSPB reserve with choughs, guillemots, razorbills, and even peregrine falcons. Boat trips go to the island; look out too for pods of dolphins and even whales.

Stained-glass window, St Davids Cathedral

🚗 *Take the A487 direct to Fishguard and park in the town center parking lot or in the Lower Town.*

Pembrokeshire Coast National Trail

Running along Britain's only true coastal park, the Pembrokeshire Coast National Trail (*01646 689076; www.pcnpa.org.uk*) is 186 miles (300 km) and covers some spectacular scenery. The Puffin bus service enables walkers to follow the path and not have to walk back at end of the day.

⑬ Fishguard

Pembrokeshire; SA65

This is a town of three parts: Lower Town with its fishing harbor, Upper Town with its shops and main streets, and Goodwick to the north with its ferry terminal. Park in the center and visit the **Royal Oak** on Market Square. The pub is decorated with objects relating to the "Last Invasion of Britain"

(1797). The tale goes that a French force of 1,400 troops in four warships found their way, in bad weather, into a cove nearby. However, the invasion was foiled when local women dressed in traditional tall hats and red clothes were taken for British grenadiers – a tapestry in the **Town Hall** portrays the event. The **West Wales Gallery** *(closed Sun; www.westwalesartscentre.com)* is one of the best regional galleries in Wales.

🚗 *Take A487 out of Fishguard, turn right on B4313 and left for Cilgwyn – a hilly drive with stunning views – and Newport.*

⑭ Newport

Pembrokeshire; SA42

Set on the estuary of the River Nevern, Newport was once a very busy port, but has long since silted up. The town has good access to the Pembrokeshire Coastal Path and is a popular base for walks into the Preseli Hills, famous as the source of the Stonehenge bluestones. For a closer Neolithic site, head east on the A487 and follow the signs right to **Pentre Ifan**, a tomb dating from c. 3500 BC and built from a series of upright stones with a huge 17-ft (5-m) capstone. Return toward the A487 but cross over to the pretty Norman village of **Nevern**. The church is famous for several items: it has a 13-ft (4-m) high, 10th-century, two-piece **Celtic Cross**; a smaller **Vitalian Stone**, possibly from AD 500; an avenue of "bleeding yews" which exude a bright red sap and, inside, the **Maglocunus Stone**, inscribed with a 5th-century example of Ogham script (an ancient southern Irish alphabet).

Above The picturesque harbor in Fishguard's Lower Town

EAT AND DRINK

ST DAVIDS

Cwtch *moderate*
Enjoy relaxed dining at this modern restaurant with seasonal menus and local produce. Enjoy sea trout, cockles, or leek and mushroom pudding.
22 High Street, SA62 6PG; 01437 720 491; www.cwtchrestaurant.co.uk

Morgans Restaurant *moderate*
This acclaimed restaurant offers great food in a contemporary setting. Enjoy Pembrokeshire beef, good vegetarian dishes, and delicious desserts.
20 Nun Street, SA62 6NT; 01437 720 508; www.morgans-restaurant.co.uk

AROUND ST DAVIDS

The Sloop Inn *inexpensive–moderate*
At Croes-goch, turn left off the A487 to Fishguard, to this perfect 18th-century harborside pub serving a wide range of bar meals, from simple sandwiches to fish and chips or hearty steak pie.
Porthgain SA62 5BN; 01348 831 449; www.sloop.co.uk

NEWPORT

Cnapan *moderate*
Established restaurant serves quality modern British cuisine using local produce such as black beef and Welsh cheeses. Also a B&B with friendly hosts.
East Street, SA42 OSY; 01239 820 575; www.cnapan.co.uk

DAY TRIP OPTIONS

Castles, gardens, churches, and beaches – this drive has it all.

Castles and Gardens

From Llandovery ❶, see its castle and Myddfai – famed for its physicians, then pack a picnic and head for Llandeilo ❷ and the colorful gardens at Aberglasney. Climb the hill to stunning Carreg Cennen Castle ❸. Finally, visit the spectacular National Botanic Garden of Wales ❹.

Follow this drive's instructions and then retrace the journey.

Camarthen Bay

Visit the beach at Tenby ❽, skirt the bay to sandy Pendine ❼ and its Museum of Speed. Head to Laugharne ❻ for bay views from both the castle and Dylan Thomas' home. Carry on to the stout bastion of Kidwelly Castle ❺. If there's time, stop off at Carew Castle ❾, before returning to Tenby for some of its lively nightlife.

Follow this drive's instructions in reverse, taking the A477 to Carew Castle.

Coastal Fun

From Newport ⑭, head down to pretty Fishguard ⑬ to learn about the last invasion of Britain. Then on to St Davids ⑫ to visit the cathedral and enjoy a clifftop walk. Have a bracing swim or surf at Whitesands Bay and finish off with supper in Solva ⑪.

Follow the A487 there and back.

Eat and Drink: inexpensive, under £25; moderate, £25–£50; expensive, over £50

Through Snowdonia National Park

Machynlleth to Llandudno

Highlights

- **Spectacular mountain peaks**
  Enjoy the magnificent scenery around Cadair Idris, and take a train or walk up to Wales' highest peak, Mt. Snowdon

- **Glacial lakes and waterfalls**
  Be stunned by the sparkling jewel-like lakes and streaming waterfalls of Snowdonia National Park

- **Redoubtable castles**
  Tour the finest 13th-century military buildings in Europe – Harlech, Conwy, Caernarfon, and Beaumaris castles

- **Traditional seaside fun**
  Build a castle (made of sand) on the beach at Llandudno, Wales' biggest and most beautiful seaside resort

Picturesque countryside in Snowdonia National Park

Through Snowdonia National Park

This drive runs through north Wales past some staggering mountain scenery, with sorties to the peaks of Cadair Idris and Mount Snowdon. Most of the route follows a trail through the pristine Snowdonia National Park, a very special part of the country where many locals speak Welsh as their first tongue. On the way to the island of Anglesey, there are pretty mountain villages – ideal bases from which to explore the countryside – and frequent stops at some fearsome castles. Returning to the mainland, the drive finishes at lively Llandudno, Wales' largest and most attractive seaside town.

Above Spectacular lakeside scenery around Llyn Gwynant north of Beddgelert, *see p151*

ACTIVITIES

Fish for brown and sea trout on the idyllic waters of Tal-y-Llyn, a glacial lake outside Machynlleth

Climb to the mighty summit of Cadair Idris' beautiful and peaceful southern Snowdonia National Park

Storm the mighty Harlech Castle and walk along the walls, admiring the vertiginous views

Ride one of the most thrilling rail routes in the UK up to the dramatic peak of Mt. Snowdon

Take a boat trip to see the seals and seabirds around Puffin Island, from Beaumaris, Anglesey

Swing through the tree tops or go rock climbing in Betws-y-Coed

Soar above Llandudno in a cable car up to the top of the Great Orme, and do some skiing on the way down

0 kilometres   10

0 miles   10

KEY

Drive route

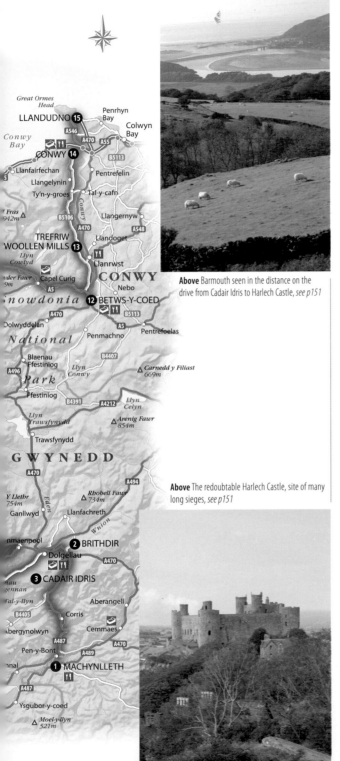

Above Barmouth seen in the distance on the drive from Cadair Idris to Harlech Castle, *see p151*

Above The redoubtable Harlech Castle, site of many long sieges, *see p151*

PLAN YOUR DRIVE

Start/finish: Machynlleth to Llandudno.

Number of days: 4, allowing time to explore Snowdonia National Park and walk on Anglesey Island.

Distance: Around 183 miles (295 km).

Road conditions: Well-paved and marked – the roads below Cadair Idris are narrow but have passing places.

When to go: Summer is best for outdoor activities, some places in the north close in the winter.

Opening times: Museums and attractions are generally open 10am–5pm, but close earlier (or are closed altogether) Nov–Easter. Shop times are longer. Churches are usually open until dusk.

Shopping: Local crafts, including traditional double-weave blankets.

Main market days: Dolgellau (near Brithidir): Farmers' Market, 3rd Sun of month; Porthmadog (near Harlech): Fri; Anglesey (at Menai Bridge, near Llanfair PG): 3rd Sat of month; Conwy: Farmers' Market, Wed.

Major festivals: Llanberis: Snowdonia Marathon, Oct; Anglesey: Oyster and Welsh Food Festival, Oct; Beaumaris: Arts Festival, May; Conwy: Honey Fair, Sept; Feast, Oct.

DAY TRIP OPTIONS

For photographers, stay at Machynlleth, see **glacial lakes,** then Brithdir's **church** and on to the **peaks** of Cadair Idris. Stay at Caernarfon for the **castle**, then go to Llanberis and take the thrilling **train ride** up Mt. Snowdon. Tour huge **tunnels** inside a mountain and then see the **pretty village** of Beddgelert. Discover Anglesey from Beaumaris – enjoy the **castle** and a **cruise**; see Moelfre's **maritime memorials** and then tour the **stately home** of Plas Newydd. For family fun, stay at Llandudno with its **sandy beach, tramway,** and Great Orme **Neolithic mines**. Head to Conwy for the **castle** and then Betws-y-Coed for some **tree-top fun**. For full details, *see p157*.

Above left Dark stone and painted house façades in Machynlleth **Above right** Welsh hill-farming country on the drive to Brithdir

VISITING MACHYNLLETH

Parking
Parking lot on Maengwyn St opposite the Tourist Information Centre.

Tourist Information
Heol Maengwyn, SY20 8EE (next to Owain Glyndŵr Museum); 01654 702 401

VISITING BEDDGELERT

Snowdonia National Park Information Centre
Canolfan Hebog, LL55 4YD; 01766 890 615; www.eryri-npa.gov.uk

WHERE TO STAY

AROUND MACHYNLLETH

Penrhos Arms Hotel moderate
Enjoy pleasant rooms with crisp bed linen and antiques in this country inn, 7 miles (11 km) northeast on the A470.
Cemmaes, SY20 9PR; 01650 511 243; www.penrhosarms.com

AROUND BRITHDIR

Ffynnon moderate–expensive
This 19th-century rectory is in Dolgellau, 5 miles (8 km) southeast of Brithdir. It has four suites with roll-top baths.
Ffynnon, Love Lane, Dolgellau, LL40 IRR; 01341 421 774; www.ffynnontownhouse.com

HARLECH CASTLE

Cemlyn Tea Shop inexpensive
There are just two neat, comfortable ensuite rooms above this lovely tea shop. One of them has stunning views of Harlech Castle and the sea.
High Street, LL46 2YA; 01766 780 425; www.cemlynrestaurant.co.uk

BEDDGELERT

Sygun Fawr inexpensive–moderate
Lovely old house in pretty gardens, with friendly atmosphere and lots of character – try for a mountain view. Take A498 north and then first right.
Beddgelert, LL55 4NE; 01766 890 258; www.sygunfawr.co.uk

① Machynlleth
Powys; SY20

This historic market town is where Owain Glyndŵr first assembled his Parliament and was crowned as Prince of Wales in 1404. Owain started his revolt against the English in 1400 during the reign of Henry IV. In 1412, after the revolt foundered, legends say that Owain went into hiding around Machynlleth, and he was never seen again. A copy of his seal can be seen in the **Old Parliament House** (Easter–Sep: closed Sun). This low stone house was actually built in the 16th century, but is now a museum about Owain Glyndŵr. The Tourist Information Centre is next door.

The **Tabernacle**, a Neo-Classical Wesleyan chapel dating from the late 18th century, has been converted to a center for the performing arts. The **MOMA Wales** (open Mon–Sat; www. momawales.org.uk) has evolved around it with four art galleries displaying the work of Welsh artists from 1900.

There is also a craft gallery, **Fforwm Crefft Cymru** (www.fforwmcrefftcymru. co.uk), which represents a wide range of artists and craft workers from silversmiths to furniture makers and sculptors to textile workers.

Below Leafy wooded avenue by the Art Nouveau Church of St. Mark's, Brithdir

Head north on the A487 and take a sharp left on B4405 to **Tal-y-Llyn** a stunningly beautiful glacial lake in the shadow of Cadair Idris. Enjoy a walk or take a boat out onto the lake. Its shallow reedy beds are stocked with brown trout, and the lake is visited by sea trout and salmon in October. Obtain permits from **Tynycornel Hotel** (01654 782282; www.tynycornel.co.uk).

🚗 *Leave on A487 north, then turn left on A470 toward Dolgellau and follow signs to Brithdir church. Park on B4416 at church entrance.*

② Brithdir
Gwynedd; LL40 1RE

Brithdir's major attraction is the **Church of St. Mark's**. Its dark stone exterior conceals an Italian-style interior (open most of the year) with red-ochre walls and a blue-sky ceiling. Designed by Henry Wilson (known for his commissions for Liberty's) and built 1895–98, it is one of the few Art Nouveau churches in Wales. See the ebony and abalone inlay on the doors and naturalistic carvings on the chestnut choir stall pews – squirrels, rabbits, a tortoise, and an owl – all created in the Arts and Crafts tradition. Notice, too, the beaten copper panels on the pulpit and altar.

🚗 *Return to A470 west. Turn left into Dolgellau along Ffos-y-Felin, which bears*

slightly right into Felin Isaf, then right into Porth Canol, which becomes Fford Cader Idris. After 5 miles (8 km), parking lot at Llynnau Cregennan is on the right.

Above One of the many rivers running off the peaks around Beddgelert

③ Cadair Idris
Gwynedd

A huge 7-mile (11-km)-long ridge, 2,927-ft (892-m) high, Cadair Idris dominates the surrounding area. The name means "Chair of Idris," after the giant warrior of Welsh legend. It's an area of outstanding scenic beauty and very popular with walkers. The tough paths to the top from the waters of **Llynnau Cregennan** take 4 to 6 hours to complete – on the way there are some standing stones and cairns over 4,000 years old. Climb to the small hill just above the parking lot for splendid views of Barmouth and Snowdonia.

🚗 Take the road up and down to A493 and turn right to Penmaenpool. Here, take a left over the toll bridge to A496. Turn left for Barmouth and on to Harlech. Park in front of the castle.

Below Impressive Harlech Castle, looking as though it has grown from the rocky hillside

④ Harlech Castle
Gwynedd; LL46 2YH

Impressively situated on a bluff over Tremadog Bay, **Harlech Castle** was built between 1283–90 at a cost of £8,190 by Edward I's master mason, James of St. George, who was also responsible for Caernarfon, Conway and Beaumaris castles. One of Edward's "iron ring" of castles, Harlech was designed to be supplied by sea, but the waters have since receded, leaving the castle high and dry. In 1404 Owain Glyndŵr took the castle, using it for his parliament. It was retaken after a long siege in 1408 by Harry of Monmouth, later Henry V. In the Wars of the Roses, it endured the longest siege in British history (1461–68) before being taken by the Yorkists, giving rise to the well-known military song "Men of Harlech."

🚗 Continue on A496 north and turn left to Penrhyndeudraeth; leave on A4085, which joins A498. In Beddgelert, take second left to parking lot.

⑤ Beddgelert
Gwynedd; LL55

Perhaps Snowdonia's prettiest village, Beddgelert has a lovely tea shop, and several cafés, bars, and bistros. The town is centered on a rustic bridge from where, along the south bank of the river, a path leads to the supposed monument to Llywelyn the Great's deerhound, Gelert. The story goes that, while Llywelyn was hunting, the dog saved his child from a wolf but Llywelyn, seeing the blood, thought the hound had killed his boy. He slew Gellert, but found his son safe and the wolf dead. He set a cairn of stones over the dog's grave, **Beth Gelert**. A short drive east on the A498, **Llyn Gwynant** is a lake in some simply stunning scenery.

🚗 Turn left from parking lot to A498 and left onto A4086 to Llanberis, left at roundabout and right to railway parking lot.

Above Stone houses overlooking the river at Beddgelert, crossed by a rustic bridge

EAT AND DRINK

MACHYNLLETH

The Wynnstay *inexpensive–moderate*
Local suppliers provide the ingredients for the dishes here, from pheasant breast to Welsh cheese cannelloni. There's also a separate pizzeria.
Heol Maengwyn, SY20 8AE; 01654 702 941; www.wynnstay-hotel.com

AROUND BRITHDIR

Dylanwad Da *moderate*
This little restaurant and coffee shop in Dolgellau, about 5 miles (8 km) southeast of Brithdir, uses lots of local produce. Dishes might include rosemary and garlic roast lamb, with Welsh whisky and honey ice cream for dessert.
2 Ffos-y-Felin, Dolgellau, LL40 1BS; 01341 422 870; www.dylanwad.co.uk

HARLECH CASTLE

Castle Cottage Restaurant *moderate–expensive*
An award-winning family-run restaurant in the heart of Harlech, Castle Cottage adds a sophisticated twist to Welsh produce, such as aromatic Welsh lamb pancakes with hoisin sauce. There's a good wine list, and rooms, too.
High Street, LL46 2YL; 01766 780 479; www.castlecottageharlech.co.uk

BEDDGELERT

Tanronnen Inn *inexpensive*
For a traditional bar meal, head for this busy inn, conveniently situated in the center of town. The inn has rooms and also does packed lunches for day trips.
Beddgelert, LL55 4YB; 01766 890 347; www.tanronnen.co.uk

Above View of the beautiful countryside of the Snowdonia National Park

VISITING MOUNT SNOWDON

Snowdonia National Park Information
*41a High Street, Llanberis, LL55 4EU;
01286 870 765*

SHOPPING IN BEAUMARIS

Try Cole & Co *(13 Church St, L58 8AB;
01248 811 391)* for hand knits, and
home-made barabrith (a traditional
Welsh fruit cake).

WHERE TO STAY

AROUND CAERNARFON

Plas Dinas *expensive*
Enjoy a taste of country house living at
this 17th-century, grade II-listed house
on the A487 not far south of Caernarfon.
It has lovely gardens and elegant rooms,
and serves local bacon for breakfast.
*Bontnewydd, LL54 7YF; 01286 830 214;
www.plasdinas.co.uk*

Ty'n Rhos *moderate–expensive*
Comfortable country hotel set in grand
grounds less than 5 miles (8 km)
northeast of Caernarfon, off the A4866.
It offers good-sized rooms, suites, and
self-catering cottages. The hotel
restaurant is pretty good, too.
*Seion, Llanddeiniolen, LL55 3AE; 01248
670 489; www.tynrhos.co.uk*

BEAUMARIS

Bulls Head Inn *moderate*
Country-style bedrooms with a modern
touch can be found at this established
inn. Next door, their contemporary town
house has stylish color-themed rooms
and luxurious bathrooms.
*Castle Street, LL58 8AP; 01248 810 329;
www.bullsheadinn.co.uk*

Right The award-winning new Hafod Eryri
visitor center at the summit of Snowdon

⑥ Mount Snowdon
Gwynedd; LL55 4TY

A popular destination, **Llanberis** has
many significant attractions, not least
Wales' highest mountain, Snowdon, at
3,560 ft (1,085 m). Walk to the top or
take the train. The 4-mile (7-km) trip
passes through stunning scenery
and is perhaps the most exciting
train journey in the UK. The **Snowdon
Mountain Railway** *(Apr–Oct: open daily;
Nov–Mar: partial service; 0844 493 8120;
www.snowdonrailway.co.uk)* is weather
dependent, so check beforehand.

At the top of Snowdon, **Hafod Eryri**,
the new railway terminus and visitor
center, awaits. Britain's highest building
and possibly one of its most unusual
was designed by architect Roy Hole,
after the original 1930s cafe was
demolished in 2006. Created from
stone and slate and with a large flat
roof, Hafod Eryri does not seem out of
place in Snowdon's rugged landscape.

Inside, the walls are lined in timber and
the hugh window afford thrilling views.

Nearby, the **Electric Mountain Centre**
*(open daily: tours Easter–end Oct; 01286 870
636; www.electricmountain.co.uk)* has a
café and activity rooms, and runs
tours of the Dinorwig Power Station,
deep in Europe's largest man-made
cavern, inside Elidir Mountain (not
suitable for wheelchair users or anyone
who suffers from claustrophobia).

Don't miss the often overlooked
Dolbadarn Castle *(open daily)*, perched
on the hillside over the main road
beside the lake, Llyn Peris. Built in the
13th century by Llywelyn the Great, it
is simple but masterful – the 40-ft
(12-m) tower once had three levels.

Steam buffs will love the **Llanberis
Lake Railway** *(May–Sep: open daily; call
at other times; 01286 870 549; www.lake-
railway.co.uk)*. The narrow-gauge steam
railway runs along the pretty wooded
lakeside. Nearby is the **National Slate
Museum** *(open Sun–Fri; 01286 870 630;
www.museumwales.ac.uk)*, telling the story
of slate in a series of Victorian workshops
with walks and demonstrations.

🚗 *Take A4086 to Caernarfon. Head
into the center and park by the castle.*

⑦ Caernarfon
Gwynedd; LL55

By the Menai Straits and with sea
access, Caernarfon is the ideal site for
a castle. **Caernarfon Castle** *(open daily)*
was built in 1283 as part of Edward I's
ring of castles to subjugate the Welsh.
With its polygonal towers and twin-
turreted gateway, Caernarfon Castle is

a fine example of late 13th- and early 14th-century military architecture. The color-banded masonry was inspired by Constantinople's walls. King Edward wanted the castle to be a royal residence and seat of government for north Wales. Its symbolic status was emphasized when Edward made sure his son, the first English Prince of Wales, was born here in 1284. It was more recently used for the investiture of the present Prince of Wales in 1969.

On the A4085, on the edge of town, stands the Roman fort of **Segontium** *(closed Mon; 01286 675 625)* dating from AD 77–78 . The large fort was built to control the approach to Anglesey and see off Irish seaborne raiders. It was in use until AD 395 and its internal layout is still visible. There is also a museum.

🚗 *Leave by A487 to Bangor. Take the A5 left across Menai Suspension Bridge (1826). Take A545 right to Beaumaris. Park by pier or opposite castle.*

⑧ Beaumaris
Anglesey; LL58

With medieval, Georgian, Victorian, and Edwardian buildings and a wide range of shops, Beaumaris is an attractive town for visitors. See the **Church of St. Mary** for the carved tomb of Joan, Llywelyn the Great's wife. The main draw here is **Beaumaris Castle** *(open daily)*, a military masterpiece and the last and largest of Edward I's Welsh castles. Built in 1295 with concentric symmetry and four lines of defence, to a design by Master James of St. George, it was meant to control the Menai Straits and there are great views of Snowdonia. The low-lying castle has 16 towers and a chapel with

a vaulted ceiling and lancet windows. However, the money ran out before the fortifications had reached full height.

Seafaring types can take a cruise to see seals and puffins, or go wreck fishing. Book with **Starida Sea Services** *(01248 810 251; www.starida.co.uk)*.

Take the coastal road north to the tranquil tip of Anglesey, to **Penmon Priory** at the entrance to the Menai Straits. Founded in the 6th century, it was destroyed by the Danes in the 10th. The present **St. Seiriol's church** dates from around 1140. Inside are some beautiful early stone Welsh crosses. The well, outside, is believed to be part of the original 6th-century building, which would make it the oldest ecclesiastical site in Wales.

🚗 *Leave on B5109, turn right onto the A5025, turning right for Moelfre. Drive on to the seafront parking lot.*

Above left Caernarfon Castle, built to recall the walls of Constantinople **Above top right** Café culture in the quiet center of Caernarfon **Above right** Cozy Beau's Tea Room, in a historic building close to the castle, Beaumaris

EAT AND DRINK

MOUNT SNOWDON

Snowdon Mountain Railway Station Café & Caffi y Copa at Hafod Eryri *inexpensive*
The café at Hafod Eryri on Snowdon's summit offers baked savories from the Village Bakery (since 1934). Alternatively, the café at Llanberis serves all-day brunch, snacks, and tea. *Snowdon Summit/Llanberis, LL55 4TY; 01286 870 223; www.snowdoniarailway.co.uk*

Caban Cyf *inexpensive*
Near Llanberis, this restaurant uses organic produce from its own garden. *Yr Hen Ysgol, Brynrefail, LL55 3NR; 01286 685 500; www.caban-cyf.org open lunch, Sat eve.*

Heights Hotel *moderate*
This hotel has an extensive bar menu of home-cooked food with good vegetarian options. *74 High Street, Llanberis, LL55 4HB; 01286 871 179; www.heightshotel.net*

BEAUMARIS

Beau's Tea Room *inexpensive*
This is the place to fill up on tea and fresh *barabrith*. In a cozy 400-year-old building, the café also sells hot meals – and antique bone china. *30 Castle Street, LL58 8AP; 01248 811 010; www.beaustearoom.co.uk*

Left Beaumaris Castle, the largest of Edward I's Welsh fortifications

Eat and Drink: inexpensive, under £25; moderate, £25–£50; expensive, over £50

Above Cottages in the coastal village of Moelfre, on the Island of Anglesey

VISITING MOELFRE

Parking
Free parking close to the village and a pay-and-display parking lot on seafront.

Tourist Information
01248 713 177;
www.visitmoelfre.fsnet.co.uk

WHERE TO STAY

AROUND MOELFRE

Llwydiarth Fawr *moderate*
This Georgian home is at the heart of a working farm about 5 miles (8 km) from Moelfre. Its spacious, elegant interior is furnished with antiques and includes a library.
Llanerch-y-medd, LL71 8DF (take A5108 out of Moelfre, at roundabout take second exit onto A5025, turn left, left again and bear left, then take second right toward B5111 and turn left; farm is on left); 01248 470 321; www.angleseyfarms.com/llwydiarth.htm

AROUND LLANFAIRPWLL

Cleifiog Uchaf *moderate*
A 16th-century Welsh longhouse in superb location, this small hotel has a relaxing interior and its own access to the Anglesey Coastal Path.
Valley, LL65 3AB (take A5/A55 toward Holyhead, exit 3 for A5 to Valley, fourth exit at the roundabout, left at Lon Spencer, then right); 01407 741 888; www.cleifioguchaf.co.uk/index.html

Neuadd Lwyd Country House
expensive
In an old grey-stoned Victorian rectory, this country residence is stylishly furnished for a relaxing break and boasts seriously good cooking.
Penmynydd, LL61 5BX (take A5/ Holyhead Rd out of town and follow signs to Ffordd Penmynydd, then B5240 and first right); 01248 715 005; www.neuaddlwyd.co.uk

⑨ Moelfre
Anglesey; LL61

The sleepy village of Moelfre looks north into the Irish Sea, over the ships going to and from Mersey port. This walk follows the headland around the village, past memorials highlighting the dangers of the sea and the bravery of the Royal National Lifeboat Institution (RNLI) crews.

A two-hour walking tour

From the seafront parking lot, walk with the sea on your right to the **Seawatch Centre** ① *(Easter–Sep: closed Mon)*, which chronicles the island's maritime and natural history, and the lives of locals such as Richard Evans who saved the lives of two boat crews.

Outside, walk down to the sea to the bronze sculpture of coxswain Evans MBE who retired in 1970. Then turn left and follow the coastal path to the **RNLI Lifeboat Station** ② *(open daily; 01248 410 367; www.moelfrelifeboat. co.uk)*, which has information about the work of the RNLI – run by volunteers – and rescuing hundreds of people a year from the sea. Further along the footpath, see terns, gannets, and fulmars on the island of Ynys Moelfre, just offshore. Continue along the coast and go through two gates and up a slight hill and some steps and over a style. Go through another gate, and along a path. Walk down the path toward a small bridge, over a stream, and then up the steps to the top. Here is the

RNLI logo at Moelfre Lifeboat Station

Monument to the Royal Charter ③, a passenger steam clipper returning to Liverpool from Melbourne, which sank off the coast of Anglesey in October 1859 during one of the fiercest storms of the century. It was a catastrophe with 459 lives lost and only 21 passengers and 18 crew surviving. No women or children survived. It was the highest death toll of any shipwreck off the Welsh coast in the days before Moelfre had a lifeboat. Walk back down the steps and up the path and take a right past the caravans. Keep on the track and cross the cattle grid, past a cottage and onto the road. Turn left into a housing estate, past the house Ty Mawr followed by a school, a library, and Maes Hydryd. Continue straight on and take a left past Anne's Pantry, a family-run café and restaurant, and the Kinmel Arms Hotel, with fine ales and pub food. The parking lot is over the road.

🚗 *Drive back on the A5025, through Pentraeth and under the A55 to Llanfair PG. Use the train station parking lot beside Pringles Weavers.*

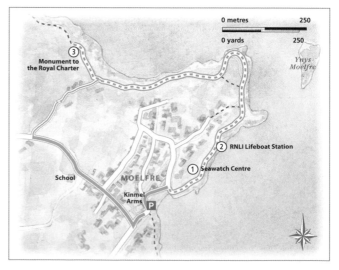

Right Headland and Monument to the Royal
Charter, near Moelfre

⑩ Llanfairpwllgwyngyll- gogerychwyrndrobwll- llandysiliogogogoch

Anglesey; LL61

The name means "Church of St. Mary
in the hollow of the white hazel trees,
near a fierce whirlpool and the Church
of St. Tysilio, near the red cave." Often
shortened to Llanfair PG or Llanfairpwll,
at 58 letters long it is the longest
place name in Britain. It was devised
by the Victorians to attract tourists. The
train station sign is the usual subject
for photos. Nearby is the **Marquess of
Anglesey's Column** (open daily), a 89-ft
(27-m) monument to Henry William
Paget who lost his leg at the Battle of
Waterloo. Climb the 115 steps for a
fabulous panorama. **Oriel Ty Gorsaf**
(summer: closed Mon, Thu; winter: closed
Mon, Tue; www.orieltygorsaf.co.uk) is a
stained-glass gallery with work from
glass artists from around the world.

🚗 Turn right out of parking lot onto
Holyhead Rd and turn right onto A4080
to Plas Newydd and parking lot. A
minibus shuttles visitors to the house.

⑪ Plas Newydd

Anglesey; LL61 6DQ

Just outside Llanfair PG, **Plas Newydd**
(open mid-Mar–end Oct: Sat–Wed; 01248
715 272) is the ancestral home of the
Marquess of Anglesey. The house
was redesigned in the 18th century
by renowned architect James Wyatt
in a mixture of Neo-Gothic and Neo-
Classical styles. It is set in parkland
with beautiful walks and dramatic
views over the Menai Straits and
Snowdonia.The long dining room
features a massive 58-ft (18-m) mural
of a mythological harbor scene by
the artist and set designer Rex
Whistler c.1936-40, who died in
World War II. There is a small military
museum about the 1st Marquess
of Anglesey, who was the Duke of
Wellington's cavalry commander at
the Battle of Waterloo.

🚗 Return on A4080, turn right onto A5
and under flyover to cross back to mainland (to bypass Bangor take A55). Keep
on A5 to Betws-y-Coed. In town center,
turn left over bridge to parking lot.

Below left Llanfairpwllgwyngyllgogerych-
wyrndrobwllllandysiliogogogoch **Below**
Neo-Gothic and Neo-Classical Plas Newydd

Eat and Drink: inexpensive, under £25; moderate, £25–£50; expensive, over £50

Above The highest waterfall in Wales, Swallow Falls, Betws-y-Coed

VISITING BETWS-Y-COED

Snowdonia National Park Information Centre
Royal Oak Stables, LL24 0AH; 01690 710 426

Adventure Activities
For rock climbing and canyoning activities, including lessons, try **Seren Ventures** *(Treetop Lodge, LL24 0HA; 01690 710 754; www.serenventures. com);* for tree-top activities, suitable for all ages, contact **Tree Top Adventure** *(Ffridd Rhedyn, Llanrwst Road, LL24 0HA UK; 01690 710 914; www.ttadventure.co.uk).*

WHERE TO STAY

AROUND BETWS-Y-COED

St. Curig's Church *inexpensive*
Snuggle up in this cozy converted church about 5 miles (8 km) west on the A5. There are original stained-glass windows, and a hot tub in the garden. *Capel Curig, LL24 0EL; 01690 720 469; www.stcurigschurch.com*

Pengwern Guesthouse *moderate*
Enjoy friendly Welsh-speaking hosts and immaculate, individually furnished rooms at this country house, a short distance south on the A5. Local produce for breakfast, free Wi-fi, and fine views. *Allt Dinas, LL24 0HF; 01690 710 480; www.snowdoniaaccommodation.co.uk*

CONWY

Sychnant Pass House
moderate–expensive
Situated about 2 miles (3 km) west of Conwy this is a friendly and relaxed country guesthouse, with comfortable rooms, highly rated food, and a swimming pool and hot tub. *Sychnant Pass Rd, LL32 8BJ; 01492 596 868; www.sychnant-pass-house.co.uk*

12 Betws-y-Coed
Conwy; LL24

The principal village in the Snowdonia National Park, **Betws-y-Coed**, the "prayer house in the wood", is a popular tourist spot along with the nearby **Swallow Falls**, the highest continuous waterfall in Wales. Nestled in a wooded valley at the confluence of the rivers Conwy, Llugwy, and Lledr, it is well-appointed with galleries, cafés, shops, pubs, and hotels. Its oldest building is the 14th-century **St. Michael's Church** with a stone effigy of Gruffydd ap Dafydd Goch, related to Llywelyn, the last free Welsh Prince of Wales. It is ideally situated for walks into the gorgeous countryside with rivers, pools, and

Traditional designs at Trefriw Woollen Mills

waterfalls and dense mountain woods. Several walks start from the ancient stone Pont-y-Pair bridge, built in 1468, in the town center. Those looking for more extreme activities can go rock climbing, abseiling, or canyoning, or try clambering around an adventure obstacle course among the tree tops.

🚗 *From the parking lot, take B5106 north to Trefriw. Park across the road from the mills by the war memorial.*

13 Trefriw Woollen Mills
Conwy; LL27 0NQ

Established in 1859 and run ever since by the Williams family, **Trefriw Woollen Mills** *(open daily; 01492 640 462; www.t-w-m.co.uk)* use 50-year-old machines and do their own blending, spinning, dying, and weaving. The mill is best known for its traditional Welsh, double-weave blankets. There is a weavers' garden with a display of the plants which provide fibers, soap, and natural dyes and, in the summer, there are hand-spinning and weaving demonstrations. Walk or drive on the road, alongside the river that supplies the mill, to the lakes of Llyn Geirionydd and **Llyn Crafnant**. There's a café beside Llyn Crafnant with great cakes and ice cream.

🚗 *Turn right out of parking lot to leave Trefriw on B5106 north to Conwy, and pass through break in city wall. At the roundabout, turn left into Rose Hill Street and park next to the castle.*

Below left Betwys-y-Coed, nestled in a deep wooded valley at the confluence of three rivers

⑭ Conwy

Conwy; LL32

At the mouth of an estuary spanned by Telford's 1826 suspension bridge, Conwy is best known for its castle. The turreted **Conwy Castle** *(open daily)* was built by Master James of St. George using local stone in four years (1283–87). The castle and the medieval town walls have World Heritage status and are Britain's finest example of a *bastide* or fortified town, with 21 towers, three double gateways and a 4,200-ft (1,280-m)-long wall.

There are other interesting historic buildings in the town. **Aberconwy House** *(Apr–Oct: closed Tue)* is a 14th-century merchant's house with period displays; **Plas Mawr** *(closed Mon)* is one of the finest surviving Elizabethan town houses (1558–1603). Admire its symmetry, the crow-stepped gables and pedimented windows. **The Potters Gallery** *(www.thepottersgallery.co.uk)*, further down the High Street has a great collection of local ceramics. And finally, on Conwy Quay, squeeze into the **Smallest House in Britain** *(Apr–Oct: open daily)* – it is 9 ft (2.75 m) high and 5 ft (1.5 m) wide and was last owned by a fisherman over 6-ft (2-m) tall!

🚗 *Leave Conwy on A547 over the bridge and take A546 left to Llandudno. Head for the seafront and promenade.*

⑮ Llandudno

Conwy; LL30

Wales' largest seaside resort, Llandudno lies in a wide bay sheltered by two limestone headlands, the Ormes. Most of the town was laid out in 1849 with grand buildings, a promenade – the Parade and the longest pier in Wales. The Great Orme is a 679-ft (207-m)-high promontory reached by road, **cable car** *(mid-Mar–Oct: open daily)*, and a **funicular tramway** *(open daily)* with spectacular views from the top.

Explore the **Great Orme Mines** *(Mar–Oct: open daily; www.greatormemines.info)*, the world's largest Bronze-Age copper mine, through tunnels dug over 3,500 years ago. The Great Orme is a good place for walking following the marked nature trails, and winter sports fans will enjoy skiing or tobogganing at the **Llandudno Ski and Snowboard Centre** *(open daily; www.llandudnoskislope.co.uk)*.

Among the town's other attractions is the outstanding contemporary art gallery **Oriel Mostyn** *(01492 879 201; www.mostyn.org)* on Vaughan Street.

Above left Inside the impressive outer ward in World Heritage status Conwy Castle **Above center** The Knight's Shop, selling suits of armour opposite Conwy Castle **Above right** Small fishing station on pretty Conwy Estuary

EAT AND DRINK

BETWS-Y-COED

Ty Gwyn Hotel *inexpensive–moderate*
This former coaching inn serves a range of restaurant and bar meals such as roast goose, smoked cod, and cottage pie. *Betws-y-Coed, LL24 0SG; 01690 710 383; www.tygwynhotel.co.uk*

AROUND TREFRIW WOOLLEN MILLS

The Tannery *moderate*
This modern café/bistro on the A470 near Trefriw serves imaginative dishes with Welsh flavors on a riverside terrace. *Willow St, Llanrwst; LL26 0ES; 01492 640 172*

CONWY

The Mulberry *inexpensive–moderate*
This pub on the Marina serves a range of dishes from meat pies to pasta. *Ellis Way, Marina; LL32 8GU; 01492 583 350; www.themulberryconwy.com*

Bistro Conwy *moderate–expensive*
Enjoy quality contemporary dishes using Welsh produce at this little bistro tucked under the old town walls. *26 Chapel St, LL32 8BP; 01492 596 326*

DAY TRIP OPTIONS

Several stops along the route make ideal bases from which to explore the area's spectacular scenery, historic sites, and visitor attractions.

A Photographers' Treat

Starting from historic Machynlleth ❶, visit beautiful Tal-y-Llyn and enjoy boating or fishing on the lake. Carry on to Brithdir ❷, to see the church and head to Llynnau Cregennan for a walk in the shadow of Cadair Idris ❸.

Follow the drive's instructions.

Exploring Snowdonia

From Caernarfon ❼, see the castle before heading for Llanberis, and a train ride up Mt. Snowdon ❻. Then travel through a mountain with the Electric Mountain Centre. Finally, drive to pretty Beddgelert ❺ for the stunning scenery.

Take the A4086 and A498; but return to Caernarfon via the A4085.

Anglesey Adventure

Staying at Beaumaris ❽, see the castle and enjoy a morning cruise around Puffin Island. Head to Moelfre ❾, and

learn about the island's maritime history. Then tour the beautiful home of the Marquess of Anglesey, Plas Newydd ⑪.

Follow the drive's instructions.

Family Fun

Explore the beach, take the tram up the Great Orme to see the copper mines at Llandudno ⑮, then head to Conwy ⑭ to tour the castle and have lunch. Drive into the heart of Snowdonia to Betws-y-Coed ⑫, for a walk to Swallow Falls or thrilling tree-top adventure.

Take the A470 and A55.

Along Offa's Dyke

From Ludlow to Holywell

Highlights

- **England's finest market town**
  Wander through Ludlow's historic center with its half-timbered buildings, medieval street plan, ancient church, and mighty castle

- **Stately castle homes**
  Explore the beautiful residences of Powis, Chirk, and Bodelwyddan castles, packed full of interesting artifacts and set in magical grounds

- **Heaven on earth**
  Spend some time at Llangollen, with its society haunts, looming hilltop castle, ancient ruined abbey, and spectacular canal and aqueduct

- **The Lourdes of Wales**
  Take the waters at Holywell – probably the oldest pilgrimage site in Britain, and appreciate its air of piety and faith

View of the Long Mynd, a series of dramatic hills in Shropshire

Along Offa's Dyke

This drive takes the visitor from the English borders over Wenlock Edge and around the Long Mynd, an ancient hog's-back ridge, into the beautiful Welsh countryside. The route now runs parallel to Offa's impressive but ultimately ineffective dyke, heading north to the estuary of the River Dee. On the way, the drive winds past the remains of once-mighty castles and still grand country houses, and Thomas Telford's fabulous feat of Victorian engineering, the aqueduct on the Llangollen Canal at Pontcysylite. There are cultural and spiritual highlights, too. See a copy of William Morgan's first translation of the Bible into Welsh in the Cathedral at St Asaph and the "Jesse Tree" window of St. Dyfnog's Church, and experience the tranquillity of St. Winefride's Well in Holywell.

Above Ruins of Denbigh Castle, overlooking the surrounding countryside, *see p166*

ACTIVITIES

Learn about old rural crafts at Acton Scott Farm Museum

Look out for rare red kites hovering over Powis Castle

Be pulled by a historic steam locomotive through the Welsh countryside on the Welshpool & Llanfair Light Railway

Clamber up to Castell Dinas Bran for the astonishing views

Glide over the 121-ft (37-m) high Pontcysyllte Aqueduct in a canal barge

Step through 600 years of housing history in Ruthin

Follow a nature trail in the grounds of Bodelwyddan Castle

Take the healing waters at the Lourdes of Wales, Holywell

Below Bodenham's, one of many striking half-timbered buildings in Ludlow, *see p162*

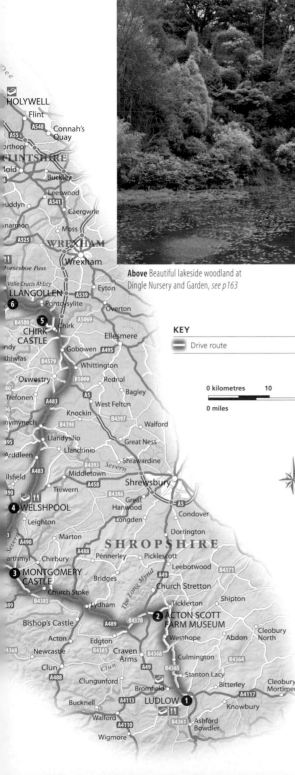

Above Beautiful lakeside woodland at Dingle Nursery and Garden, *see p163*

HOLYWELL
Flint
A548 Connah's
A55 Quay
orthop
FLINTSHIRE
Mold
Buckley
uddyn Leeswood
A541
Caergwrle
narmon Moss
A525
WREXHAM
Wrexham
Horseshoe Pass
Valle Crucis Abbey Eyton
LLANGOLLEN A539
6 Pontcysylite
Overton
B4500 Chirk A5069
5 Ellesmere
CHIRK
CASTLE Gobowen A495
ndy
thiwlas B4579 Whittington
Oswestry B5009 Rednal
Trefonen A483 A5 Bagley
West Felton
nymynech Knockin B4397
B4398 Walford
Llandysilio Great Ness
Arddleen Llandrinio
A483 B4393 Shrawardine Severn
ilsfield Middletown
A458 Shrewsbury
190 Trewern
Great
WELSHPOOL Hanwood B4386
4 Longden Condover A5
Leighton
Marton Dorrington
A490
SHROPSHIRE
arthmyl Chirbury Pennerley Picklescott
3 MONTGOMERY Leebotwood B4371
CASTLE Bridges A49
Church Stoke Church Stretton
89 B4385
Lydham Ticklerton Shipton
Bishop's Castle A489 B4370
Acton Edgton ACTON SCOTT
2 FARM MUSEUM
1368 Newcastle B4385 Craven Westhope Abdon Cleobury
Clun Arms B4368 North
A488 Clun Culmington B4364
Clungunford A49 B4365
Stanton Lacy
89 B4385 Bromfield Bitterley Cleobury
Bucknell A4113 Mortimer
LUDLOW 1 A4117
Walford Knowbury
A4110 B4361 Ashford
Wigmore Bowdler

KEY

Drive route

0 kilometres   10

0 miles   10

PLAN YOUR DRIVE

Start/Finish: Ludlow to Holywell.

Number of days: 4, allowing half a day at Ludlow and half a day at Llangollen.

Distance: About 129 miles (207 km).

Road conditions: Good, well-paved and marked.

When to go: Spring and summer is best for walks in the hills.

Opening times: Galleries, museums, and attractions are generally open 10am–5pm, but often close earlier Nov–Easter. Shops are often open longer. Churches are usually open until dusk.

Main market days: Ludlow: 4 days a week, Castle Square; Sat am, Church St; Welshpool: 1st Fri of month, Farmers' Market, Town Hall; Llangollen: Fri am, Town Hall; Denbigh: last Fri of month, Town Hall; Holywell: Thu & Sat am.

Shopping: Plenty of Shropshire produce and local foods around Ludlow and pottery at St Asaph. Carved wooden lovespoons can be found all over Wales.

Major festivals: Ludlow: Arts festival, Jun–Jul; Food Festival, beginning Sep (*www.foodfestival.co.uk*); St Asaph: North Wales International Classical Music Festival, end Sep (*www.northwalesmusicfestival.co.uk*); Llangollen: International Musical Eisteddfod, Jul.

DAY TRIP OPTIONS

Families will enjoy staying at Ludlow to visit the **castle** and a **farm museum** for a **picnic**, before heading to Welshpool for the **steam train** and maybe a tour of the **castle**. Alternatively, spend a day near Llangollen – climb a hill to the **castle**, walk along a **canal**, see the **aqueduct**, admire the **views** at Horseshoe Pass, visit an **abbey,** and then drive to Chirk Castle for its **interiors** and **gardens**. For those interested in cultural and religious treasures, see Denbigh's **castle** and **churches**, the **Welsh Bible** at St Asaph, **treasures** and **gardens** at Bodelwyddan Castle, the **pilgrimage site** and **well** at Holywell, and the **Jesse window** at St. Dyfnog's. For full details, *see p167*.

Above Carved wooden façade of the Feathers Hotel, Ludlow

VISITING LUDLOW

Parking
Follow signs to town centre and park as near as possible to Castle Square: there is pay-and-display parking on Mill Street and Dinham, down the side of the castle, and a parking lot off Castle Street.

Tourist Information
Castle St, SY8 1AS; 01584 875 053; www.shropshiretourism.co.uk

WHERE TO STAY

LUDLOW

De Grey's Town House *moderate*
This picturesque Tudor half-timbered building above a lovely tea shop has nine quality ensuite rooms with fine furnishings and roll-top baths.
Broad Street, SY8 1NG; 01584 872 764; www.degreys.co.uk

AROUND LUDLOW

The Clive *moderate*
This former farmhouse, north of Ludlow on the A49, has 15 immaculate ensuite rooms and serves fresh produce for breakfast. It also has a superb restaurant and bar, open to non-residents.
Bromfield, SY8 2JR; 01584 856 565; www.theclive.co.uk

WELSHPOOL

The Royal Oak Hotel *moderate*
Once a Georgian coaching inn, this hotel has comfortable boutique-style rooms with a contemporary or classic décor.
The Cross, SY21 7DG; 01938 552 217; www.royaloakhotel.info

---

❶ Ludlow
Shropshire; SY8

The market town of Ludlow is a great base for exploring the glorious Marches countryside. Growing from the wealth of the medieval wool trade, Ludlow became an important political center. Much of its medieval street pattern has survived almost intact and there are some fine examples of timber-framed buildings and a ruined castle. This walk gives a good introduction to the town.

A two-hour walking tour

From Mill St, turn left to 11th-century **Ludlow Castle** ① *(open daily)*, one of a series of Norman castles built in the Marches to control the Welsh. Return to Castle Square, and across Mill St on the right to the **Assembly Rooms** ② – a Tourist Information Centre and museum with local history and geology exhibits. Continue down the narrow Market St and turn right into the fine **Broad Sreet** ③. Appreciate the seamless mix of timber-framed Tudor and elegant brick buildings. Return back up Broad St and turn right into King St toward the restored 15th-century toll house, **The Tolsey** ④. Now occupied by solicitors' offices and shops, this is where tax was collected for every head of cattle brought for sale at market. At the Old Bull Ring pub, turn left onto Bull Ring and continue to the **Feathers Hotel** ⑤,

Carved stone arch at Ludlow Castle

built in 1619, with its skillfully carved half-timbered frontage. The balconies were added in the 19th century. Return back up the street, admiring the woodwork on the buildings. Turn right and head back to the **Butter Cross** ⑥, which was rebuilt in 1744 in Neo-Classical style as a town hall and served as a butter market. Take a right past Barclays Bank to **St. Laurence's Church** ⑦. Established in the 11th century, this was rebuilt in 1199 and heavily modified in the 15th century. Look out for the tomb of Arthur Tudor (Henry VII's son) and the carved misericords of medieval scenes. Climb the 138-ft (42-m) tower for fabulous views. Admire the stained glass – the Palmer's window tells of King Edward the Confessor's visit to the Holy Land. The cherry trees in the graveyard commemorate the poet AE Housman (1859–1936), author of *A Shropshire Lad,*

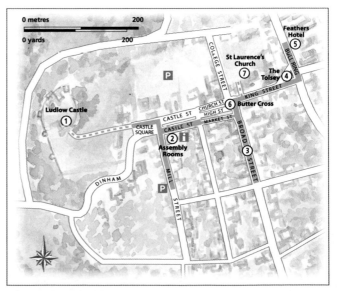

Above View of the Shropshire countryside around Ludlow

whose ashes are buried in the church wall near the West Door. Exit the church and return to King St. Turn right and carry on down Church St to Castle Square, turning left to return to Mill St.

🚗 *Take A49 towards Shrewsbury, then B4365 right to a T-junction (B4368). Turn left, then first right to Ticklerton and the museum, 2 km (1½ miles) beyond.*

❷ Acton Scott Farm Museum
Shropshire; SY6 6QN

This living history farm museum *(Apr–Oct: closed Mon)* recreates life on a Shropshire farm at the turn of the last century. Visitors are returned to the days of shire horses, hay ricks, and milkmaids, and the farm is stocked with pigs, poultry, cows, and sheep, including some rare breeds. Kids will enjoy the daily demonstrations by farm workers dressed in period costumes. There are also marked walks starting from the farm.

🚗 *Turn left from parking lot and straight across to A49. Turn right, then left onto B4370, then take A489 right. Take B4385 to castle and parking lot.*

❸ Montgomery Castle
Powys; SY15

It was the Norman knight Roger de Montgomerie (the very first Earl of Shrewsbury) who built the first fort here in c.1070 – the motte-and-bailey Hen Domen, at the bottom of Castle Hill. The present castle *(open daily)* was built in 1223 during the reign of Henry III to defend the border against the Welsh Prince, Llywelyn the Great (1173–1240). It was demolished during the Civil War. There are great views out over a wide expanse of countryside to the north and east.

🚗 *Head northwest on B4385, joining the A483 north, with the floodplain of*

the Severn flowing south on the right. Fork left onto the A490 into Welshpool. Park in Church St in the town center.

❹ Welshpool
Powys; SY21 8RF

Set in the picturesque countryside of the Severn Valley, Welshpool makes an excellent base for exploring the surrounding area. The big attraction, off the A490 into town (with parking lot) or a 1-km/2-mile walk across parkland), is stunning **Powis Castle** *(Mar–Oct: open Thu–Mon; Jul–Aug: open Wed–Mon).* Originally a 13th-century fort, it is the only Welsh castle to have remained a residence from the medieval to the modern period. The castle's golden age was in Elizabethan times, when it was acquired by the Herbert family (1587) and altered extensively. In 1784, Henrietta Herbert married Edward Clive, the son of Clive of India. Clive's collection in the museum is probably the greatest display of Indian Mughal art outside the subcontinent.

The "red castle" (Castell Coch in Welsh) sits in a delightful Baroque 17th-century Italianate terraced garden dotted with sculptures and manicured hedges. Look out, too, for sentinel red kites which hover above.

At the western edge of town, the **Welshpool & Llanfair Light Railway** *(Apr–Aug: open daily; Sep: closed Mon; 01938 810 441; www.wllr.org.uk),* built in 1903, takes visitors on a 16-mile (26-km) round trip through rural Powys on a narrow-gauge steam railway. The **Dingle Nursery and Garden** *(open daily; www.dinglenurseries.co.uk)* at Frochas, north of Welshpool on the A490, has a superb small garden.

🚗 *Continue along A490, then A483 and A5, taking B5070 to Chirk. Follow signs left for Chirk Castle (with parking lot).*

Below The imposing, red Powis Castle, set in exquisite terraced gardens

Above left Decorative topiary in the grounds of Chirk Castle **Top right** Pub sign, Llangollen **Bottom right** The ruins of Valle Crucis Abbey, set in glorious countryside

WHERE TO STAY

AROUND CHIRK CASTLE

The West Arms Hotel *moderate*
The drive to this ancient inn set in the tranquil Ceiriog Valley is long – but a real treat. The hotel is 11 miles (18 km) west of Chirk on the B4500 with pretty ensuite rooms and lovely views.
Llanarmon Dyffryn Ceiriog, LL20 7LD; 01691 600 665; www.thewestarms.co.uk

LLANGOLLEN

Gales of Llangollen *inexpensive*
This hotel has 15 ensuite rooms with original features, plus widescreen TVs and wifi. Some rooms are over the wine bar, others in a timber-framed building..
18 Bridge Street, LL20 8PF; 01978 860 089; www.galesofllangollen.co.uk

RUTHIN

Firgrove Country House *moderate*
This charming Georgian house, just west of Ruthin on the B5105, has extensive gardens, two attractive B&B rooms plus a self-catering suite. Can do evening meals.
Llanfwrog, LL15 2LL; 01824 702677; www.firgrovecountryhouse.co.uk

Manorhaus *moderate*
This boutique hotel has eight modern, stylish rooms. There are luxurious touches like fine bedlinen, DVD players, sleek bathrooms, and there's even a private cinema for guests.
Well Street, LL15 1AH; 01824 704 830; www.manorhaus.com

Right The colourful hills and valley of Horseshoe Pass, near Llangollen

Where to Stay: inexpensive, under £80; moderate, £80–£150; expensive, over £150

⑤ Chirk Castle
Wrexham; LL14 5AF
Built as a border fortress at the end of the 13th century by Roger Mortimer, a warlord of Edward I, Chirk Castle *(Feb–Oct: open Wed–Sun)* is full of beautiful furniture and paintings. Bought in the 16th century by Sir Thomas Myddleton, his descendants hired Augustus Pugin (1812–52), Gothic revivalist and architect of the Houses of Parliament, to carry out major alterations. There are also some wonderful Neo-Classical rooms by Joseph Turner. The library has many fine books and the garden, laid out in the 18th century with dramatic clipped yews, is a particular highlight. There is also an impressive set of intricate iron-lacework gates.

🚗 *Return to Chirk, taking B5070 north to A5 and on to Llangollen. Park in the center, or cross the bridge and turn right into Mill St for the long-term parking lot.*

⑥ Llangollen
Denbighshire; LL20
British Prime Minister and Welshman, David Lloyd George (1863–1945), described the area around Llangollen as "a little bit of heaven on earth." Llangollen itself is best known for the International Musical Eisteddfod. This was set up in 1947 to encourage good relations between all nations after World War II. The town gets very busy during the festival in July. Visit the black and white half-timbered **Plas Newydd** *(Easter–Oct: open daily)*, the former home of the "Ladies of Llangollen," Lady Eleanor Butler and Miss Sarah Ponsonby, who ran away from Ireland together to live here between 1780 and1829. Famed in Regency society, their visitors included the Duke of Wellington, Wordsworth, Byron, Shelley, and the Darwins. Above the town looms 700-ft (213-m) the ruins of **Castell Dinas Bran**. Follow the path marked from the Canal Wharf bridge up to the top for superb views. The 46-mile (74-km) **Llangollen Canal**,

Offa's Dyke
The Anglo-Saxon King Offa of Mercia (AD 757–96) is best known for his dyke, a defensive earthwork, running north to south, built to protect the border between Mercia and Wales. Built from AD 780–90, it was up to 88 ft (27 m) wide and 26 ft (8 m) high, with probably a wall or palisade at the top. However, it was of limited success and was soon overrun. Today, the 177-mile (285-km) **Offa's Dyke Footpath** *(www.nationaltrail.co.uk/offasdyke)* is a pretty national trail passing close to Montgomery, Powis Castle, Chirk Castle and Castell Dinas Bran.

over the Dee valley, is a beautiful spot for a walk. It crosses the stunning 121-ft (37-m) high **Pontcysyllte Aqueduct**, designed by Thomas Telford and William Jessop. Completed in 1805, it is the longest and highest aqueduct in the UK. For a better look, head 3-miles (5-km) east on the A539. Here visitors can hire a barge for the day to cruise the canal from **Trevor Wharf Services** (*Canal Wharf, LL20 7TY; 01978 821 749*).

West of Llangollen, along the A542 (with car park), lies **Valle Crucis Abbey**, a ruined Cistercian Abbey dating from 1201. Walk further along the road to **Eliseg's Pillar**, set up in the 9th century by the King of Powys in memory of his great-grandfather. Driving further on, the road rises up to **Horseshoe Pass** (416 m/1,367 ft, often snowbound in winter) and the Ponderosa Café – worth a stop for the views, but beware of chip-snatching mountain sheep.

🚗 *Take the A542, then A525 to Ruthin. Park in the center off Station Road.*

Above Barges cruising serenely along the Llangollen Canal

⑦ Ruthin
Shropshire; LL15

This town's historic center is filled with timber-framed buildings. **Nantclwyd y Dre** is a c.1435 historic house in Castle Street displaying rooms from seven periods from the 15th to the 20th century. The new **Ruthin Craft Centre** (and TIC) is also worth a stop, showing crafts from across the British Isles. **Ruthin Gaol** (*Feb–Oct: open daily; Nov–Jan: weekends; www.ruthingaol.co.uk*) opposite the Watergate Tea Room, has been restored as a prison museum.

🚗 *Leave on the A525 for Denbigh. Look out for a sign to Llanrhaeadr on left (easy to miss) and park by church.*

⑧ St. Dyfnog's Church
Denbigh; LL16 4NN

In the tiny village of Llanrhaeadr, St. Dyfnog's Church holds one of the most important Welsh ecclesiastical treasures. It is the most complete "Jesse Tree" window (showing Jesus' descent from Jesse, King David's father). The work dates from 1544 and was paid for by pilgrims seeking the healing powers of the holy well of St. Dyfnog – visible in the woods behind the church. It is regarded as the finest pre-Reformation stained glass in Wales. Admire its powerful depth of color, revealed in 23 portraits from Jesse, reclining at the base, to other figures associated with Jesus' lineage. Next door is the **Anvil Pottery**, in an old smithy, where the two potters make beautiful but functional glazed stone- and earthenware pots.

🚗 *Take the A525 north to Denbigh, then A453 – parking lot is on the right.*

Above Half-timbered houses line the street in the market town of Ruthin

Above Plas-Newydd, the pretty home of the "Ladies of Llangollen"

EAT AND DRINK

AROUND CHIRK CASTLE
The West Arms Hotel *moderate*
Cozy fireplaces and low beams add character to this historic inn, 11 miles (18 km) west of Chirk on the B4500. There's a restaurant and bar, serving mixed grills, local trout, and vegetarian dishes. *Llanarmon Dyffryn Ceiriog, LL20 7LD; 01691 600 665; www.thewestarms.co.uk*

LLANGOLLEN
The Corn Mill *moderate*
Gorgeous riverside setting at this converted corn mill, now an award-winning pub. Come for delicious steak sandwiches, ploughmans' lunches, fishcakes, and sticky toffee pudding. *Dee Lane, LL20 8PN; 01978 869 555; www.brunningandprice.co.uk*

AROUND LLANGOLLEN
The Sun Inn *inexpensive*
There's lots of character at this 14th-century drovers' inn, west of Llangollen on the B103 off the A542. It has wooden beams, open fires, and serves good bar meals and real ale. *Rhewl, LL20 7YT; 01978 861 043*

Ponderosa Café *inexpensive*
The splendid views are the selling point here, more than the food. It's cheap, cheerful, and child-friendly. *Horseshoe Pass, LL20 8DR; 01978 790 307; www.ponderosacafe.co.uk*

RUTHIN
Wynnstay Arms *inexpensive–moderate*
This 16th-century coaching inn offers a modern tapas menu, as well as traditional Sunday lunches, such as roast Welsh lamb, and bar meals. Try Eton mess for dessert. *Well Street, LL15 1AN; 01824 703 147; www.wynnstayarms.com*

Eat and Drink: inexpensive, under £25; moderate, £25–£50; expensive, over £50

Above The former St Asaph Union Workhouse, now HM Stanley Hospital

WHERE TO STAY

AROUND DENBIGH

Pentre Mawr Country House *moderate*
Head east from Denbigh on the Ruthin Rd, taking the minor road further east to the B5429. Turn left and left again to this historic family home. It has beautiful bedrooms, some with four-poster beds and freestanding baths. There are lovely views, a swimming pool and hot tubs, and home-cooked dinners, if required.
Llandyrnog, LL16 4LA; 01824 790 732; www.pentremawrcountryhouse.co.uk

Tan-yr-Onnen *inexpensive*
In the country just south of Junction 28 on the A55, this B&B offers modern rooms with Wi-Fi and DVD players, and serves homemade bread for breakfast.
Waen, LL17 0DU; 01745 583 821; www.northwalesbreaks.co.uk

AROUND ST ASAPH

Bach y Graig *inexpensive*
This 16th-century farmhouse is set in quiet countryside, south of St Asaph off the A541. It has five cozy ensuite rooms and a beamed lounge with a log fire.
Tremeirchion, LL17 0UH; 01745 730 627; www.bachygraig.co.uk

HOLYWELL

Greenhill Farm *inexpensive*
This working dairy farm on the outskirt of Holywell has four rooms. Enjoy hearty farmhouse breakfasts as the cows are being milked.
Bryn Celyn, CH8 7QF; 01352 713 270; www.greenhillfarm.co.uk

Right One of the towers of Denbigh castle, built to subdue the Welsh

⑨ Denbigh
Denbighshire; LL16
Dominating the town, **Denbigh Castle** *(open daily)* was built in 1282 under Henry de Lacy, Edward I's councillor. Marvel at the triple-towered Great Gatehouse with a statue of King Edward – only grand Caernarfon Castle has something similar. Even the town walls were built to integrate with the castle. Walk north down to the **Burgess Gate**, the main gate of the town wall with checkered stonework. On the way, look out for the tower of **St. Hilary's Chapel**, built in 1300, and **Leicester's Church**, the remains of Robert Dudley, Earl of Leicester's unfinished church. It was important because it was the only large church built (1579–80) between the Dissolution of the Monasteries and the rebuilding of St. Paul's Cathedral in London after the Great Fire of 1666.

🚗 *Leave on the A525 to St Asaph. Park next to the cathedral (on the A525).*

⑩ St Asaph
Denbighshire; LL17
This tiny city, set amid glorious scenery with views over the Vale of Clwyd, is home to Britain's smallest cathedral. **St. Asaph's Cathedral** *(open daily)* was founded in AD 560 by exiled Scottish bishop Saint Kentigern. However, its turbulent history – it was sacked by Henry III in 1245, Edward I in 1282, and Owain Glyndŵr in 1402 – means that the current building is mostly 14th century with more modern additions made by the Victorian architect Sir George Gilbert Scott (1867–75). Importantly, it houses a copy of the 1588 translation of the Bible into Welsh by William Morgan who later became bishop here. The revised version, published in 1620, enabled the survival of the Welsh language and its continued everyday use in the face of pressure from English. The cruciform **St Asaph Union Workhouse** was built in 1838. One of its inmates was five-year old orphan John Rowlands, who later changed his name to Henry

Item from Earthworks Pottery, St Asaph

Morton Stanley and, as a journalist, found missing explorer, Dr. Livingstone.

🚗 *Leave on B5381 towards Betws-yn-Rhos, over roundabout and sharp right. Follow brown signs to castle.*

⑪ Bodelwyddan Castle
Denbighshire; LL18 5YA

A "fortified" house and museum set in expansive grounds, **Bodelwyddan Castle** *(open weekends; open weekdays, summer and school holidays; 01745 584 060; www.bodelwyddan-castle.co.uk)* was named after Flwyddan, a 5th-century Romano-British chieftain. Although the estate dates back to the 15th century, most of what is visible today – the limestone turrets and battlements – was created by John Hay Williams between 1830 and 1852 with the architects Hansom and Welch.

As an outpost of the National Portrait Gallery, it is a real trove of art treasures, and also houses furniture from the V&A Museum and sculptures from the Royal Academy of Arts. The interiors are sumptuous and there are galleries on the upper floor. Outside there are formal gardens and parkland with woodlands walks and nature trails. The grounds also have trenches used to train soldiers for World War I.

🚗 *Turn right out of castle, over the flyover, and onto A55 towards Chester. Turn off for A5026 on the left, turning left at the sign for St. Winefride's Well.*

⑫ Holywell
Flintshire; CH8 7PN

Close to the estuary of the River Dee, Holywell is a historic market town whose name derives from its main attraction, **St. Winefride's Well** *(open daily)*. Legend has it that in AD 660, the son of local chieftain, Caradoc, beheaded the young Winefride after she refused his advances. Water sprang from the earth at the spot where her head fell, and she was restored to life by her uncle, St. Beuno. The spring rises in the crypt of a 16th-century hall and flows into a large bathing pool. Look out for the sculpture of a pilgrim being carried to the well on a friend's back. The waters of the "Lourdes of Wales" have been said to cause miraculous cures since the 7th century and today, pilgrims travel from all over the world to worship at the shrine and take the water. In the Middle Ages, the Holywell to St David's road linked the two most important Welsh shrines and was known as "The Pilgrims Road" right up to the 19th century.

DAY TRIP OPTIONS

Ludlow, Llangollen and Denbigh are all excellent bases for exploring the treasures of Wales.

One for the Kids

From Ludlow ❶, see the castle and buy food for a picnic, then head to Acton Scott Farm Museum ❷ to see the animals and enjoy lunch in the country. On to Welshpool ❹, for a ride on the steam train and a visit to Powis Castle, if there's time.

Follow the drive route but return on the A490, A489 and A49 for speed.

Local Llangollen

Start at Llangollen ❻ with a visit to the society ladies' house of Plas Newydd, then a climb up Dinas Bran for some stunning views. After a visit to the canal and aqueduct, have lunch at Horseshoe Pass, and see Valle Crucis Abbey. Drive south to Chirk Castle ❺ to admire its interiors and gardens.

Follow the drive's instructions in reverse.

Cultural and Religious Treasures

Staying at Denbigh ❾, see the castle and churches before heading to St Asaph ❿ to see the William Morgan Bible; head on to Bodelwyddan Castle ⑪, filled with fine treasures, and on to the pilgrimage site of Holywell ⑫. Return toward Denbigh, going past it and on to Llanrhaeadr and St. Dyfnog's Church ❽ to see the Jesse Window.

Follow the drive's instructions all the way there and back.

Eat and Drink: inexpensive, under £25; moderate, £25–£50; expensive, over £50

Around the Peak District

Ashbourne to Matlock Bath

Highlights

- **The Peak landscapes**
  Travel through some of England's most scenic country – walk up to the lofty crags of Stanage Edge, drive through winding Winnats Pass, and enjoy sheltered Dovedale

- **Towns and villages with character**
  Discover Georgian Buxton, quaint Bakewell with its courtyards, and soak up the local atmosphere in the old village pubs of Edale and Eyam

- **Grand mansions**
  Admire one of the most majestic of aristocratic palaces at Chatsworth, set in sublime grounds, and one of the most intact medieval manor houses in England at Haddon Hall

View across the River Wye from Haddon Hall, England's finest medieval manor house

Around the Peak District

The Derbyshire Peak District has long been renowned as a place of beauty, becoming the country's first national park in 1949. Despite being in the heart of industrialized England, the area's villages and towns have a remote feel and retain an individuality often lost elsewhere – within minutes of parking the car, visitors can be exploring secluded valleys, or striding up over hills with fabulous views. The Peak District divides in two, between the limestone "White Peak" to the south, where water has scooped out the soft rock into deep caves and sheltered valleys, and the "Dark Peak" north of Buxton, where the harder millstone grit has created a dramatic landscape of ridges and windswept moorland.

Above Typical Peak District scenery on the lovely road to Edale, *see p173*

ACTIVITIES

Cycle along the beautiful Tissington Trail from Ashbourne

Walk through amazing Peak District scenery at Ilam

Take the waters at the handsome spa town of Buxton

Hike the Pennine Way, or at least part of it, from Edale

Climb down into Castleton's watery caverns to see the area's unique blue minerals

Get lost in the maze at Chatsworth and marvel at the sheer grandeur of the country house and gardens

Feast on an original Bakewell Pudding and other goodies on a stroll around Bakewell's shops and markets

Travel back in time to the Middle Ages at Haddon Hall

Look down on the world from the cable car at Matlock Bath

KEY

— Drive route

0 kilometres   10

0 miles   10

erwent Moor
Hollow Meadows
A57
Hallam Head
Fulwood
Greystones
Ecclesall
Bamford
Thornhill
Hallam Moors
Whiteley Wood
Stanage Edge
A6187
6 HATHERSAGE
A625
Abbeydale
Dore
Bradway
Abney
Totley
B6001
B6521
Nether Padley
Owler Bar
Brctton
B6064
Grindleford
A625
EYAM **7**
Froggatt
A623
B6521
Big Moor
A621
Calver
Curbar
Great ongstone
B6001
Hassop
Baslow
ford
A6020
Pilsley
A619
A619
Edensor
8 CHATSWORTH
East Moor
B6012
9 BAKEWELL
A6
Beeley
Derwent
10 HADDON HALL
Over addon
Rowsley
B5057
Stanton in-Peak
Youlgreave
B5056
Two Dales
iddleton
Darley Bridge
Upper Hackney
Birchover
A6
Winster
Wensley
Matlock
Tansley
A615
ehall
A5012
MATLOCK BATH **11**
Lea
Aldwark
Cromford
Holloway
Middleton
A6
Brassington
B5056
Wirksworth
Carsington
Millers Green
Bradbourne
Carsington Water
B5035
Hognaston
Kniveton
Kirk Ireton
Biggin
Hulland
A517
Bradley
3smaston

Above Wild-garlic-lined steps off Lover's Walk, above Matlock Bath, *see p175*

Below The High Street, Matlock Bath, below the Heights of Abraham, *see p175*

PLAN YOUR DRIVE

Start/finish: Ashbourne to Matlock Bath.

Number of days: 2–3, allowing half a day for the Dovedale walk.

Distances: Around 60 miles (97 km).

Road conditions: The roads are in good condition.

When to go: Peak District weather is notoriously changeable, but from May to September is usually when there is the best chance of good weather.

Opening times: Museums and attractions are generally open 10am–5pm, but close earlier (or are closed altogether) Nov–Easter. Shops are often open longer. Churches are usually open until dusk.

Shopping: For the area's most famous dish, try the Bakewell Pudding Shop on Bridge St, Bakewell. Look out, too, for David Mellor's cutlery at Hathersage, and Blue John, as pure stone or jewelery, in Castleton and Bakewell.

Main market days: Ashbourne: Thu, Sat; Buxton: Tue, Sat, Farmers' Market 1st Thu of month; Castleton, Farmers' Market, 1st Sun of month; Bakewell: Mon, Farmers' Market last Sat of month; Matlock: Market Hall open Mon–Sat, Farmers' Market 3rd Sat of month.

Main festivals: Ashbourne: Shrovetide Football Match, Shrove Tuesday and Ash Wednesday; Buxton: Festival of Music and Arts, Jul; Castleton: Garland Ceremony, 29 May; Bakewell: Bakewell Show (farming show), 1st week Aug; Matlock: River illuminations, end Sep.

DAY TRIP OPTIONS

Tour the White Peak from Ashbourne with its **pub** and **church**, go on to Ilam for a **walk** in the prettiest of **dales**, and finish in the **spa town** of Buxton. Or, to see the Hope Valley, try a **hike** in Edale and then visit the **caves** at Castleton before eating **sweet treats** at Bakewell. History lovers should start at Bakewell, buy a **picnic**, and tour the grand **house and estate** at Chatsworth, then visit the medieval **manor house** Haddon Hall and ascend the **cable car** at Matlock Bath. For full details, *see p175*.

Above One of several pretty "Swiss chalet-style" houses in Ilam

VISITING ASHBOURNE

Parking
Park in the Market Place or nearby Shawcroft Car Park off Park Road.

Tourist Information
13 Market Place, DE6 1EU; 01335 343 666; www.visitpeakdistrict.com

Ashbourne Cycle Hire
Mapleton Lane, DE6 2AA; 01335 343 156; www.peakdistrict.org/cycle.htm

WHERE TO STAY

ILAM AND DOVEDALE

Hillcrest House *inexpensive*
Charming B&B on the road from Ilam to Ashbourne, with spacious rooms and modern comforts. Breakfasts are generous, and the location is glorious.
Thorpe, DE6 2AW; 01335 350 436; www.hillcresthousedovedale.co.uk

BUXTON

Old Hall Hotel *inexpensive*
Perhaps the oldest hotel in England, this now has modern facilities to add to its character. There's a bar and cozy lounges and the restaurant uses top local produce.
The Square, SK17 6BD; 01298 22841; www.oldhallhotelbuxton.co.uk

Buxton Hilbre *inexpensive*
A welcoming three-room B&B known for its quality organic breakfasts.
8 White Knowle Road, SK17 9NH; 01298 22358; www.buxtonhilbre.co.uk

AROUND CASTLETON

Losehill House Hotel & Spa *expensive*
This hotel is intimate, luxurious, and as comfortable, light rooms. Hope is on the A6187, take the Edale Rd north, forking left down a track and keeping right.
Edale Road, Hope, S33 6RF; 01433 621 219; www.losehillhouse.co.uk

① Ashbourne
Derbyshire; DE6
This charming market town is full of fascinating corners, such as the 15th-century half-timbered **Ashbourne Gingerbread Shop** and the **Green Man & Black's Head Royal Hotel**, whose extraordinary pub sign runs across the main street. Ashbourne is famed for its yearly Shrovetide Football Match – a chaotic ancestor of modern soccer, played all day and with half the village on each side. A walk along Church St, past the beautiful 1585 **Grammar School** and 1640s almshouses, leads to the magnificent Gothic **St. Oswald's Church**, with finely sculpted tombs from the 14th to the 18th centuries in the Cockayne-Boothby chapel.

To explore the stunning countryside, get a bike from **Ashbourne Cycle Hire** and ride along the **Tissington Trail**, a 13-mile (21-km) out-of-use railway line.
🚗 *Leave by A515 north and turn left at the sign for Thorpe, Ilam and Dovedale. Park near the obelisk in Ilam village.*

② Ilam and Dovedale
Staffordshire; DE6 2AZ
Starting from quaint Ilam, this bracing walk explores Dovedale, a winding, hidden gorge of dramatic rock formations and woods by the sparkling River Dove. Its beauty has been long celebrated – so it's popular – but during the week, it's still possible to avoid the crowds.

A three-hour walk
From the **obelisk at Ilam** ①, walk up the road beside the river until you pass the last cottage. Go through a gate on the left into fields. Climb up to a wider footpath, turn left, and at a green footpath sign go right on the path for **Stanshope**. This goes up the side of **Bunster Hill** ②, the giant peak between Ilam and Dovedale. At a dry-stone wall, do not go through the gate but head up the steep path, with the wall to the left, to the top of hill.

At the top, rest and enjoy the views. Return to the path and go through a gate and the next field to a large five bar gate onto a broad track between stone walls. Outside **Ilamtops Farm** ③, turn right to walk down to **Air Cottage** ④. Just before the cottage, follow the sign leading off to the right. Stop on the crags nearby to enjoy the full view of Dovedale below.

Below the cottage, the well-marked path curves through the woods before it climbs up again to the small gate

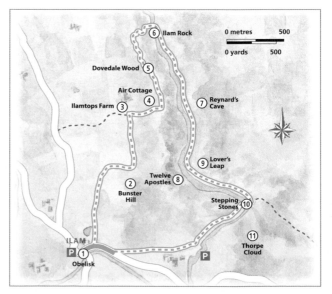

Above left Walkers beside the River Dove, in Dovedale **Above right** Edale Parish Church and the National Park's Moorland Centre

into **Dovedale Wood** ⑤. The path goes through the wood before a right turn starts a very steep winding descent to the bottom of Dovedale itself, to a stone pillar known as **Ilam Rock** ⑥.

Turn right, and cross a footbridge to the main path down the east side of the dale. Compared to the windswept hills, it feels sheltered here. On the walk through the woods, look out for cave entrances and natural landmarks, such as the rock arch to **Reynard's Cave** ⑦, the stone towers of the **Twelve Apostles** ⑧ (through the trees), **Lover's Leap** ⑨, and the dale's most picturesque sight, the **Stepping Stones** ⑩ to the west bank. Here, the Dove turns, below another hill, **Thorpe Cloud** ⑪. Follow the path back to the Dovedale parking lot and, beyond it, take the path to the right back to Ilam.

🚗 *Go up hill to Stanshope, through the village and at next junction left through Wetton. Take left fork at bottom of hill, next right, then left signed Hulme End. After tunnel, turn left for Hulme End, left again at junction and right at Manifold Inn (B5054). Take left to Sheen and Longnor, then B5053 and A515 to Buxton. Park near the Crescent.*

③ Buxton
Derbyshire; SK17
Famous for its mineral waters since Roman times, Buxton was transformed in the 1780s, when the fifth Duke of Devonshire decided to create a stylish spa here in imitation of Bath, and commissioned Neo-Classical buildings such as the elegant **Crescent** and giant domed **Stables**, now Derby University. Buxton remained popular in the 19th century, gaining the lovely **Pavilion Gardens** and the ornate 1905 **Opera House** (www.buxtonoperahouse.org.uk) – the center of the Buxton Festival of Music and Arts (July). The water from

St. **Ann's Well**, in the town center, is still valued. The baths are now a shopping centre, still with beautiful Victorian tiles.

🚗 *Leave on A6 north, turn right onto A623. At Sparrowpit, take left to Edale (B6061). At junction keep left for Barber Booth, then left again toward Chapel-en-le-Frith. Turn sharp right for Barber Booth and parking lot on left in Edale.*

④ Edale
Derbyshire; S33
Nestling in a broad valley, pretty Edale is a magnet for hikers as the start of the **Pennine Way**, the 256-mile (412-km) footpath to Scotland – but there are many shorter walks in the area. Visit the National Park's **Moorland Centre**, for maps, information, and walking routes. The two village pubs, the **Rambler Inn** and **Old Nag's Head**, are favorite spots for a restorative drink after a hike.

🚗 *Retrace the route back to the B6061 and turn second left for Edale (Winnats Pass) to Castleton.*

⑤ Castleton
Derbyshire; S33
Winnats Pass, a spectacular gash in the landscape, leads to lovely **Castleton**, overlooked by the romantic ruins of 11th-century **Peveril Castle** (open mid-Mar–Oct daily; Nov–mid-Mar: closed Tue, Wed), which gave Castleton its name. This old stone village is also close to dramatic **caves** (open daily) from which minerals such as Blue John, a unique local purple fluorspar, were mined for centuries. The best caves to visit are **Blue John Cavern** at the top of Winnats Pass, **Peak Cavern**, **Treak Cliff Cavern**, and **Speedwell Cavern**, a "drowned mine" reached by boat. Further down the valley, **Hope** is another attractive village, with a fine 14th-century church.

🚗 *Continue down the Hope Valley Rd (A6187) to Hathersage.*

EAT AND DRINK

ASHBOURNE

St. John Street Gallery & Café
inexpensive
A former magistrates' court has been turned into a lively arts center, which also has a friendly café, with delicious salads, snacks, and main dishes. There are vegetarian choices and homemade specialities include Stilton and walnut pâté – beers and wines are available.
50 St. John Street, DE6 1GH; 01335 347 425; www.sjsg.co.uk

AROUND ILAM AND DOVEDALE

The Manifold Inn *moderate*
This classic stone coaching inn, on the route from Ilam to Buxton, has a garden terrace and serves some of the county's best pub food, including delicious beef and ale pies, and lighter options – it also has rooms.
Hulme End, Hartington, SK17 0EX; 01298 84537; www.themanifoldinn.co.uk

BUXTON

Pavilion Gardens *moderate*
Occupying the magnificent Victorian conservatories in Buxton's grand park, this café makes the most of its space and light. Choose between the main café, or the Art Café above, decorated by local artists. The menu, based on local produce, runs from breakfasts and snacks to larger dishes for lunch.
St. John's Road, SK17 6XN; 01298 23114; www.paviliongardens.co.uk

AROUND BUXTON

Vanilla Kitchen *inexpensive*
Take the A6 east, then the B6049 north to Tideswell to find this bright, award-winning café. Ingredients are seasonal and local, whether used in tasty lunches or the scrumptious range of cakes. Beers, wines, and great Fairtrade coffee are also served.
Queen Street, Tideswell, SK17 8PF; 01298 871 519; www.vanillakitchen.co.uk

Eat and Drink: inexpensive, under £25; moderate, £25–£50; expensive, over £50

Above Glorious Chatsworth Park, created by Capability Brown in the 1760s

WHERE TO STAY

HATHERSAGE

Cannon Croft *inexpensive*
A pretty – and environmental – B&B in a Hathersage cottage with superb views of the hills from its garden and indoor conservatory. The helpful owners provide generous organic breakfasts.
Cannonfields, S32 1AG; 01433 650 005; www.cannoncroftbedandbreakfast.co.uk

AROUND EYAM

Bretton Cottage *moderate*
This distinctive guesthouse in a 17th-century hillside farmhouse, off Sir William Hill Rd just north of Eyam, offers huge rooms with sitting areas, fridges and coffee- and tea-making facilities. The breakfasts are substantial, too. There are also three self-contained cottages for rent.
Bretton, near Eyam, S32 5QD; 01433 631 076; www.peakholidayhomes.com

AROUND CHATSWORTH

Bubnell Cliff Farm *inexpensive*
Enjoy two charming rooms with large bathrooms and lovely views on all sides in this homely farmhouse B&B in Baslow off the A619 on the edge of the Chatsworth estate. As usual in the Peaks, generous breakfasts of local farm produce make a great start to the day.
Wheatlands Lane, Baslow, near Bakewell, DE45 1RF; 01246 582 454; www.bubnellcliff.co.uk

AROUND HADDON HALL

East Lodge Hotel and Restaurant *expensive*
In Rowsley, off the A6, south of Haddon Hall, this fine old house has been beautifully restored with a blend of country-house and modern boutique-hotel style. It has just 12 sumptuous rooms and the gourmet restaurant, looking out onto the gardens, provides seasonal modern menus to match.
Rowsley, Matlock, DE4 2EF; 01629 734 474; www.eastlodge.com

Where to Stay: inexpensive, under £80; moderate, £80–£150; expensive, over £150

⑥ Hathersage
Derbyshire; S32
On the drive down the Hope Valley, a dramatic wall of red rock, **Stanage Edge**, is visible to the northeast of Hathersage. Head up to the "Edge" from town for fabulous views – many walking paths begin near Hathersage's tranquil 14th-century church. In the churchyard lies **Little John's Grave** where, according to local legend, Robin Hood's best friend is buried. On the south side of the village is the **Round Building**, the workshop and shop of the celebrated cutlery designer David Mellor (1930–2009).
🚗 *Take B6001 through Grindleford, then right (B6521) to Eyam. Follow signs to Eyam museum for large parking lot.*

⑦ Eyam
Derbyshire; S32
Eyam became famous as an amazing example of self-sacrifice. In 1665, when the Great Plague was raging in London, the disease also took hold of Eyam. The village agreed to cut off all contact with the outside world until the plague had run its course, to avoid infecting the surrounding villages. They maintained this for nearly a year, during which 257 people died. The story is told in the **Eyam Museum** *(late Mar–early Nov: open Tue–Sun)* and through monuments around the village, such as the **Riley Graves**, where all seven of the Hancock family were buried in a field. Despite this grim history, today Eyam is a charming village of old stone houses. The imposing mansion of **Eyam Hall** hosts a craft center and is open to visitors *(for opening times, see www.eyamhall.co.uk)*.
🚗 *Take the B6521 south and then A623 left to Baslow, where Chatsworth is well marked. The B6012 leads through the Chatsworth estate.*

Peak District Pubs
Snug old stone pubs are among the jewels of the Peak District, and many provide well-priced food. As well as the **Manifold Inn** *(see p173)*, other pubs to look out for are **Smith's Tavern** and the historic **Green Man & Black's Head Royal Hotel** *(see p173)* in Ashbourne, the **Bluebell Inn** in Tissington near Ilam, the **Old Nag's Head** and the **Ramblers' Inn** in Edale, the **Cheshire Cheese** in Hope near Castleton, the **Miners' Arms** in Eyam and the **Plough Inn**, just south of Hathersage.

⑧ Chatsworth
Derbyshire; DE45 1PP
One of the grandest of Britain's great houses and a model of 18th-century elegance, the Palladian mansion of Chatsworth *(open daily)* has been home to the Dukes and Duchesses of Devonshire since the early 1700s. Truly palatial, the house has sumptuous furnishings and works of art, but is made still more magnificent by its setting, as the centerpiece of a majestic park created by "Capability" Brown in the 1760s with huge formal gardens with fountains, a maze, and cascading waterworks. There's also an adventure playground, shops, and special exhibitions. Opposite the Chatsworth entrance, **Edensor** is a pretty model village, built in the 1830s when the then Duke decided the original Edensor village was too close.
🚗 *Turn right from Chatsworth, back toward Baslow, then left on a road marked for Pilsley and Bakewell (B6048). Turn left again onto A619 into Bakewell. Use pay parking lot off main street.*

Below The church at Eyam, a village decimated during the Great Plague of 1665

⑨ Bakewell
Derbyshire; DE45

A bustling market town at the heart of the Peaks, Bakewell is a charming place just to wander and window-shop. It's also known for good food, with food stores in the courtyards off the main street and plenty of tea shops offering the local speciality, Bakewell Pudding – it's never called a tart in its home town. In addition to its weekly market, the town hosts a monthly **Farmers' Market** attracting many local independent food producers. The **Old House Museum** (Apr–Oct: open daily), Bakewell's oldest house, begun in 1543, has been made into a fascinating museum of everyday life.

🚗 **Take the A6 south – Haddon Hall is on the left but park on the right.**

Above Extravagant topiary in the grounds of Haddon Hall

⑩ Haddon Hall
Derbyshire; DE45 1LA

The most complete medieval and Elizabethan manor house in England, Haddon Hall (Apr, Oct: open Sat–Mon; May–Sep: wopen daily; www.haddonhall. co.uk) has remained virtually unaltered, except for upkeep, since the 1600s, and still owned by the Manners family. Original features include massive medieval kitchens, flagstoned courtyards, a 12th-century chapel with 15th-century wall paintings, and a Long Gallery with exquisite wood paneling.

🚗 **Turn right out of the car park and continue down A6 to Matlock Bath. Pay-and-display parking along main street.**

⑪ Matlock
Derbyshire; DE4

Matlock developed in the 19th century as a spa with mass-market appeal. It is still a popular destination, especially **Matlock Bath** to the south of the main town, where the River Derwent runs through an impressive narrow gorge. The main street (A6) beside the river is lined with budget restaurants and ice-cream and souvenir shops. The most popular family attraction is the **Heights of Abraham** (mid-Feb–Nov: open daily; www.heightsofabraham.com) at the top of the gorge – reached via a dramatic cable car trip – with views, gardens, playgrounds, nature trails, and caverns.

Above left Stone houses in the hilly market town of Bakewell **Above center** Pretty gardens and medieval manor house of Haddon Hall **Above right** Matlock Bath, perched beside the River Derwent

EAT AND DRINK

HATHERSAGE

The Walnut Club moderate
Much acclaimed for its inventive, organic cooking, this eaterie has a hip and stylish décor and live jazz in the evenings. Open Fri–Sun – reservations are essential.
The Square, Main Road, S32 1BB; 01433 651 155; www.thewalnutclub.com

AROUND CHATSWORTH

Rowley's Restaurant moderate
This stylish bar-restaurant in Baslow, on the A619 just north of Chatworth, serves creative modern British food of a very high standard.
Church Street, Baslow, DE45 1RY; 01246 583 880; www.rowleysrestaurant.co.uk

BAKEWELL

Piédaniel's moderate
Chef Eric Piédaniel combines his own French skills and culinary traditions with local produce, and his restaurant is a beautifully calm, relaxing space.
Bath Street, DE45 1BX; 01629 812 687; www.piedaniels-restaurant.com

MATLOCK BATH

The Strand Restaurant inexpensive
There is something for everyone at this friendly, buzzing brasserie and the midweek set menus are a bargain.
Dale Road, Matlock, DE4 3LT; 01629 584 444; www.thestrandrestaurant.com

---

DAY TRIP OPTIONS
Take in stunning countryside, historic houses and pretty towns.

Through the White Peak
Explore Ashbourne ❶ and then take a long walk in the country at Dovedale ❷ before driving north through quaint Peak villages to relax in Buxton's elegant Georgian pavilions ❸.

Follow the drive route north but return via the A515 to save time.

Along the Hope Valley
Staying at Buxton ❸, drive to Edale ❹ for a walk above the village, and then visit the caves at Castleton ❺. Drive on through Hathersage ❻, with views of Stanage Edge and finally stop at Bakewell ❾ for some food shopping.

Follow the drive route but return via A6.

Great houses in the Peaks
From Bakewell ❾, buy some treats for lunch and visit majestic Chatsworth ❽ to enjoy a picnic in the park. Drive around to the smaller but older Haddon Hall ❿ and end the day with some family fun at Matlock Bath ⓫.

Take the A6 there and back.

Eat and Drink: inexpensive, under £25; moderate, £25–£50; expensive, over £50

Yorkshire Dales and Abbeys

Harrogate to Bolton Abbey

Highlights

- **Health-giving Harrogate**
  Test the restorative waters in this gracious Victorian spa resort with its fine architecture and pretty parks

- **Crumbling abbeys**
  Wander through the historic, romantic ruins of these once-great Yorkshire abbeys, set in marvelous countryside

- **Gorgeous gardens**
  Admire a charming kitchen garden, orderly civic flowerbeds, a national hyacinth collection, and a beautiful ornamental water garden

- **Great dale views**
  Walking or driving, there are always breathtaking views over the beautiful Yorkshire Dales National Park

Rolling green Wensleydale, perfect for sheep whose milk is used to make cheese

Yorkshire Dales & Abbeys

Departing from the beautiful spa town of Harrogate, this drive follows a circuit through the Yorkshire Dales National Park, with some truly sublime stretches that demand to be taken at an easy pace. Along the way are the estate village of Ripley with its castle, the small cathedral city of Ripon, the pretty market towns of Middleham and Leyburn, linked by an ancient bridge across the Ure, and Hawes, home of Wensleydale cheese. Star features of the tour are the ruins and grounds of Jervaulx, Fountain, and Bolton abbeys. Plundered in the 16th-century on the orders of Henry VIII, these once-glorious monastic buildings are now poignant monuments to the transience of power.

Above Middleham castle, dating to 1170, favorite home of the young Richard III, *see p182*

ACTIVITIES

Take the plunge in a steamy Turkish bath in the beautiful spa town of Harrogate

Set your watch in Ripon when the Hornblower blows in the market place at 9pm every evening

Explore the poignant ruins of Jervaulx Abbey, laid waste by Henry VIII's henchmen

Watch the young racehorses galloping out in the morning on the moors outside Middleham

Walk into the beautiful Yorkshire Dales having packed a delicious Wensleydale picnic from Hawes

Learn how to fly fish at Bolton Abbey, or ride a steam train, pet the farm animals, or just enjoy the scenery

KEY

⬌ Drive route

Above Glorious Yorkshire Dales' scenery between Hawes and Bolton Abbey, *see p183*

PLAN YOUR DRIVE

Start/finish: Harrogate to Bolton Abbey.

Number of days: 3 days, taking it at a gentle pace.

Distance: Around 100 miles (160 km).

Road conditions: The roads are in good condition and not challenging.

When to go: The best time is between spring and early autumn – Harrogate, with its green spaces, is especially wonderful at blossom time.

Opening times: Museums and attractions are generally open 10am–5pm, but close earlier (or are closed altogether) Nov–Easter. Shop opening hours are longer. Churches are usually open until dusk.

Main market days: Harrogate: Farmers' Market, 2nd Thu of month; **Ripon**: Thu; Farmers' Market, Sun **Leyburn**: Fri; North Dales Farmers' Market, 4th Sat of month; **Hawes**: Produce and Antiques Market, Tue.

Shopping: Stock up on some Harrogate toffee and various types of Wensleydale – young, mature, smoked, etc. Look out, too, for produce from Nidderdale farms, such as beef or chicken. And there is also good local beer to be enjoyed along the way.

Major festivals: Harrogate: Music Festival, Jul; **Ripon**: Ripon International Festival, Sep (music, arts, architecture, and nature); **Leyburn**: Dales Festival of Food, May.

DAY TRIP OPTIONS

Families can enjoy a day **shopping** in Harrogate and then take the **steam railway** and visit the **children's farm**, and **parkland** at Bolton Abbey. Garden lovers and history buffs will enjoy the **market town** of Ripon, the magnificent **ruined Fountains Abbey** and **water gardens** nearby, as well as the **castle** and **gardens** at Ripley. Follow the steps of royalty through the **picturesque Dales**, from Middleham with its **castle**, to Leyburn with its **great views**, on to Hawes for its famous **cheese** and then to Jervaulx Abbey for its enchanting **ruins**. For full details, *see p183*.

Above Pretty flowers of Crescent Gardens in front of the Royal Hall, Harrogate

VISITING HARROGATE

Parking
Follow signs for center, for parking on Montpellier Road or Union Street

Tourist Information
Royal Baths, Crescent Rd, HG1 2RR; 0845 389 3223; www.harrogate.gov.uk

WHERE TO STAY

HARROGATE

Balmoral Hotel *moderate*
Plush boutique hotel in an old building with opulent rooms and ensuite Victorian bathrooms at good prices.
16–18 Franklin Mount, HG1 5EJ; 01423 508 208 ; www.balmoralhotel.co.uk

Grants *moderate–expensive*
In a quiet but central location, this Victorian town house has smart ensuite rooms and a smalll seafood bistro.
3–13 Swan Road, HT1 2SS; 01423 560 666; www.grantshotel-harrogate.com

April House *inexpensive*
This small, friendly B&B in a Victorian house in a quiet avenue offers rooms with ensuite or private bathrooms.
3 Studley Road, HG1 5JU; 01423 561 879; www.aprilhouse.com

RIPLEY

Boar's Head Hotel *moderate*
Friendly hotel owned by the Ingilbys has "olde worlde" but comfortable rooms that include access to the castle.
Ripley Castle Estate, HG3 3AY0; 01423 771 888; www.ripleycastle.co.uk

RIPON

The Old Deanery *moderate*
This small historic, central hotel offers individually designed ensuite rooms. There's also a decent restaurant.
Minster Road, HG4 1QS; 01765 600 003; www.theolddeanery.co.uk

❶ Harrogate
North Yorks; HG1 1

This vibrant and elegant spa town, on the edge of the Dales, grew up around a sulphur well, enclosed within the Royal Pump Room built in 1842. Modern visitors will find a wide choice of boutiques, antique shops, restaurants, and bars, and plenty of green spaces in Crescent Garden and Valley Gardens. The vast open park, "The Stray," was created in 1778 so that the people of Harrogate could access the springs.

A two-hour walking tour

From the parking lot go up Montpellier Rd to the tourist office, housed in the **Royal Baths** ① on Crescent Rd. Dating from 1897, the baths were once a key destination for the health-conscious super-rich, who came for the sulphur water, peat baths, and other delights. Inside, the Turkish baths, with original Victorian tiles, have been restored to their 19th-century glory. Facing away from pretty Crescent Gardens, and with the baths on the right, turn left into Parliament St past the Royal Hall, built in 1903, and take Swan Rd on the left. It was at the **Old Swan Hotel** ② that crime writer Agatha Christie was found after crashing her car and going missing in 1926. Booked in as Theresa Neele – her husband's mistress – she claimed amnesia, but it is not known what really lay behind it all. Visit the **Mercer Art Gallery** ③ *(closed Mon except Bank Hols; Sun, pm only)* on Swan Rd, with its fine art collection of some 2,000

works, mainly from the 19th and 20th centuries. At the 19th-century **Royal Pump Room Museum** ④ *(open daily)* on Crown Place, built around the Old Sulphur Well, try some of the strongest sulphur water in Europe. Head into **Valley Gardens** ⑤ *(open daily)* opposite and follow the stream to see the restored 1930s Colonnade, Sun Pavilion and Magnesia Pump Room. Return to the Royal Pump Room and head right up Royal Parade and right at the roundabout, past the stately Crown Hotel, up Cold Bath Rd, noting the fine Georgian houses. Turn left into Queens Rd and left into Lancaster Rd to West Park Stray. Turn right down Beech Grove and left onto Otley Rd toward the Prince of Wales roundabout. Turn right onto Trinity Rd. Admire the Gothic-style, 19th-century **Trinity Church** ⑥, then cross Leeds Rd and enter the marvelous public amenity of **The Stray** ⑦. The tree-shaded path across the park leads to the domed

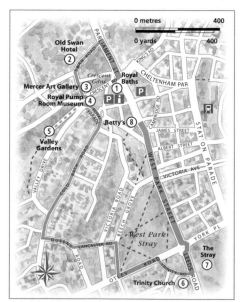

Tewit Well, England's oldest spa. Here, in 1571, William Slingsby came upon a spring, and, tasting from it, was reminded of the health-giving waters of European spas. Either follow Slingsby Walk across the railway to appreciate the size of the park, or head back to town along West Park St for refreshments at Yorkshire's famous tea rooms, **Betty's** ⑧, on the left, before heading back to the parking lot.

🚗 *Head north along Parliament St (the A61), and take the left fork to enter Ripley. There is free parking by the castle.*

② Ripley
North Yorks; HG3 3AY

Home to the Ingilby family since the 14th century, **Ripley Castle** *(Nov & Mar: closed Mon, Wed, Fri; Dec–Feb: closed Mon–Fri)*, is set amongst walled gardens and wooded walks, lakes, and a deer park with venerable oaks. The kitchen garden grows many herbs and rare vegetable varieties and the castle also houses a National Hyacinth Collection – from March to October the flower borders are spectacular. Inside, seven rooms are open to the public for guided tours. Explore a family history of political, military, religious, and social turbulence, from the Renaissance to the Industrial Revolution. The delightful **estate village of Ripley**, adjoining the castle, was built in the 1820s on the eccentric whim of Sir William Ingilby, who, inspired by his European travels, endowed it with a *Hotel de Ville* (town hall) on a square with stocks, a market cross, and a war memorial.

🚗 *Exit village, bearing right on the A61. After 6 miles (10 km) take the first exit off the roundabout onto the A6108; follow signs to center.*

③ Ripon
North Yorks; HG4 1QT

Stained-glass window, Ripon Cathedral

Small but perfectly formed, Ripon is centered on its market square and has plenty for the visitor – including an impressive 13th-century **cathedral**. On the square, the Hornblower "sets the watch" by blowing his horn in each corner at 9pm – a tradition dating from the 11th century.

For an excellent day out, take the B6265 west, turning left for **Fountains Abbey and Studley Royal** *(open daily)*. This World Heritage Site contains a Cistercian abbey founded in 1132, the largest abbey ruins in the country, and a truly spectacular and ornate Georgian water garden.

🚗 *Head northwest on the A6108 and follow signs for Jervaulx Abbey. There is on-site parking.*

Above left Agatha Christie's hideout, the Old Swan Hotel, Harrogate **Above center** The East end window of Ripon Cathedral **Above right** Ripley Castle, the Ingilby family home for 700 years

EAT AND DRINK

HARROGATE

Betty's Café Tea Rooms *inexpensive*
The original Betty's has been tempting in visitors since 1919, with the promise of "something fresh and dainty." There is an extensive choice of cooked food, as well as over 300 breads, cakes, and 50 different teas and coffees.
1 Parliament Street, HG1 2QU; 01423 877 300; www.bettys.co.uk

Hales Bar *inexpensive*
The town's oldest pub has retained its Victorian character using mirrors and working gas lights, and has friendly staff, real ale, and good simple food. The odd whiff of sulphur wafts from the springs that flow below the cellar.
1 Crescent Road, HG1 2RS; 01423 725 570; www.halesbar.co.uk

Drum and Monkey
moderate–expensive
A fish restaurant in an attractive building over two floors. Fresh fish and shellfish – lobster, Dover sole, oysters, halibut, and sea bass, etc – is delivered daily. It's not cheap, but there are lunchtime sandwiches for those on a budget.
5 Montpellier Gardens, HG1 2TF; 01423 502 650; www.drumandmonkey.co.uk

RIPON

Lockwoods *inexpensive–moderate*
This is a popular family-run lunchtime café bar and evening restaurant just off the square, serving brunch, sandwiches, light, zesty lunches and more ambitous dinners from an eclectic menu.
83 North Street, HG4 1DP; 01765 607 555; www.lockwoodsrestaurant.co.uk

Left The wrought iron Art-Deco canopy of Betty's Café Tea Rooms, Harrogate

Above Jockeys taking the young racehorses out for exercise, Middleham

WHERE TO STAY

JERVAULX ABBEY

Park House
Set in the grounds of the abbey, this is a perfectly situated small B&B housed in two converted former workers' cottages. It is also home to the Abbey's owners, who welcome guests with tea and delicious homemade cake.
Jervaulx Abbey, HG4 4PH; 01677 460 184; www.jervaulxabbey.com

MIDDLEHAM

Domus House *moderate*
One of a number of decent inns and guest houses clustered around the town's square. This ivy-clad Georgian house offers three ensuite rooms.
Market Place, DL8 4NR; 01969 623 497; www.myspace.com/domushouse

The Black Swan *moderate*
This charming "olde worlde" 17th-century real-ale inn right by the castle comes complete with log fires and oak beams. The bedrooms, however, may be a little chintzy for some tastes.
Market Place, DL8 4NP; 01969 622 221; www.blackswan-middleham.co.uk

The White Swan *moderate*
Overlooking Market Square, the White Swan subsumed the old post office and underwent refurbishment, adding more and a smart brasserie.
Market Place, DL8 4PE; 01969 622 093; www.whiteswanhotel.co.uk

BOLTON ABBEY

Devonshire Arms *expensive*
This country house has been in the Devonshire family since 1753. Furnished with antiques, it is gloriously situated and offers every comfort, including a spa, sauna, tennis courts, and a range of good restaurants, too.
Bolton Abbey, BD23 6AJ; 01756 710 441; www.thedevonshirearms.co.uk

4 Jervaulx Abbey
North Yorks; HG4 4PH
Founded in 1156, this once-great Cistercian monastery is today in private hands, but allows public access. Declared forfeit to the Crown under Henry VIII *(see p192)*, its roof was stripped of lead and the church destroyed by gunpowder. What survived such vandalism is a place of utter peace and charm, in a beautiful wildflower meadow amidst the Yorkshire Dales. Tour the remains of this enchanting building, including the dormitory, kitchen, parlour, infirmary and cloister. The homemade cakes in the tea rooms are excellent, too.

🚗 **Continue on A6108 to Middleham; park for free on the cobbled square.**

5 Middleham
North Yorks; DL8 4QG
This historic town boasts an impressive castle, two market places and racehorse training stables. Visitors can watch the jockeys riding out in the morning on the moors beyond **Middleham Castle** *(Oct–Mar: closed Thu & Fri)*. This castle was from 1461 home to Richard, Duke of York, who would ascend to the throne for a brief reign as Richard III in 1483. Chambers and lodgings were added over time to the 12th-century keep to create a more luxurious palace.

Take the A6108 northwest across a 19th-century bridge over the River Ure to pretty **Leyburn**, filled with craft shops, galleries, a chocolatier, and a tea pottery. It's also an excellent place for walking. At the top of the marketplace, follow signs for the **Leyburn Shawl**, supposedly where Mary

Queen of Scots dropped her shawl in her flight from Bolton Castle, where she was imprisoned in 1538–9. Climb the escarpment for a short walk and great views across Wensleydale. Power walkers can try the 7-mile (11-km) walk to Bolton Castle (and get the bus back) – for instructions, visit *www.dalesbus. info/richmond/walk_5.htm.*

🚌 **From Leyburn, take the A684 west through the Yorkshire Dales National Park to Hawes. Aysgarth Falls, on the way, is a good place to stop for a picnic.**

Above Aysgarth Falls in the picturesque Lower Wensleydale valley

Wensleydale
This wonderful cheese is handmade using milk from cows grazing on the sweet pastures in Upper Wensleydale. White Wensleydale is a young cheese, with a clean, mild, slightly sweet flavor. It can be bought, along with mature and oak-smoked and ewes' milk versions at the **Wensleydale Creamery** shop and visitors' center on the left on Gayle Lane on the way out of Hawes *(www.wensleydale.co.uk).*

Below The haunting ruins of Jervaulx Abbey in beautiful bucolic surroundings

Where to Stay: inexpensive, under £80; moderate, £80–£150; expensive, over £150

⑥ Hawes

North Yorks; DL8 3NT

Pretty, bustling Hawes, at the head of Wensleydale, valley of the waterfalls, is Yorkshire's highest market town. There are some fine walks to be enjoyed from here; visit *www.wensleydale.org* for instructions. Pick up picnic supplies from the **Wensleydale Creamery** *(open daily)* and see how they make the famous cheese. Tuesday is market day and stalls of produce line the streets. **Dales Countryside Museum** *(open daily)* is also well worth a visit, with displays about the history, people, and landscape of the region, housed in the converted train station.

🚗 *Head south on Gayle Lane to Buckden. Turn right on the B6160 all the way to Bolton Abbey. Use on-site parking lots.*

Wensleydale Creamery sign, Hawes

⑦ Bolton Abbey

Skipton on Swale; N Yorks; BD23 6EX

Now owned by the Duke and Duchess of Devonshire, Bolton Abbey *(open daily; www.boltonabbey.com)*, located on the banks of the River Wharfe, was founded by Augustinian monks in 1154. Although the priory buildings were partially destroyed during the Dissolution of the Monasteries, the Parish Church of St. Mary and St. Cuthbert survived, and continues to this day. The ruins are best explored in the company of a volunteer guide, or by downloading a detailed map from the website and planning a visit.

Bolton Abbey offers a very different experience to dreamy Jervaulx. There is simply so much to do in its 12,140 hectares (30,000 acres): it has over 80 miles (130 km) of paths for riverside or moorland walks, a steam train for a nostalgic trip to Embsay, stocked rivers for fly fishing (with lessons available, if required), woods and parkland for picnics, a children's farm, and a range of visitors' shops as well as places to eat.

Above (all) Bolton Abbey, extensively damaged during the Dissolution of the Monasteries in 1539

EAT AND DRINK

AROUND MIDDLEHAM

The Sandpiper Inn *moderate*
Well-kept ales and inventive cooking from a changing menu can be sampled at this traditional inn. Try some home-made soup, a Wensleydale sandwich, fish and chips or pressed Dales lamb. *Market Place, Leyburn, DL8 5AT; 01969 622 206; www.sandpiperinn.co.uk*

George and Dragon
inexpensive–moderate
This 17th-century coaching inn on the A684 between Hawes and Leyburn, serves soup, sandwiches, and full meals, using local ingredients in season such as roast Nidderdale chicken breast with smoked applewood risotto. *Aysgarth, DL8 3AD; 01969 663 358; www.georgeanddragonaysgarth.co.uk*

DAY TRIP OPTIONS

Choose from family fun around Harrogate, touring the beautiful gardens of Fountains Abbey and Ripley Castle, or a day out in the Dales.

Town and Country
Explore Harrogate ❶, taking in its pretty flower gardens, fine architecture, and spa facilities. Head to Bolton Abbey ❼ to ride a steam train, see some farm animals, go fishing, and just enjoy the glorious countryside.

From Harrogate take the scenic A59, then b6160 to Bolton Abbey.

Gardens and History

Staying at Ripon ❸, visit its cathedral before heading off to Fountains Abbey and Water Gardens. After walking around the best-preserved Cistercian abbey in England, go on to historic Ripley ❷ for a picnic in the castle's deer parks, gardens, or the estate village, or just make use of the tea rooms. Then return to Ripon for dinner and to hear the Hornblower.

Take the B6265 to Fountains Abbey; head down Fountains Lane to B6165 to Ripley. Return via the A61 and A6108.

Royalty in the Dales

Visit the castle at Middleham ❺, former haunt of Richard III; pop across to quaint Leyburn and walk in the steps of Mary Queen of Scots up to Leyburn Shawl to see the great views. Enjoy the drive to Hawes ❻ to stock up on cheese for a picnic on the way through the Dales to the graceful ruins of Jervaulx Abbey ❹, destroyed by King Henry VIII.

Follow the instructions in the drive to Hawes and on to the B6160, but turn off left at Kettlewell back to Middleham.

Eat and Drink: inexpensive, under £25; moderate, £25–£50; expensive, over £50

North Yorkshire Moors & Coast

York to Sutton Park

Highlights

- **Historic York**
  Walk through this living museum of a city with its great Minster, medieval streets, and Georgian town houses

- **The grandest stately homes**
  Admire the splendors of Castle Howard and lovely Sutton Park

- **Wild North York Moors**
  Explore this airy expanse of heather, woodland, and rollercoaster dales on foot, by bike, or by steam train

- **Atmospheric abbeys**
  See the poignant ruins at Rievaulx and Gisborough, and Gothic Whitby, an inspiration for the story of Dracula

- **Fun and fishing on the coast**
  Make a splash in the fishing towns and seaside resorts on this beautiful coast

Heather adds colour to the hills and valleys of the North York Moors, Rosedale, Yorkshire.

North Yorkshire Moors & Coast

England's largest county, North Yorkshire is strewn with picturesque villages, old market towns, stately homes and castles, historic churches, romantic ruins, and so much more. Its coastline is variously quaint, bustling, and unspoiled. Its high, heather-clad moor land is stirringly beautiful with great vistas where sheep graze demurely. There are some purely scenic stretches of dramatic road. This drive, which passes through the Howardian Hills and the center of the North York Moors National Park, before reaching the seaside, provides more than a glimpse of all of these aspects. The trip takes the historic city of York for its point of departure, with a walk at the heart of this wonderful city.

Above Sandsend, just north of Whitby, a small town with a long sandy beach, *see p191*

ACTIVITIES

Climb York Minster's 275 steps and look out over the delightful warren of medieval streets and buildings

Enjoy a warm Yorkshire Fat Rascal – a traditional rich fruit and nut scone – at Betty's Tea Rooms, York

Revisit Brideshead, actually Castle Howard, the palatial home used as a setting in the TV series and film of Evelyn Waugh's classic novel

Cycle through beautiful Yorkshire forests near Pickering

Walk through time in historic buildings chronicling 400 years of rural history at Hutton-le-Hole, one of the country's prettiest villages

Hop aboard a steam train on the Rail Trail over the Yorkshire moors from Grosmont to charming Goathland, and stroll back

Go deep-sea fishing in Whitby, a center of Yorkshire coastal fishing

Look down on Rievaulx Abbey from above – England's foremost Cistercian abbey looks fabulous when seen from Rievaulx Terrace

Walk along the Cleveland Way National Trail from the pretty town of Helmsley

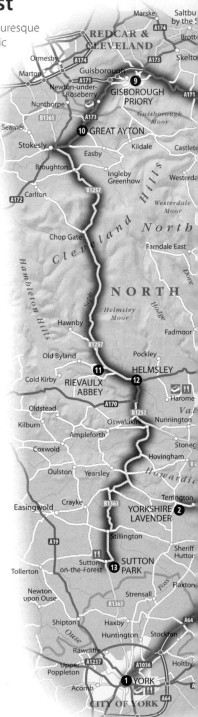

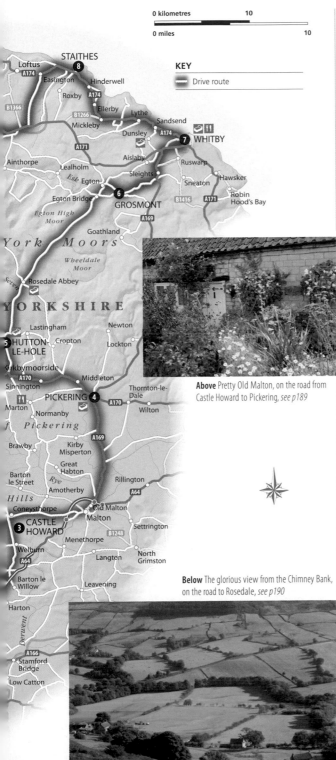

Above Pretty Old Malton, on the road from Castle Howard to Pickering, *see p189*

Below The glorious view from the Chimney Bank, on the road to Rosedale, *see p190*

PLAN YOUR DRIVE

Start/finish: York to Sutton Park.

Number of days: 4 allowing half a day in York.

Distances: 145 miles (233 km).

Road conditions: The roads are generally well-maintained. The steepest routes over the high moors require the use of low gears.

When to go: Best from late April through to mid-September. In summer the heather covering the moors blooms a rich purple.

Opening times: Galleries, museums, and attractions are generally open 10am–5pm, but often close earlier Nov–Easter. Shops are often open longer. Churches are usually open until dusk.

Main market days: York: open market, Newgate, daily; **Pickering**: street market, Mon; **Whitby**: Sat; Helmsley: Fri; Gisborough: Thu & Sat.

Shopping: Look out for Whitby jet jewellery and local smoked kippers; heather honey from the Yorkshire moors; and knitwear made with wool from local sheep breeds.

Major festivals: York: Spring Festival of New Music, May; Early Music Festival, July; National Book Fair, Sep; Food and Drink Festival, Sep; **Whitby**: Regatta and Carnival, early Aug; Folk Week, late Aug.

DAY TRIP OPTIONS

See the **Minster** and **medieval streets** of York, then explore the **palace** and **grounds** of Castle Howard, enjoy some **aromatic lavender**, and finish at the **Georgian mansion** of Sutton park. From Pickering, explore the **moors** by **foot**, **bike**, or **steam train** and marvel at some **frescoes**; in Hutton-le-Hole, see **historic buildings** and a take a thrilling **high moor drive**. From Whitby, see the **ruined abbey**, take a **fishing** trip, visit Grosmont for a **steam-train ride**, then **walk** home. For full details, *see p193*.

Above Example of Georgian architecture in the heart of the city of York

VISITING YORK

Parking
York can be difficult to navigate for drivers, so take advantage of one of the park-and-ride sites, clearly marked on the major routes into the city.

Tourist Information
Buy a York Pass from the Tourist Office if visiting a number of attractions.
The De Grey Rooms, Exhibition Square, YO1 7HB; 01904 550 099; www.visityork.org

WHERE TO STAY IN YORK

The Bloomsbury *inexpensive*
Lovely Victorian house in a leafy area, close to the center. Very friendly service; there is also parking available.
127 Clifton, YO30 6BL; 01904 634 031; www.bloomsburyhotel.co.uk

Galtres Lodge *inexpensive*
Welcoming and smart, this small, central hotel is a Georgian red brick building with thirteen rooms, not all ensuite, and a brasserie.
54 Low Petergate, YO1 7HZ; 01904 622 478; www.galtreslodgehotel.co.uk

Deancourt *moderate–expensive*
Centrally-situated right on the Minster, this attractive hotel is run by Best Western and has nice, smart rooms.
Duncombe Place, YO1 7EF; 01904 625 082; www.deancourt-york.co.uk

The Grange *moderate–expensive*
Upmarket hotel in substantial Regency town house, offers 30 lovely tasteful rooms, some furnished with antiques.
1 Clifton, YO30 6AA; 01904 644 744; www.grangehotel.co.uk

❶ York
Yorkshire; YO1 7JN

A walled city on the River Ouse and spiritual capital of the North of England for 2,000 years, York is best explored on foot. Its rich architectural tapestry mixes the medieval with half-timbered Tudor and elegant Georgian. Amid the high culture of churches, galleries, and museums, cool bars, smart restaurants, and open spaces abound.

A three-hour walking tour
Start at the **Minster** ① *(open daily)*, York's most striking landmark. Built of magnesian limestone between 1220 and 1470, this is the largest Gothic cathedral in Northern Europe, with awe-inspiring stained-glass windows. Climb the tower's 275 steps to take in the views. In Minster Yard nearby lie the **Treasurer's House and Garden** ② *(closed Fri)* with interiors covering 400 years of design. From the Minster go left up Deangate. Carry on along Goodramgate, by Lady Row, the oldest houses in York, dating back to 1316. These are fine examples of jettied houses, where the upper story overhangs the lower. Ahead, in the tallest of York's four medieval gatehouses, is the **Richard III Museum** ③ *(open daily)*, stripping away the myths around the last Plantagenet

Sign for Betty's Café Tea Rooms

king. Next, turn left along Lord Mayor's Walk, then left again down Gillygate. Cross to Exhibition Square and **York Art Gallery** ④ *(open daily)*, with an impressive collection of paintings and ceramics. Cross back to the gateway into the old shopping street of High Petergate. Stop in Café Concerto for possibly the best cappuccino in town. Continue down Low Petergate, and after Church St bear right for the higgledy-piggledy **Shambles** ⑤. This is one of the best-preserved medieval streets in Europe, lined with timber-framed buildings dating from 1350. Once home to York's butchers, it is named for the "shammels" or shelves used to display the meat. From here, turn right down The Pavement and onto Coppergate, then left into Castlegate. At its end stands a fine Georgian townhouse,

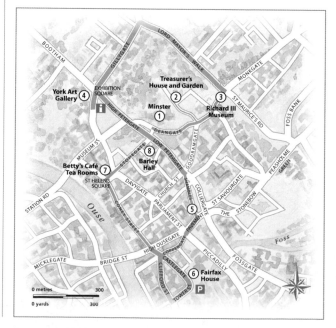

(map of York)

0 metres 300
0 yards 300

Fairfax House ⑥ *(open Mon–Thurs and pm on Sun, also Fri by appt)*, home to a world-class collection of furniture and clocks. Walk down Tower St, right onto Clifford St, then Coney St, then right again into St. Helen's Square for yet another York tradition – tea and cakes in the Art-Deco **Betty's Café Tea Rooms** ⑦. Cross Davygate and halfway up Stonegate turn right down Coffee Yard to **Barley Hall** ⑧ *(May–Oct: open daily; Nov–Apr: closed Mon, Tue except school holidays)*, which recreates life in a 15th-century house. Cross High Petergate back to the Minster.

🚗 *Take A64 north from outer ring road, After 7 miles (11 km) take the left signed Castle Howard. Pass the monument and branch left. Tourist signs lead through Terrington to the farm.*

② Yorkshire Lavender

Terrington, North Yorks; YO60 6PB
This lavender farm and herb nursery *(closed Dec–Mar; www.yorkshirelavender. com)* grows hundreds of different lavender varieties, creating a haze of blue in summer on its south-facing slopes. Admire the gardens, buy

plants, herbs, scented candles, and essential oils, and feast on blueberry and lavender jelly with herb scones in the tea room.

🚗 *Return to Terrington and take the Malton Road, following signs to Castle Howard (with parking lot).*

③ Castle Howard

North Yorks; YO60 7DA
Vast gardens surround this veritable palace *(open daily; www.castlehoward. co.uk)* built over three centuries from 1699 by the Howard Family, who still live here. In 1981, Castle Howard became Brideshead for the TV series of Evelyn Waugh's *Brideshead Revisited* (and again in 2007 for the film). The sumptuous interiors and landscaped grounds with fantastic fountains are both open to the public. Admire the Great Hall under the dome, wander in the Rose Garden or Potager, and visit the striking Turquoise Drawing Room.

🚗 *Return to the Malton Road and continue east, passing through Malton and sedate Old Malton; take the A169 to Pickering. Use parking lot over the roundabout in the center of town.*

Above left Pubs along the river Ouse, York
Above center Yorkshire Lavender farm, overlooking the Vale of York **Above right** The magnificent stained glass of York Minster

SHOPPING IN YORK

For beautiful soft knitwear, made from the wool of rare-breed sheep saved from slaughter, try **Responsibly Gorgeous** *(1 Peter Lane, York; 01904 675 987)*. The shop also sells other ethical and fairtrade designer fashions.

EAT AND DRINK IN YORK

Betty's Café Tea Rooms *inexpensive*
One of a small, venerated chain of Yorkshire tea rooms, Betty's menu is a unique mix of Swiss and Yorkshire food – try Betty's fruit cake with Wensleydale cheese or maybe a Gruyère rösti. Cooked meals and snacks all day.
6-8 St. Helen's Square, YO1 8QP; 01904 659 142; www.bettys.co.uk

Café Concerto *inexpensive*
This is an attractive, modern-European café-bistro, whose walls are papered with sheet music. Great coffee, wraps, salads, baguettes, club sandwiches, and more substantial dishes.
21 High Petergate, YO1 7EN; 01904 610 478; www.cafeconcerto.biz

Melton's Too *inexpensive*
This is a cool café-bar-cum-bistro in a three-story 17th-century building. Nice and informal, it serves all-day breakfast, sandwiches, and tapas.
25 Walmgate, YO1 9TX; 01904 629 222; www.meltonstoo.co.uk

Melton's *moderate*
Excellent restaurant with a firm commitment to home-cooking and Yorkshire ingredients such as Whitby crab, Swaledale lamb, and herbs.
7 Scarcroft Rd, YO23 1ND; 01904 634 341; www.meltonsrestaurant.co.uk

Left Castle Howard, one of Britain's finest historic houses and gardens

Eat and Drink: inexpensive, under £25; moderate, £25–£50; expensive, over £50

④ Pickering
North Yorks; YO18 8DY

This market town is an excellent base for exploring the North Yorkshire Moors National Park. Do it on foot *(www.northyorkmoors.org.uk)* or by bike: the **Purple Mountain Bike Centre** *(01751 460 011; www.northyorkmoors.org. uk)*, in Dalby Forest, rents out bikes and has details of trails for all abilities. A more sedate way to see the moors is by steam train: the **North York Moors Railway** *(Apr–Oct; www.nymr.co. uk)* runs all the way to Whitby. There's a lot to see in Pickering, too. The charming 15th-century **Church of St. Peter and St. Paul** contains striking frescoes, discovered in 1878, that were hidden under limewash during the 16th-century Reformation. Explore **Pickering Castle** *(Apr–Oct: open daily)*; first built of wood and earth in 1079 and rebuilt in stone in the 13th century.

🚗 *Head west on A170, turning right to Hutton-le-Hole. Park at top of the village.*

⑤ Hutton-le-Hole
North Yorks; YO62 6UA

Hutton is built around a series of greens on which local Swaledale and Blackface sheep graze. Hutton Beck runs through the village, spanned by pretty bridges and perfect for a picnic. **The Ryedale Folk Museum** *(open daily)* is an amazing village within a village. Thirteen historic buildings reveal the lives of local folk over the centuries to the 1950s. Look inside an Elizabethan manor, a thatched cottage, a 1950s village store – even a witch's hovel.

Leaving the village, turn right on the road marked for Lastingham and then fork left (unsuitable for caravans)

Above Charming houses of Hutton-le-Hole, built around a series of sheep-grazed greens

on the stunning road to **Rosedale**. This crosses the Chimney Bank, from the top of which the valley spread below resembles a vast green patchwork quilt. Check the brakes before attempting this drive – the descent to the village of Rosedale Abbey is said to be the steepest road in England.

🚗 *In Rosedale Abbey, take the road by the Milburn Arms, opposite the green, marked for Egton. Turn right at sign for Grosmont. Park at Grosmont station.*

⑥ Grosmont
North Yorks; YO22 5QE

In the beautiful Esk Valley, this village is known for two reasons; the first is **Grosmont Station** *(Apr–Oct; www.nymr. co.uk)*. Volunteers run this delightful old station for the North York Moors Railway from Pickering to Whitby. Hop aboard for a nostalgic journey and visit the village of Goathland. Walk

Below left North York Moors Railway steam train at Grosmont Station **Below right** Shop selling traditional beach equipment and that sugary seaside staple – rock

back via the 3-mile (5-km) **Rail Trail**. Its other claim to fame is as the setting for popular TV drama series *Heartbeat*.

🚗 *Leave on Front St, turning left at Sleights on A169 and right onto A171. Veer left onto Prospect Hill and take 3rd exit at the roundabout for seafront.*

7 Whitby
North Yorks; YO21 1YN
Visually dramatic, the buzzing fishing port and resort of Whitby clings to the hills on the banks of the River Esk, its hilltop abbey ruins dramatically silhouetted against the sky. Other architectural highlights includes fine Georgian houses and humbler white fishermen's cottages, linked by ginnels (alleys). **Whitby Abbey** *(open daily)* was founded by St. Hilda in AD 655, but today's ruins destroyed by Henry VIII and further damaged by German battleships in 1914. Sharing the windswept hillside is **St. Mary's Church** *(open daily)* and its graveyard, reached by 199 steps. The two edifices provided a dramatic setting in Bram Stoker's Gothic vampire novel *Dracula* (1897). Leeds-born artist Frank Sutcliffe set up a studio in Whitby in 1876, taking photos of fishermen, farmers, ships, and moorland. See his work at the **Sutcliffe Gallery**, *(Flowergate, www.sutcliffegallery.co.uk)*.

Whitby fudge shop sign

It's a short walk to **Sandsend** which has a nice, sandy beach and plenty of surf; or a longer one to family-friendly **Robin Hood's Bay**; or just climb up past the Abbey and explore the Cleveland Way *(www.northseatrail. co.uk)*. It's even possible to catch a fish supper at sea with a half-day fishing trip *(01947 605 658; www.wsatsite.com)*.

🚗 *Head inland, turning right on the A174 through Sandsend and right to Staithes; use the pay-and-display car park.*

8 Staithes
North Yorks; TS13 5BH
As a young man, the explorer James Cook (1728–79) once worked in the draper's shop in this fishing village, and it is here that he first dreamt of becoming a sea captain and navigator. Still ringed by cliffs offering spectacular walks, this pretty harbor village has probably changed little to this day. To the north lie the dramatic **Boulby Cliffs**, the highest on England's east coast.

🚗 *Go west on A174. Turn left at Easington on a minor road to A171. Turn right and follow signs to Guisborough.*

Above Crab and lobster pots in Whitby, still a busy fishing center

SHOPPING IN WHITBY

Whitby Jet
Mourning for Prince Albert, Queen Victoria set a fashion for lustrous black jet jewelery. Whitby's shore proved a rich source of this beautiful gemstone. Buy it from **Whitby Jet Heritage Centre** and **W Hamond** *(both on Church St)*.

Whitby Kippers
W R Fortunes *(22 Henrietta St)* produces richly flavored kippered herrings, smoked using oak and beech shavings.

EAT AND DRINK

AROUND PICKERING

Appletree Country Inn *moderate*
This dining pub serves excellent local produce – Whitby crab cakes, Marton beef, and Marton Mess – lavender meringue, fruit, and cream.
Marton, Nr Pickering YO6 6RD (on Marton Rd, left off the A170); 01751 431 457; closed Mon, Tue

WHITBY

Elizabeth Botham & Sons *inexpensive*
This family-run tea house is delightfully old fashioned. Choose a speciality tea to wash down gingerbread with Coverdale cheese or buttered plum bread.
35 Skinner Street, YO21 3AH; 01947 602 823; www.botham.co.uk

Magpie *inexpensive*
This Whitby portside institution serves tip-top fish dishes, including oysters, chowders, prawn cocktail, and Whitby crab – can get busy at lunchtime.
14 Pier Road, YO21 3PU; 01947 602 058; www.magpiecafe.co.uk

Green's Seafood Bistro and Restaurant *moderate*
Serves seafood fresh from the quay each morning, as well as local meat and game. Bistro menu is simpler with a changing catch of the day.
13 Bridge St, YO22 4BG; 01947 600 284; www.greensofwhitby.com

Above Yorkshire, Moors And Coast, driving over the Rosedale Chimney Bank

Eat and Drink: inexpensive, under £25; moderate, £25–£50; expensive, over £50

WALKING THE CLEVELAND WAY NATIONAL TRAIL

The 109-mile (176-km) Cleveland Way National Trail crosses the North Moors National Park in a horseshoe-shaped route from the market town of Helmsley to Saltburn on the coast and along to Filey. Several companies offer a luggage-transfer service for long-distance walkers, or there are plenty of possibilities for shorter, circular walks. Information about both can be found on the trail website *(www. nationaltrail.co.uk/ClevelandWay).*

WHERE TO STAY

AROUND GISBOROUGH PRIORY

King's Head *moderate*
Award-winning B&B comprising two adjoining 17th-century cottages at the foot of Roseberry Topping. Eight ensuite rooms. Breakfast of local bacon, black pudding, sausages and Whitby kippers.
The Green, Newton-under-Roseberry TS9 6QR; 8 km (5 miles) on A171 and A173; 01642 722 318; www.kingsheadhotel.co.uk

AROUND HELMSLEY

Pheasant Hotel *moderate*
Family-run country hotel in quiet village setting 3 miles (5 km) southeast of Helmsley. Twelve ensuite rooms have picturesque views of the village pond, deer park, or walled garden.
Harome, Helmsley YO62 5JG; 01439 771 241; www.thepheasanthotel.com

Right Rievaulx Abbey, once one of the great abbeys in Yorkshire **Far right** Statue of James Cook the explorer, Great Ayton

Above The splendid Gothic east gable of Gisborough Priory

⑨ Gisborough Priory
North Yorks; TS14 6HG

Little remains of this 14th-century **Augustine monastery** *(closed Mon, Tue),* but the towering skeleton of the eastern gable gives an idea of what a masterpiece the building must have been. Founded in AD 1119 by the Bruce family, who became kings of Scotland, the priory was twice rebuilt. After the Dissolution of the Monasteries under Henry VIII, the priory was acquired by the Chaloner family, who created a magnificent garden on the site. Volunteers are working to restore it as a public space. In summer, plays are staged here.

🚗 *Go west on the Middlesborough Road (A171), then left on the A173 to Great Ayton.*

The Dissolution of the Monasteries

When the Pope refused to annul his marriage to Catherine of Aragon in 1531, Henry VIII had himself declared Head of the Church of England. As well as helping solve his marriage problems, this enabled him and his minister, Cromwell, to sieze power from the Catholic Church in England. Taking his lead from the Protestant Reformation in Europe, Henry VIII claimed to be fighting the greed and corruption of the Church. By 1540, over 850 monasteries and shrines had been closed and their wealth and property diverted to the Crown.

⑩ Great Ayton
North Yorks; TS9 6NB

For eight years the boyhood home of explorer Captain James Cook, this is a delightful village with views of the distinctively shaped sandstone hill, the Roseberry Topping. The High Green has a statue of 16-year-old Cook looking towards Staithes and the sea. Low Green, on the banks of the Leven, is a great picnic spot. The Postgate School is now the **Captain Cook School Museum** *(Apr–Oct: open daily pm).* The 12th-century **All Saints Church** on Low Green, where Cook's family is buried, is still used for candlelit worship *(Sun pm, Wed am).*

🚗 *Continue on A173, taking B1257 left for a fabulous 20-mile (32-km) drive. Turn right at the sign for Rievaulx Abbey. Park by the entrance.*

Above Flowers outside a pub in the attractive market town of Helmsley

⑪ Rievaulx Abbey

North Yorks; YO62 5LB
This partially ruined building *(Apr–Sep: open daily; Oct–Mar: closed Tue, Wed; www.english-heritage.org.uk)* is widely regarded as England's foremost Cistercian abbey. The atmospheric remains of soaring pillars and graceful arches set on a slope in a quiet valley, fire the imagination. Founded in 1131, by the 13th century it was home to 150 monks and over 500 lay brothers. An indoor exhibition explores the farming, commercial, and spiritual aspects of the abbey. The café serves fresh locally sourced food – and cider from Ampleforth Abbey. Nearby, and close to the main road, **Rievaulx Terrace and Temples** *(open daily)* has two classical Georgian temples and fabulous views over Rievaulx Abbey.
🚗 *Drive on the B1257 to Helmsley. Park on the market square or Cleveland Way.*

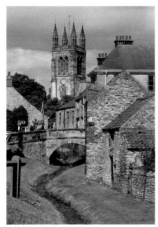

Above Unspoiled Helmsley, a favorite destination for walkers on the North York Moors

⑫ Helmsley

North Yorks; YO62 5AB
This small but bustling market town on the River Rye is dominated by the ruins of 13th-century **Helmsley Castle** *(Mar–Oct: open daily; Nov–Feb: closed Tue, Wed)*. Against this backdrop, **Helmsley Walled Garden** *(open Apr–Oct)* is a pretty 18th-century fruit and vegetable garden and a nice place for a picnic. At the start of the Cleveland Way National Trail, the town is a popular base for walkers.
🚗 *Leave on B1257, then A170, then B1257 again. Turn right onto B1363 south towards York. At Sutton-on-the-Forest, follow signs to Sutton Park.*

⑬ Sutton Park

Sutton-on-the-Forest, N Yorks; YO61 1DP
The home of Sir Reginald and Lady Sheffield *(Apr–Sep: Wed, Sun & Bank Hols, pm; ring ahead, 01347 811 251)*, this is a fine early Georgian stately house (1730) set in pretty parkland. The furniture came from Buckingham House (before it became a palace). There are woodland walks, a Georgian ice house, and the gardens – especially the roses – are stunning in summer.

EAT AND DRINK

AROUND HELMSLEY

Star Inn *moderate*
Award-winning pub restaurant offers imaginative cooking using fresh, local produce flavored with herbs from the garden. Grilled black pudding with pan-fried foie gras and Pickering watercress; North Sea fish pie with Montgomery Cheddar topping; or pan-roasted haunch of Duncombe Park roe deer.
High Street, Harome, YO62 5JE (3 miles/ 5 km) southeast of Helmsley); 01439 770 397; www.thestaratharome.co.uk

SUTTON PARK

Rose and Crown *moderate*
Gastropub serving imaginative cooking such as tuna carpaccio, Yorkshire rib-eye steak with rocket and smoked cheese salad, and sea bass with buttered summer greens.
Sutton-on-the-Forest, YO61 1DP; 01347 811 333; www.rosecrown.co.uk

---

DAY TRIP OPTIONS

Wherever you stay, history is not far away, and neither are the moors.

Architectural Indulgence

In York ❶, see its Minster and medieval "shambles." Tour the splendid Castle Howard ❸ and go on to Yorkshire Lavender ❷ for aromas, fresh air, and lunch. Finish off with the exquisite interiors and gardens of Sutton Park ⑬.

Take the A64 north. Turn off for Castle Howard and Yorkshire Lavender, then continue west to the B1363 and south.

Moorland Adventures

Staying at Pickering ❹, see the church frescoes before enjoying a few hours of energetic cycling in the Dalby Forest. Next head for Hutton-le-Hole ❺ and explore the historic rural buildings of Rydale Folk Museum. Finish the day with a thrilling rollercoaster of a drive over Rosedale Chimney Bank, enjoying the views.

Head west on A170, turning right to Hutton-le-Hole, then follow the signs to Rosedale. Take Moor Lane south.

Coastal Fun

Be scared by the Gothic ruins of the abbey and spooky graveyard at Whitby ❼. If the vampires aren't biting, maybe the fish will be, so try to catch some on a boat trip. If there is time, drive to Grosmont ❻ to take the restored steam train to pretty Goathland. Those feeling fit can walk back to Whitby on the Rail Trail.

Head out of Whitby on the A171, turn left on the A169, turning right down Eskdaleside to Grosmont.

The Poetry of the Lakes

Carlisle to Coniston

Highlights

- **Handsome Carlisle**
  Tour the border county town of Cumbria, with its splendid cathedral complex and historic castle

- **Natural wonders**
  Drive through luxuriant forests and mountain passes; see nesting ospreys, lofty waterfalls, and an enormous rock brought from Scotland by a glacier

- **Jewels of the Lakeland**
  Make the most of the Lake District's prettiest and most unspoiled waters – cruise, row, go trout fishing, or just relax by their lapping shores

- **Literary landscapes**
  Visit the home of Wordsworth, the celebrated lake poet; the marvelous house of John Ruskin; and Beatrix Potter's charming cottage

Rowing boat on the still, clear waters of Derwent water, Lake District

The Poetry of the Lakes

This tour winds its way around the Lake District, starting with gentle miles through green open pastures grazed by sheep. There are also a few long stretches to cover, amid some of the most stupendous natural scenery in all of Britain. The route entails two lovely, unchallenging passes; taking in scattered slate-roofed farms, it runs alongside lakes great and small, touristy and tranquil. Stop-offs along the way include the small town of Cockermouth, bustling Keswick on Derwent Water and the famous Dove Cottage in Grasmere, once home to the poet William Wordsworth, who drew his inspiration from the surrounding natural beauty.

Above Typical Lake District cottage built with local stone, matching the dry-stone walls

ACTIVITIES

Soak up the history of Carlisle, close to the Scottish borders, taking in the magnificent cathedral and the doughty castle

Visit a traditional brewery to see Cockermouth beer in production and sample the real ales in the brewery's bar

Watch ospreys nesting via CCTV at the Whinlatter Forest Park

Go walking, hiking, off-road biking, sailing, canoeing – the Lake District is one vast adventure playground

Go underground in the last working slate mine in Britain at the stunning Honister Pass

Spend an evening at the theatre in Keswick and emerge to find Derwent Water lapping the shore before you

Try and work out Sarah Nelson's secret recipe by eating her traditional Cumbrian gingerbread in Grasmere

Watch skilled glassblowers at work and buy a memento from Ambleside

Tour the inside of the lakeside Victorian home of John Ruskin the poet, artist, commentator, and conservationist

Take a pleasure cruise across Coniston on a steam yacht

KEY

Drive route

Below Traditional cruiser skimming across the surface of Ullswater lake near Keswick, *see p201*

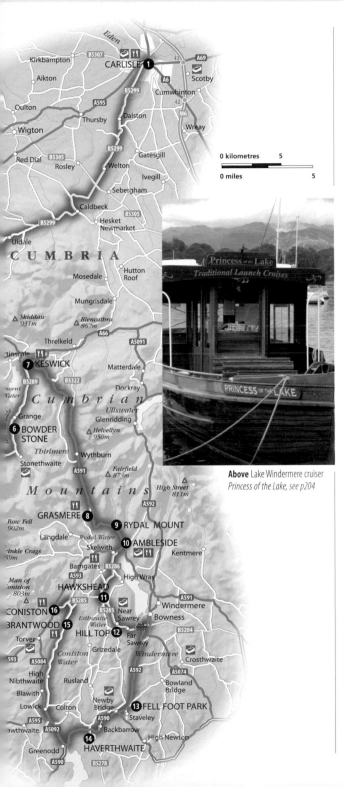

Above Lake Windermere cruiser *Princess of the Lake, see p204*

PLAN YOUR DRIVE

Start/finish: Carlisle to Coniston.

Number of days: 5, including a half day at Carlisle.

Distances: Approximately 135 miles (217 km).

Road conditions: The roads are good, but watch out for straying sheep.

When to go: Spring is the ideal time to see hosts of golden daffodils; May–Jun is when the azaleas are ablaze; summer is fun but busy; and Oct for the blaze of autumn color.

Opening times: Galleries, museums, and attractions are generally open 10am–5pm, but often close earlier Nov–Easter. Shops are often open longer. Churches are usually open until dusk.

Main market days: Keswick: Sat; Carlisle: Carlisle Farmers' Market, first Fri of month; Covered Market, closed Sun.

Shopping: Look out for gingerbread in Grasmere, ice cream in Buttermere, fine relishes in Hawkshead, and fudge in Coniston. There are also wool products and glass products from Ambleside.

Major festivals: Cumbria-wide: Cumbria Life Food and Drink Festival, Apr–May; Lake District Summer Music Festival, Aug; **Carlisle**: International Summer Festival, Jul; **Cockermouth**: Summer Festival, Jul; **Keswick**: Film Festival, Feb; Words by the Water, Mar; Jazz Festival, May; **Grasmere**: Lake Artists Society Summer Exhibition, Aug; **Coniston**: Water Festival, Jul.

DAY TRIP OPTIONS

Families will love discovering Carlisle with its **fortifications** and **cathedral**, followed by a visit to Cockermouth with its **castle ruins**. Continue to Whinlatter Forest Park for a **walk** or **bike ride**. Learn about Lakeland stone at Keswick's **ancient stone circle**, climb the **Bowder Stone**, cross **Honister Pass**, go down a **slate mine** and take in the **scenery** on a **walk** by Buttermere Lake. Poetry lovers will relish seeing Wordsworth's **cottage** and **burial place** at Grasmere; his home at **Rydal Mount**, as well as Ambleside and Hawkshead – good spots for a **walk** or **fishing trip**. For full details, *see p205*.

Above Ancient wooden door at Carlisle's 12th–14th-century castle

VISITING CARLISLE

Parking
Exit M6 at junction 43, then drive down A69 Rotary Way to Warwick Rd until you see Lowther St. Turn right to The Lanes parking lot on the left, or follow signs to station for short- and long-stay parking (pay-and-display parking lots are clearly marked). There is street parking on Main Street, Station Street, and Market Place.

Tourist Information
Old Town Hall, Market Square, CA3 8JE;
01228 625 600; www.visitcumbria.com

WHERE TO STAY

CARLISLE

Cornerways Guest House *inexpensive*
A conveniently-situated and good value B&B. Not all rooms are ensuite. Serves full English and continental breakfasts.
107 Warwick Road, CA1 1EA; 01228 521 733; www.cornerwaysbandb.co.uk

Number Thirty-One *moderate*
This award-winning guesthouse offers a set dinner plus B&B, with menus based on what is best and freshest that day.
31 Howard Place, CA1 1HR; 01228 597 080; www.number31.co.uk

AROUND CARLISLE

Willowbeck Lodge *moderate*
A purpose-built Scandinavian-style lodge offering breakfast with Craster kippers, free-range eggs, and Scotch pancakes.
Lambley Bank, Scotby, CA4 8BX; 5 km (3 miles) east on A69; 01228 513 607; www. willowbeck-lodge.com

❶ Carlisle
Cumbria; CA3 8JA

Streets of handsome terraces surround the ancient center of this border city, which is still intact, atmospheric and accessible behind the bland store fronts of the pedestrian precinct. Neither chic nor cosmopolitan, Carlisle has character, with a strong sense of civic pride and the small but beautiful cathedral at its spiritual heart. Visitors won't go hungry in town, but the best gastronomic treats await in the nearby countryside.

A two-hour walking tour

Start at the **Railway Station** ① with its imposing Tudor-Gothic-style façade. It was designed in 1847 by Sir William Tite, designer of the Bank of England and London's Royal Exchange. From the station it is impossible to miss the **Citadel** ② *(open Jul–Aug: Mon–Fri)*; its oval East and West Towers were begun in 1810–11 to a design by Thomas Telford and contained courts and a prison. The West Tower has oak-paneled courtrooms, a grand jury room, and cells. Walk between the towers up English St towards the city's shopping center. At the center of the pedestrianized area is Carlisle Cross, dated 1682. The tourist office is here, housed in the **Old Town Hall** ③ which was founded in 1122 and has been rebuilt many times. Just outside stands a "Victorian" pillar box marking the fact that England 's first such box was erected in Carlisle in 1853. Turn right out of the tourist office and enter grey and red stone **Carlisle Cathedral** ④. Admire its glorious interior, lit by exquisite stained-glass windows, some dating from the 14th century. Beneath a stunning barrel-vaulted, starred ceiling are excellent paintings, a carved

oak Antwerp triptych dating back to 1510 and 15th-century choir stalls.

Clustered around the cathedral are some fine 17th-century buildings, such as the Old Registry, dated 1699, The Deanery with its defensive Pele tower *(see p209)* and the Fratry, a 13th-century monastic dining room. Turn left and left into Abbey Street and go through the wrought-iron gates to **Old Tullie House** ⑤ *(open daily)*, a museum and gallery housed in a Jacobean mansion dating from 1689. Its collections are devoted to local social history, archaeology, wildlife, geology and fine arts. Leave by the rear exit to find the **Millennium Gallery** ⑥. This is actually a bright subway running beneath the road, with artifacts celebrating the city. These include the 16th-century cursing stone, recording the scathing words of the Bishop of Glasgow aimed at the marauding reivers of the borders *(see p209)*. Enter the **Castle** ⑦ by its 14th-century gatehouse and portcullis onto the 12th-century keep, with the dank dungeons that once held Mary Queen of Scots. Walk around the outside of the castle and enter Bitts Park at the junction with Castle Way. Cross the park to the River Eden and climb the steps

Below The remains of what was an earlier, larger version of Carlisle Cathedral

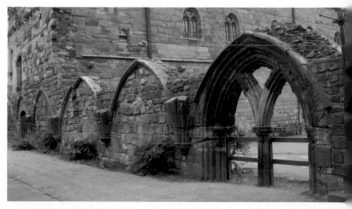

Where to Stay: inexpensive, under £80; moderate, £80–£150; expensive, over £150

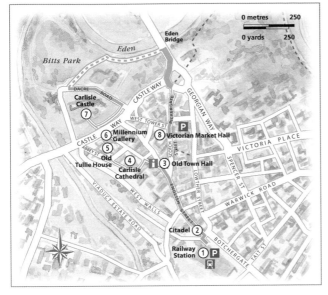

Above Colorful and quirky independent coffee shop, Cockermouth

EAT AND DRINK

CARLISLE

La Pergola *inexpensive*
Family-run Italian restaurant offering tried and trusted fare in a great location.
28 Castle Street, CA3 8TP; 01228 534 084; www.ristorantelapergola.co.uk

The Spice Enterprise *inexpensive*
In a former pub, this place serves staple dishes and interesting specials – chilli lime-infused grilled king prawns, rabbit with pickling spices and yogurt sauce. There are Fairtrade and organic wines, and children are welcome.
Briar Bank, CA3 9SN; 01228 599 888; www.thespiceenterprise.co.uk

La Mezzaluna *inexpensive*
This Italian restaurant serves traditional dishes for breakfast, lunch and dinner, including vegetarian options.
6 The Crescent, CA1 1QW; 01228 534 472; www.lamezzalunacarlisle.co.uk

Alexandros *inexpensive*
Small, intimate restaurant offering an authentic Greek menu with a few imaginative modern twists.
68 Warwick Road, CA1 1DR; 01228 592 227; www.thegreek.co.uk

COCKERMOUTH

The Bitter End *inexpensive*
This friendly real-ale pub with in-house brewery serves traditional sandwiches, steak-and-ale pie, and fish and chips.
Kirkgate, CA13 9PJ; 01900 828 993; www.bitterend.co.uk

Old Stackyard Tearooms *inexpensive*
A lovely place to enjoy award-winning homemade snacks and light meals.
Wellington Farm, CA13 0QU (just off the A66/A5086 roundabout); 01900 822 777; www.wellingtonjerseys.co.uk

Quince and Medlar *moderate*
Offering an inventive vegetarian menu with organic wines and great fruit drinks, this restaurant is located close to the castle in a superb Georgian building.
13 Castlegate, CA13 9EU; 01900 823 579

---

of Eden Bridge. To the right stands the high-rise Civic Centre; to the left, hidden to all but historical imagination, the course of **Hadrian's Wall**, along Stanwix Bank on the far side of the Eden. Head back into the town center along Rickergate to pass the glass-roofed **Victorian Market Hall** ⑧, built in 1890, and return through the precinct to the station.

🚗 *Leave via A6 (Lowther Street). Take first exit on roundabout onto A595, turn left at B5299, then branch left to Uldale. Take B5291 toward Bassenthwaite/Keswick and A66. At roundabout take B5089 into Cockermouth and join B5292 in center.*

② Cockermouth
Cumbria; CA13 9NP
At the meeting of the rivers Derwent and Cocker, this small market town, the birthplace of William Wordsworth (1770–1850), is easily explored on foot. Step inside the Georgian **Wordsworth House** *(closed Sun)* townhouse, where the poet spent his early years, to see what life was like in the 1770s. Cooking demonstrations and tastings are held in the kitchen, and the walled garden is planted with traditional varieties of flowers, fruit, and vegetables. The mostly ruined

Cockermouth Castle, best viewed from the riverside, is only opened to the public during the Summer Festival in July. There are antiques shops on Station Street, and real-ale drinkers should book a tour of 19th-century **Jennings Brewery** *(www.jenningsbrewery. co.uk; 0845 1297 185)*.

🚗 *Leave on the B5292 for Lorton. Take left branch to stay on B5292 to Whinlatter Forest.*

Whinlatter Forest Park sign

③ Whinlatter Forest Park
Cumbria; CA12 5TW
The road climbs through England's only true mountain forest (planted for timber after WW1), affording fabulous views of the Lake District and across the water of the Solway Firth into Scotland. See breeding ospreys via CCTV, or feeding siskins and the shy red squirrels scampering over the feeding station. The **Visitors' Centre** *(www.forestry.gov.uk/whinlatterhome; 01229 860 373)* has details of woodland walks, or go mountain biking on the longest purpose-built trail in the Lake District, the Altura Trail. Hire bikes and clothing from Cyclewise Whinlatter *(www.cyclewise.co.uk; 017687 78711)*.

🚗 *Return through High Lorton and turn left on to B5289 to Buttermere. There is a parking lot in the village.*

Eat and Drink: inexpensive, under £25; moderate, £25–£50; expensive, over £50

Above left Traditional water launch, Derwent Water, near Keswick **Above right** Panoramic view over Keswick, Derwent Water, and the Fells

VISITING KESWICK

Parking
There is pay parking by the theater on the lake and at various well-marked sites around the town.

Boating
At **Derwent Water Marina**, west off the A66, rent kayaks, rowing boats, sail boats, and windsurfers, or take some lessons. *(Portinscale, CA12 5RF; 01768 772 912; www.derwentwatermarina.co.uk)*

WHERE TO STAY

AROUND BUTTERMERE

New House Farm *moderate–expensive*
This top-notch 17th-century guest house located on B5289 to Buttermere offers impressive wood-paneled rooms. *Lorton, Cockermouth, CA13 9UU; 07841 159 818; www.newhouse-farm.com*

AROUND HONISTER PASS

Langstrath Country Inn *inexpensive*
There are eight very nice ensuite rooms in this relaxed, attractive, walker-friendly inn just off the B5289 after Honister Slate Mine. It has bags of personality and serves great food – try the local lamb, Cumbrian cheeses, and ales. *Stonethwaite, Borrowdale, CA12 5XG; 017687 77239; www.thelangstrath.com*

AROUND KESWICK

Swinside Lodge *moderate*
This Georgian country house, near Stair on the west shore of Derwent Water, offers seven good rooms with great views. The daily changing menu based on fresh local ingredients includes homemade bread, soups, ice cream, and Cumbrian cheeses. *Newlands, CA12 5UE; 017687 72948; www.swinsidelodge-hotel.co.uk*

④ **Buttermere**
Cumbria; CA13 9UZ
This hamlet is scenically situated beneath looming lakeland pikes and crags between tranquil Buttermere Lake and larger Crummock Water. Try the eminently walkable footpath – allow 2–3 hours – around Buttermere (meaning "lake of the dairy pastures"); usually there's a welcome ice-cream van at the end of the walk. It is also a short walk from the village to the spectacular **Scale Force**, the highest waterfall in the Lake District, with a single drop of 170 ft (52 m).

🚗 *Continue along the B5289 over Honister Pass to the mine.*

⑤ **Honister Pass**
Cumbria; CA12 5XN
The drive across **Honister Pass** is simply glorious, passing skipping streams and rushing torrents, tough grass slopes and rock-studded scree patches, and everywhere shaggy Herdwick sheep.

On the B5289, **Honister Slate Mine** *(open daily; 017687 77230; www.honister-slate-mine.co.uk)* is Britain's last working slate mine and produces traditional Westmoreland green slate. It offers four daily 90-minute tours within the 11 miles (18 km) of tunnels. See the vast caverns being worked, and learn about the extraction and processing of slate (reservations essential).

🚗 *Continue on B5289 to Bowder Stone. Note the double stone bridge into Grange village, but don't cross in high summer, when the village is packed.*

The Lady of the Lake
Mary Robinson, the pretty daughter of the landlord at the Fish Hotel, was widely known as the "Beauty of Buttermere." In 1802 she married the Hon. Alexander Augustus Hope, Lieutenant-Colonel of the 14th Regiment of Foot. However, he was really John Hatfield, an imposter and bigamist and was hanged in 1803 in Carlisle for forgery. Her story was the inspiration for the novel by author and broadcaster Sir Melvyn Bragg, *The Maid of Buttermere.*

⑥ **Bowder Stone**
Grange, Cumbria
Weighing 2,000 tons and standing some 30 ft (9 m) high, this stone, you might suppose, had simply broken loose from the rock face – but it is not

Below A visitor from Scotland, the colossal Bowder Stone, Grange

Far left The old stone bridge over the River Greta at Keswick **Left** Dove Cottage, home of celebrated lake poet William Wordsworth

SHOPPING IN GRASMERE

Sarah Nelson's Grasmere gingerbread is sold at **Grasmere Gingerbread Shop**, in what was once the Lych Gate village school where Wordsworth taught. *(Portinscale, CA12 5RF; 01768772 912; www.derwentwatermarina.co.uk)*

EAT AND DRINK

KESWICK

Luca's Ristorante *inexpensive*
This bills itself as Keswick's premium Italian restaurant and has a loyal local following. It has an extensive menu and a riverside location.
High Hill, Greta Bridge, CA12 5NX; 017687 74621; www.lucasristorante.co.uk

Square Orange *inexpensive*
Continental-style café-bar offering great coffee, stone-baked pizzas, and tapas. It also has indoor games for rainy days.
20 St. John's Street, CA12 5AS; 017687 73888; www.thesquareorange.co.uk

Highfield Restaurant *expensive*
With a menu that draws on local seasonal produce, this hotel-restaurant serves Cumbrian beef, wild venison, and award-winning Cumbrian cheeses.
The Heads, CA12 5ER; 017687 72508; www.highfieldkeswick.co.uk

GRASMERE

The Jumble Room *moderate*
This quirky restaurant with a suitably eclectic menu serves delights such as traditional Graythwaite game pie and less traditional Italo-Thai ravioli.
Langdale Rd, LA22 9SU; 015394 35188; www. thejumbleroom.co.uk

Below The enigmatic Castlerigg Stone Circle, one of the earliest stone circles in Britain

local rock, and was probably carried here all the way from Scotland by the glaciers of the Ice Age. It is traditional to shake hands with a friend under the stone and climb to the top.
🚗 *Continue on B5289 into Keswick.*

⑦ Keswick
Cumbria; CA12 5JR

A tourist magnet, this buzzy town has a stunning setting on Derwent Water, surrounded by the fells of Saddleback, Helvellyn, and Grizedale Pike. Attractions include the beautifully situated **Theatre by the Lake**, *(www.theatrebythelake. co.uk)* with its professional drama company and art galleries. Alternatively, take to the water in a rowing boat or kayak, or on a cruise. East of town, on the A591, stands the enigmatic **Castlerigg Stone Circle** with distant views of Skiddaw, Blencathra, and Lonscale Fell. With an astrologically significant alignment, the circle of 38 stones holds a rectangle of 10 more and dates from around 3,000 BC.
🚗 *Head south on A591 to Grasmere.*

Sign for local ice cream, Buttermere

The Hardy Herdwick
Incredibly enduring, Herdwick sheep are native to the Lake District, where they have grazed since the 12th century or earlier. The meat is prized by Cumbrian gourmets. It gets its distinctive taste from a diet of fell grasses, and heather. The wool is tough, wiry, and longlasting.

⑧ Grasmere
Cumbria; LA22 9SH

On the Wordsworth trail, Grasmere has the sturdy little village church of **St. Oswald's**. Inside, there is a glass case holding the poet's prayer book

and outside are eight yew trees that he planted. One now marks the grave that Wordsworth shares with his wife, Mary. Nearby are buried his sister Dorothy, four of his children, Mary's sister, and Samuel Taylor Coleridge's son, Hartley. Just beyond the village, on A591 there is free parking on the left for **Dove Cottage** *(closed Dec 24–26 and 3 weeks in Jan)*, home to William, and Dorothy from 1799 to 1808. Here, the poet enjoyed a golden age of creativity, and the whitewashed walls, flagged floors and dark paneling resonate with his presence. Here, too, Dorothy wrote her *Grasmere Journals*. In 1802 William married Mary Hutchinson, who joined the household. Guests included fellow poet Samuel Taylor-Coleridge, and novelists Sir Walter Scott and Thomas de Quincey. The garden, a "domestic slip of mountain," has been restored to the semi-wild state planned for it by William and Dorothy.
🚗 *Follow A591 alongside glorious Rydal Water to Rydal Mount.*

VISITING AMBLESIDE

Parking
Pay-and-display parking lot on the right on the drive into town.

Tourist Information
Central Buildings, Market Cross LA22 9BS; 015394 32582; www.amblesideonline.co.uk

WHERE TO STAY

AMBLESIDE

Cote How Organic Guest House *moderate*
This guest house has a beautiful setting, six ensuite rooms, and serves organic, sustainable, and Fairtrade produce.
Rydal, LA22 9LW; 015394 32765; www.cotehow.co.uk

Barnes Fell B&B *moderate*
A boutique B&B with three delightful ensuite rooms. Breakfasts feature organic produce and local bacon.
Low Gale, LA22 0BD; 015394 33311; www.barnesfell.co.uk

AROUND HILL TOP

Ees Wyke Country House *moderate*
This lovely Georgian country house overlooks Esthwaite Water.
Near Sawrey, LA22 0JZ; 11 km (7 miles) south from Hill Top; 015394 36393; www.eeswyke.co.uk

Below left Terrace of Victorian stone B&Bs, Ambleside **Below right** Rydal Water, one of the smallest lakes in the area **Bottom left** The Old Corn Mill, Ambleside, dating back to 1680 **Bottom right** Rydal Mount, Wordsworth's final home

⑨ Rydal Mount
Rydal, near Ambleside; LA22 9LU
William and Mary Wordsworth moved to 16th-century **Rydal Mount** *(closed Jan; Mon & Tue in winter & Dec 25–26; 015394 33002; www.rydalmount.co.uk)* in 1813, with three of their children (two had died the previous year), William's sister Dorothy, and sister-in-law Sara. It was to be his home for the last 37 years of his life. Use a guide leaflet to tour the house and garden and see touching relics such as the poet's leather picnic box, and correspondence concerning his appointment as Poet Laureate. Walk to nearby Rydal Water, one of Wordsworth's favorite places.

🚗 **Continue on the A591 to Ambleside, find pay parking on right.**

⑩ Ambleside
Cumbria; LA22 9BS
A favorite destination for walkers, Ambleside lies at the heart of the Lake District National Park and abounds in pubs, restaurants, and hotels. It was here that Wordsworth carried out his job as distributor of stamps. Visit the **Glass Blowing Workshop** *(see right)*, and the tiny National Trust office in the two-story **Bridge House**, built on the old packhorse bridge. In this 13 x 6 ft (4 x 2 m) former apple store, Mr. and Mrs. Rigg brought up six children in the 1850s.

🚗 **Start off on A591, turn right for A593**

toward Coniston, fork left onto B5286 to Hawkshead. Park in pay parking lot outside village.

The Lake Poets
The first mention of the Lake School of poetry – Romantic poets who lived in the Lake District – appeared in 1817. These were Samuel Taylor Coleridge, Robert Southey, Thomas de Quincey, and William Wordsworth, although Wordsworth alone was born here. Much of his poetry was confessional and autobiographical – highly original in its day. His *Daffodils*, a delirious evocation of spring beauty in the Lakes, is probably his best-known poem and one of the most loved in the English language.

⑪ Hawkshead
Cumbria; LA22 0NT
This is a charming village, with pretty cottages, an old Court House, and the **Beatrix Potter Gallery** *(closed Fri)* devoted to the children's author, with some of her original artwork. For eight years from 1779, Wordsworth was one of 100 boys attending **Hawkshead Grammar School** *(closed Nov–Mar; Sun am)*. You can see where he (allegedly) carved his name on a desk. Nearby is the vast Esthwaite Water, described in Wordsworth's *Prelude* as "our little lake," stocked with fish and popular with anglers. Permits,

tackle, tuition and boat rentals are available from the **Esthwaite Water Trout Fishery** *(015394 36541; www. hawksheadtrout.co.uk)* on the southwest shore. Walkers should head for **Tarn Hows**, 3 miles (5 km) to the northwest, a beautiful body of water, with splendid views. Set in woods, it is skirted by a good 1.5-mile (2.5-km) path, suitable for wheelchairs. Visit *www.hawkshead-village.co.uk/walks/tarn_hows.html* or buy a map from the tourist office.

There are five walking routes from **Grizedale Forest Park Visitor Centre** *(01229 860 010; www. forestry.gov.uk/grizedalehome)* where a guide map can be bought. To find it, travel south on Main Street, then take the first right at the sign for "Theatre in the Forest." Or rent some mountain bikes and enjoy some safe off-roading.

🚗 *From Main St, turn left on B5285 to Near Sawrey (some parking available).*

WORDSWORTH STREET
FORMERLY LEATHER.RAG & PUTTY STREET

Hawkshead street sign

⑫ Hill Top

Near Sawrey, Ambleside; LA22 0LF
Home to children's author Beatrix Potter from 1905, **Hill Top** *(015394 36369; www.nationaltrust.org.uk; closed Fri)* was bought with the proceeds from *The Tale of Peter Rabbit*, her first book. This 17th-century farmhouse and cottage garden with flowers, vegetables, and herbs, have been kept as they were at the author's wish. Fans of her work will recognize elements from her stories such as the long-case clock from *The Tailor of Gloucester*, and the dresser from *The Tale of Samuel Whiskers*. In the village, note the flower-filled gardens of Buckle Yeat Guesthouse, inspiration for Potter's *Tale of Tom Kitten*.

🚗 *Continue on B5285 to Far Sawrey and Lake Windermere and take the 15-minute ferry journey to the eastern shore (open daily; queues in high season). Travel down the A592 along lake shore to Fell Foot Park.*

Above left Colorful Buckle Yeat Guesthouse, Near Sawrey **Above center** Tower Bank Arms, Near Sawrey, just behind Beatrix Potter's home **Above right** Eccentric teapot topiary in Hawkshead, Cumbria

SHOPPING IN AMBLESIDE

Contemporary glass lighting is made using traditional methods at the **Glass Blowing Workshop** *(Rydal Rd, LA22 9AN; 01539 433 039)*, while Jane Exley produces unique hand-tufted rugs from Herdwick wool in her riverside studio, the **Woolly Rug Co** *(Old Mill Bridge, North Road, LA22 9DT; www.woollyrug.com; 01539 433 003)*.

SHOPPING IN HAWKSHEAD

The **Hawkshead Relish Company** produces homemade preserves, on sale at at Buttercups and Hawkshead Fine Teas *(The Square, LA22 0NZ)*, and outlets in the area. For Beatrix Potter memorabilia and figurines, try the "official stockist," Haddows Gifts *(The Car Park, LA22 0NT)*.

EAT AND DRINK

AMBLESIDE

The Giggling Goose *inexpensive*
This riverside terrace and upstairs tea room serves good coffee, homemade soups, sandwiches, and cakes. Enjoy the alfresco seating by the mill race. *The Old Mill, LA22 9DT; 01539 433 370; www.gigglinggoose.co.uk*

Glass House *moderate*
Feast on sandwiches, tortilla wraps, and burgers on foccacia for lunch. The evening menu is posher and pricier. *Rydal Road, LA22 9AN; 01539 432137; www.theglasshouserestaurant.co.uk*

AROUND HAWKSHEAD

Drunken Duck *moderate*
On the route to Hawkshead – turn right off B5286 opposite Outgate Inn – this acclaimed gastropub and inn serves quality sandwiches and inventive food. *Barngates, LA22 0NG; 01594 36347; www.drunkenduckinn.co.uk*

Below Hawkshead Grammar School, founded by the Archbishop of York in 1585

Eat and Drink: inexpensive, under £25; moderate, £25–£50; expensive, over £50

Above left Part of the refurbished Haverthwaite & Lakeside Railway **Above right** Britain's earliest working locomotive, Haverthwaite Station

WHERE TO STAY

AROUND FELL FOOT PARK

Punch Bowl Inn *expensive*
After the ferry, take the A5074 south, turning off to Crosthwaite for nine distinctive rooms in this 18th-century country inn. Imaginative cooking extends to breakfast – freshly squeezed orange juice, potato and dill pancakes with quails' eggs and hollandaise.
Crosthwaite, Lyth Valley, LA8 8HR; 015395 68237; www.the-punchbowl.co.uk

Newby Bridge Hotel *expensive*
Grand hotel in lovely setting on the shores of Windermere (just off the A590 south of Fell Foot), with leisure center including pool and mini gym. Daily changing menu, with fresh produce from their kitchen garden and farm.
Newby Bridge, LA12 8NA; 015395 31222; www.newbybridgehotel.co.uk

AROUND CONISTON

Old Rectory *moderate*
This hotel, south of Coniston on the A593 – take first left after Little Arrow – is in a 19th-century house set in extensive gardens and woodland. Close to Coniston Water, the Old Rectory offers nine individually styled rooms and traditional Cumbrian breakfasts cooked to order, using local meat and eggs.
Torver, Coniston, LA21 8AX; 015394 41353; www.theoldrectoryhotel.com

Right Sheep grazing in fields with morning mist rising off Coniston Water beyond

Lake Windermere
Running north to south for 11 miles (18 km), Windermere is the largest lake in England and has been an important waterway since Roman times. It is fed by the Rivers Brathay and Rothay at the northern head and feeds into the River Leven at Newby Bridge in the south. On its eastern shore, sprawling Bowness-on-Windermere is the main resort town with many hotels, shops, pubs, and attractions, as well as plenty of access to the lake. In high season the town is full to bursting with visitors. The glorious lakeside road south passes along thickly wooded banks holding covetable houses with some truly sublime views.

⑬ Fell Foot Park
Cumbria; LA12 8NN
A late-Victorian garden of sweeping lawns, rhododendrons, oaks, and pines at the south end of Windermere, Fell Foot Park *(open daily; 015395 31273; www.nationaltrust.org.uk)* has great shoreline access and splendid views of the Fells. There are good picnic areas, rowing-boat rentals and a lovely

tearoom housed in an old Victorian boathouse, which serves light lunches.
🚗 *Carry on to Newby Bridge, turning right on to A590 and left on B5278.*

⑭ Haverthwaite
Cumbria; LA12 8AL
This is where children's book author and spy Arthur Ransome *(Swallows and Amazons)* ended his days, but the main reason to visit Haverthwaite is the nearby **Haverthwaite & Lakeside Railway** *(open daily, trains run Apr–Oct; 015395 31594; www.lakesiderailway.co. uk)*. The station is on the A590 (on right from Newby Bridge). Once used to carry goods to the steamers on Windermere, the service closed in 1967. But thanks to enthusiasts, the locomotives once more ply alongside the River Leven. See the engines or try the short run to **Lakeside**. This tourist town offers lake cruises and the fun **Lakes Aquarium** *(open daily)*.
🚗 *Rejoin A590, turn right on A5092, fork right on A5084 and turn right at Lowick (marked Nibthwaite/east of lake), then left for Brantwood.*

SHOPPING IN CONISTON

Buy some delectable fudge – hand-made from local dairy ingredients – from the **Coniston Fudge Co** *(Post Office, LA21 8DU; 015394 41259; www.conistonfudge.co.uk)*. Flavors include Coniston Cookie Crunch and Ginger Biscuit. Best of all, visitors can taste before buying.

EAT AND DRINK

BRANTWOOD

Jumping Jenny Coffee House and Restaurant *inexpensive*
Enjoy lunch on the terrace with sublime views over Coniston in this restaurant-café, located in the former stables in Brantwood grounds. The menu includes homemade soups, flans, casseroles, pasta, cakes, and pastries. *Brantwood, LA21 8AD; 015394 41715; www.jumpingjenny.com*

CONISTON

Black Bull Inn *inexpensive*
This old coaching inn has played host to poet Samuel Taylor Coleridge, artist JMW Turner, and the late Donald Campbell, who died on Coniston in an attempt to set a new water speed record. Enjoy sandwiches, baked potatoes, and hearty cooked meals such as Cumberland sausage, shoulder of lamb, and haddock and chips. Wash it all down with ales such as its own Bluebird. It also has a few rooms. *Coppermines Rd, LA21 8HL; 015394 41133; www.conistonbrewery.com*

⑮ Brantwood
Cumbria; LA21 8AD;

John Ruskin (1819–1900), artist, writer, poet, critic, and social reformer, lived at Brantwood *(open daily; mid-Nov–mid-Mar: closed Mon–Tue; 015394 41396; www.brantwood.org.uk)* from 1871. The house is so imbued with his personality that it feels as though he has just gone out for a stroll. His own watercolors and drawings are hung with those of other prominent painters. Views across Coniston, especially from the turret, are sublime and there are wonderful gardens. The best time to visit is in late May, when the azaleas are at their showiest. Aged 81, Ruskin died of influenza and is buried at St. Andrew's Church, Coniston.

🚗 *Head north, turning left around the lake to join the B5285 to Coniston and pay parking at Coniston Pier.*

Railway insignia, Haverthwaite Station

⑯ Coniston
Cumbria; LA21 8AJ

Situated at the head of Coniston Water – third-largest of the central Cumbrian lakes – this village was once a center for the local copper-mining industry, which boomed in the 18th and 19th centuries. It is overlooked by the 2,631 ft (802 m) fell, the Old Man of Coniston, and is also close to **Tarn Hows**. The graceful Victorian steam yacht the **Gondola** *(Apr–Oct; www.nationaltrust.org.uk)* – so called because of its high prow – glides across the water from Coniston Pier to Brantwood jetty. The 45-minute round trip gives passengers the chance to appreciate the beauty of the lake amid the surrounding Coniston Fells. Or rent a kayak, canoe, or rowing boat from **Coniston Boating Centre** *(015394 41366)*, also located near the pier, to explore the lake.

DAY TRIP OPTIONS
Carlisle, Keswick and Ambleside are all good bases for exploring the sublime countryside, and following in the footsteps of the Lakeland poets.

War and Peace
Take a tour around Carlisle ❶, a border city often attacked by raiders from the north. See the citadel, castle, and cathedral. Then set out on the glorious drive southwest to Cockermouth ❷, having a look at the castle and an ice cream at the Old Stackyard Tearooms. Time permitting, head to Whinlatter Forest Park ❸ for a walk or a bike ride in the quiet woodland countryside.

Follow driving instructions to Whinlatter Forest Park. Continue towards Keswick

on B5292 and return to Carlisle up the east side of Bassenthwaite Lake.

Lakeland Stone
Based at Keswick ❼, enjoy the lake location and Castlerigg Stone Circle, then set off to climb the Bowder Stone ❻. Head for Honister Pass ❺ and Honister Slate Mine, the last working slate mine in the UK. Drive on to Buttermere ❹; enjoy a picnic and walk around the lake admiring the pikes and crags. Head north to Lorton and through Whinlatter Forest Park ❸ to return to Keswick.

Follow the drive's instructions in reverse from Keswick to Whinlatter Forest Park. Then head east back to Keswick.

Wander o'er Vales and Hills
Follow the Wordsworth trail from Grasmere ❽, for the church and cottage with links to the poet, then continue to Rydal Mount ❾ and the nearby lake – two of his favorite places. Ambleside ❿, where the poet worked – is a good place for lunch. Next go on to Hawkshead ⑪, where Wordsworth was schooled, to enjoy a walk or go fishing, before pushing on past Hill Top ⑫, across the lake on the ferry and returning up Windermere's eastern shore.

Follow the drive's instructions to Hill Top and across Lake Windermere. Turn left on A592 through Bowness to return to Ambleside or Grasmere.

Eat and Drink: inexpensive, under £25; moderate, £25–£50, expensive, over £50

Wild Northumbria

Kielder Water to Lindisfarne

Highlights

- **Lakeside adventures**
  Enjoy a wealth of exciting activities beside northern Europe's largest man-made expanse of water at Kielder Water

- **Castles galore**
  See medieval strongholds, romantic coastal ruins, an island's defense and a magnificent ducal home

- **Nature close up**
  Look out for elusive otters and shy deer in Kielder Forest; colorful puffins and terns off Amble; and migrating sea birds and seals on Lindisfarne Island

- **Cradle of Christianity**
  Cross the tidal causeway to Holy Island (Lindisfarne), a special place of pilgrimage with an ancient monastery

Alnwick Castle, familiar to Harry Potter fans as the exterior of Hogwarts

Wild Northumbria

Sparsely populated and with a large pristine moorland habitat, Northumberland is a county of wild beauty. The long and low coastline has seen more development than the wilder, more hilly interior, but as much as a quarter of the county is protected as part of the Northumberland National Park. This makes the area one of the best in the country for a driving holiday – the roads are generally empty and the scenery simply stunning. Architecturally, the area is also surprisingly rich. Sharing a border with Scotland and facing the North Sea, Northumberland was often subjected to attacks from marauding Scots and pillaging Vikings. As a result the coast and interior is studded with more castles than any other county.

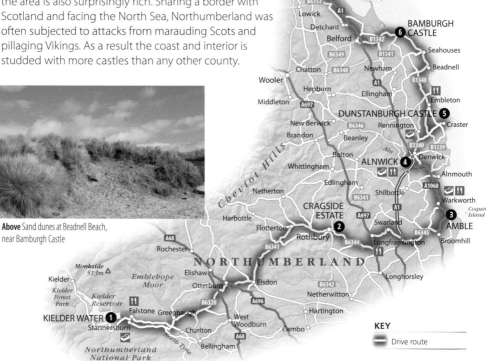

0 kilometres 10

0 miles 10

Above Sand dunes at Beadnell Beach, near Bamburgh Castle

KEY

Drive route

PLAN YOUR DRIVE

Start/finish: Kielder Water to Lindisfarne Island.

Number of days: 2, including a wait for the tide.

Distances: 79 miles (126 km).

Road conditions: Roads are well-maintained.

When to go: From late May to early August – but the weather can be windy at all times of year.

Main market days: Alnwick: Market Square, Sat & Thu (Mar–Sep); Farmers' Market last Fri of the month.

Festivals: Alnwick: International Music Festival, Aug; **Cragside**: Rothbury Traditional Music Festival, Jul; Brinkburn Priory Music Festival, early Jul.

Above On the approach road to the impressive Bamburgh Castle

① Kielder Water
Northumberland; NE48 1BX

With 27 miles (43 km) of shoreline set among cool pine forest and heather moorland, Kielder Water is northern Europe's largest man-made lake. Visit the **Tower Knowe Visitor Centre** (closed Nov through Mar; www.nwl.co.uk) to find out about the activities in the area, such as walking, fishing, lake cruises, mountain biking, and horseback riding. Further west along the shoreline is the **Leaplish Waterside Park** (0870 240 3549; www.nwl.co.uk/planyourbreak.aspx) with lodges for rent, Bird of Prey Centre, swimming pools, saunas, boat rental and ferry rides – for non-residents, too.

The forest teems with wildlife such as otters, roe deer, and osprey, and is home to nearly three-quarters of the UK's red squirrels. The lakeside is also home to works by renowned artists.
🚗 *Turn left out of the visitor center, following the minor roads towards Greenhaugh. Turn right just before this hamlet then left on B6320 to Otterburn. Turn right on A696 and left on B6341 just beyond Rothbury to Cragside.*

② Cragside Estate
Rothbury, Northumberland; NE65 7PX

One of the great Victorian houses of the Northeast and the first to be lit by hydro-electricity in 1880, **Cragside Estate** (open Mar–Sep; www.nationaltrust.org.uk) was commissioned by scientist and arms manufacturer Sir William Armstrong. It is best seen from below, looming over its woodland estate, and the largest hand-made rock garden in Europe. The sumptuous interiors also contain a wealth of gadgetry. There is some rough going in the grounds, so wear walking shoes and keep a lookout for glimpses of red squirrels and England's tallest tree, a Douglas

Fir, in the pinetum. Children will enjoy playing with the hands-on mini electrical generators inside the house and the newt colony, adventure play area, and rhododendron maze outside.
🚗 *Return toward Rothbury on B6341, turn left on B6344; turn left on A697 and right on B6345, then A1068 to Amble.*

③ Amble
Northumberland; NE65

A key center for coal distribution in the 19th century, Amble's fortunes declined along with the mining industry. Sitting at the mouth of the River Coquet, Amble is now a pleasant and relaxed town. Head north along the Coquet to **Warkworth** to see the **castle** – a former stronghold of the mighty Percy family – with its cross-shaped keep, and enjoy lunch in the Mason's Arms (see right) or picnic on the wide sandy beach. In summer, take a boat from the marina to **Coquet Island** with its 80-ft (24-m) high lighthouse, and watch nesting seabirds – puffins, eider ducks and the rare roseate tern. Or walk south along the coast and picnic in the dunes at lovely **Druridge Country Park**.
🚗 *Take the A1068 north for 9 miles (14.5 km) to Alnwick. Turn right onto Greenwell Road for the car park.*

A Man's House is His Castle

Over the centuries, Northumberland has been the site of many battles and border raids with the Scots, so it is no surprise that it boasts more castles than any other part of England. There are also many smaller houses fortified with square bastions or pele towers, which were virtually impregnable. In Elizabethan times these oddities also harbored raiding clans known as the Border Reivers (see p198).

Above left Cragside towering above its large rock garden **Above right** The technologically advanced Victorian manor house at Cragside

GETTING TO KIELDER WATER

From the south, take the A1, turning left on the A68 after Darlington, then left to Bellingham and the road to Kielder.

WHERE TO STAY

AROUND KIELDER WATER
Pheasant Inn *inexpensive–moderate*
On the road (2 miles/1 km) from Kielder Water, this friendly farmhouse-inn has a great location and comfy rooms.
Stannersburn, Falstone, NE48 1DD; 01434 240 382; www.thepheasantinn.com

AROUND AMBLE
Roxbro House *moderate*
This boutique B&B in an old stone house 2 miles (3 km) north of Amble on the A1068 is charming and friendly and serves great locally sourced breakfasts.
5 Castle Terrace, Warkworth, NE65 0UP; 01665 711 416; www.roxbrohouse.co.uk

EAT AND DRINK

AROUND KIELDER WATER
Old School Tea Room *inexpensive*
Attractive tea rooms and craft shop housed in a Victorian school building, ideal for inexpensive snacks.
Falstone, NE48 1AA; 01434 240 459

AROUND CRAGSIDE
Angler's Arms *moderate*
This 1760s coaching inn is on the River Coquet, off the A697 around 6 miles (10 km) east of Cragside. Meals are served in an old railway carriage.
Weldon Bridge, Longframlington, NE65 8AX; 01665 570 271

AROUND AMBLE
Mason's Arms *inexpensive*
Home-cooked meals include Craster smoked kipper pâté and Northumbrian sausage at this pub in Warkworth, 2 miles (3 km) north of Amble on the A1068.
3 Dial Place, Warkworth, NE65 0UR; 01665 711 398

Eat and Drink: inexpensive, under £25; moderate, £25–£50; expensive, over £50

Above The Bailey at Alnwick Castle, used in the Harry Potter films

VISITING ALNWICK

Parking
Turn right just before Bondgate archway onto Greenwall Road for parking.

Tourist Information
The Shambles, NE66 1TN; 01665 511 333;
www.visitnorthumberland.com/alnwick

VISITING LINDISFARNE

Tide Information
Look for tables displayed on posts; 01289
389 200; www.visitnorthumberland.com

WHERE TO STAY

ALNWICK

Tate House B&B *inexpensive*
Three rooms, two ensuite, in a late-Victorian house just outside the center.
11 Bondgate Without, NE66 1PR;
01665 604 661

Oaks Hotel *inexpensive-moderate*
There are 12 comfortable rooms in this friendly pub-hotel on the mini roundabout on leaving Bondgate.
South Road, NE66 2PN; 01665 510 014;
www.theoakshotel.co.uk

White Swan *moderate–expensive*
This 300-year-old coaching inn, with 57 bedrooms, has a handy central location, good food, and guest parking.
Bondgate Within, NE66 1TD; 01665 602
109; thewhiteswan.classiclodges.co.uk

AROUND DUNSTANBURGH

The Mason's Arms *inexpensive*
This welcoming inn is 2 miles (3 km) north of Denwick on the B1340. It has 17 comfortable ensuite rooms and serves good pub fare in the restaurant.
Rennington, NE66 3RX; 01665 577 275;
www.masonsarms.net

Where to Stay: inexpensive, under £80; moderate, £80–£150; expensive, over £150

---

④ Alnwick

Northumberland; NE66 1TN
This attractive market town is a compact warren of cobbled streets, old stone buildings and narrow alleys tucked between its main attractions, Alnwick Castle and Garden. It is also ideally located for countryside or coastal trips. Allow at least half a day to tour the town and its sights.

A two-hour walking tour

From the parking lot head down Greenwell Road to the 15th-century **Bondgate Tower ①** (or Hotspur Tower), originally one of four town gateways. Walk up Bondgate Within, past the Market Place and Cross and Northumberland Hall on the left, into Narrowgate, curving round to the right. Turn left down Bailiffgate, with its charming old houses, and visit the **Bailiffgate Museum ②** *(closed Mon; www.bailiffgatemuseum.co.uk)*, in the former St. Mary's Church and dedicated to the people and places of the area. Keen walkers can continue down Ratten Row for 1 km (half a mile) to explore **Hulne Park ③**, a vast area of estate forestry, farm, and sawmills. Head for 13th-century Carmelite Hulne Friary, in the distance. Otherwise, turn left onto Northumberland St and pass Pottergate Tower into Dispensary St. Go left on Clayport St, up Market St, and right to arrive back on Bondgate Within. Return through the Tower, down Bondgate Without. After passing the War Memorial on the left, across from the Percy Tenantry Lion Column, look for the 19th-century Alnwick Station building, home to **Barter Books ④**, a terrific second-hand bookshop with a model train that shuttles around on top of the shelves. Return to the parking lot on Greenwell Road.

A path from behind the Greenwell Road car park leads up to **Alnwick Castle ⑤** *(Apr–Oct: open daily; www.alnwickcastle.com)*, the second-largest inhabited castle in the country and seat of the Dukes of Northumberland since 1309. Fans of the first two Harry Potter films will recognize the exterior as Hogwarts school. Dominating the town, the castle dates from the 11th century but has seen major expansion since the14th century. Visitors can tour the grand state rooms, a library, a fabulous Renaissance drawing room and an art collection that includes works by Van Dyke and Canaletto.

Walk back down the path to delightful **Alnwick Garden ⑥** *(open daily; www.alnwickgarden.com)*. In 1997 Jane Percy, Duchess of Northumberland, decided to bring an overgrown garden close to the castle back to life. it is still a work in progress, created by Belgian garden designers Jacques and Peter Wirtz. The Grand Cascade, visible on entry, is the largest water feature of its kind in the UK. From the sweet to the sinister, the Rose Garden to the Poison Garden, and the Tree Walk for children, there is much to enjoy. Return down the path to the car park.

🚗 *Leave Alnwick on Bondgate Without turning left on B1340. After Denwick, follow signs to Dunstanburgh, fork right to Craster to park. Walk to the castle.*

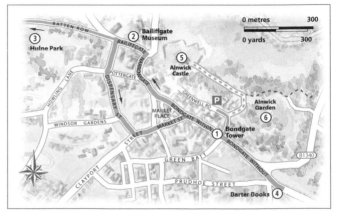

⑤ Dunstanburgh Castle

Craster, Alnwick; NE66 3TT

From the fishing village of Craster the massive, brooding ruins of this grand edifice are visible rising out of the sands atop a cliff. The castle was not built for convenience, so wear strong, waterproof shoes to walk along the beach and be prepared for a scramble up to Dunstanburgh Castle. It was begun in the 14th century by the Earl of Lancaster, and enough survives of its walls, watchtower, and gatehouse to fire the imagination and transport the visitor back some 700 years.

🚗 *Return inland, turning right on the B1339 and then B1340 to Bamburgh.*

⑥ Bamburgh Castle

Bamburgh, Northumberland; NE69 7DF

On a stunning basalt crag, Bamburgh Castle *(Mar–Sep: open daily; www. bamburghcastle.com)* looks across the sea to the Farne Islands. Originally built by the Normans, it was all but destroyed in the 15th-century Wars of the Roses by Edward IV. Restoration began in the mid-18th century, and was later continued by Sir William Armstrong *(see p209)* in 1894. It is still the Armstrong family home, but visitors can tour 16 rooms of armour, antiques, and paintings, including the magnificent King's Hall and Cross Hall, and the armoury, bake house, and scullery. There is also a small museum.

🚗 *Take the B1342, then right on A1 and right for Lindisfarne. Park on the island.*

⑦ Lindisfarne Island

Northumberland; TD15

Also known as Holy Island, this tidal islet is inaccessible by car at high tide *(see opposite)*, adding to the thrill of a visit to the cradle of English Christianity. Lindisfarne Monastery was founded in AD 635, and was a powerful center of Christianity. Prepare to be captivated by this place of pilgrimage. Tour the ruined priory and clamber up to the castle and walled garden, walk around the headland and harbor, and sample the famous crab sandwiches and Lindisfarne mead. A nature reserve, the island is a great place to see migrating birds and grey seals.

Above left Bistro restaurant Lilburns in the centre of Alnwick **Above right** The imposing Bamburgh Castle, the Armstrong family home

SHOPPING

Craster Kippers
At Craster, the Robsons produce their famous oak-smoked kippers, using the best herrings and traditional methods. *L Robson & Sons Ltd, NE66 3TR; 01665 576 223; www.kipper.co.uk*

EAT AND DRINK

ALNWICK

The Art House *inexpensive–moderate*
Restaurant and Gallery in Bondgate Tower serving soups, sandwiches, burgers, and salads at lunch time, and more ambitious food for dinner. *14 Bondgate Within, NE66 1TD; 01665 602 607; www.arthouserestaurant.com*

Lilburns *inexpensive-moderate*
With a handy location just off Bondgate Within, this bistro has a pleasant family atmosphere and serves good food. *7 Paikes Street, NE66 1HX; 01665 603 444*

AROUND DUNSTANBURGH

Dunstanburgh Castle Hotel *moderate*
This hotel restaurant, 2 miles (3 km) north of Craster on the B1339, serves good pub fare including homemade soups, Northumbrian meat, smoked salmon, and Whitby scampi. *Embleton, NE66 3UN; 01665 576 111; www.dunstanburghcastlehotel.co.uk*

Left The crumbling ruins of Dunstanburgh Castle, north of Craster village

---

DAY TRIP OPTIONS

Kielder Water and Alnwick make ideal bases for exploring the area.

Family Day by the Lake
Kielder Water ① is the perfect place for a day trip or to stay in a lodge, learn to fish, sail or horseback ride; go cycling or walking by the lake; and then soak tired muscles in the spa.

Castles and Coast
Staying at Alnwick ④, see the Castle and Garden, then head to Amble ③ for a walk to Warkworth Castle and a beach picnic. Return to Alnwick via the ingenious Cragside Estate ②, with its grand interiors and outside adventures.

Reverse the driving instructions to get to Amble and Cragside; return on B6341.

Castles and Christianity
Walk to see the ruins of Dunstanburgh Castle ⑤, then drive to the impressive Bamburgh Castle ⑥. Continue on to Lindisfarne Island ⑦ for a walk around the island, castle, and priory. Vary the order of these, depending on the tide.

Follow the instructions for the drive. Return via the A1.

Eat and Drink: inexpensive, under £25; moderate, £25–£50; expensive, over £50

History and Romance in the Borders

Edinburgh to Rosslyn Chapel

Highlights

- **Cultural capital**
  Wander round Edinburgh, Scotland's stunning capital city, filled with history and grand architecture, where the medieval mingles with the modern

- **Coastal pleasures**
  Watch the myriad seabirds and rich marine wildlife from the rugged cliffs on the glorious East Lothian coast and enjoy the surprisingly sandy beaches

- **Historical romance**
  Visit ancient crumbling abbeys and grand historic houses in the spectacular and wild countryside of the Borders, the land that inspired the novels of Sir Walter Scott

Glorious view of the Borders, seen from Scott's View, on the road to Abbotsford

History and Romance in the Borders

The city of Edinburgh may be the jewel in Scotland's crown, but just a short drive south is a glorious landscape that many people have yet to discover. This circular route takes in coastal towns and villages standing on rugged cliffs by inviting golden sands, as seabirds screech and wheel overhead. It then sweeps inland to the Borders, where mighty rivers like the Tweed flow past bustling towns and ancient abbeys, and where grand historic houses sit in tranquil countryside. The route finally heads north to its last stop at Rosslyn Chapel, famous for its extraordinary – and mysterious – carvings.

Above North Berwick Law, the hill south of the Scottish Seabird Centre, *see p217*

ACTIVITIES

Go ghost hunting in Mary King's Close, the warren of alleys under Edinburgh

Sup a few drams of whisky in the Whisky Experience, Edinburgh

Take a Seafari in a boat to see puffins and guillemots, from the Scottish Seabird Centre

Walk along the Berwickshire Coastal Path to the lighthouse at St. Abb's Head

Sample a Jacobite Ale in the historic 18th-century brewery at Traquair House

Decipher the secret code in the mysterious carvings at Rosslyn Chapel

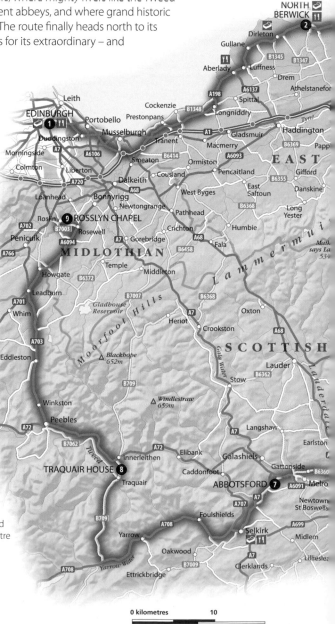

0 kilometres   10

0 miles   10

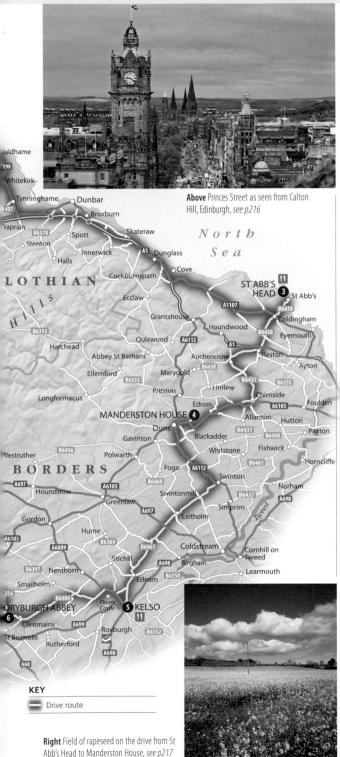

Above Princes Street as seen from Calton Hill, Edinburgh, *see p216*

North Sea

KEY

━━ Drive route

Right Field of rapeseed on the drive from St Abb's Head to Manderston House, *see p217*

PLAN YOUR DRIVE

Start/finish: Edinburgh to Rosslyn Chapel.

Number of days: 2–3 days, with at least half a day in Edinburgh.

Distance: Approx 225 miles (362 km).

Road conditions: Generally good roads and well marked; some Border roads can be very narrow and the scenic B709 to Traquair House often gets snowbound in winter.

When to go: Best for birdlife in spring and early summer, best for colour in the autumn.

Opening times: Museums and attractions are generally open 10am–5pm, but may close earlier (or are closed altogether) Nov–Easter. Shops are often open longer. Churches are usually open until dusk.

Main market days: Kelso: Farmers' Market, 4th Sat of month; **Traquair House**: Peebles Farmers' Market, 2nd Sat of month.

Shopping: Shop for fine cashmere and woollens in the Borders – especially around Selkirk and Kelso, the heart of Scotland's knitwear industry.

Main festivals: Edinburgh: Festival and Festival Fringe, mid Aug–early Sep; **Manderston House**: Duns Summer Festival, Jul; **Dryburgh Abbey, Abbotsford & Traquair House**: Selkirk, Melrose & Peebles: Common Ridings, Jun.

DAY TRIP OPTIONS

Families staying in Edinburgh will enjoy looking around a **royal palace** and some **haunted alleyways**, before exploring the **ancient bastion** of Edinburgh Castle. Then drive off to North Berwick to see the **puffins** and **seals** at the Scottish Seabird Centre and go on an **island boat trip**, before relaxing on the **beach**. History-lovers should head to Kelso to see the local **abbey** and magnificent **castle**, then on to the **abbey** at Dryburgh and Sir Walter Scott's interesting **house**, Abbotsford, before enjoying the glorious **countryside** on the way to a historic **country house**, dating back to 1107. For full details, *see p219*.

Above Princes St, Edinburgh with the Balmoral Hotel and Scott's Monument on the left

VISITING EDINBURGH

Parking
There are lots by Waverley Station, at Castle Terrace, and at Greenside Place.

Tourist Information
3 Princes Street, EH2 2QP; 0845 22 55 121; www.edinburgh.org

WHERE TO STAY

EDINBURGH

The Bonham *moderate–expensive*
This chic townhouse in a leafy corner of the West End has boutique rooms.
35 Drumsheugh Gdns, EH3 7RN; 0131 226 6050; www.townhousecompany.com

NORTH BERWICK

The Glebe House *moderate*
This lovely mansion has four charming rooms and picturesque views.
Law Rd, EH39 4PL; 01620 892 608; www.glebehouse-nb.co.uk

AROUND NORTH BERWICK

The Castle Inn *inexpensive*
There are five beautiful bedrooms at this recently refurbished coaching inn on the A198 to Edinburgh.
Manse Road, Dirleton, EH39 5EP; 01620 850 221; www.castleinndirleton.com

❶ Edinburgh
Lothian; EH1

With its brooding castle, dramatic crags and rich history, Edinburgh is Scotland's most romantic city as well as its capital. Visitors have long been fascinated by the medieval streets of the Old Town and charmed by the Georgian squares of the New Town, before being entertained in the city's many bars and restaurants. It's no wonder that it has inspired generations of writers, from Robert Louis Stevenson to J K Rowling.

A three-hour walking tour

Start from Waverley Station parking lot. Walk uphill on New Street, turn right onto Market St, and then left at a roundabout up Cockburn St. Traverse the medieval Old Town, with its cobbled streets, wynds (alleys), and high buildings – the city was once enclosed by a wall, so built upward. At the top, turn left and walk down the High Street – the Royal Mile. Pass **John Knox House** ❶ *(open Mon–Sat; Jul–Aug also Sun pm)*, a distinctive 16th-century building said to have been home to the religious reformer. Next is **Canongate Kirk** ❷ *(open daily)*: the 18th-century economist Adam Smith and David Rizzio, the secretary to Mary Queen of Scots killed by her jealous husband, Lord Darnley, are both buried here. At the end of the Royal Mile is the new Scottish Parliament, opposite the Queen's official residence in Scotland, the **Palace of Holyroodhouse** ❸ *(open daily, except mid-Jun–mid-July & royal visits)*.

Head back up the Royal Mile, past Cockburn St to **St. Giles' Cathedral** ❹ *(open daily)*, founded in the 12th-century. It was from here that Knox led the Scottish Reformation. Nearby is **Mary King's Close** ❺ *(open daily)*, a warren of ancient, supposedly haunted streets beneath the city.

Beyond the cathedral, turn left onto George IV Bridge, then right down charming Victoria St, lined with specialist shops. At the bottom, bear right into the **Grassmarket** ❻ – now bustling with pubs and shops, but once the haunt of 19th-century body-snatchers Burke and Hare. They lured their victims here and sold the bodies to a local surgeon. Part way down the Grassmarket, turn right up Castle Wynd South. Go up the steep steps, cross the road at the top, and up more steps to Castle Hill. Edinburgh's great **castle** ❼ *(open daily)* is on the left. Set on an extinct volcano, it dates back to the 12th century, but has been a fortress since AD 600. Its treasures include the Honours of Scotland (the Scottish Crown Jewels) and Mons Meg, one of the world's oldest cannons.

Walk down Castle Hill, stopping to sample a few "drams" at the **Scotch Whisky Experience** ❽ *(open daily)* on the right. At Bank St, turn left and go down The Mound, then walk down Playfair Steps. The **National Gallery of Scotland** ❾ *(open daily)* is on the left, and good views of the monument to Sir Walter Scott, to the right. Cross Princes St, then walk up Hanover St, to the grand avenues and buildings of the 18th-century Georgian New Town, built so the wealthy could escape the squalor of the Old Town.

Continue to George St, the city's smartest shopping area. Turn left to Charlotte Square, designed by Robert Adam, and bear right to the north

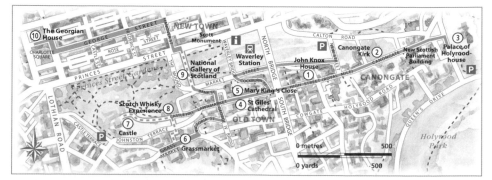

Where to Stay: inexpensive, under £80; moderate, £80–£150; expensive, over £150

side of the square to **The Georgian House** ⑩ *(open daily)*, a fine example of an Edinburgh townhouse. Retrace the route to Princes St, turn left back up to the station parking lot.

🚗 *From station lot, turn left onto New Street, left along Carlton Rd to a T-junction, left on Leith St, and then left onto A1. Beyond the fringes of the city turn left onto A198, taking coastal road to North Berwick. Park on streets near harbor and seabird centre.*

② North Berwick
The Harbour, North Berwick; EH39 4SS
With hi-tech cameras on its islands, the **Scottish Seabird Centre** *(open daily; www.seabird.org)* allows visitors to view wildlife all year round. In summer, there are puffins and gannets rearing their young; in winter, grey seals and their dark-eyed pups. Visitors control the cameras, and there are telescopes on the viewing deck. Seabird Seafaris also runs trips around the islands in fast boats. Head to the town's seafront for a game of mini golf or just take it easy on the sandy beach.

🚗 *Continue on A198 to rejoin A1. After Cockburnspath, turn left onto A1107 and then left on B6438 to St Abb's. The Reserve is to the left just before town.*

③ St Abb's Head
Nr Eyemouth,Berwickshire; TD14 5QF
The **St Abb's Head National Nature Reserve** has an unmanned visitor center detailing various coastal walks, which offer dramatic clifftop views. The most interesting walk goes to the remote lighthouse, built in 1862 by the Stevenson family (relatives of author R L Stevenson): once lit by an oil lamp

it's now fully automated. Next to the visitor center is a little café *(May–Aug: open daily)*. Continue into **St Abb's** to see the charming harbor.

🚗 *Leave on B6438, cross the A1 (right then left), staying on B6438, and turn left on B6437. Then right on A6105 to the main gates, from where signs lead to the parking lot and entrance.*

④ Manderston House
Duns, Berwickshire; TD11 3PP
A superb Edwardian country mansion, Manderston *(May–Sep: open Thu & Sun pm; www.manderston.co.uk)* was built by Sir James Miller, a wealthy baronet, to impress society. Its most extravagant feature must be the silver staircase. The house is now home to Lord and Lady Palmer, of Huntley and Palmers biscuits.

🚗 *Drive into Duns and take A6112 to Swinton, then take B6461 to Kelso. Park in or around the main square.*

Above left The grand façade of Manderston House, remodeled in 1871 **Above top right** View south across the grass terrace at Manderston House **Above right** The hi-tech Scottish Seabird Centre, North Berwick

EAT AND DRINK

EDINBURGH

David Bann *moderate*
Delicious, imaginative vegetarian food such as roast aubergine chickpea cake or risotto with asparagus, fennel and peas.
56–8 St Mary's St, EH1 1SX; 0131 556 5888; www.davidbann.com

NORTH BERWICK

The Grange *moderate*
The seasonal menu at this popular restaurant might include steak from the local butcher and garden herbs.
35 High Street, EH39 4HH; 01620 893 344

Osteria No 1
Excellent Italian food at this acclaimed restaurant, which serves a good value 3-course lunch. Entrees might feature chicken breast stuffed with pancetta. Try the creamy pannacotta for dessert.
7 High Street, EH39 4HG; www.osteria-no1.co.uk

AROUND NORTH BERWICK

Ducks at Aberlady
This award-winning restaurant on the A198 to Edinburgh has 26 rooms too.
Main Street, Aberlady, EH32 0RE; 01875 870 682; www.ducks.co.uk

ST ABB'S HEAD

The Old Smiddy Cafe *inexpensive*
Pleasant little café in a former cottage on the outskirts of St Abbs. Serves soups, baguettes, and cakes and has seats outside for fine days.
By Nature Reserve Visitor Centre, TD14 5QF; 01890 71707; open daily May–Aug; Mar & Apr weekends only

Below View of the craggy coastline looking north from St Abb's Head

Eat and Drink: inexpensive, under £25; moderate, £25–£50; expensive, over £50

Above Charming Abbotsford House, once home to Sir Walter Scott **Top right** Floors Castle, still home to the Duke of Roxburgh **Above right** Ruined stone archway of 12th-century Kelso Abbey

VISITING KELSO

Parking
If there are no spaces on the square, there are several small lots nearby, just off the B6461 in Bowmont St, East Bowmont St and Jamieson's Entry.

Tourist Information
Town House, The Square, TD5 7HF; 01835 863 170; www.visitscotland.com

WHERE TO STAY

AROUND KELSO

The Roxburghe Hotel *expensive*
Staying at the Roxburgh is a real treat. It's a little way south of Kelso, just off the A698. This imposing historic house has real fires in winter and is set in extensive grounds. As well as luxurious rooms and suites, the hotel also boasts its own golf course and a fine, candlelit restaurant. *Heiton, TD5 8JZ; 01573 450 331; www.roxburghe.net*

AROUND ABBOTSFORD

Sunnybrae Guest House *inexpensive*
There are two suites at this friendly guest house in Selkirk. Each has a sitting room, as well as a bathroom, and there are fine views of the surrounding hills. Breakfast features organic, local produce.
5 Tower St, Selkirk, TD7 4LS; 01750 21156

Below The pretty gardens at 15th-century Rosslyn Chapel, Roslin

⑤ Kelso
Roxburghshire; TD5
Kelso is a handsome town on the River Tweed. Near the main square are the ruins of 12th-century **Kelso Abbey**, once one of Scotland's richest abbeys, still with traces of beautifully carved stonework. On the edge of town is **Floors Castle** *(Easter–Oct: open daily; www.floorscastle.com)*, a grand stately home (1721) set in vast grounds and still home to the Duke of Roxburghe. The sumptuous rooms boast vibrant tapestries and paintings by masters such as Turner, Gainsborough, and Hogarth. Golfers may want to try the **Roxburgh Hotel Golf Course** *(see left)*.
🚗 *Leave on A6089 toward Edinburgh, exit left onto B6397, then turn left on B6404. Turn right on B6356 through Clintmains and then left to Dryburgh Abbey and parking lot.*

The Common Ridings
The Borders were once lawless: there were wars with England and "reivers" (cattle thieves) plagued the area. So, around the 13th century, people had to patrol their land on horseback. Over the years, this evolved into the annual Common Ridings, where a man carrying the local flag gallops around the town's boundaries, followed by hundreds of riders. In summer, each Border town has its own spectacular Common Riding.

⑥ Dryburgh Abbey
St Boswells, Melrose; TD6 0RQ
Founded in the 11th century and built in soft red sandstone, **Dryburgh Abbey** *(open daily)* was frequently damaged in the Border wars between the Scots and the English. However, its beauty is still evident, making for a delightful stroll around the ruins: the refectory's ornate rose window, for example, is still intact. Two famous Scots are buried here: the historical romance writer Sir Walter Scott, and WWI commander Field-Marshal Earl Haig. Their graves are in the ruined north transept chapel.
🚗 *Take B6356 marked Earlston up to Scott's View, with views of the Eildon Hills. Beyond, turn left and left again at two unmarked junctions and onto B6360. Pass under a viaduct, through Gattonside and turn left on B6374. Go right toward A7 and A68, straight over roundabout onto A6091, then left on B6360 to Abbotsford and parking lot.*

⑦ Abbotsford
Melrose; TD6 9BQ
There's more than a touch of drama about Abbotsford *(mid-Mar–Oct: open daily; www.scottabbotsford.co.uk)*, which is not surprising as it was the home of 19th-century novelist Sir Walter

Far left The historic Traquair House, dating back to the 12th century **Left** Intricate stonework exterior of Rosslyn Chapel, Roslin

SHOPPING

Look for wool, cashmere, and tartans in the Borders, especially from places that offer mill tours. Try **Locharron Scottish Cashmere and Wool Centre** *(Waverley Mill, Dunsdale Rd, Selkirk, TD7 5DZ; 01750 726 100; www.lochcarron.com)*. Hawick is a traditional textile-making town: to get there, take the A698 from Kelso or A7 from Selkirk. As well as a museum of textiles, visit **Trinity Mills** *(Duke St, TD9 9QA; 01450 371 221)*.

Scott, the author of classic tales such as *Ivanhoe*. He commissioned the house himself and it's full of character, with suits of armor in the oak-paneled hall, his battered leather writing chair in the study, and thousands of books crammed onto the shelves of his well-used library. The windows of the house overlook the Tweed, the river he loved.

🚗 *From parking lot go left on B6360, then A7 to Selkirk. Here take A707, then A708 through dramatic scenery, turning right onto B709. This is the remote Borders: there's not a settlement to be seen. Follow signs for Traquair House.*

⑧ Traquair House
Innerleithen, Peeblesshire; EH44 6PW
Scotland's oldest inhabited house, Traquair *(Apr–Oct: open daily; www.traquair.co.uk)* dates back to at least 1107. It is home to the Maxwell-Stuart family and is steeped in history. With sloping floors and a fascinating jumble of rooms, the house boasts relics such as Mary Queen of Scots' son's cradle, as well as a concealed room with secret stairs – a means of escape for priests, when Catholics were persecuted in the 16th to 18th centuries. The family were loyal supporters of James II and VI and

the Stuart monarchs, and today make a Jacobite Ale, based on an 18th-century recipe, in their historic brewery.

🚗 *From Traquair, go left on B709 toward Innerleithen, then take A72 toward Peebles. On the outskirts of the town pick up A703 going north; at Leadburn turn right on A6094 to Rosewell, then descend steeply left on B7003. Turn right on B7006 and right again to Rosslyn Chapel.*

⑨ Rosslyn Chapel
Chapel Loan, Roslin; EH25 9PU
Stepping inside Rosslyn Chapel *(open daily; www.rosslynchapel.org.uk)*, it is hard to decide where to look first, there are so many extraordinary – and mysterious – carvings. An angel plays the bagpipes; pagan "Green Men" peer down from pillars; there is even maize, carved here years before the New World was "discovered." The chapel, built for the St. Clair family in 1450, is perhaps best known for the lavishly carved Apprentice Pillar, thought by some to conceal the Holy Grail, brought here by the Knights Templar – a theory popularized in the book and film *The Da Vinci Code*.

🚗 *Drive north on B7006, then turn right onto A701 to central Edinburgh.*

EAT AND DRINK

KELSO

Oscar's *inexpensive*
Lively wine bar and restaurant, with polished wooden floors, serving modern Mediterranean dishes. Mains include asparagus and thyme risotto, or home-made fishcakes, and daily specials such as sea bass on tomato and basil risotto. *35–37 Horsemarket, TD5 7HE; 01573 224 008; www.oscars-kelso.com*

The Cobbles Inn *moderate*
This popular restaurant serves modern British dishes. The menu might feature local pork with mustard mash, or Cheviot hills lamb with potatoes and pea purée. Leave room for sticky date pudding with toffee sauce for dessert. *7 Bowmont Street, TD5 7JH; 01573 223 548; www.thecobblesinn.co.uk*

AROUND ABBOTSFORD

The Waterwheel *inexpensive*
On the A708 road just beyond Selkirk on the drive to Traquair House, this attractive wooden cabin has an outside deck and lovely countryside views. It serves good value hot meals, as well as soups, and sandwiches. *Philiphaugh Old Mill, Selkirk, TD7 5LU; 01750 22258; closed Sun, Mon*

DAY TRIP OPTIONS

Edinburgh and Kelso would make good bases for families and history-lovers to explore the area.

Ghosts and Coasts
Staying in Edinburgh ❶, walk around the city, visit the Palace of Holyrood-house and listen to tales of how people lived cheek-by-jowl in Mary King's Close and the Grassmarket, before stocking up on picnic supplies

and heading to North Berwick ❷ for the Scottish Seabird Centre and a Seafari to see the birds up close. Finish the day relaxing on the beach.

Follow the A1, then the A198. Retrace the route to return.

Border Romance
From Kelso ❺, see Kelso Abbey and Floors Castle. Next, head for the romantic ruins of Dryburgh Abbey ❻, burial place of Sir Walter Scott,

before heading to his former home, Abbotsford ❼. Tour Scott's home, evocative of his dashing fictional tales, with suits of armor and memorabilia, before visiting Traquair House ❽, steeped in history and drama. Drive back through the wild and beautiful Scottish Border countryside.

Follow the drive instructions to get to all the stops, but return via the A72 and A699, if pressed for time.

The Kingdom of Fife

St Andrews to Culross

Highlights

- **The home of golf**
  Explore the ancient university town of St. Andrews, with its tightly packed medieval street plan, cathedral, and castle, and the oldest golf course in the world

- **Pleasures of the East Neuk coast**
  Stride out along the coastal walking path, take to the seas to watch the abundant wildlife, or stroll around a pretty fishing village

- **Royal retreats**
  Tour fabulous Renaissance Falkland Palace, built for James IV of Scotland, and the romantic ruins of the castle in beautiful Loch Leven where Mary Queen of Scots was imprisoned

Fishing paraphernalia at pretty Pittenweem in the East Neuk of Fife, along the coast from Anstruther

The Kingdom of Fife

Squeezed between the Firth of Tay and the Firth of Forth, Fife was for centuries isolated from the rest of Scotland and still retains its distinctive character. The region was once the seat of Scottish kings and this tour includes some of its most fascinating sights. From St. Andrews, with its hallowed golf courses, ancient university – and bracing North Sea winds – the route leads to a former military bunker, hidden deep underground. This subterranean secret is followed by a succession of picturesque fishing villages that line the Fife coast. The route then winds inland past fertile fields, castles, and palaces, before returning to the coast in the immaculately preserved mercantile town of Culross.

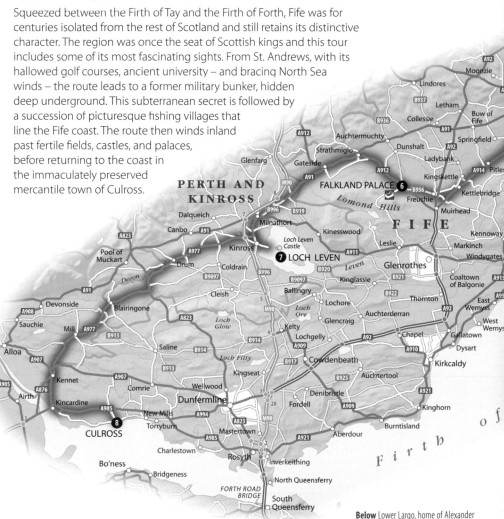

PERTH AND KINROSS

FIFE

Moonzie
Lindores
Letham
Collessie
Bow of Fife
Springfield
Auchtermuchty
Dunshalt
Ladybank
Pitle
Strathmiglo
Kingskettle
Glenfarg
Gateside
FALKLAND PALACE 6
Kettlebridge
Freuchie
Muirhead
Dalqueich
Milnathort
Lomond Hills
Kennoway
Canbo
Kinesswood
Leslie
Markinch
Loch Leven Castle
Windygates
Pool of Muckart
Kinross
7 **LOCH LEVEN**
Leven
Glenrothes
Drum
Coldrain
Kinglassie
Coaltown of Balgonie
Devon
Cleish
Ballingry
Thornton
East Wemyss
Devonside
Blairingone
Lochore
Auchterderran
West Wemys
Sauchie
Mill
Loch Glow
Kelty
Glencraig
Chapel
Gallatown
Saline
Lochgelly
Dysart
Alloa
Loch Fitty
Cowdenbeath
Kirkcaldy
Kennet
Kingseat
Auchtertool
Airth
Comrie
Wellwood
Denibristle
Kincardine
Dunfermline
Fordell
Kinghorn
New Mills
Burntisland
8
Torryburn
Mastertown
Aberdour
CULROSS
Charlestown
Rosyth
Bo'ness
Inverkeithing
Bridgeness
North Queensferry
FORTH ROAD BRIDGE
South Queensferry

F i r t h   o f

Below Lower Largo, home of Alexander Selkirk, the real Robinson Crusoe, *see p226*

ACTIVITIES

Play a round of golf on the famous Old Course in St Andrews

Walk the invigorating Fife Coast Path from Anstruther

Go canoeing, abseiling, or mountain biking in the East Neuk of Fife

Take a boat trip to see the wildlife on the Isle of May

Go birdwatching to spot the lapwings and pink-footed geese at Loch Leven

Take a ferry to the island on Loch Leven to see Mary Queen of Scots' prison

Walk up the hill to the abbey overlooking Culross

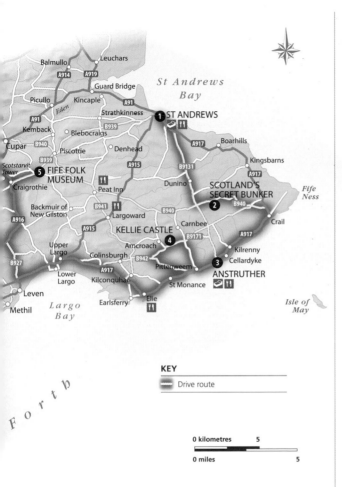

KEY

![Drive route] Drive route

0 kilometres 5

0 miles 5

Below Fertile farmland on the East Neuk of Fife, near Anstruther, *see p225*

PLAN YOUR DRIVE

Start/finish: St. Andrews to Culross.

Number of Days: 1–2 days, possibly 3, if spending more than a day at St. Andrews.

Distances: Approx. 92 miles (148 km).

Road conditions: Generally good, though the roads can be busy – fairly well-marked.

When to go: Late spring and early autumn are good times to visit, though golfers might prefer the long summer days for endless hours on the links.

Opening times: Museums and attractions are generally open 10am–5pm, but close earlier (or are closed altogether) Nov–Easter. Shop times are longer. Churches are usually open until dusk.

Main market days: St. Andrews: Farmers' Market, 1st Sat of month.

Shopping: Pick up hand-thrown items from Crail Pottery; local artworks from the Fisher Studio in Pittenweem; and golf clubs and apparel from Auchterlonie's in St. Andrews.

Major festivals: St. Andrews: Golf Week, Apr; **Anstruther**: East Neuk Festival (arts), Jul; Pittenweem Arts Festival, late Jul/early Aug; **Ceres**: Highland Games (last Sat of month); **Culross**: Culross Festival (arts), Jun.

DAY TRIP OPTIONS

St. Andrews makes a great base for exploring Fife and there is plenty to guarantee happy families. In St. Andrews, see the **home of golf** at the Old Course, visit the **ancient university** and the **cathedral**, and take a stroll on the **beach**; then head off to Ceres for the **folk museum** and finish off at Falkland for a **royal palace**. Alternatively, visit **St. Andrews castle**, with its dungeon, and then head to Scotland's **secret underground bunker**. Continue to Anstruther for **canoeing**, **abseiling**, **cycling**, **walking**, or watching the wildlife on a **boat trip**. Finally, do some **ghost hunting** on a tour of a spooky castle. For full details, *see p227*.

Above Victorian bandstand in the seafront park at St Andrews

VISITING ST ANDREWS

Parking
There is parking by the harbor.

Tourist Information
70 Market St, KY16 9NU; 01334 472 021

Playing golf
There are seven links (seaside) golf courses. A daily ballot decides who plays on the Old Course. For all courses, contact **St Andrews Links** (01334 466 666; www.standrews.org.uk).

WHERE TO STAY

ST ANDREWS

Doune House *inexpensive*
Close to the Old Course and the center, this Victorian townhouse B&B has nice, modern rooms with tartan touches.
5 Murray Place, KY16 9AP; 01334 475 195; www.dounehouse.com

The Macdonald Rusacks Hotel
moderate–expensive
The Rusacks is set beside the Old Course and West Sands, the beach featured in the film *Chariots of Fire*.
Pilmour Links, KY16 9JQ; 0844 879 9136; www.macdonaldhotels.co.uk/rusacks

ANSTRUTHER

Laggan House *inexpensive*
Close to the coastal path, this B&B is comfortable and charming. Rooms have sea views and there's a garden.
The Cooperage, Cellardyke, KY10 3AW; 01333 311 170

Craw's Nest Hotel *moderate*
Ask for a room with a sea view at this 3-star hotel, which is close to the 9-hole golf course. It's also a good choice for families, with its attractive gardens and friendly staff.
Bankwell Road, KY10 3DA; 01333 310 691; www.symphonyhotels.co.uk

Where to Stay: inexpensive, under £80; moderate, £80–£150; expensive, over £150

① St Andrews
Fife; KY16
The **Old Course**, the oldest golf course in the world, attracts thousands of visitors to St Andrews each year. Yet it was religion that first made the city famous. Legend tells that, in the 4th century, St. Rule brought the relics of St. Andrew from Constantinople to Scotland and kept them in a chapel here, founding the city. They were moved to **St. Andrews Cathedral** *(open daily)*, after it was built in 1160. Nearby **St. Andrews Castle** *(joint ticket with cathedral)* was the residence of senior clergy. Both buildings are now ruined but they still make an imposing pair. Visitors can peer into the castle's bottle-shaped dungeon, into which prisoners were dropped with no hope of release. The **university**, founded in 1410, is the oldest in Scotland. It is possible to visit two of the colleges – St. Salvator's in North St and St. Mary's in South St. The latter has a thorn tree, supposedly planted by Mary Queen of Scots.

🚗 **From harbor parking lot drive uphill to North St (A917) and turn left. Turn right onto B9131, then left onto B940 following signs for Scotland's Secret Bunker. There is parking on site.**

Highland Fling
Highland Games are an established part of the summer scene In Scotland. Contestants take part in events such as "tossing the caber" (throwing a large wooden post), swinging the hammer, and piping and dancing competitions. They have their origins in ancient gatherings such as *wappinschaws* – where clans gathered to test their military skills. Modern, formal Games date to 1820 and the revival of Highland culture encouraged by writer Sir Walter Scott.

② Scotland's Secret Bunker
Crown Buildings, Troywood; KY16 8QH
Enter the secret world of surveillance in this former military bunker, hidden far beneath an isolated farmhouse. Scotland's Secret Bunker *(mid-Mar–Oct: open daily; www.secretbunker.co.uk)*, encased in thick concrete, was to have been the HQ of operations, had the UK come under nuclear attack during the Cold War. In the vast labyrinth, visitors can see the basic dormitories, communications equipment, and the little chapel.

🚗 **Return to the B940 and turn right, then right again to take A917. Drive along coast road to Anstruther. Park by harbor.**

Below Anstruther Harbour, once busy with the Scottish herring fleet **Below top right** The Isle of May, seen from the cliffs at Anstruther **Below right** Anstruther beach, sheltered by the harbor walls

❸ Anstruther

Fife; KY10

A charming fishing village typical of the East Neuk (corner) of Fife, Anstruther was once one of the busiest ports in Scotland. The harbor now mainly holds yachts, but the town still has plenty of character with its pubs, award-winning fish and chip shop, and charming buildings. Visitors can also walk the Fife Coastal Path, enjoy a multitude of outdoor activities, or take a boat to the Isle of May to see the wildlife.

A two-hour walking tour

From the parking lot, bear left (if facing the harbour) and walk past the RNLI lifeboat station to visit the **Scottish Fisheries Museum** ① *(open daily; www.scotfishmuseum.org)* telling the history of the local fishing industry. Walk along James St by the shore. When the 16th-century Tolbooth and council chamber is visible, continue on John St and then George St, keeping the sea to the right. Look for clues that the houses were for fishermen: some upper windows have posts used for drying fishing nets. Other properties have external staircases (good for drying nets and creels) and Dutch-style gables on the roofs (Holland was a historic trading partner).

Walk past **Cellardyke Harbour** ②, after which there is a trailer park on the left-hand side. Out to sea lies the Isle of May, on which stands a ruined 12th-century monastery and the oldest lighthouse in Scotland (1635). A National Nature Reserve, the island is home to seals and colonies of puffins, guillemots and razorbills.

Soon after Cellardyke, the path turns into a grassy track and passes a pig farm on the left. Go through a gate next to a seat, then another gate. Look out for fishing boats bobbing on

the sea. To the left are fields where, in summer, the long grasses and wild flowers come alive with clouds of bees, butterflies, and other insects.

Eventually, climb a few steps over a low wall, and go straight ahead – look out for the cormorants that often perch on rocks by the shore. Cross a tiny bridge above a brook and continue on beside the sea. Climb a few more steps over a wall, and follow the shore to a large **outcrop of rocks** ③ – the layers of sediment deposited over the centuries can be seen in the exposed stone. Around a corner, the path enters a grassy area with lots of gorse growing on the left.

Cross another bridge over a brook to see the village of Crail in the distance. If the tide is out, the pretty **shell beach** ④ here is a good place for a breather, with large rocks as convenient seats. For those with stamina, the path goes on to Crail, otherwise retrace the walk back to the car park for some well-earned fish and chips by the harbour.

🚗 *Drive back to A917 and follow to Pittenweem. Then turn right into Charles St; follow the road taking the right fork and then turn left onto B9171. Turn right for castle and parking lot.*

Below Beautiful scenery on the Anstruther to Crail coastal path

For canoeing, abseiling, climbing, cycling, and archery, try **East Neuk Outdoors** *(01333 311 929; www.eastneukoutdoors.co.uk)*. For boat trips to the Isle of May, buy tickets from **Anstruther Pleasure Trips** from the harbor *(01333 310 054; www.isleofmayferry.com)*.

EAT AND DRINK

ST ANDREWS

The Glass House *inexpensive*
This laid-back restaurant in the center of town serves pizzas, pastas, and salads. *80 North Street, KY16 9AH; 01334 473 673; www.houserestaurants.com*

The Doll's House *moderate*
Popular restaurant serving Scottish-French dishes such as Scottish lamb with puy lentils, and sticky toffee pudding. *3 Church Square, KY16 9NN; 01334 477 422; www.houserestaurants.com*

ANSTRUTHER

Anstruther Fish Bar *inexpensive*
This legendary fish and chip shop consistently wins awards for its food. *42–4 Shore Street, KY10 3AQ; 01333 310 518; www.anstrutherfishbar.co.uk*

The Cellar *moderate*
This restaurant serves modern Scottish dishes, with an emphasis on seafood. *24 East Green, KY10 3AA; 01333 310 378; www.cellaranstruther.co.uk; closed Sun; lunch served Fri & Sat*

Eat and Drink: inexpensive, under £25; moderate, £25–£50; expensive, over £50

Above Victorian-style gardens surround the ancient home of Kellie Castle, rumored to be haunted **Above top right** Imposing walls and turrets of Kellie Castle **Above right** Falkland Palace, once a royal hunting lodge

⑤ Fife Folk Museum
Fife; KY15 5NF

The attractive village of Ceres is home to the **Fife Folk Museum** (*Apr–Oct: open daily; www.fifefolkmuseum.org*), which sheds light on the history of the working people of Fife. Housed in a 17th-century building, the museum contains a vivid array of items, from agricultural implements to patchwork quilts and a Victorian "bone-shaker" bicycle. A cottage living room has been reconstructed to recreat the feel of a home in the pre-industrial age.

🚗 *Return on B939 to A916. Turn right, then after Scotstarvit Tower, fork left down a minor road. At A914, turn left (signed Glenrothes), then right on a minor road beyond Kettlebridge, crossing A92 onto B936 through Freuchie and on to Falkland. Turn right briefly onto A912, then left into East Port to High St, palace, and town parking lot.*

④ Kellie Castle
Pittenweem; KY10 2RF

Kellie Castle (*Apr–May & Sep, Oct: open Fri–Tue; Jun–Aug: open daily*) dates as far back as the 14th century and is said to be haunted. It was largely rebuilt by the Lorimer family in the 19th century, after it had almost fallen into ruin. The rooms contain fine paintings, grand plaster ceilings, and furniture designed by Arts and Crafts architect Sir Robert Lorimer. There are superb views of the Bass Rock and a Victorian-style garden, with roses and herbaceous plants.

🚗 *Turn right onto B9171, then left at B942 to A917. Turn right and at Upper Largo, go straight onto A915 (or detour to Lower Largo – see box), then turn right onto B927 to travel away from the coast. Turn right on A916 north, then right onto B939 into Ceres. The museum is on High St, on the right.*

The Real Robinson Crusoe

Alexander Selkirk, born in Lower Largo in the 17th century, was the inspiration for Daniel Defoe's novel *Robinson Crusoe*. Selkirk went to sea as a youth and in 1704 was serving as a sailing master on the vessel *Cinque Ports*. He quarrelled with the captain and asked to leave the ship. His wish was granted, and he was put ashore on Juan Fernandez, an uninhabited island off Chile. He lived there for over four years until being rescued in 1709.

---

⑥ Falkland Palace
Falkland; KY15 7BU

The magnificent Renaissance **Falkland Palace** (*Mar–Oct: open daily*) dominates the village. Built as a royal hunting lodge for James IV of Scotland in the 15th century, it became the Stuart monarchs' favorite retreat – Mary

---

WHERE TO STAY

AROUND FALKLAND PALACE

Ladywell House *inexpensive*
This handsome detached house, set in its own grounds off the A912 just outside Falkland, once belonged to Princess Diana's mother. Now it's a B&B with six elegant rooms, furnished in country house style. Guests take breakfast in the large conservatory.
Falkland, KY15 7DE; 01337 858 414; www.ladywellhousefife.co.uk

Right RSPB Vane Farm, set on the beautiful shores of Loch Leven

Where to Stay: inexpensive, under £80; moderate, £80–£150; expensive, over £150

Queen of Scots was also very fond of it. As well as touring the palace itself, with its Flemish tapestries and painted ceilings, visitors can visit the gardens and the Real Tennis court, built in 1539.

🚗 *Return to A912, turn left to A91. Turn left again, then merge onto B996 to Milnathort. Turn left onto A992, then straight onto B996 into center of Kinross. Turn left onto Burns Beggs St, then right onto Pier Rd to the parking lot for the ferry to Loch Leven Castle.*

Above Falkland Palace gardens, home to Britain's oldest tennis court

⑦ Loch Leven
By Kinross; KY13 8UF

Loch Leven is famed for the lonely **castle** *(Apr–Sep: open daily)*, perched on an island in its waters, only accessible by ferry. Mary Queen of Scots was imprisoned here on the order of Elizabeth I. While here, Mary was forced to abdicate in favour of her son, James VI. She escaped after a year with the help of her jailer, but was locked up again at Fotheringay in England. The 14th-century castle is now a ruin, but full of atmosphere.

The loch is also noted for its rich bird life. Head south on B996, then left on B9097 to the **Royal Society for the Protection of Birds Vane Farm** *(open daily)*, with nature trails and viewing points – from here look for regular visitors such as pink-footed geese.

🚗 *From Loch Leven Pier, return to B996 and turn right, then left onto Station Rd. Continue on to the A977 and follow it all the way to Kincardine, then head left to join A985 (towards Forth Road Bridge). After 4 miles (6 km) turn right down Gallows Loan to Culross. Park in the town centre near the palace.*

⑧ Culross
Culross; KY12 8JH

Culross (pronounced "koo-ross") was one of Scotland's largest ports in the 16th century: ships took coal and salt from Fife to the Low Countries and returned with red pantiles, which were used as roofing. This once prosperous town, with its Dutch-influenced architecture and cobbled streets, is almost perfectly preserved. Main sights include **Culross Palace** *(Apr–May, & Sep, Oct: open Thu–Mon; Jun–Aug: open daily)*, which was built for a local merchant; and **The Study** *(joint admission with palace)* a 17th-century tower house. It is also worth walking up to the ruined **abbey**, founded by the Cistercians in the 13th century, which can be found on the hills above town.

Above The 17th-century Town House, an example of Dutch-style architecture in Culross

EAT AND DRINK

AROUND KELLIE CASTLE
The Inn at Lathones *moderate*
This former coaching inn has a popular restaurant, serving traditional dishes: game suet pudding with root vegetable mash, for example, or a saffron seafood chowder. Take B942, then B941 to Largoward, then right on A915.
Largoward, KY9 1JE; 01334 840 494; www.theinn.co.uk

Sangsters *moderate–expensive*
This Michelin-starred restaurant serves fine Scottish produce such as venison, crab, beef, and salmon. Vegetarians catered for with notice. Take the coastal road (A917) from Pittenweem to Elie.
51 High St, Elie, KY9 1BZ; 01333 331 001; www.sangsters.co.uk; closed Sun eve, Mon, Tue & Wed, Sat lunch; best to book

AROUND FIFE FOLK MUSEUM
The Peat Inn *moderate–expensive*
Award-winning food at this country inn, with the focus on fresh Scottish produce. Enjoy imaginative dishes such as cannelloni of langoustines and scallops. From Ceres, head north on B939, then right on B940 to Peat Inn.
Peat Inn, KY15 5LH; 01334 840 206; www.thepeatinn.co.uk

DAY TRIP OPTIONS
St Andrews is an excellent base from which to explore Fife.

Royal and Ordinary Fife
Spend the morning in St Andrews ①, with its famous royal golf course, university and ancient cathedral. Stroll along the golden beach, then drive to pretty Ceres to visit the Fife Folk Museum ⑤ and gain an insight

into the lives of the locals. Drive on to the Stuart monarchs' wonderful Renaissance Falkland Palace ⑥.

From St Andrews take A915, then B939 to Ceres. Follow drive instructions to Falkland. Retrace journey to return.

Family Fun in the East Neuk
In St Andrews ①, visit the castle dungeon and then drive to Scotland's

Secret Bunker ②, with lots for kids to enjoy. Next, visit Anstruther ③ for canoeing, cycling, a boat trip, or just relaxing on the beach. If more excitement is needed, go ghost hunting at Kellie Castle ④.

Follow the drive instructions as far as Kellie Castle. To return, head back to B9171, turn left and continue to B9131. Then turn left here to St Andrews.

The Wild West Coast of Scotland

Inveraray to Plockton

Highlights

- **Meeting the locals**
  See abundant wildlife: grey and common seals, playful otters, shy pine martens, majestic red deer and rare eagles

- **Natural splendour**
  Travel through some of the most stunning landscapes in Europe – deep sea lochs framed by wild, craggy mountains, and tumbling rivers running through steep-sided glens

- **Historic adventures**
  Visit Glencoe, scene of an infamous betrayal; take a boat to the cave that sheltered Bonnie Prince Charlie, and explore ancient castles with many colorful and historic connections

Glenelg Bay in the distance, seen from the road to Kylerhea Otter Hide

The Wild West Coast of Scotland

Scotland's west coast is the most dramatic, jagged coastline in Great Britain. The route starts on the shores of Loch Fyne, at the pretty town of Inveraray, whose grand castle is still a family home. It continues past stunning mountains and woodland, and through Glencoe, scene of a terrible massacre in 1692. Every now and then you'll see a mighty castle, testimony to the turbulent history of the area. Winding coastal routes lead to the remote Ardnamurchan Peninsula, before heading north to take the ferry across to the craggy mountains and sandy beaches of the Isle of Skye. The final stop is back on the mainland, among the palm trees of Plockton, warmed by the waters of the Gulf Stream.

Above White sand made of crushed seashells on the fabulous beach at Sanna, Ardnamurchan Peninsula, *see p234*

KEY

 Drive route

ACTIVITIES

Travel deep inside a mountain at Cruachan Power Station

Climb up McCaig's tower at Oban for views of the Isle of Mull

Come eye-to-eye with an inquisitive stingray at the aquarium in the Scottish Sea Life Sanctuary

Explore the waterfalls and mountains at Glencoe and see the sites of the infamous massacre

Watch for rare pine martens and eagles in the remote Ardnamurchan Peninsula

Take a boat trip from Elgol to see Bonnie Prince Charlie's cave

Watch the otters that inspired the book *Ring of Bright Water* at the Kylerhea Otter Hide

Below Boats moored in the still waters of the port of Oban, *see p233*

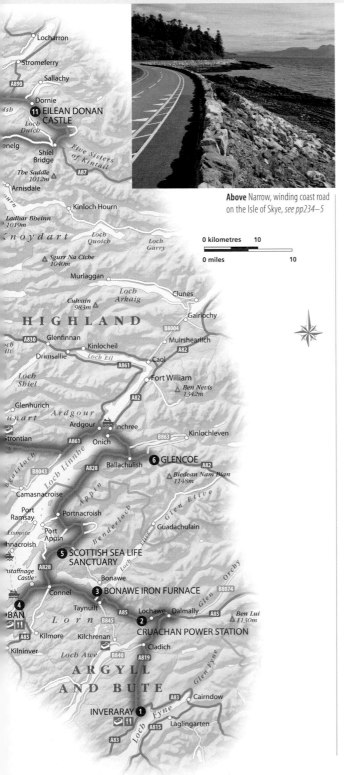

Above Narrow, winding coast road on the Isle of Skye, *see pp234–5*

0 kilometres 10

0 miles 10

PLAN YOUR DRIVE

Start/finish: Inveraray to Plockton.

Number of days: About 5–6 days.

Distances: Approx. 297 miles (478 km).

Road conditions: Generally good, but with long stretches of single track roads (with passing places) which should be driven with care. The scenic track to Glenelg, on Skye, is not useable in snow or ice – use Skye Bridge.

When to go: High summer (Jul–Aug) offers long hours of daylight, but can get surprisingly busy. May, Jun, Sep, and Oct are ideal. Please note, routes likely to get snowbound in winter.

Opening times: Museums and attractions are generally open 10am–5pm, but close earlier (or are closed altogether) Nov–Easter. Shop times are longer. Churches are usually open until dusk.

Main market days: Oban: Farmers' Market at Benderloch, near Oban, 1st and 3rd Thu of month.

Shopping: Skye has plenty of craft outlets, selling sheepskins, Celtic jewellery, pottery, and knitwear. The island and other parts of the west coast, also attracts many artists, whose studios can be visited.

Major festivals: Inveraray: Highland Games, Jul; **Oban**: Highland and Islands Music & Dance, 4 days at the end of Apr; **Skye**: Highland Games, Aug.

DAY TRIP OPTIONS

With beautiful countryside and wildlife, Scotland is great for children. Stay at Inveraray to see its **castle**, before heading off to the **power station** at Cruachan and going deep inside the **mountain**. Picnic by the **loch** at the **iron furnace** at Bonawe and then see the **seals**, **rays**, and other **fish** at a **sea life sanctuary**. Older romantics might prefer to stay at Plockton with its **palms** and **harbor** and then visit the **gardens** at Armadale. Continue on to Elgol to see the craggy Cuillin **mountains** and relive the **exploits** of a prince. Then take a **ferry** and drive to dreamy **castle ruins**. For full details, *see p235*.

Above View of Argyll Hotel and church tower from Loch Fyne

VISITING INVERARAY

Tourist Information
Front Street, PA32 8UY; 08452 255 121;
www.visitscottishheartlands.com; Apr–
Oct: open daily; Nov-Mar: closed Sun.

Parking
There is parking off The Avenue, in the center of Inveraray, and by the castle.

WHERE TO STAY

INVERARAY

Creag Dhubh *inexpensive*
A large, detached house set in neat gardens, this family-run B&B has five bedrooms and great views over Loch Fyne.
Main Street South, PA32 8XT; 01499 302 430; www.creagdhubh.freeuk.com

Rudha-Na-Craige *moderate*
This handsome house was built in the 19th century by the Duke of Argyll. Now it is a 4-star B&B, with six unfussy, stylish bedrooms, all with views of Loch Fyne.
Inverarary, PA32 8YX; 01499 302 668; www.rudha-na-craige.f2s.com

Loch Fyne Hotel and Spa *expensive*
Near the harbour, with stunning views of Loch Fyne, this hotel has comfortable, stylish rooms, a swimming pool and spa.
Main Street South, PA32 8XT; 01499 302 980; www.crerarhotels.com

BONAWE IRON FURNACE

Ardanaiseig Hotel *moderate*
Wildly romantic hotel on the shores of Loch Awe (take B845 from Taynuilt), this historic house has luxurious bedrooms.
Kilchrenan, by Taynuilt, Argyll, PA35 1HE; 01866 833 333; www.ardanaiseig.com

OBAN

Kimberley House *moderate*
In an old maternity hospital, this friendly B&B has rooms combining antique and modern décor with sea views.
Dalriach Rd, PA34 5EQ; 01631 571 115; www.kimberley-hotel.co.uk

❶ Inveraray
Argyll; PA32

Sitting on the banks of Loch Fyne, Inveraray is small but imposing. The town was built by the 3rd Duke of Argyll in the 18th century and has two main visitor attractions – its 19th-century jail and castle. The walk explores the surrounding woodland and starts with a visit to the castle.

A one-and-a-half-hour walking tour

From the parking lot, visit **Inveraray Castle ①** *(Apr–Oct: open daily; www.inveraray-castle.com)*. The building belongs to the Duke of Argyll, and the family is head of the Campbell clan – the 1st Duke's regiment carried out the notorious massacre at Glencoe *(see p234)*. It is crammed with tapestries, silverware, and porcelain, and unusual items such as Rob Roy's sporran.

From the castle entrance, look for the "Dun na Cuaich walk" signs and follow the blue arrows along a tarmac track. This soon passes a **monument ②**, commemorating the execution of 17 Campbell leaders by the 1st Marquis of Atholl in 1685. This was punishment for rising against the Stuart King James II in protest at his assertion that he was divine head of the church.

Cross the charming 18th-century **stone bridge ③** – built by John Adam – that spans the River Aray, then bear right to go through the woods. At a gate, go straight ahead on the grassy track to reach another gate, which leads into woodland – in springtime

the ground is carpeted with bluebells. The track soon passes a ruined former **lime kiln ④** on the left-hand side. Continue uphill, then branch right after a few minutes, still following the blue arrows.

Eventually the path bears to the right and flattens out a little, and the fresh scent of pine trees fills the air. After passing the remains of a wall, the woodland opens out, providing a glimpse of the surrounding hills. Zig-zag uphill now, to reach the summit, which is covered with wild flowers in summer and also has a welcome seat. The views of the castle, the town and the loch spread out far beneath are wonderful. **Dun na Cuaich ⑤** means something like "fort of cups" in Gaelic and this peak was the site of an Iron-Age hillfort. The summit is topped with a monument, built by another of the famous Adam family of architects. Some say it was used as a watchtower by the Campbells, others that it was simply built to enhance the landscape.

After enjoying the views and taking a well-earned rest, simply follow the path back down to Inveraray. The

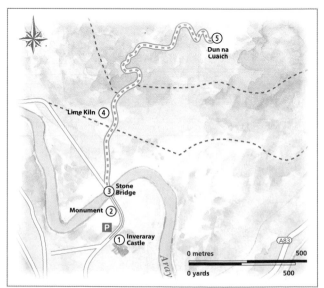

castle at the bottom has a café, where walkers can refuel on tea and cakes.

🚗 *Take A819 north (marked for Oban) then, after views of Kilchurn Castle, turn left on A85 to reach Cruachan Power Station and parking lot.*

② Cruachan Power Station
Dalmally, Argyll; PA33 1AN

Hidden deep inside Ben Cruachan, this hydro-electric power station, *(Apr–Oct: open daily; Nov–Mar: open Mon–Fri; closed Jan)* runs on water fed from a reservoir high on the mountain. Tours take visitors on a bus into a vast cavern in the heart of the mountain. Seeing the workings of this mighty structure feels like entering the world of James Bond. After a visit, try a brisk walk around the loch or to the top of Ben Cruachan, for views of the dam.

🚗 *Carry on A85, then turn right (toward Brochroy), when road splits, bear right to Bonawe Iron Furnace. Park on site.*

③ Bonawe Iron Furnace
By Taynuilt, Argyll; PA35 1JQ

It is hard to imagine industry in this tranquil spot by Loch Etive, but Bonawe *(Apr–Sep: open daily)* was once a flourishing iron furnace and what remains is Britain's best example of a charcoal-fueled ironworks. The ironworks were built here in the 18th century because of the vast supply of wood from which charcoal could be made. Bonawe produced large numbers of cannonballs – some used by Lord Nelson in his sea battles.

🚗 *Return to the A85, follow the road to Oban and park on street.*

④ Oban
Oban, Argyll; PA34

Attractive Oban is a bustling working port, with fishing boats bobbing amid the passenger ferries running to the Hebridean islands. Overlooking the town is **McCaig's Tower**, a monument

resembling the Colosseum in Rome. It was intended as a family memorial and to provide work for local masons. Started in 1897, it remained unfinished when McCaig died in 1902. Climb up for fine views to the islands.

Just outside town, on the A85, stand the romantic ruins of **Dunstaffnage Castle** *(Apr–Sep: open daily; Oct–Mar: open Sat–Wed)*, one of Scotland's oldest stone fortifications. It was built in the 13th century to defend against marauding Norsemen and was the stronghold of the MacDougall lords until it fell to the kings of Scotland. Centuries later, Flora MacDonald was imprisoned here for helping Bonnie Prince Charlie escape after the Jacobite rebellion. She was later removed to the Tower of London.

🚗 *Head north on A85, turn right onto A828 across the Connel Bridge. Follow signs to Sea Life Sanctuary and parking.*

⑤ Scottish Sea Life Sanctuary
Barcaldine, Argyll; PA37 1SE

Situated on the shores of Loch Creran, the Scottish Sea Life Sanctuary *(open daily; www.sealsanctuary.co.uk)* rescues seal pups found on the coast, nursing them and rehabilitating them for return to the wild – there are resident seals to admire. The aquarium holds sea creatures from starfish to stingrays and there is an adventure playground and woodland trail – it's a fascinating place for both adults and children.

🚗 *Drive north on A828 along the coast, take A82, toward Crianlarich. Turn right for Glencoe Visitor Centre and parking.*

Above top left 18th-century Bonawe Iron Furnace **Above** Oban, overlooked by the imposing McCaig's Tower **Above left** Tower at Inveraray Castle, home to the Duke of Argyll **Below left** Popular attraction of Inveraray Jail

EAT AND DRINK

INVERARAY

The George Hotel *inexpensive*
This popular seafront pub serves a wide range of traditional and vegetarian dishes. Look out for fresh mussels and chips, Scottish steak pie, or haggis. *Main Street East, PA32 8TT; 01499 302 111; www.thegeorgehotel.co.uk*

OBAN

Oban Chocolate Company *inexpensive*
Relax into sofas and enjoy sea views at this modern café for coffee, cakes, and ice cream – or hand-made chocolates. *34 Corran Esplanade, PA34 5PS; 01631 566 099; www.obanchocolate.co.uk; closed Jan*

Coast *inexpensive–moderate*
Contemporary restaurant in a former bank, specializing in locally caught seafood. *102–104 George Street, PA34 5NT; 01631 569 900; www.coastoban.co.uk*

Room 9 Restaurant *moderate*
Visit this waterside restaurant for simple sandwiches, or smoked salmon pâté and beef with Stornoway black pudding. *9 Craigard Rd, PA34 5NP; 01631 564 200; closed Sun*

Temple Seafood *moderate*
This small restaurant has waterside views and offers scallop chowder, lobster and seafood platters. Reservations essential. *Gallanach Rd, PA34 4LW; 01631 566 000; www.templeseafood.co.uk; open Thu–Sun*

Eat and Drink: inexpensive, under £25; moderate, £25–£50; expensive, over £50

Above The lush Ardnamurchan Peninsula, a haven for Scottish wildlife

CROSSING TO SKYE

Car ferry services
The ferry crossing to Skye from Mallaig takes about 30 minutes and is run by **Caledonian Macbrayne** (08000 665 000; www.calmac.co.uk). The **Glenelg–Skye Ferry** (Easter–Sep: runs daily every 20 mins; www.calmac.co.uk) crosses from Kylerhea to Glenelg.

WHERE TO STAY

AROUND GLENCOE

Kilcamb Lodge Hotel *moderate*
Peaceful hotel in a stunning lochside location on the A861, beyond Strontian on the drive to Ardnamurchan Peninsula. Combines luxury with friendliness and attention to detail. Excellent food, too.
Strontian, Argyll, PH36 4HY; 01967 402 257; www.kilcamblodge.co.uk

AROUND ARMADALE CASTLE GARDENS

Kinloch Lodge *moderate*
Cozy atmosphere at the home of the chief of the Macdonald clan and his culinary-writer wife. A log fire burns in the drawing room and the charming bedrooms are individually furnished.
Sleat, Isle of Skye, IV43 8QY (on A851); 01471 833 333; www.kinloch-lodge.co.uk

Tigh an Dochais *moderate*
Sleek rooms at this spotless B&B by the beach, with views of Broadford Bay. Homemade bread and jam for breakfast.
13 Harrapool, Isle of Skye, IV49 9AQ; 01471 820 022; www.skyebedbreakfast. co.uk; closed Dec–Feb

PLOCKTON

The Plockton Hotel *moderate*
This hotel sits right on the seafront in Plockton, so try and get a room with a view across the loch. Bedrooms are ensuite and there's a busy bar and restaurant downstairs.
41 Harbour View, IV52 8TN; 01599 544 274; www.plocktonhotel.co.uk

Right Splendid waterfall in Glencoe, scene of the brutal massacre in 1692

⑥ Glencoe
Glencoe; PH49 4LA
The mountains of Glencoe, described by Queen Victoria as: "stern, rugged, precipitous," are truly dramatic and home to wildlife as varied as mountain hares and golden eagles. But it is for the brutal massacre of 1692 that this somber place is best known. **Glencoe Visitor Centre** (Mar–Oct: open daily; Nov–Feb: open Thu–Sun; www.nts.org.uk) has an excellent exhibition and film on the history and wildlife of the glen; a viewing platform, and information on walks and climbs in the area.
🚗 *Follow A82 toward Fort William. After Onich, follow signs for Corran Ferry and cross to Ardgour. Then follow the A861 to Salen, and take B8007 to the Natural History Centre and parking lot.*

⑦ Ardnamurchan Peninsula
Argyll; PH36 4JG
This remote peninsula has a wet but mild climate and is home to a wide array of plants and wildlife. The **Natural History Centre** (Apr–Oct: open daily) introduces visitors to the flora and fauna with displays, remote CCTV cameras, specially constructed pine marten dens and a live "eagle cam." Continue on B8007 to Ardnamurchan

Point, generally regarded as mainland Britain's most westerly point. Built in 1849 and automated in 1988, the **lighthouse** (Apr–Oct; 01972 510 210; www. ardnamurchanlighthouse.com) is also a museum – climb the 152 steps to the top to enjoy glorious views. Just below there's also a fabulous beach at **Sanna**, where the white sand is made of shells.
🚗 *Follow B8007 back to Salen, go left on A861 and left on A830 to Mallaig. Take the ferry to Skye. Once on the island, take A851 to the castle.*

⑧ Armadale Castle Gardens
Armadale, Isle of Skye; IV45 8RS
Now largely ruined, the castle was once home to members of the Clan Donald, former rulers of this area – Jacobite heroine Flora Macdonald was married here. Visitors can stroll in the **Castle Gardens** (Apr–Oct: open daily; www.clandonald.com) and woodlands. There's also a **Museum of the Isles** (same hours), full of history of the area and the Clan Donald. The library helps those tracing their family history.
🚗 *Continue on A851 and A87 into Broadford, then turn left onto B8083. Follow this scenic single track road into Elgol. Park above the harbor.*

9 Elgol

Isle of Skye; IV49 9BJ

Elgol offers fine views of the Cuillins of Skye, a fierce craggy mountain range that challenges even experienced climbers. Bonnie Prince Charlie was hidden here in a remote cave, by loyal members of the Mackinnon clan, after defeat at Culloden in 1746. He was then rowed across to Mallaig and taken to France. Visitors can take a boat trip to the cave, or join a trip to Loch Coruisk in the heart of the Cuillins.

🚗 *Follow B8083 to Broadford, turn right on A87 and right to Kylerhea, turn left to Otter Haven Hide parking lot.*

10 Kylerhea Otter Hide

Kylerhea, Isle of Skye; IV42 8

This forest hide *(open daily)* offers great views across the Kylerhea waters to Glenelg. Visitors can watch otters on the shore, common and Atlantic grey seals in the water, and even the occasional white-tailed sea eagle. The otters here inspired Gavin Maxwell's famous novel, *Ring of Bright Water*.

🚗 *From Kylerhea take ferry to Glenelg, take the coast road then turn left to Shiel Bridge. Stop at viewpoint for Five Sisters of Kintail mountains above Loch Duich. In Shiel Bridge turn right on A87 then left to castle. In winter, when ferry is not running, leave Skye on A87, cross bridge to Kyle of Lochalsh, turn left for Plockton.*

11 Eilean Donan Castle

Dornie, by Kyle; IV40 8DX

This gloriously romantic castle *(Mar–Nov: open daily; www.eileandonancastle. com)* reached by an arched stone bridge sits on a rocky island, settled in the 6th century by Saint Donan. The castle was built much later, to defend against invading Vikings. The building was carefully restored in the 1930s – visitors can now see the grand halls, bedrooms, and kitchens. Eilean Donan may well look familiar: it has featured in many films, including the James Bond thriller, *The World is Not Enough*.

🚗 *Continue on the A87 – at Balmacara turn right onto a pretty country road into Plockton. Park on street.*

12 Plockton

Plockton, Ross-shire; IV52

The warm winds of the Gulf Stream give the little village of Plockton a surprisingly lush appearance: there are palm trees, colorful flowers, and all sorts of exotic plants flourishing in the gardens that line the harbor. It started life as a fishing village, planned in the 18th-century by the Earl of Seaforth. It makes a relaxing base and is popular with sailors, who moor their yachts in the harbor. Visitors can enjoy loch and hill walks or go on a sea cruise to see the coast with **Calum's Boat Trips** *(01599 544 306; www.calums-sealtrips.com).*

Above left Craggy mountains around Elgol **Above center** Female red deer on the shore, Ardnamurchan Peninsula **Above right** The pretty village of Plockton in its lush setting

EAT AND DRINK

AROUND ARMADALE CASTLE GARDENS

Harbour View *moderate*
This former fisherman's cottage is now a popular restaurant specializing in fish and seafood. Try the fish pie or *moules*. *7 Bosville Terrace, Portree, Isle of Skye, IV51 9DG (on A87 north); 01487 612 069; www.harbourviewskye.co.uk*

The Three Chimneys *expensive*
Acclaimed restaurant in the north of Skye, serving modern Scottish cuisine. The menu might include saddle of wild rabbit, or pan-fried sea trout, followed by hot marmalade pudding. *Colbost, Dunvegan, Isle of Skye (on A87 north), IV55 82T; 01470 511 258; www.threechimneys.co.uk*

PLOCKTON

The Haven Hotel *inexpensive*
This pleasant little bistro located in a central hotel offers varied dishes such as fillet steak and lime fish cakes. *3 Innes Street, IV52 8TW; 01599 544 223; www.havenhotelplockton.co.uk*

Plockton Shores *moderate*
This is part-grocer's shop, part-restaurant, on the waterfront in Plockton. Locally sourced food might include scallops, or venison cooked with juniper and thyme. *30 Harbour St, IV52 8TN; 01599 544 263; www.plocktonshoresrestaurant.co.uk*

DAY TRIP OPTIONS

This route can easily be split into day trips from Inveraray and Plockton.

Family Adventure

From Inveraray ❶, buy some picnic provisions and visit the castle, with its splendid interiors, then head north to Ben Cruachan Power Station ❷, to go deep inside the mountain. Next, it's a short drive to Bonawe Iron Furnace

❸, for a picnic in the idyllic grounds before driving to the Scottish Sea Life Sanctuary ❺, to see the seals, aquarium, and walk in the woods.

Follow A819, then join A85 north. Turn off right on A828. Reverse to return.

Castles and Skye

Enjoy Plockton's ❶ temperate climate and pretty palm-lined harbor, then cross the bridge to the Isle of Skye and

walk around pretty Armadale Castle Gardens ❽. Go to Elgol ❾, close to the cave that hid Bonnie Prince Charlie and cross back to the mainland on the Glenelg-Skye ferry to visit the romantic ruins of Eilean Donan Castle ⓫.

From Plockton, head to the Kyle of Lochalsh and take A87, then A851 to the castle gardens. Then follow the drive instructions all the way back.

Eat and Drink: inexpensive, under £25; moderate, £25–£50; expensive, over £50

The Heart of Scotland

Perth to Loch Lomond

Highlights

- **Fairytale castles**
  Visit the great Scottish castles at Blair Atholl and Glamis, as well as historic Scone Palace, where the kings of Scotland were once crowned

- **Rivers and lochs**
  Enjoy the beautiful scenery from the great River Tay as it flows from Dunkeld down to Perth; from slender Loch Voil to the largest expanse of freshwater in the UK, Loch Lomond

- **Literary associations**
  Follow the literary links: see the home of JM Barrie; Birnam Wood mentioned in Shakespeare's *Macbeth* and visited by Beatrix Potter; and the highland glens and grave of Rob Roy, hero of Sir Walter Scott and Daniel Defoe

A sun-dappled road through Argyll Forest Park, west of Loch Lomond

The Heart of Scotland

This tour characterizes perfectly the variety that Scotland has to offer. It takes visitors through the very heart of the country: where the Lowlands meet the Highlands, where famous figures like Rob Roy once lived and historic battles were fought. Here the landscape – which encompasses Loch Lomond and the Trossachs, Scotland's first National Park – is a picturesque mixture of brooding hills, open glens, ancient trees and tranquil lochs. It is superb walking country, offering trails for all abilities. Food lovers will enjoy the chance to taste some of Britain's finest food – soft fruit from Angus and fresh salmon and trout caught in the River Tay.

Above Balfour Castle in the Kirkton of Kingoldrum, near Kirriemuir, *see p241*
Below Ben Lomond seen in the distance over Loch Lomond, *see p243*

BLAIR CASTLE
A9 B8079 **7** Blair Atholl
Calvine B847
Killiecrankie
PASS OF KILLIECRANKIE **6**
B8019
Tummel Strathtummel
Bridge Foss Pitlochry
Schichallion B846
1081m △
Tay A827
Carn Mairg △
1042m
Invervar Dull Aberfeldy
Bridge of **8**
Balgie THE FORTINGALL Kenmore
YEW A826
Ben Lawers △ Milton
1215m Loch
Tay Amulree
Meall nan △ Lawers
Tarmachan A827
1043m Ardeonaig PERTH AND
Killin Ben Chonzie △ Glen A822
929m Almon
A85 St Fillans Gilmerton
A85 Lochearnhead Loch Earn A85 Crieff
Comrie B8062
Loch Voit **9** A84 Ben Vorlich △ Muthill Kinke
BALQUHIDDER 1013m Earn Bridge
Strathyre Dalchruin A822 Auchterarder
STIRLING Loch A823
Loch Lubnaig Braco Blackford
Katrine Ben Ledi △ Pass of
876m Leny **10** CALLANDER Greenloaning
Brig o' Turk Loch
Ben Venue △ Venachar A9
730m A821 A81 A84
B829 Doune
Kinlochard Port of B822 Dunblane
Aberfoyle Menteith Lake of Thornhill 11
INCHMAHOME **11** Menteith
Gartmore PRIORY B8034 Forth A84
A81 A811
Arnprior
Luss Buchlyvie
BALMAHA ACTIVITIES
Loch **12** B837
Lomond Drymen **Go on a ghost hunt** at spooky Glamis Castle
A82 Killearn
A811 Gartocharn A81 **Enjoys a day's trout fishing** on the Tay at Dunkeld
LOCH LOMOND **13** A809
SHORES Balloch **Walk through the wooded gorge**, the scene of the
Alexandria Battle at Killiecrankie
A82
Watch for red squirrels in the woods of Blair Castle

Take the ferry across to the island of Inchmahome Priory in the Lake of Menteith

Paddle a kayak on beautiful Loch Lomond or explore via a cruise boat

0 kilometres 10

0 miles 10

KEY

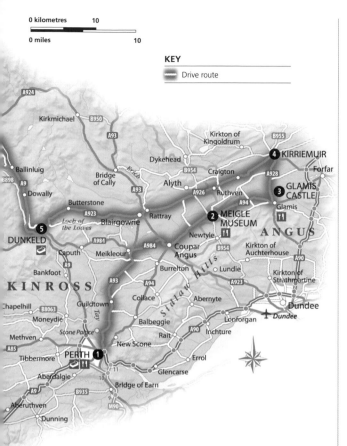

Drive route

Below The spectacular rocks at Bracklinn Falls, near Callander, see pp242–3

PLAN YOUR DRIVE

Start/finish: Perth to Loch Lomond.

Number of days: Around 3–4 days.

Distances: Approx 248 miles (400 km)

Road conditions: The roads are mostly good and well marked, although there are some winding, hilly sections and narrow single-track roads. The road to Bridge of Balgie is unsuitable for trailers, and impassable in bad weather, icy conditions, and snow; use A827 as an alternative.

When to go: Spring is a pleasant time to visit. Summer brings better weather, but also more visitors and the Scottish midge. Autumn is beautiful when the trees change color. Sections of the drive may be snowbound in winter.

Opening times: Museums and attractions are generally open 10am–5pm, but close earlier (or are closed altogether) Nov–Easter. Shops are often open longer. Churches are usually open until dusk.

Main market days: Perth: Farmers' Market, 1st Sat of month.

Shopping: Jams made from local berries; woollens, Celtic jewelry and fine foods at Loch Lomond Shores, the National Park Gateway, Balloch.

Main festivals: Perth: Scottish Game Fair (Scone Palace), Jul; **Glamis**: Strathmore Highland Games, 2nd Sat in Jun; **Dunkeld**: Birnam Highland Games, last Sat in Aug; **Blair Castle**: International Horse Trials, Aug; Glenfiddich Piping and Fiddling Championships, Oct; **Balloch**: Loch Lomond Highland Games, Jul.

DAY TRIP OPTIONS

Staying at Perth, visit its fine **gardens**, **church**, and **gallery** and the **palace** at Scone. Then head to Dunkeld for a walk by the **river**, with its huge stone **bridge**, ruined **cathedral**, and mighty **trees**. Romantics can walk beside the **river** at Callander, see the **shops**, and then drive by a **loch** to Balquhidder **glen** to see Rob Roy's **grave**, then head south to visit the **island priory** at Inchmahome. For full details, see p243.

VISITING PERTH

Parking
There is long-stay parking by the railway station, on the High St and on South St.

Tourist Information
Lower City Mills, West Mill St, PH1 5QP; 01738 450 600; www.perthshire.co.uk

VISITING DUNKELD

Parking
There is a large car park in the town centre, behind the High Street.

Tourist Information
The Cross, PH8 0AN; 01350 727 688; www.perthshire.co.uk

WHERE TO STAY

PERTH

Ardfern House *inexpensive*
Enjoy pretty rooms at this comfortable Victorian house. There's a fire in the lounge and many options for breakfast.
15 Pitcullen Crescent, PH2 7HT; 01738 637 031; www.ardfernguesthouse.co.uk

Beechgrove Guest House *inexpensive*
Attractive B&B overlooking the Tay, just outside the centre, offers traditional ensuite rooms and has its own grounds.
Dundee Road, PH2 7AQ; 01738 636 147

Halton House *moderate*
Arts and Crafts architecture is a feature at this attractive B&B. The guest lounge has an open fire in winter. Wifi in rooms.
11 Tullylumb Terrace, PH1 1BA (just off main Glasgow Rd); 01738 643 446

AROUND DUNKELD

Kinnaird Hotel *expensive*
A superb 18th-century country house in tranquil countryside by the River Tay. Elegantly furnished rooms offer stunning views. Delicious breakfasts of fresh fruit, pastries and pancakes.
Kinnaird Estate, by Dunkeld (on B898 north of Dunkeld); PH8 0LB; 01796 482 440; www.kinnairdestate.com

① Perth
Perthshire; PH1

The "Fair City", as Sir Walter Scott dubbed Perth, sits on the banks of the River Tay – Scotland's longest river. It's a lovely green city: **Branklyn Gardens** *(Dundee Rd; open daily)* are famed for their brilliant blue Himalayan poppies; and **Cherrybank Gardens** *(Glasgow Rd; open daily)* contain the National Collection of heathers. The **Museum and Art Gallery** *(closed Sun)* contains watercolours by Beatrix Potter, creator of Peter Rabbit *(see opposite)*.

Just north of the city, off the A93, stands **Scone** (pronounced "scoon") **Palace** *(Apr–Oct; open daily; www.scone-palace.co.uk)*. In the grounds lies Moot Hill where ancient Scottish kings such as Macbeth and Robert the Bruce were crowned. The Stone of Destiny stood here until Edward I took it to London in 1296: it sat under the Coronation Chair until 1996. It's now in Edinburgh Castle.

🚗 *Continue on the A93, past the 30-m (100-ft) high Meiklour beech hedge, planted in 1745. Soon after, turn right onto A984 signed Coupar Angus and at crossroads go right on the A923. At Coupar Angus take the A94 to Meigle.*

② Meigle Museum
Meigle, Perthshire; PH12 8SB

Meigle Museum *(Apr–Sept: open daily)* contains a superb collection of Pictish stones, dating back to the 8th century. Amongst the images carved on these mysterious stones by the Picts are a camel, a bear and mythical beasts.

🚗 *From Meigle, continue on the A94, turning left to reach Glamis Castle.*

Above The wonderful Italian Garden at Glamis Castle, laid out in 1910

③ Glamis Castle
Glamis, Angus; DD8 1RJ

With its grand towers, turrets and tiny windows, **Glamis Castle** *(Mar–Dec: open daily; guided tours only; www.glamis-castle.co.uk)* looks like a French château or something out of a fairytale. The seat of the Earls of Strathmore since 1372, it was the childhood home of the late Queen Elizabeth the Queen Mother: visitors can see her sitting room and bedroom. The castle is said to be the most haunted building in Scotland and the creepy crypt contains a secret room: according to legend, it was where one of the lords of Glamis played cards with the Devil. The room was later sealed up. In summer, the Strathmore Highland Games are held in the grounds.

🚗 *Take A928 north and park in centre.*

④ Kirriemuir
Angus; DD8

Known in the 19th century for its jute factories, Kirriemuir is now more famous as **J M Barrie's Birthplace** *(Easter–Oct: open Sat–Wed; Jul, Aug: open daily; www.nts.org.uk)*. The museum is signposted, just off the central square. The creator of Peter Pan was the 9th of 10 children and it's hard to imagine how they all squeezed into the tiny upper rooms. Barrie's father, a weaver, worked downstairs. Outside is the little wash house, in which the 7-year-old author acted out his first plays – it inspired Wendy's House in Peter Pan.

🚗 *Pick up A926 towards Blairgowrie, then take A923 past the Loch of the Lowes Visitor Centre (ospreys can be seen in late spring) and into Dunkeld.*

Far left The compact and pretty city of Perth, set beside the River Tay **Left** The elegant tea garden and peacock at 14th-century Scone Palace, Perth

⑤ Dunkeld

Perthshire; PH8

This charming market town, with shops, restaurants and a 14th-century cathedral makes a relaxing place to stop. It stands on one bank of the River Tay, with the town of Birnam on the other. As well as excellent salmon and trout fishing on the Tay, the nearby woods and hills offer plenty of fine walks – ask about these activities in the Tourist Office.

A one-and-a-half-hour walking tour

From the car park, walk down Bridge St and over **Dunkeld Bridge** ① across the Tay. It was built in the early 19th century by Thomas Telford, and cost £15,000 (about £1m today). It's a magnificent structure over 200 m (685 ft) long. Keep to the left and, just over the bridge, take the steps down to the river – a sign says Birnam Walk. Once under the bridge, go left to follow a path which offers picturesque views of **Dunkeld Cathedral** ②, much of which is in ruins, the result of damage during the Reformation in the 16th century.

The most scenic and enjoyable option from here is to retrace the alk route under the bridge, keeping the river now on the left-hand side.

After crossing a small footbridge, there's a mighty sycamore tree and the **Birnam Oak** ③, its lower branches propped up with posts, like an elderly gentleman leaning on a stick. This is the last survivor of Birnam Wood, mentioned in Shakespeare's *Macbeth*.

Follow this lovely tree-lined path along the river to a blue painted **fishing hut** ④ by the waters of the Tay. Then return the same way along the riverside but, just before reaching the Birnam Oak, turn left up a set of steps. Follow the path to the road in Birnam, and cross over to visit the **Beatrix Potter Exhibition** ⑤ (open daily). The children's author Beatrix Potter used to holiday in Birnam as a child, and spent

hours exploring with a local naturalist, Charles Macintosh. The wildlife and countryside inspired Beatrix to create such enduring characters as Peter Rabbit and Mrs Tiggy Winkle, years later. The exhibition includes a Victorian schoolroom, information panels and a Beatrix Potter Garden – the museum is an ideal place for young children. There's also a café.

To return to Dunkeld, either walk back along the river or follow Perth Rd in Birnam to cross the bridge again.

🚗 *Take A9 north, after Pitlochry turn left, onto B8019, then right onto B8079 to Killiecrankie. The Pass Visitor Centre is clearly signposted.*

Above left Neo-Gothic fountain at the market cross, Dunkeld **Above center** detail of ruined Dunkeld Cathedral **Above right** Impressive Dunkeld Bridge, spanning the River Tay

EAT AND DRINK

PERTH

63 Tay Street *moderate*
There's a contemporary feel to this fine restaurant in the heart of Perth. Enjoy risotto of Scottish lobster and scallops.
63 Tay Street, PH2 8NN; 01736 441 451; www.63taystreet.com; closed Sun, Mon

MEIGLE

The Joinery Coffee Shop *inexpensive*
Lovely little café in a former joinery in Meigle. Come for home-made soups, freshly made *panini* and delicious cakes.
The Square, PH12 8RN; 01828 640717; www.meiglecoffeeshop.co.uk

AROUND GLAMIS CASTLE

Castleton House Hotel *moderate*
This hotel, 10 minutes west of Glamis on the A94, serves excellent roasts with pork from its own Tamworth pigs and venison from the Angus glens, in season.
Glamis, Angus DD8 1SJ; 01307 840 340; www.castletonglamis.co.uk

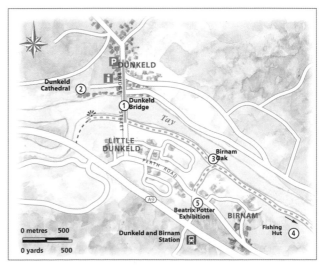

Eat and Drink: inexpensive, under £25; moderate, £25–£50; expensive, over £50

VISITING CALLANDER

Tourist Information
Ancaster Square, FK17 8ED; 01877 330 342; www.visitscotland.co.uk

WHERE TO STAY

PASS OF KILLIECRANKIE
Killiecrankie House Hotel *expensive*
Enjoy crisp white bedlinen and tasteful furniture at this small country hotel with rural views and locally sourced breakfasts.
Pass of Killiecrankie, PI I16 5LG; 01796 473 220; www.killiecrankiehotel.co.uk

CALLANDER
Arden House *inexpensive*
This handsome Victorian house has comfortable, good-sized rooms.
Bracklinn Rd, FK17 8EQ; 01877 330 235; www.ardenhouse.org.uk

Leny Estate *moderate*
This peaceful estate on the edge of Callander has six attractive, heated lodge-style cabins and a flat in the castle.
Leny House, FK17 8HA; 01877 331 078; www.lenyestate.com

Roman Camp Country House
moderate–expensive
A 17th century hunting lodge, this country house with wood paneling and ornate ceilings offers traditional comforts.
Off Main Street, FK17 8BG; 01877 330 003; www.roman-camp-hotel.co.uk

INCHMAHOME PRIORY
Lake of Menteith Hotel *expensive*
This hotel looks across the water toward Inchmahome Priory and has bright rooms. Breakfast on Scottish produce.
Port of Menteith, FK8 3RA; 01877 385 258; www.lake-hotel.com

⑥ Pass of Killiecrankie
Pitlochry, Perthshire; PH16 5LG
On the evening of July 27 1689, the wooded gorge at Killiecrankie became a bloody battleground, when Highland troops led by John Graham of Claverhouse routed government forces in the first battle of the Jacobite rebellion. The **Visitor Centre** *(Apr–Oct: open daily)* tells the story of the battle and also has displays on the wildlife and natural history of the gorge, which looks particularly beautiful when the trees turn russet and gold in autumn. A path leads down to a viewpoint over **Soldier's Leap**, where a government soldier, leapt 18 ft (5.5 m) across the River Garry to escape the Highlanders.
🚗 *Turn left out of parking lot and follow B8079 to Blair Castle and parking lot.*

⑦ Blair Castle
Blair Atholl, Pitlochry; PH18 5TL
Strategically situated to defend the highland passes, gleaming Blair Castle *(Apr–Oct: open daily; www.blair-castle. co.uk)* is an imposing sight. The ancestral home of the Dukes of Atholl, it dates back to the 13th century, but has been greatly expanded over the years. In the summer, a uniformed piper may well be playing outside – an Atholl Highlander, the only private army in Europe, raised by the 4th Duke in 1778. There is lots to see here, with items as varied as the furniture used

by Queen Victoria to an ivory compass carried by Bonnie Prince Charlie. The grounds include a deer park, gardens, and woods, the haunt of red squirrels.
🚗 *Return past Killiecrankie on B8079, then go right on the scenic B8019. At Tummel Bridge, go left on B846 and turn right to Fortingall. Park at the church.*

⑧ The Fortingall Yew
Fortingall, Aberfeldy; PH15 2NQ
In a corner of the churchyard stands the Fortingall Yew: probably the oldest living thing in Europe, it is thought to be 5,000 years old. Legend has it that Pontius Pilate knew this tree, not so unlikely as his father, an army officer, was stationed here during the Roman occupation.
🚗 *Continue down the road to Bridge of Balgie and turn left to A827. Turn right, drive through Killin, then pick up A85 toward Perth. At Lochearnhead, take the A84, then turn right to Balquhidder.*

⑨ Balquhidder
Perthshire; FK19 8PA
This small village is set by Loch Voil under spectacular mountains. In its **churchyard** is the grave of one of Scotland's most famous figures: Rob Roy Macgregor (1671–1734). Rob Roy, whose nickname came from his red hair ("roy" comes from the Gaelic for red), fought at Killiecrankie. After a dispute with the Duke of Montrose, he embarked on a campaign of cattle rustling and eventually became an outlaw. Avoiding capture, he became a romantic hero, immortalized by writers Sir Walter Scott and Daniel Defoe.
🚗 *Return to A84 south to Callander and park in the center.*

⑩ Callander
Callander, Stirling; FK17
Popularly known as the "gateway to the highlands," Callander, with its shops and restaurants, makes an excellent base for exploring. In the 1960s and 70s it gained fame as Tannochbrae in the TV version of *Dr Finlay's Casebook* by AJ Cronin. Visitors can enjoy signed walks along the River Teith and to

Far left Shaded woods in the gorge at the Pass of Killiecrankie **Above left** The magnificent white-painted exterior of 13th-century Blair Castle **Below left** The grave of Rob Roy bearing its defiant motto

Where to Stay: inexpensive, under £80; moderate, £80–£150; expensive, over £150

Bracklinn Falls, climbs up nearby Ben Ledi, and bike rides on the national cycleway – see Tourist Information *(left)*.

🚗 *Take A81 toward Glasgow. Go left at B8034 to Port of Menteith ferry parking.*

⑪ Inchmahome Priory

Lake of Menteith; FK8 3RA

There can be few more picturesque places than **Inchmahome Priory** *(Apr–Sep: open daily; www.historic-scotland.gov. uk)*. This Augustinian monastery sits on a small island in the Lake of Menteith, and can only be reached by ferry. The priory, built in 1283, was home to a small religious community for 300 years. Visitors can stroll around the tranquil ruins, which once provided a refuge for young Mary, Queen of Scots.

🚗 *Continue along B8034, turning right on A811. At Drymen, turn right on B837 to Balmaha and parking lot.*

⑫ Balmaha

Loch Lomond; G63 0JQ

Balmaha is a tiny village on the east bank of **Loch Lomond**, nestling amid ancient oak woods. These support so much wildlife they are a Site of Special Scientific Interest. Walk the **Millennium Forest Path** through the woods or take a ferry from the boatyard to visit the island of **Inchcailleach**. At 24 miles (39 km) long and 5 miles (8 km) wide, Loch Lomond is the largest expanse of freshwater in Britain. The loch is dotted

with thickly wooded islands, including **Inchconnachan**, which is home to an unlikely colony of wallabies, introduced in the early 20th century.

🚗 *Return to Drymen, then take A811 toward Glasgow to Balloch. Follow signs to Loch Lomond Shores parking lot.*

⑬ Loch Lomond Shores

Ben Lomond Way, Balloch; G83 8QL

Visitors to Balloch should head for **Loch Lomond Shores** *(open daily; www. lochlomondshores.com)*, gateway to the Loch Lomond National Park, to pick up local crafts and walk maps. Here, it is also possible to hire bikes, canoes and kayaks, or book tickets to take a cruise on the loch itself. Visitors with children will enjoy a visit to the aquarium, which offers close up views of creatures such as starfish and sharks.

Above left Unspoiled Callander, set in the beautiful Trossach hills **Above right** Boats on serene Loch Lomond as seen from Balmaha **Below** Lake cruise ship on Loch Lomond awaiting passengers, Balloch

EAT AND DRINK

AROUND BLAIR CASTLE

Loch Tummel Inn *inexpensive*
This inn by Loch Tummel is on the B8019 about 15 minutes from Killiecrankie. Bar meals include big sandwiches, mussels in wine, or Aberdeen Angus burgers. *Strathtummel, PH16 5RP; 01882 634 272; www.lochtummelinn.co.uk*

THE FORTINGALL YEW

Fortingall Hotel *moderate*
Beside the famous Fortingall Yew, this hotel restaurant serves good Scottish produce, such as fresh salmon from the Tay and locally raised lamb. *Fortingall, PH15 2NQ; 01887 830 367; www.fortingall.com*

BALQUHIDDER

Monachyle Mhor *moderate–expensive*
Enjoy chic eating on the north shore of Loch Voil. The menu is modern Scottish, and there are vegetarian dishes, too. Also has nice rooms. *Balquhidder, FK19 8PQ; 01877 384 627; www.monachylemhor.com*

CALLANDER

Ciro's *moderate*
This popular Italian restaurant in the center of town, serves pasta and pizza dishes, as well as Scottish rib-eye steak. *114 Main Street, FK17 8BG; 01877 331 070; www.cirositalianrestaurant.co.uk; closed Wed*

DAY TRIP OPTIONS

Perth and Callander are excellent bases for day trips.

Gardens and River Tay

Staying at Perth ❶, spend the morning enjoying its sights – the river, gardens, and galleries – and then enjoy a tour of Scone Palace, where Scotland's kings were

crowned. Drive to Dunkeld ❺ to see its cathedral, and historic trees beside the River Tay, and walk into Birnam.

Take A93 to Scone Palace and then return to Perth center and take the A9. Return to Perth on the A9.

Romance of the Lochs

From Callander ❿, explore the town and enjoy a walk by the river, before

driving up the loch to Balquhidder ❾ to see Rob Roy's grave and the glens. Then return to Callander and head south to take a boat to romantic Inchmahome Priory ⑪, set on an island in Lake Menteith.

From Callander take A84, then follow signs to Balquhidder. Retrace route and then take A81 to Inchmahome Priory.

Eat and Drink: inexpensive, under £25; moderate, £25–£50; expensive, over £50

On the Highlands Whisky Trail

Inverness to Aberdeen

Highlights

- **Fairytale castles**
  Visit some of Scotland's finest castles, including Cawdor, immortalized in Shakespeare's *Macbeth*, and clifftop Dunnottar Castle, once the keeper of the Scottish Crown jewels

- **Spectacular Speyside**
  Watch dolphins on the Moray coast, then follow the River Spey to sample the finest malt whiskies, made amongst the heather-clad hills

- **Cities of stone**
  Explore Inverness, notable for its pink sandstone buildings by the River Ness, and historic Aberdeen, the grey granite city on the North Sea

The dramatic shoreline of Spey Bay, at the WDCS Wildlife Centre

On the Highlands Whisky Trail

This drive is Scotland distilled: the route runs through a landscape of brooding mountains and sparkling rivers, dotted with picture-book castles, barrel-makers and world famous whisky producers. Starting from Inverness, the drive visits Culloden to see the site of the famous battle, continues to Cawdor Castle, then heads north to enjoy some dolphin watching on the Moray coast. Heading south through Speyside, the home of whisky, visitors get the chance to taste a dram or two, before travelling back in time at the Grampian Transport Museum. On reaching the east coast, there are spectacular craggy cliffs at Dunnottar Castle, before the drive ends at the historic granite city of Aberdeen.

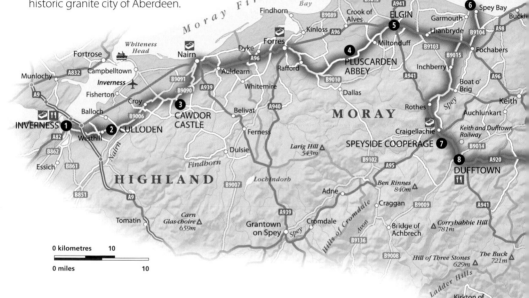

ACTIVITIES

Go on a monster hunt with a boat cruise over the mysterious depths of Loch Ness

March across a battlefield and see the memorial at the poignant meadows of Culloden

Watch for wildlife at the Whale and Dolphin Conservation Society Wildlife Centre, Spey Bay

Walk along the Speyside Way in Craigellachie

Climb aboard a vintage train on the Keith & Dufftown Railway

Taste a dram or two of single-malt whisky on a tour of the Glenfiddich Distillery

Enjoy a picnic in the grounds of Leith Hall

Watch the salmon leaping on the waters of the Feugh

Below Archway in the pretty Flower Garden, Cawdor Castle, *see p248*

Above Peaceful boating pond in the park close to the centre of Elgin, *see p249*

KEY

🟰 Drive route

PLAN YOUR DRIVE

Start/Finish: Inverness to Aberdeen.

Number of days: Around 3–4 days, with half a day in Aberdeen.

Distances: Approx. 181 miles (291 km).

Road conditions: Good roads, liable to become snowbound in winter.

When to go: This drive is lovely in the autumn, when the trees are changing color. In summer, the roads will be busier – but the weather can be fine and the days will be long.

Opening times: Museums and attractions are generally open 10am–5pm, but close earlier (or are closed altogether) Nov–Easter. Shops are often open longer. Churches are usually open until dusk.

Main market days: Inverness: Farmers' Market, 1st Sat of month; Aberdeen: Farmers' Market, 1st and last Sat of month.

Shopping: Scottish whisky is famed the world over, so take the chance to buy a good-quality single malt here. Look out for excellent jams, tablet (the Scottish version of fudge), and buttery shortbread, too.

Main festivals: Inverness: Highland Games, Jul; Dufftown: Spirit of Speyside Whisky Festival, May; Dunnottar Castle: Stonehaven Folk Festival, Jul; Stonehaven Fireballs Ceremony, Dec; Aberdeen: Highland Games, Jun.

DAY TRIP OPTIONS

History lovers will enjoy the **cathedral** and **museum** at Inverness, before walking on Culloden **battlefield** and exploring the **dungeons** at Cawdor Castle. Finish the day at Nairn on its **sandy beach**. **Whisky buffs** should stay at Craigellachie, watch **dolphins** in Spey Bay and see coopers at work at Speyside Cooperage. End the day with a visit to Dufftown to taste **whisky** and ride on a **heritage train**. Staying at Aberdeen, visit the **transport museum** at Alford, the **waterfalls** and **castle** at Banchory, and the **cliffside castle** at Dunnottar, then return for Aberdeen's **beach funfair**. For full details, *see p253*.

Above St. Mary's Catholic Church by the River Ness, Inverness

VISITING INVERNESS

Parking
For long-term parking close to the castle try the Rose St car park, off A82/B865.

Tourist Information
Castle Wynd, IV2 3BJ; 0845 2255 121

WHERE TO STAY

INVERNESS

Trafford Bank Guest House *moderate*
Enjoy chic, designer rooms at this 5-star B&B. There are features such as Victorian roll-top baths, DVD players, and luxury toiletries – and sherry decanters.
96 Fairfield Road, IV3 5LL; 01463 241 414; www.traffordbankguesthouse.co.uk

Glenmoriston Town House Hotel
moderate–expensive
Crisp cotton sheets and sleek rooms can be found at this boutique riverside hotel, which also has good restaurants. Rooms have modern televisions and free Wi-fi.
20 Ness Bank, IV2 4SF; 01463 223 777; www.contrastbrasserie.co.uk

AROUND CAWDOR CASTLE

Sunny Brae Hotel *moderate*
Follow B9090 to the seafront in Nairn for comfortable ensuite rooms, some with views of the Moray Firth, and an attractive guest lounge.
Marine Road, Nairn, IV12 4EA; 01667 452 309; www.sunnybraehotel.com

AROUND ELGIN

Milton of Grange Farmhouse
inexpensive
There are three ensuite rooms and lovely views of the countryside at this working arable farm. Guests can enjoy a full Scottish breakfast, or a fruit and cheese platter. From Elgin, take A96 to Forres, then turn right on B9011.
Forres, Moray, IV36 2TR; 01309 676 360; www.forres-accommodation.co.uk

① Inverness
Highland; IV1
Sitting serenely on the River Ness, Inverness is acknowledged as the capital of the Highlands. The river is flanked on one side by a substantial pink stone **castle**, built in the 19th century on the site of a much earlier structure destroyed by the Jacobite army after 1746. On the other side stands **Inverness Cathedral**, with some fine stained-glass windows. *The City Museum (open Mon–Sat)* contains a variety of items associated with the Highlands. Visitors can also enjoy a cruise on **Loch Ness** *(www.jacobite.co.uk)* and learn more about Loch Ness wildlife including, of course, the mythical monster. Buses to the boats leave from Inverness Bus Station.

🚗 *From Rose St parking lot drive onto A82 roundabout, turning right, then join A9 south for a short distance, turning left on B9006. The Culloden Visitor Centre is just off the road and clearly marked; there is a parking lot.*

② Culloden
Culloden Moor, Inverness; IV2 5EU
The wind never seems to stop blowing across the bleak expanse of Culloden Moor where, on April 16 1746, the last battle of the Jacobite Risings took place. It lasted only an hour, but heralded the end of the distinctive clan system, bringing many changes to Highland Scotland. The excellent **Visitor Centre** *(open daily; www.nts.org. uk)* gives the historical context to the battle, together with memorabilia such as Jacobite medals and first-

hand accounts from those involved in the events. Visitors can also walk the battlefield for a soldier's-eye view.

🚗 *Continue on B9006, bearing right onto B9091. Turn right onto B9090 to Cawdor Castle.*

The Mystery of Loch Ness
Stories of a monster lurking in Loch Ness date back to St. Columba, who is said to have saved a man from the beast. However, modern sightings started in 1933, when a creature with a long neck was reported in the loch. Murky photographs and film of the creature have appeared: many consider them to be hoaxes, others are sure that Nessie exists. Scientific expeditions have been unable to find the beast, and the mystery lingers on.

③ Cawdor Castle
Cawdor, Nairn; IV12 5RD;
Although Cawdor Castle's *(May–Oct: open daily; www.cawdorcastle.com)* only associations with the real Macbeth were in Shakespeare's imagination, that does not lessen its appeal. It was built in the late 14th century, long after Macbeth had died, and retains a medieval feel with stone staircases, atmospheric passageways and a dungeon. It is still home to the Cawdor family and photos mingle with Flemish tapestries, four-poster beds, and artwork by Landseer and Edward Lear. There are several colorful gardens – Walled, Flower, and Wild – which are delightful places to explore .

🚗 *Continue on B9090 to Nairn (consider a detour to the beach). Then*

Below The imposing west towers of Gothic Inverness Cathedral, built in 1866

take A96 east and branch off onto B9011 in Forres, to turn right on B9010. Drive through fertile fields and turn left at a sign for an unclassified road to reach the abbey, and park on the left-hand side.

④ Pluscarden Abbey

Elgin, Moray; IV30 8UA

Sitting serenely in a sheltered valley surrounded by trees, Pluscarden Abbey *(open daily; www.pluscardenabbey.org)* seems to radiate tranquillity. Founded in the year 1230 by King Alexander II of Scotland, this venerable building is still home to a community of Benedictine monks – the only such medieval monastery in Britain still used for its original purpose. The abbey church contains contemporary stained-glass windows, most of which are made in the abbey workshop by monks.

🚗 *Continue on the minor road to turn left onto B9010 near Elgin. A 80-ft (24-m) high column, erected in memory of the 5th Duke of Gordon in 1839, can be clearly seen rising above the town. Take B9010 into Elgin; there is parking near the cathedral, off the High Street and also by North Street.*

⑤ Elgin

Elgin, Moray; IV30

With historic buildings, a medieval street plan, and pretty park, Elgin is a pleasant town for a stroll. Undoubtedly, its finest sight is the ruined **Elgin Cathedral** *(Apr–Oct: open daily; Nov–Mar; open Sat–Wed),* which was once so large

it was known as the Lantern of the North; intricate carvings on the exterior and its almost complete Chapterhouse provide a glimpse of its former glory. **Elgin Museum** *(Apr–Oct: open Mon–Sat; www.elginmuseum.org.uk)* has a vast collection of fascinating items, from ancient Pictish stones, Roman coins, fossils and, paintings by local artists to a display on the county and its people.

🚗 *Leave Elgin on A96, toward Keith. After the Baxters Visitor Centre (the food company), turn left onto B9104, follow it to Spey Bay. The WDCS visitor center and parking lot is at the road's end.*

Above left The ruins of Elgin Cathedral, once one of the finest in Scotland **Above** The field where the decisive Battle of Culloden was fought in 1746 **Below right** Detail of Pluscarden Abbey, still home to Benedictine monks

EAT AND DRINK

INVERNESS

Riva *inexpensive*
This smart Italian restaurant offers classic dishes such as mushroom risotto, pasta with meatballs, and pizzas.
4–6 Ness Walk, IV3 5NE; 01463 237 377; www.rivainverness.co.uk; closed Sun lunch

The Kitchen on the River *inexpensive–moderate*
This relaxed, contemporary restaurant beside the River Ness serves modern Scottish food. Imaginative dishes include pheasant and venison patties, or breast of chicken stuffed with haggis. There are vegetarian options, too.
15 Huntly Street, IV3 5PR; 01463 259 119; www.kitchenrestaurant.co.uk

The Rocpool *moderate*
This cool city center brasserie offers fusion food, made with as much local produce as possible. Come for dishes such as Venetian-style calves' liver, sea bream with chorizo, or venison with Parma ham and black pudding.
1 Ness Walk, IV3 5NE; 01463 717 274; www.rocpoolrestaurant.com

Above Impressive ruins at Elgin Cathedral with almost intact Chapterhouse

Eat and Drink: inexpensive, under £25; moderate, £25–£50; expensive, over £50

Above Statue of an osprey outside the WDCS Wildlife Centre, Spey Bay

VISITING DUFFTOWN

Parking
Park at the top of Balvenie Street under the clock – although most of Dufftown's sights are outside the village.

Tourist Information
2 The Square, AB55 4AD; 01340 820 501

WHERE TO STAY

AROUND SPEYSIDE COOPERAGE

Craigellachie Hotel *moderate*
Built in 1893, the Craigellachie Hotel offers country house accommodation on the River Spey, just north of the Speyside Cooperage. It makes an ideal stop on the whisky trail, especially as its Quaich Bar has over 700 whiskies to choose from. It's also handy for walks as the Speyside Way runs beside the hotel. The restaurant is worth visiting, too. *Craigellachie, Speyside, AB38 9SR; 01340 881 204; www.craigellachie.com*

AROUND LEITH HALL

Castle Hotel *moderate*
Built in the 18th century as a home for the Dukes of Gordon (powerful Scottish nobles), the hotel is set in quiet parkland and has comfortable, traditionally furnished rooms. It's a delightful place for a relaxing break. *Huntly, Aberdeenshire, AB54 4SH (follow driving instructions from Dufftown to Leith Hall); 01466 792 696; www.castlehotel.uk.com*

⑥ WDCS Wildlife Centre
Spey Bay, Moray; IV32 7PJ
Perched beside the unspoilt sands of Spey Bay, the Whale and Dolphin Conservation Society Wildlife Centre *(Apr–Oct: open daily; Mar & Nov: weekends; www.wdcs.org)* constantly monitors the water for dolphin activity. This part of the coast is noted for its bottlenose dolphins and visitors have a good chance of spotting them – especially with the help of the wildlife wardens. This area is also home to minke whales, ospreys, otters, and wildfowl. The staff here offer informative talks, as well as guided walks on the nature reserve.

🚗 *Return to A96 and turn right, then left on B9015 to Rothes. There, take A941 south, passing the Glen Grant Distillery. Stay on A941 through Craigellachie and on to Speyside Cooperage, with parking.*

⑦ Speyside Cooperage
Craigellachie, Banffshire; AB38 9RS
Nearly all the casks in Scotland are made at this family-run cooperage. The **Visitor Centre** *(open Mon–Fri; www.speysidecooperage.co.uk)* introduces this ancient industry, explaining how they make the oak casks, and how sherry and bourbon casks are repaired, and then used to give distinctive flavors to whiskies. Visitors can watch the coopers and apprentices at work – it's a four-year apprenticeship – using the traditional tools of their trade.

There are also some good walks on the Speyside Way from Craigellachie.

🚗 *Turn right from the cooperage onto A941. Before Dufftown, on the left-hand side, is the Keith & Dufftown Railway, with parking.*

The Honours of Scotland
After Charles I was executed, the Scots crowned his son, Charles II, at Scone Palace. Then in 1650 Oliver Cromwell, (the anti-monarchist leader) ordered an invasion of Scotland. To prevent him destroying the country's Crown Jewels –the Honours of Scotland – they were taken to Dunnottar Castle and later to Kinneff Old Church – where they lay under the floor for eight years. Eventually they were taken to Edinburgh Castle and hidden again – too well, in fact, for everyone forgot where they were until Sir Walter Scott rediscovered them.

⑧ Dufftown
Keith, Banffshire; AB55
Dufftown is popularly known as "the town that was built on seven stills", a reference to the distilleries that dot the surrounding countryside. Founded in 1817, the so-called malt whisky capital of the world is a pleasant town with an imposing central clock tower.

Just outside Dufftown is the **Keith & Dufftown Railway** *(Easter–May & Sep: open weekends; Jun–Aug: open Fri–Sun; www.keith-dufftown-railway.co.uk)*, run by volunteers, which makes a great family expedition (a round trip lasts an hour and a half). A restored diesel train chugs through stunning Highland scenery, crossing the Fiddich Viaduct, passing distilleries and ruined castles, before reaching the market town of Keith, home of the Strathisla Distillery.

Immediately south of the railway station stands the family-owned **Glenfiddich Distillery** *(Easter–Oct: open daily; Nov–Easter: open Mon–Fri; www.glenfiddich.com)*, which has been

Below Looking out to sea from the WDCS Wildlife Centre, Spey Bay

Where to Stay: inexpensive, under £80; moderate, £80–£150; expensive, over £150

producing single malt whisky since 1887, using water from local springs. Visitors can join an informative tour of the buildings, see the shiny copper stills and the warehouses where the whisky is stored in traditional oak barrels. Tours end with a delicious free dram. Whisky buffs might prefer to join a connoisseurs' tour (with an entry charge) which includes a tutored tasting of more whiskies.

🚗 *Continue through Dufftown on A941, then bear left on A920 to Huntly, to pick up the A96, then A97 south. Follow this through fertile farmland, eventually turning left on the B9002. After 1 mile (1.6 km), look out for Leith Hall, with parking, on the left.*

9 Leith Hall

Nr Kennethmont, Huntly; AB54 4NQ
This 17th-century mansion house *(grounds open daily)* has been home to the Leiths – a family that long supported the Jacobite cause – for hundreds of years. Although the house (reputed to be haunted) is now closed to the public, the gardens

Below Impressive Leith Hall, home to the Leith family for 350 years **Below right** Whisky barrels at the Glenfiddich distillery, near Dufftown **Bottom right** The pretty gardens at Leith Hall, perfect for a picnic

make a lovely place for a picnic on a fine day. There are also several easy walks to follow. In the grounds, visitors can see an old sycamore tree known as a 'dule tree' (gallows tree) – said to have been used to hang criminals.

🚗 *From Leith Hall, continue along B9002, then turn right at the crossroads onto B992. Head south to A944 and turn right to Alford. Park by the museum.*

10 Grampian Transport Museum

Alford, Aberdeenshire; AB33 8AE
This excellent museum *(Apr–Oct: open daily; www.gtm.org.uk)* contains a fascinating variety of vehicles, ranging from a horse-drawn mail coach to the electric "car," the Sinclair C5. There are early bicycles and motorbikes, an eccentric steam tricycle built by a postman in 1895, gleaming vintage cars, and a green Jaguar from the James Bond film *Die Another Day*, with a missile launcher in the front grille. Visitors even get the chance to sit in the saddle of a penny farthing bicycle. Great fun for all ages.

🚗 *Leave Alford on A944 west, soon bearing left on A980, then at the junction with the A93, turn right to Banchory. Take B974 off the High Street to Bridge of Feugh parking lot.*

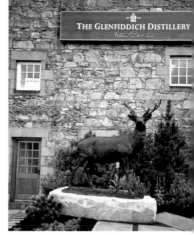

Above Glenfiddich Distillery – the name means "Valley of the Deer" in Gaelic

Above The dramatic 15th-century ruins of Dunnottar Castle **Above center** The Triple Kirk spire and Union Terrace Gardens, Aberdeen **Above right** St Mark's Church, Aberdeen, modeled on St Paul's Cathedral

VISITING ABERDEEN

Parking
Park in College Street near the railway station, or Bon Accord shopping center.

Tourist Information
23 Union Street, AB11 5BP; 01224 288 828; www.aberdeen-grampian.com

WHERE TO STAY

BANCHORY

Old West Manse *inexpensive*
This B&B in a Victorian house has three cozy bedrooms, two of which are ensuite and one with private facilities. It is conveniently located for the town center and the famous Falls of Feugh.
71 Station Rd, AB31 5YD; 01330 822 202; www.deeside-bed-and-breakfast.com

AROUND BANCHORY

Raemoir House Hotel *expensive*
Head north from Banchory on the A980 and keep on going to this impressive Georgian mansion set in large grounds. There are 16 comfortable rooms and some have fine views.
Banchory, AB31 4ED; 01330 824 884; www.raemoir.com

ABERDEEN

The Marcliffe Hotel and Spa *expensive*
Lovely hotel with luxurious rooms that blend contemporary style with traditional comfort. Expect fluffy white towels in spotless bathrooms, plasma screen televisions and an excellent selection of local produce for breakfast.
North Deeside Road, AB15 9YA; 01224 861 000; www.marcliffe.com

Where to Stay: inexpensive, under £80; moderate, £80–£150; expensive, over £150

⑪ Banchory
Aberdeenshire; AB31 6NL

A popular holiday spot since Victorian times, Banchory is in Royal Deeside, known for its beautiful countryside and castles. Just south of town on the A974 stands the 18th-century stone **Bridge of Feugh**, over a tributary of the mighty River Dee. The waters foam furiously down below and there is a good chance of spotting salmon leaping over the rocks to reach the calm waters beyond. The best times to see them are Sep–Nov and Feb–Mar. Take the A93 east to the fairytale **Crathes Castle** *(Jun–Aug: open daily; Sep–Oct: closed Fri; Nov–May: closed grounds open daily)*, built in the 16th century. With exquisite interiors – original painted ceilings – and delightful gardens, this is a must-see visitor attraction.

🚘 *Return to A93, turn right, then take A957 to Stonehaven. Bear right onto A90/A92 for a short distance and follow signs to the castle. There is a parking area (which gets busy in summer) a short walk from the castle itself.*

⑫ Dunnottar Castle
Nr Stonehaven; AB39 2TL

Perched dramatically on the clifftops with gulls swirling overhead and waves crashing below, **Dunnottar Castle** *(Easter–Oct: open daily; Nov–Easter: open Fri–Mon; www.dunnottarcastle.co.uk)* makes a compelling sight. The castle, built in the 15th century, was once home to one of Scotland's most powerful families. Visited by William Wallace, Mary Queen of Scots,

the Marquis of Montrose, and the future King Charles II, it gained its place in history when the Honours of Scotland *(see p250)* were hidden here following Oliver Cromwell's invasion. The castle was under siege for eight months, but the Honours were smuggled away to Kinneff Old Church further along the coast. Today, Dunnottar is a picturesque ruin, reached by a steep set of steps.

🚘 *Rejoin A92/A90 north to Aberdeen, turning onto A956 to city center. Go straight over two roundabouts and the River Dee into College St to park beside the train station.*

⑬ Aberdeen

Aberdeen; AB11

Known as the Granite City because of its silvery granite buildings, Aberdeen faces out to the North Sea and, not surprisingly, is a city with a strong maritime tradition. For centuries it had firm trading links with Scandinavia and is still an important fishing port. Its historic buildings are interspersed with shops, lively bars, and restaurants.

Above View of Old Aberdeen seen from Union Street Bridge

A two–three-hour walking tour

Start at the Tourist Information Centre on Union St. Turn right and walk down Shiprow to the **Maritime Museum** ① *(open Tue–Sun)*, which gives a fascinating insight into the city's maritime heritage, as well as good views of the harbor. Leaving the museum, turn left up Shiprow, then left along Union St, the city's main shopping area. Turn right up Belmont St to the **Art Gallery** ② *(Tue–Sun)*, with a large collection of portraits, Impressionist paintings, and works by the Scottish Colourists and the Victorian artists known as the Glasgow Boys. Turn right and walk along Schoolhill, continuing into Upper Kirkgate – look out for the imposing Neo-Gothic **Marischal College** ③, part of Aberdeen University.

Turn left up Gallowgate to the large roundabout, cross to the right; walk a short distance up Mounthooly Way, then go left up Kings Crescent which soon becomes Spittal, then College Bounds, a nice street lined with fine old houses. Go past magnificent King's College, on the right, part of the university, founded in the 15th century. **King's College Chapel** ④ *(open Mon–Fri)* is topped with a distinctive "crown

Neo-Gothic Marischal College, Aberdeen

tower", symbolizing the authority and independence of the Scottish king.

Carry on to see a Georgian town-house up ahead, once a meeting place for the city's trade organizations. Cross over the road ahead. Walk up the historic cobbled Chanonry where the university **Botanic Gardens** ⑤ *(open daily)* provide a short detour. In medieval times Chanonry was home to the canons of **St Machar's Cathedral** ⑥ – which is reached soon. The cathedral dates to the 13th century and has some fine stained-glass windows. Follow Chanonry past the cathedral to Don St, then turn right to rejoin the High St and pass King's College again. At the start of Spittal turn left down Orchard Rd, go right at the end and cross King St to turn left down Pittodrie Place. At its end turn right on Golf Rd – with golf links on the left and the football stadium on the right. Walk up the steps onto a grassy hill to reach the seafront with a stretch of golden sand and **funfair** ⑦. To return to the city center, continue south along the coast, then turn right at Beach Boulevard. Cross carefully at the roundabout to go down Justice St, past the Mercat Cross and back into Union Street.

EAT AND DRINK

AROUND BANCHORY

The Irvine Arms *Inexpensive*
This village pub, a short way east on the A93, has milk churns as bar stools and offers good home-cooked bar meals – hearty soups and pasta.
North Deeside Road, Drumoak, AB31 5AU; 01330 811 423

AROUND DUNNOTTAR CASTLE

The Creel Inn *inexpensive*
In Catterline, a few miles south of the castle off the A92, former fisherman's cottages have been turned into this popular inn. There's seafood on the menu, such as pan-seared scallops.
Catterline, Stonehaven, AB39 2UL; 01569 750 254; www.thecreelinn.co.uk

ABERDEEN

Bistro Verde *inexpensive–moderate*
This popular bistro specializes in fish– try roasted sea bass, Basque-style monkfish, or sea bream in Parma ham.
59 The Green, AB11 6NY; 01224 586 180; closed Sun

The Marcliffe Hotel and Spa *moderate–expensive*
Enjoy the relaxing atmosphere at this popular hotel restaurant – and produce such as Scottish lobster, roe deer, and roast rabbit. There are vegetarian options and homemade ice creams.
North Deeside Rd, AB15 9YA; 01224 861 000; www.marcliffe.com

DAY TRIP OPTIONS

Children and adults will enjoy historic castles and stunning coastline.

War and Peace

From Inverness ❶ it's a short drive to Culloden ❷, where Bonnie Prince Charlie's campaign ended. Take a tour of Cawdor Castle ❸, then it's off to Nairn for a spell on the sandy beach.

Take B9006 from Inverness to Culloden, then B9091 and B9090 to Cawdor and on to Nairn. Return on the A96.

Speyside Delights

From Craigellachie, drive to the WCDS Wildlife Centre ❻ at Spey Bay to look for dolphins. Then head back to make a tour of Speyside Cooperage ❼, take a heritage railway trip at Dufftown ❽ and taste the whisky at the Glenfiddich Distillery, before dinner in a Dufftown restaurant.

Follow drive instructions in reverse to the WCDS Wildlife Centre, return on the same roads and take A941 to Dufftown.

Vintage Fun

From Aberdeen ⑬, visit the transport museum ❿ at Alford, with tanks and vintage cars. Then head to Banchory ⓫ to watch salmon leaping up the falls and perhaps see Crathes Castle. Visit dramatic Dunnottar Castle ⑬ on the cliffs, before returning to Aberdeen and the beachside funfair.

From Aberdeen, take A944 to Alford, then A980 south Banchory. Then follow the drive instructions to Aberdeen.

General Index

Acknowledgments

Dorling Kindersley would like to thank the many people whose help and assistance contributed to the preparation of this book.

Main Contributors

Patricia Aithie lived and travelled in the Middle East for 25 years, writing extensively about travel, culture and faith there, before returning to her native Cardiff. She has written several books about Wales, including *Cardiff: Rebirth of a Capital* and *Cardiff and Beyond***.**

Robert Andrews has been working on travel guides for 20 years, writing for DK, Rough Guides and Fodor's. He has authored, or co-authored, books on Devon and Cornwall, Sicily and Sardinia, and has written about all areas of Italy and southern England.

Rebecca Ford is an award-winning travel journalist who lives in London. She writes for national newspapers and magazines on everything from railway journeys to eco-travel, and has contributed to more than 30 guidebooks.

Nick Rider has a PhD on the history of Barcelona and has written travel books on Spain, Mexico and France. He has contributed to DK guides including those to France, Mexico, Great Britain and Poland. He is a regular reviewer for the *Time Out London Eating & Drinking* guide.

Rose Shepherd started her career as a freelance writer and editor at the *Good Food Guide*. Since then she has contributed regularly to newspapers and magazines including *Condé Nast Traveller*, the *Observer* and the *Sunday Times Magazine*. She is also a published novelist.

Gillian Thomas and **John Harrison**, who are married with three grown-up children, are both freelance travel writers who started their careers at the BBC. Members of the British Guild of Travel Writers, they have been visiting the West Country since their own childhood holidays. They are contributors to the *Good Holiday Cottage Guide*.

Roger Williams is a prolific writer who began his career in journalism. Formerly chief sub-editor on the *Sunday Times Magazine*, he is currently associate editor of *Cornucopia*. He has published several novels – the latest is *Burning Barcelona* – and non-fiction works, as well as contributing to countless travel guides.

Fact checker
Mary Villabona

Proofreader
Jane Ellis

Indexer
Hilary Bird

Americanization
Nichole Morford

Special Assistance
Julia Brownsword, Zara Camble, Clare Currie, Donna Dailey, Ian Gardiner at National Trust for Scotland, Jude Henderson at Visit Scotland, Martin Jackson, Stuart James, Sarah Lee, Anna Richards, John Richards, Rupert Small, Jocelyn Waterfall, Christian Williams

Photography
Charles and Pat Aithie, John Harrison, Alex Havret, Lynne McPeake, Robert Schweizer, Tony Souter, Linda Whitwam, Roger Williams

Additional Photography
June Buck, Lucy Claxton, Joe Cornish, Andy Crawford, Bethany Dawn, Steve Gorton, John Heseltine, Rose Horridge, Bob Langrish, Gerald Lopez, Stephen Oliver, Rob Reichenfeld, Rough Guides/Tim Draper, Kim Sayer, Chris Stowers, Stephen Whitehorn, Paul Wilkinson

Maps
John Plumer, JP Map Graphics Ltd, www.jpmapgraphics.co.uk
Maps on pages 71, 80, 87, 93, 113, 123, 144, 180, 199, 210, 252 are derived from @ www.openstreetmap.org and contributors, licensed under CC-BY-SA, see www.creativecommons.org for further details

Picture Credits

Every effort has been made to trace the copyright holders of images, and we apologize in advance for any unintentional omissions. We would be pleased to insert the appropriate acknowledgments in any subsequent edition of this publication.

The Publishers would like to thank the following individuals, companies and picture libraries for their kind permission to reproduce their photographs:

t=top; tc = top centre; tl=top left; tr=top right; c=centre; cl=centre left; cr=centre right; bc = bottom centre; bl=bottom left; br=bottom right.

Alamy Images: AA World Travel Library 154tl; Elmtree Images 15bc.
Corbis: Macduff Everton 204br; Angelo Hornak 189tr; Richard Klune 155bl.
Dorling Kindersley: Cass Sculpture Foundation *One of us on a Tricycle* 2006 Steven Gregory bronze 220 x 140 x 155 cm edition of 9 96tc; Andy Crawford Crown copyright material is reproduced with the permission of the Controller of HMSO and Queen's Printer for Scotland 13tl.
Ees Wyke: 23bl.
English Heritage: 114br, 178cl, 192tc, 198tl.
Flickr.com: simone_brunozzi/3604939324/ 10bl.
Getty Images: Scott Barbour 17tr; Matt Cardy 16br; Antony Edwards 194-195; Christopher Furlong 18br, 152br; Gavin Hellier 200tr; William S Helsel 189tl; David Hughes 10br; Photonica/Martin Tothill 17bl; The Image Bank/Chris Close 14br; Travel Ink 11bl, 13tc, 205tl; Jake Wyman 15tc.
iStockphoto.com: Aliaksandr Kazlou 15tr; Timothy Large 12br; Andy Medina 12tr.
The National Trust Photo Library ©NTPL: 77tc, 78br, 81bc, 86t, 101tl, 124cra, 209tl, 209tr, 211bc; Matthew Antrobus 164tl; Nick Meers 155br; Brenda Norrish 106bl; Kevin Richardson 163br; David Sellman 106br.
Photolibrary: Jon Arnold Images 146-147.
Al Richardson: 118-119.
von Essen Group: 22br.

Jacket

Front – **Getty Images**: Photographer's Choice/David C Tomlinson.
Spine – **Getty Images**: Photographer's Choice/David C Tomlinson t.
Back – **Dorling Kindersley**: Alex Harvet tr; Anthony Souter tc; Linda Whitwam tl.

All other images © Dorling Kindersley
For further information see: www.dkimages.com

Road Signs

SPEED LIMITS AND GENERAL DRIVING INDICATIONS

Yield

Compulsory stop

Roundabout

Crossroads

Congestion charge zone

Give way to oncoming traffic

No overtaking

No left turn

No access for vehicles over 14 ft 6 in height

Traffic enforcement cameras in use

Speed limit

National speed limits apply

Minimum speed limit

Entrance to 20 mph speed limit zone

End of 20 mph zone and start of 30 mph zone

WARNING SIGNS

Unspecified danger

Succession of bends

Slippery road

Risk of strong crosswinds

Risk of rockfalls

Speed bumps

Road narrows

Road narrows on the left

Level crossing with barrier

Level crossing with no barrier

Steep descent

Wild animals

Children crossing, or school

Pedestrian crossing

Road works